FIFTY HOLLYWOOD DIRECTORS

Fifty Hollywood Directors introduces the most important, iconic and influential filmmakers who worked in Hollywood between the end of the silent period and the birth of the blockbuster. By exploring the historical, cultural and technological contexts in which each director was working, this book traces the formative period in commercial cinema when directors went from pioneers to industry heavyweights.

Each entry discusses a director's practices and body of work and features a brief biography and suggestions for further reading. Entries include:

- Frank Capra
- Cecil B. DeMille
- John Ford
- Alfred Hitchcock
- Fritz Lang
- Orson Welles
- D. W. Griffith
- King Vidor.

This is an indispensable guide for anyone interested in film history, Hollywood and the development of the role of the director.

Yvonne Tasker is Professor of Film and Television Studies at the University of East Anglia, UK.

Suzanne Leonard is Associate Professor of English at Simmons College, USA.

ALSO AVAILABLE FROM ROUTLEDGE

Fifty Contemporary Film Directors
Edited by Yvonne Tasker
ISBN 978-0-415-55433-6

Film Studies: The Basics
By Amy Villarejo
ISBN 978-0-415-58496-8

The Routledge Encyclopedia of Films
Edited by Sabine Haenni,
Sarah Barrow and John White
ISBN 978-0-415-68893-2

FIFTY HOLLYWOOD DIRECTORS

Edited by
Yvonne Tasker
and
Suzanne Leonard

Routledge
Taylor & Francis Group

LONDON AND NEW YORK

First published 2015
by Routledge
2 Park Square, Milton Park, Abingdon, Oxon OX14 4RN

and by Routledge
711 Third Avenue, New York, NY 10017

Routledge is an imprint of the Taylor & Francis Group, an informa business

British Library Cataloguing in Publication Data
A catalogue record for this book is available from the British Library

Library of Congress Cataloging-in-Publication Data
Fifty Hollywood directors / edited by Yvonne Tasker and Suzanne Leonard.
pages cm
Includes bibliographical references and index.
1. Motion picture industry–California–Los Angeles–History–20th century. 2. Motion picture producers and directors–California–Los Angeles–History–20th century. 3. Motion picture producers and directors–California–Los Angeles–Biography. I. Tasker, Yvonne, 1964– editor. II. Leonard, Suzanne, editor.
PN1993.5.U65F655 2015
791.43'09794'94–dc23
2014019069

ISBN: 978-0-415-50139-2 (hbk)
ISBN: 978-0-415-50140-8 (pbk)
ISBN: 978-1-315-74503-9 (ebk)

Typeset in Bembo
by Taylor & Francis Books

MIX
Paper from
responsible sources
FSC
www.fsc.org FSC® C013056

Printed and bound in Great Britain by
TJ International Ltd, Padstow, Cornwall

CONTENTS

CONTRIBUTORS

Eylem Atakav is Senior Lecturer in Film and Television Studies at the University of East Anglia where she teaches courses on women and film; women, Islam and media; and Middle Eastern media. She is the author of *Women and Turkish Cinema: Gender Politics, Cultural Identity and Representation* (Routledge, 2012) and editor of *Directory of World Cinema: Turkey* (Intellect, 2013). Her academic interests are in Middle Eastern film and television; representation of "honour" crimes in the media; and women's cinema. She writes frequently on issues around gender and culture for the *Huffington Post* (UK) and for her co-authored blog on women's cinema: *Auteuse Theories*.

Jeanine Basinger is Corwin-Fuller Professor of Film Studies at Wesleyan University, where she chairs the College of Film and the Moving Image. She is also Curator and Founder of the Wesleyan Cinema Archive, a Trustee of the American Film Institute and the National Board of Review, and the author of numerous articles in publications such as *The Washington Post, The Wall Street Journal, The New York Times, The New York Review of Books*, etc. She is the author of eleven books on film, the latest of which is *I Do and I Don't: A History of Marriage on Film*, published by Alfred A. Knopf (2013). She served as advisor on Martin Scorsese's *A Story of Movies*, co-produced an American Masters episode on Clint Eastwood, and was head consultant on the PBS series *American Cinema: 100 Years of Filmmaking* for which she also wrote the companion book. A nationally recognized expert on American film history, she has won the William K. Everson prize, the Theatre Library Association Award, Wesleyan's Binswanger Prize for Excellence in Teaching, and the Connecticut Governor's Award for her contribution to film and the arts.

Tim Bergfelder is Professor of Film at the University of Southampton. He is an editor of *Screen* and has published widely on aspects of European and international film history. Books as author and editor include *The Titanic as Myth and Memory: Representations in Visual and Literary Culture* (I. B. Tauris, 2004), *International Adventures: German Popular Cinema and European Co-Productions in the 1960s* (Berghahn 2005), *Film Architecture and the Transnational Imagination: Set Design in 1930s European Cinema* (Amsterdam University Press, 2007), and *Destination London: German-Speaking Emigrés and British Cinema 1925–1950* (Berghahn 2008).

Lucy Bolton is Lecturer in Film Studies at Queen Mary, University of London. She is the author of *Film and Female Consciousness: Irigaray, Cinema and Thinking Women* (Palgrave Macmillan, 2011) and of many articles and book chapters on film philosophy and on stardom. Upcoming publications include a chapter on *The Hours* in the second edition of Warren Buckland's *Puzzle Films* and a chapter on the figure of "the girl in British cinema" for the book *International Cinema and the Girl: Local Issues and Transnational Contexts*, edited by Fiona Handyside and Kate Taylor. She is currently co-editing, with Julie Lobalzo-Wright, a collection of essays called *Lasting Stars: Images that Fade and Personas that Endure* (Palgrave Macmillan). Her current research is for a monograph on cinema and the philosophy of Iris Murdoch, and she is also co-writing, with Catherine Wheatley, *An Introduction to Film Philosophy: Concepts, Forms and Theories* (Berghahn).

Shane Brown recently completed his PhD at the University of East Anglia in Norwich, with his thesis centred around representations of queerness and masculinity in the films of Europe and America during the silent and early sound eras. His publications include an essay co-written with Mark Jancovich on the critical reception of Boris Karloff and Bela Lugosi, published in an edited collection, and also an article on the treatment in the press of silent star Jack Pickford following the death of his wife, Olive Thomas.

Shelley Cobb is a lecturer in English and Film at the University of Southampton. Her main research interests are representations of women in film, women filmmakers and film adaptation. She has published on Jane Campion, *Bridget Jones's Diary*, postfeminism, chick-flicks, celebrity culture and film adaptation theory.

Steven Cohan is Professor of English at Syracuse University. His books include *Telling Stories: A Theoretical Analysis of Narrative Fiction* (Routledge, 1987), *Screening the Male: Exploring Masculinities in Hollywood Cinema* (Routledge, 1993), *The Road Movie Book* (Routledge, 1997), *Masked Men: Masculinity and the Movies in the Fifties* (Indiana

University Press, 1997), *Hollywood Musicals: The Film Reader* (Routledge, 2001), *Incongruous Entertainment: Camp, Cultural Value and the MGM Musical* (Duke University Press, 2005), *CSI: Crime Scene Investigation* (British Film Institute, 2008), and *The Sound of Musicals* (British Film Institute, 2010). At present he is writing a book on films about making movies and the branding of Hollywood.

Celestino Deleyto is Professor of Film Studies and English at the University of Zaragoza, Spain. His books include *The Secret Life of Romantic Comedy* (Manchester University Press, 2009) and *Alejandro González Iñárritu*, co-written with María del Mar Azcona (University of Illinois Press, 2010), as well as books in Spanish on contemporary Hollywood cinema, the films of Woody Allen and *Smoke*. At the moment he is working on a volume on the representation of the city of Los Angeles in post-1992 movies, forthcoming from Wayne State University Press.

Steven Doles is a PhD candidate in the Department of English at Syracuse University. His general research interests focus on forms and genres that blur the line between fictional and factual representations, such as the essay film, reality television, and especially the social problem film genre. He is currently completing a dissertation about the role of assertion and rhetoric in the social problem films of the 1940s and 1950s.

Peter William Evans is Emeritus Professor of Film Studies at Queen Mary, University of London. He is the author of *Written on the Wind* (BFI, 2013), *Top Hat* (Wiley-Blackwell, 2010), *The Films of Luis Buñuel: Subjectivity and Desire* (Oxford University Press, 1995), *Women on the Verge of a Nervous Breakdown* (BFI, 1996), *Carol Reed* (Manchester University Press 2005) and co-author, with Bruce Babington, of *Blue Skies and Silver Linings; Aspects of the Hollywood Musical* (Manchester University Press, 1985)*, Affairs to Remember; the Hollywood Comedy of the Sexes* (Manchester University Press, 1989), *Biblical Epics: Sacred Narrative in the Hollywood Cinema* (Manchester University Press, 1993) and "All that Heaven Allowed; Another Look at Sirkian Irony" (*Movie* 34/5, 1990, pp. 48–58).

Pete Falconer is a Lecturer in Film, and Deputy Head of Film and Television, at the University of Bristol. His work revolves primarily around the forms and genres of popular cinema. He has published writing on Westerns, horror movies, and on other aspects of popular culture (including country music). He is currently working on a book about the "afterlife" of the Western genre.

David Greven is Associate Professor of English at the University of South Carolina. His books include *Psycho-Sexual: Male Desire in Hitchcock, De Palma, Scorsese, and Friedkin* (University of Texas Press, 2013), *The Fragility of Manhood: Hawthorne, Freud, and the Politics of Gender* (Ohio State University Press, 2012), *Representations of Femininity in American Genre Cinema: The Woman's Film, Film Noir, and Modern Horror* (Palgrave, 2011), *Manhood in Hollywood from Bush to Bush* (University of Texas Press, 2009), and *Men Beyond Desire: Manhood, Sex, and Violation in American Literature* (Palgrave, 2005). He is on the editorial boards of *Cinema Journal*, *Poe Studies*, and *Genders* and is currently working on a book about post-millennial Hollywood masculinity called *Ghost Faces*.

Oliver Gruner is a lecturer in Visual Culture at the University of Portsmouth. His research focuses on cultural memory of the 1960s and the historical film. He has had essays published in the journals *Rethinking History* and *The Historical Journal of Film, Radio and Television* as well as in various edited collections.

Ina Rae Hark is Distinguished Professor Emerita of English and Film and Media Studies at the University of South Carolina. She is the author of *Deadwood* (Wayne State TV Milestones, 2012) and *Star Trek* (BFI Television Classics, 2008) and editor or co-editor of *American Cinema of the 1930s: Themes and Variations* (Rutgers, 2007), *Exhibition: the Film Reader* (Routledge, 2001), *The Road Movie Book* (Routledge, 1997) and *Screening the Male* (Routledge, 1993).

Dana Heller is Eminent Scholar and Chair of English at Old Dominion University in Norfolk, Virginia. She holds an MFA from Columbia University and a PhD from the Graduate Center, CUNY. She writes about popular culture, television, queer arts, and all things considered to be in bad taste. Her most recent books are *Loving The L Word: The Complete Series in Focus* (I. B. Tauris, 2013), and *Hairspray* (Wiley-Blackwell, 2011).

Jan Johnson-Smith has taught at universities in the USA and UK and was Senior Lecturer in Film and Television at Bournemouth University for many years. She is the author of *American Science Fiction TV: Star Trek, Stargate and Beyond* (Wesleyan University Press, 2005) and currently lectures in English, Media and Film at The Sheffield College in South Yorkshire.

Patrick Keating is an Associate Professor of Communication at Trinity University in San Antonio, where he teaches courses in film and media studies. His book, *Hollywood Lighting from the Silent Era to Film Noir* (Columbia University Press, 2009), won the Best First Book Award from the Society of Cinema and Media Studies. The Academy of Motion Picture Arts and Sciences has named him an Academy Film Scholar in support of his research on the history of camera movement.

Christopher Kelly is a writer based in New Jersey, whose film criticism has appeared in *Film Comment, Film Quarterly, Texas Monthly, The New York Times, The Chicago Tribune, Premiere, Salon. com*, Slate and numerous other publications. From 2000 to 2012, he was the chief film critic of the *Fort Worth Star-Telegram. He is also the author of a novel, A Push and a Shove (Alyson Books, 2007).*

Rob King is an Associate Professor at Columbia University's Film Program, where he is currently working on a history of short-subject slapstick during the early sound era. He is the author of *The Fun Factory: The Keystone Film Company and the Emergence of Mass Culture* (University of California Press, 2009), and co-editor of the volumes *Early Cinema and the "National"* (John Libbey Publishing, 2008), *Slapstick Comedy* (Routledge, 2011), and *Beyond the Screen: Institutions, Networks and Publics of Early Cinema* (John Libbey Publishing, 2012).

Amanda Ann Klein is Associate Professor of Film Studies in the English Department of East Carolina University. She is the author of *American Film Cycles: Reframing Genres, Screening Social Problems, & Defining Subcultures* (University of Texas Press, 2011). Her work on film and television has been published in *The Quarterly Review of Film and Video, Jump Cut, Flow, Antenna, MediaCommons* and several edited anthologies. She also blogs regularly about film, television and popular culture at *Judgmental Observer* (http://judgmentalobserver.com).

Sarah Kozloff is the William R. Kenan, Jr. Professor in the Film Department at Vassar College. In addition to her work on William Wyler, she has written *Invisible Storytellers: Voice-Over Narration in American Fiction Film* (University of California Press, 1988), and *Overhearing Film Dialogue* (University of California Press, 2000). She is also one of the co-authors of *An Introduction to Film Genres* (W.W. Norton, 2013).

Alicia Kozma is a doctoral candidate at the Institute of Communications Research at the University of Illinois. Her dissertation research is concerned with gendered authorship in U.S. independent cinema of the 1960s and 1970s, focusing on a case study of filmmaker Stephanie Rothman. Her areas of interest coalesce around the theoretical and practical issues surrounding gender in film, cultural worth/taste culture in film and television, marginalized media products, female media production, cult media, affect, and sexuality studies. She is a former adjunct lecturer of Hunter College's Department of Film and Media Studies and is an Instructor in the University of Illinois Media and Cinema Studies Program.

Suzanne Leonard is Associate Professor of English at Simmons College, where she coordinates the minor in Cinema and Media Studies. She is the author of *Fatal Attraction* (Wiley-Blackwell, 2009) and her specialties include feminist media studies, American film and television studies, and contemporary women's literature. Her articles have appeared in *Signs*, *Feminist Media Studies*, *Genders*, and *Women's Studies Quarterly*, as well as in various anthologies.

Cynthia Lucia is Professor of English and Director of the Film and Media Studies Program at Rider University. She has been an editor of *Cineaste* and of the magazine's Film Review section for more than two decades and is author of *Framing Female Lawyers: Women on Trial in Film* (University of Texas Press, 2005). She is co-editor of *The Wiley-Blackwell History of American Film* (Wiley-Blackwell, 2012), a four-volume series named an Outstanding Academic Title of the Year by *Choice*, of the American Library Association. Beyond her work published in *Cineaste*, her writing has appeared in various anthologies, including *Law, Culture and Visual Studies* (Springer, 2014); *Modern British Drama on Screen* (Cambridge, 2013); *A Companion to Woody Allen* (Wiley-Blackwell, 2013); and *Authorship and Adaptation* (Texas, 2008).

Alice Maurice is Associate Professor of English at the University of Toronto. She is the author of *The Cinema and its Shadow: Race and Technology in Early Cinema* (University of Minnesota Press, 2013). Her articles have appeared in journals including *Camera Obscura*, *Cinema Journal*, *Moving Image*, and the *Henry James Review*.

Walter Metz is a professor of film and television studies in the Department of Cinema and Photography at Southern Illinois University. He is the author of three books: *Engaging Film Criticism: Film History and Contemporary American Cinema* (Peter Lang, 2004), *Bewitched* (Wayne State University Press, 2007), and *Gilligan's Island* (Wayne State University Press, 2012), and over fifty articles and book chapters devoted to intertextuality in cinema. His website, devoted to re-inventing film criticism, "Walter's World" can be found at http://waltermetz.com. His new book about Pixar Animation Studios, Dr. Seuss, and *The Simpsons*, is under contract with Wayne State University Press.

Kristian Moen is a Lecturer in the Department of Film and Television Studies at the University of Bristol. His research focuses on the place of fantasy in cinema and modernity, the relationship of cinema with other cultural and artistic forms, and the aesthetics and history of animation. He is the author of *Film and Fairy Tales: The Birth of Modern Fantasy* (I. B. Tauris, 2013).

Giuliana Muscio is Professor of Cinema at the University of Padua, Italy, but she has taught also at UCLA and at the University of Minnesota, Minneapolis, as a Visiting Professor. She received her PhD in film at UCLA. She is author of *Hollywood's New Deal* (Temple University Press, 1996), of the forthcoming *Napoli/New York/Hollywood*, and of works both in Italian and English on screenwriting, film relations between USA and Italy, Cold War cinema, the New Deal and cinema, women screenwriters in American silent cinema, and Italian actors from the immigrant stage in Hollywood. She was a member of the European program "Changing Media, Changing Europe", and she belongs to the Steering Committee of the Women and Silent Screen.

Alan Nadel, William T. Bryan Chair in American Literature and Culture at the University of Kentucky, is the author of several books and numerous articles on post-World War II American literature, film, drama, and television. His monographs include *Flatlining on the Field of Dreams: Cultural Narratives in the Films of President Reagan's America* (Rutgers University Press, 1997) and *Television in Black-and-White America: Race and National Identity* (University Press of Kansas, 2005). Most recently he has, with Susan Griffin, co-edited *The Men Who Knew Too Much: Henry James and Alfred Hitchcock* (Oxford University Press, 2012).

Steve Neale is Professor of Film Studies at the University of Exeter. He is author of *Genre and Hollywood* (Routledge, 2000), co-author of *Epics, Spectacles and Blockbusters* (Wayne State University Press, 2010), and editor of *The Classical Hollywood Reader* (Routledge, 2012) and *Silent Features* (forthcoming).

Martha P. Nochimson is the author of six books, and has had essays reprinted in numerous anthologies; her latest publications are *David Lynch Swerves: Uncertainty from Lost Highway to Inland Empire* (University of Texas Press, 2014) and *An Introduction to Film Genres* (W.W. Norton, 2013), to which she contributed three chapters. She is currently busy editing the forthcoming Wiley/Blackwell *Companion to Wong Kar-wai*. A Professor Emerita at Mercy College, she also taught for over a decade at the Tisch School of the Arts at New York University. She is a frequent contributor to *Film Quarterly* and served as Associate Editor for six years at *Cineaste*. Between 1984 and 1990, she took time out from her academic duties to write and edit five network soap operas.

Harvey O'Brien is the author of *Action Movies: The Cinema of Striking Back* (Columbia University Press, 2012) and *The Real Ireland: The Evolution of Ireland in Documentary Film* (Manchester University Press, 2005). He has contributed to journals, magazines, edited collections, and reference works including *Cineaste* and *Historical Journal of Film, Radio and Television* and is former co-editor of the journal *Film and Film Culture*. He teaches Early and Silent Cinema, Documentary, Animation, and general film studies at University College Dublin. He is former associate director of the Boston Irish Film Festival and currently serves on the Board of Directors of the Irish Film Institute.

Marc O'Day is a freelance writer and researcher. In the 1980s he studied and taught English and American literature at the University of East Anglia. In the 1990s and 2000s he moved into Film and Media Studies, teaching adult education for Cinema City, Norwich and Ipswich Film Theatre and undertaking course leadership, administrative and management roles at Suffolk College (from 2007 University Campus Suffolk). He has published work on the novelists Angela Carter and J. G. Ballard, film directors David Cronenberg and David Lynch, action babe cinema, the television series *The Avengers* and postmodernism and television. He is currently working on a study of the bonds between men in association football, provisionally titled *The Glory and the Shame: Football, Men and Honour*.

Maria Pramaggiore is Professor and Head of Media Studies at the National University of Ireland, Maynooth in County Kildare. She has published four books and a number of articles on various topics in cinema and media studies, from feminist and queer cinemas to

Irish film to reality TV, and is the co-author of *Film: A Critical Introduction* with Tom Wallis (Pearson, 2011). She is currently writing a book on Stanley Kubrick's *Barry Lyndon*.

Sudarshan Ramani was born in 1988 in Bombay, India. Today he resides in the city, since renamed Mumbai. He completed his M. A. in English Literature at the University of Mumbai in 2010. He has worked for the UK DVD Company Mr. Bongo Films as a researcher and copywriter and is active as a programmer and film critic, contributing to such publications as *La Furia Umana* and *Projectorhead*.

Joanna E. Rapf is a professor of English and Film & Media Studies at the University of Oklahoma. She edited *Sidney Lumet Interviews* (University of Mississippi Press, 2006), a book that includes an interview she did herself with the director. Other books include *Buster Keaton: A Bio-Bibliography* (Greenwood, 1995), *On the Waterfront* (Cambridge, 2003), and with Andrew Horton, *A Companion to Film Comedy* (Wiley-Blackwell, 2012). She regularly teaches Lumet in her courses and references him in her published work.

Elizabeth Rawitsch is Visiting Lecturer in Film Studies at the University of North Carolina Wilmington. She received her PhD in Film, Television and Media Studies from the University of East Anglia, and her research on classical Hollywood film, national identity and American popular culture has appeared in *The Journal of Popular Film and Television* and *In Media Res*.

Zoran Samardzija is Assistant Professor of Cinema Art + Science at Columbia College Chicago. He has published several essays on Eastern European cinema in addition to essays on David Lynch and *Star Trek*.

Thomas Schur is a Visiting Assistant Professor at Claremont McKenna College. He is co-author of *The Films of Terrence Malick* (Praeger, 2003), and is currently working on a book that looks at cinema through the lens of systems theory.

Neil Sinyard is Emeritus Professor of Film Studies at the University of Hull, UK and Visiting Professor of Film at the University of Lincoln, UK. He is the author of twenty-five books and over 100 articles on film and has contributed to a number of radio and television programmes about the cinema, as well as doing the commentary on the DVD release of Billy Wilder's *Ace in the Hole*. His books include studies of Hollywood directors such as Billy Wilder, Fred Zinnemann, Steven Spielberg, Clint Eastwood, Woody Allen and Mel Brooks as well as studies of Marilyn Monroe, Walt Disney, and topics such as Silent Film, Film Comedy, Representations of Childhood on Film, and Film Adaptation. His most recent book is *A Wonderful Heart: The Films of William Wyler* (McFarland, 2013); and he is currently writing a book on the films of George Stevens.

Tim Snelson is a Lecturer in Media History at the University of East Anglia (UK). His research addressing the relationship between media and social history has been published in journals including *Media History*, *Cultural Studies* and *New Review of Film and Television Studies*, and in edited collections including *Explorations in New Cinema History: Approaches and Case Studies* (Wiley-Blackwell, 2011) and *Gendering the Recession: Media Culture in an Age of Austerity* (Duke, 2014). He has a forthcoming monograph titled *Phantom Ladies: Hollywood Horror and the Home Front* (Rutgers, 2014).

Shelley Stamp is the author of *Movie-Struck Girls: Women and Motion Picture Culture after the Nickelodeon* (Princeton University Press, 2000) and *Lois Weber in Early Hollywood* (University of California Press, forthcoming 2015). She is currently at work on *Women and the Silent Screen in America*, co-written with Anne Morey. With Charlie Keil she co-edited *American Cinema's Transitional Era: Audiences, Institutions, Practices* (University of California Press, forthcoming 2015). Her essays have appeared in anthologies on silent cinema, film censorship, and feminist historiography and she has provided expert audio commentary for several DVD releases. Stamp is Professor of Film & Digital Media at the University of California, Santa Cruz, where she won the Excellence in Teaching Award.

Lindsay Steenberg is a senior lecturer in Film Studies at Oxford Brookes University. Her research focuses on violence and gender in postmodern and postfeminist media culture. She has published on the subject of the crime genre, reality television and is the author of *Forensic Science in Contemporary American Popular Culture: Gender, Crime, and Science* (Routledge, 2012).

Yvonne Tasker is Professor of Film and Media Studies and Dean of Arts and Humanities at the University of East Anglia, UK. She has written extensively on gender and popular cinema and is the editor of *Fifty Contemporary Filmmakers* (Routledge, 2002, 2010).

Yannis Tzioumakis is Senior Lecturer in Communication and Media at the University of Liverpool. His research specializes in American cinema and the business of entertainment. He is the author and editor of six books, including *American Independent Cinema: An Introduction* (Rutgers University Press, 2006), *Hollywood's Indies: Classics Divisions, Specialty Labels and the American Film Market* (Edinburgh University Press, 2012), *American Independent Cinema: Indie, Indiewood and Beyond* (Routledge, 2012) and *The Time of Our Lives: Dirty Dancing and Popular Culture* (Wayne State University Press, 2013). He also co-edits the American Indies series for Edinburgh University Press, which has published five volumes on key independent films. He is currently developing Hollywood Centenary, a book series dedicated to the 100 year anniversary of the Hollywood studios.

Christopher Weedman is a Visiting Assistant Professor in the Department of English at Kutztown University of Pennsylvania, where he teaches courses on the American Genre Film and Film Production Theory. He has published articles on the films of Joseph Losey, Jean-Luc Godard, Roman Polanski, Jerzy Skolimowski, Howard Hawks, and Anthony Mann in film journals such as *Quarterly Review of Film and Video* and *Senses of Cinema*. He is currently writing a book on Joseph Losey and Harold Pinter's film collaboration.

Michael Williams is a Senior Lecturer in Film Studies at the University of Southampton. His monograph *Film Stardom, Myth and Classicism: The Rise of the Hollywood Gods*, exploring the use of antiquity in the creation of Hollywood stardom, was published by Palgrave Macmillan in 2012. He is also author of *Ivor Novello: Screen Idol*, a contextual study on Britain's first major film star (BFI, 2003), and co-editor of the collection *British Silent Cinema and the Great War* (Palgrave Macmillan, 2011). Other work includes: queer readings of the heritage film; Belgian filmmaker Bavo Defurne; film adaptations of Highsmith's *The Talented Mr. Ripley*; Anton Walbrook; and various essays on stars. He is an editorial advisor for *The Velvet Light Trap* and is currently working on a monograph for Palgrave Macmillan, *Film Stardom and the Ancient Past*, which examines stardom's relationship to antiquity from the 1930s to the present.

INTRODUCTION

By Yvonne Tasker and Suzanne Leonard

The origins of the present collection lie in the desire to provide a companion volume to an earlier anthology of writings, *Fifty Contemporary Filmmakers*, the second edition of which was published in 2010. Ironically enough, the authorship approach around which that collection was organized came to prominence as a tool for analysing Hollywood cinema of what is known as the classical period (more or less from the 1930s to the 1960s). Some of the best known criticism of the 1950s that understood the director as a central organizing presence of the cinema as art looked to Hollywood filmmakers: John Ford, Howard Hawks, Orson Welles, for example. These men – and they were indeed all men – were credited with delivering a creative vision within the confines of a studio system that operated in quite particular ways. This is not the space to engage in a protracted discussion of the value and the limitations of authorship criticism: within film studies these questions are well rehearsed. Even so, it remains the case that prominent filmmakers, many of whom served not only as director but screenwriter, producer and even sometimes performer (such as Elia Kazan, Billy Wilder, Raoul Walsh, and Alfred Hitchcock) provide a fascinating entry point for readers interested in the study of cinema history. The men and women whose work is discussed by the contributors to this volume are not the only figures of note in Hollywood filmmaking: we understand that the cinema is very much a collaborative endeavour. However, the study of film directors allows us to think about the creative and commercial imperatives of the American film industry, incorporating numerous cultural influences – theatre, radio, popular fiction – and drawing personnel from many nations.

We have organized *Fifty Hollywood Directors* in order to frame the classical period of Hollywood filmmaking in terms of what went before and what came after. Thus while the majority of the essays concern what is known as the classical Hollywood of the studio era, that investigation is bookended by shorter sections: the first exploring directors prominent within early and silent Hollywood, the last exploring the so-called "New Hollywood". The structure serves to highlight the blurred boundaries between the various categories of which cinema history consists rather than to challenge their validity. Of course several of the filmmakers considered here cross these historical boundaries pursuing filmmaking careers that persisted as the industry changed in significant ways, a dimension of Hollywood foregrounded in Kristian Moen's examination of Cecil B. DeMille, Alice Maurice's discussion of King Vidor, and Jeanine Basinger's account of Anthony Mann. These terms – early, classical, new – and the categories they denote evoke a context for film production, which crucially shaped the characteristic modes of cinematic story-telling associated with Hollywood. Writing in the 1980s, Thomas Schatz used Andre Bazin's phrase, the "genius of the system" to evoke a commercial (systematized) form of film-making, which allowed for innovation and creativity within particular limits. Whether these are technological limits or regulatory ones (the strictures of the production code for instance) the essays in the book demonstrate filmmakers who operated productively and with a degree of aesthetic and/or thematic consistency within the commercial context of Hollywood.

Given the significance and status of the figure of the director both within the industry and within cinema studies, it is not perhaps surprising that by far the majority and by far the best known names are male. While historical accounts suggest that larger numbers of women were involved in film production in the silent period – to some extent before roles became more tightly defined as Shelley Stamp shows with her piece here on Lois Weber – the classical Hollywood of the studio system gave few opportunities for women to direct. Indeed, as Eylem Atakav notes, only one woman, Dorothy Arzner, achieved the sort of prominence associated with male author-directors in the studio years. The only other prominent female director of the Hollywood years, Ida Lupino, forged her career as actor and producer, as Shelley Cobb discusses. Developing her directing career in the changing Hollywood context of the 1950s, Lupino's production company allowed greater opportunities for directorial projects. In the New Hollywood Stephanie Rothman both directed and wrote films with progressive socio-political messages in the 1970s, but, as Alicia Kozma documents, Rothman has largely been consigned to the footnotes of mainstream film history. These examples indicate that women have managed to develop directorial careers in particular circumstances. This said, the risk of being written out of film history seemingly remains high, a particular concern for us as editors.

Hollywood directors in the period covered within this book are not only mostly male, they are overwhelmingly white. Incorporating an essay on Oscar Micheaux represents a gesture towards those African American filmmakers excluded from the institutions of American cinema up to the 1970s. Micheaux himself, as Shane Brown argues in his essay here, was both an important figure in American film history and a filmmaker who worked effectively outside (and yet in relation to) Hollywood. The essays in this volume nevertheless trouble the distinction between "inside" and "outside". Even filmmakers who are today considered or remembered as American directors gleaned the basics of their craft from international – and generally European – cinemas, importing styles and techniques across national borders. As Ina Rae Hark clarifies, Michael Curtiz was already a prolific director before arriving in Hollywood, having made sixty-four previous films in Hungary, Austria, and Denmark. In the context of the 1930s, the rise of fascism led many filmmakers to leave an increasingly hostile Europe for the US, luminaries including Fritz Lang, Robert Siodmak, Douglas Sirk, Ernst Lubitsch, Max Ophüls, and Joseph von Sternberg.

Many other directors deliberately worked with international crews both behind and in front of the camera: Joseph Losey made his most memorable films in collaboration with British playwright Harold Pinter, and was at the same time a darling of French critics, as Christopher Weedman elucidates. James Whale was lauded for utilizing a style reminiscent of German expressionist horror and, as Michael Williams explains, the director made a habit of introducing British actors and writers to American audiences. Though he is little remembered as such, Orson Welles is aptly understood as a transnational figure whose directorial vision benefitted from extensive European travel, suggests Celestino Deleyto. Roman Polanksi is likewise included in this volume though he made only two films in the United States. Thomas Schur reminds us, however, that despite this international production schedule (for which there are specific reasons related to Polanski's criminal history in the United States) Polanski's films tend to be shot in English and feature prominent Hollywood stars.

Whether or not their origins were explicitly outside the American context, directors have long craved independence from the Hollywood system. This desire for greater creative control makes its first appearance in this volume with the collaboration of D. W. Griffith and Charlie Chaplin, who founded United Artists in conjunction with Douglas Fairbanks, Mary Pickford, and William S. Hart, in 1919. Other directors who attempted solo stints by either developing their own companies or working as or with independent producers include King Vidor, Lois Weber, Frank Capra, Robert Aldrich, Ida Lupino, Otto Preminger, Nicholas Ray, and Preston Sturges. In the post-studio period, Stanley Kubrick is typically esteemed for his high degree of independence from the Hollywood film industry (establishing his own production companies, negotiating financing and distribution deals with major studios, and living primarily in the UK) as Maria Pramaggiore explicates. Likewise, Roger Corman's production/distribution company, New World Pictures, helped to support the work of independent directors such as Rothman, and Corman's association with marginalized cinemas such as cult, youth, and science fiction is reflected in his patterns of influence and mentoring.

Utilizing the director as an organizing framework through which to understand Hollywood film history presents multiple opportunities, we have found, to identify key debates, pinpoint influential collaborative relationships and, most importantly, convey a sense of the continuing interest and importance of these figures. Many of the directors included here will already be familiar to readers. There remains unmistakable association, for example, between certain directors and the genres they worked primarily within: John Ford, Anthony Mann, and Samuel Peckinpah with the Western, Douglas Sirk and Vincent Minnelli with the melodrama, Frank Capra with populist drama, Samuel Fuller with the war film, and John Waters with campy exploitation. This book amplifies these shorthands, often revealing the complexity within, while at the same time remaining cognizant of the productive value of these directors' iconic visual, narrative, industrial, and ideological interventions. At the same time, there is much the book leaves out, considering at it does only those filmmakers who were exceptionally prolific. Despite these necessary omissions, the promise of the book is manifold—surveying fifty Hollywood directors in detail, it attends to their skills and visions, as well as places these directors in conversation with one another and with American film history itself.

SILENT HOLLYWOOD

CHARLIE CHAPLIN

By Rob King

A seminal figure in the history of twentieth-century culture, Charles Spencer Chaplin has been accorded a unique place in the ranks of film-makers. As a star, his unquestioned import extended worldwide across the twentieth century, inspiring homages ranging from the playfully imitative to the quasi-devotional. The "Chaplinitis" craze of the mid-1910s, which greeted his initial stardom with an epidemic of movie-mad children and adults emulating his funny walk, was in this sense only the thin end of a wedge that quickly enshrined him as something akin to a mass cultural deity (dubbed a "mob-god" by his early critics). As a director, however, he remains of more equivocal status – on the one hand, celebrated in his lifetime as the medium's most important artist and, in the words of George Bernard Shaw, its "only genius"; on the other, disparaged by others of his contemporaries as a filmmaking primitive whose formal technique failed to advance beyond the level of his slapstick performances, which his camera served simply as a means of recording.[1] What might here appear as a paradox or contradiction in critical assessments of Chaplin's filmmaking nonetheless bespeaks the singularity of his achievement; for what is found in Chaplin's films is an articulation of cinematic art that emerged not primarily in terms of the formal properties of the medium – not, that is, in terms of specifically filmic resources like montage, as in the case of D. W. Griffith – but rather through a sensibility that produced a historically unequaled trans-formation in the cultural and political resonance of the popular arts.

The Tramp

Born in poverty in London's East End in 1889, Chaplin began his professional performing career on the stage at the age of just nine, before graduating to Fred Karno's celebrated music hall troupe in 1908. Five years later, Chaplin took the leap into film when, in late 1913, Mack Sennett signed him from Karno's company (then touring the US) to appear in films for the Keystone Film Company, where he soon began appearing as a bowler-hatted comic tramp. No effective account of Chaplin's iconicity can ignore the complex valences of the tramp persona he introduced at Keystone. The "little fellow" (as Chaplin liked to term him) was first introduced during the filming of *Mabel's Strange Predicament* in January of 1914 and would feature in nearly all of Chaplin's screen appearances for the next quarter century. Chaplin would occasionally be accused of filching the tramp characterization from earlier forebears. (Billie Ritchie – a Scots comedian who had played leads with Karno's troupe before Chaplin joined – was the most vocal in this regard.) But originality, in any absolute sense, was hardly at issue. Comic tramps were hugely prevalent as stock stereotypes of turn-of-the-century popular culture, in newspaper strips, dime novels, vaudeville, and early film comedy. (The American Mutoscope and Biograph Co.'s 1897 film *The Tramp and the Bathers* has been cited as the first motion-picture appearance of the comic hobo.) What distinguished Chaplin's work within this tradition was less a matter of costuming and makeup – which Ritchie, rightly or wrongly, claimed for his own – but his success in developing a more nuanced, naturalistic performance style than was screen slapstick's madcap norm, allowing for complex effects of audience empathy and involvement.

In his autobiography, Chaplin recalled describing the persona to Keystone chief Mack Sennett as follows:

> You know this fellow is many-sided, a tramp, a gentleman, a poet, a dreamer, a lonely fellow, always hopeful of romance and adventure. He would have you believe he is a scientist, a musician, a duke, a polo-player. However, he is not above picking up cigarette-butts or robbing a baby of its candy.[2]

Chaplin is here guilty of presentism, of viewing his creation through the lens of what it became, rather than what it initially was. With the single exception, perhaps, of *The New Janitor* (1914), the character Chaplin here describes never appeared at Keystone, where the tramp was more a rollicking figure of roughhouse violence and crude appetite. Still, Chaplin's memory slip does indicate the directions in which he would develop the tramp *after* Keystone – first with the Essanay Film Company, where he signed a highly publicized deal for $1,250 a week, beginning in 1915, then the following year with Mutual, where he broke star salary records by negotiating for $10,000 a week in addition to a $150,000 signing bonus. What became distinctive about Chaplin's tramp, as a popular type, was the way the character's development linked up to standards of "high" culture, in at least two ways. In terms of the film's comic plots, there was the growing imprint in Chaplin's slapstick of the codes of Victorian sentimentalism, which translated the tramp's populist content into a genteel ethical code: the "little fellow" now becomes a sentimental victim, of unrequited love in Essanay two-reelers such as *The Tramp* (1915) and *The Bank* (1915) and Mutual's *The Vagabond* (1916), of poverty and immiseration in Mutual's *Easy Street* (1917) and *The Immigrant* (1917). In terms of his pantomime, there was a pronounced emphasis on balletic virtuosity, as Chaplin now began to conjoin slapstick physicality to a more self-consciously choreographic art – inspired, in part, by a meeting with Vaslav Nijinsky, to whom Chaplin subsequently paid homage in the dance interlude from his later short, *Sunnyside* (1919).

Some soon recognized in Chaplin's slapstick the stamp of genuine aesthetic distinction, although the terms of that recognition differed. In America, for instance, the continued sway of genteel Victorianism ensured that Chaplin's achievements were celebrated in relation to a received tradition of highbrow culture, as when theater star Minnie Maddern Fiske defended Charlie's "vulgarity" by placing it in the lineage of Aristophanes, Plautus, Shakespeare, and Rabelais.[3] In Europe, however, the gestures of Chaplin's pantomime were assimilated to a modernist investment in dance as plastic form. Thus did filmmaker and critic Louis Delluc align Chaplin with Isadora Duncan, Anna Pavlova and Nijinsky, proclaiming that "The rhythm of the plastic line has a new master!" – an opinion shared by painter Fernand Léger, who turned "Charlot" (as the tramp was known in France) into a Cubist assemblage of rectangles and cylinders in the final section of his *cinéma pur* masterpiece, *Ballet mécanique* (1924).[4] What made for Chaplin's astonishing fame and repute was in this sense nothing less than a radical reevaluation of the cultural valences of the stereotypes of popular comedy, his ability to inscribe the tramp at the historical juncture of competing ideals of "art," at once modernist and genteel.

The features

Chaplin's iconicity also made him a significant industry player, one of a handful of stars with the clout to resist the growing stranglehold of film producers over the emergent Hollywood film industry. In June 1917, he signed a deal for eight comedies with First National Exhibitors Circuit, a consortium of prominent exhibitors who wanted to combat Paramount chief Adolph Zukor's expansion into theater ownership by financing their own productions. Two years later, in early 1919, Chaplin entered an alliance with D. W. Griffith, Douglas Fairbanks, Mary Pickford, and William S. Hart to form United Artists, a company that would distribute their own films independently of any external producers' oversight. Such moves represent a jostling for power within an industry that had recently consolidated itself around the multiple-reel feature as its principle commodity. Unlike the previous companies with which he had been associated, both First National and United Artists were primarily in the business of features. If he wanted to maintain his primacy, Chaplin would now too have to adapt to the longer format.

Yet the task of transitioning to multiple-reel features could be no straightforward one, given the widespread presumption that slapstick's frenetic comic pleasures simply could not be sustained at feature length (which, for the time, typically meant five reels and above). Slapstick stars who had already made the jump had done so by more or less abandoning madcap physical comedy in favor of a more plot-driven light comedy mode – as was the case with two of Chaplin's former Keystone confrères, Mabel Normand, who transitioned into features with the comedy-drama *Mickey* in 1917, and Roscoe Arbuckle, who commenced a short-lived feature series at Paramount in 1920. Chaplin was thus hardly the first slapstick star to attempt the transition. But he *was* the first to do so under his own direction, which allowed for a unique solution to the challenge of multiple-reel comedy. Rather than simply subordinate slapstick to the demands of storytelling, Chaplin's approach was to alternate between scenes of free-flowing slapstick, on the one hand, and more plot-driven sequences of sentimental drama, on the other.[5] The dual inscription of Chaplin's tramp persona – both popular and genteel – was thus translated into a principle of narrative form, defined through the systematic alternation of slapstick and sentiment.

Chaplin later described this strategy, recalling a discussion with a short-story writer during production of his first feature, the six-reel First National picture *The Kid* (1921).

> I told him about *The Kid* and the form it was taking, keying slapstick with sentiment, he said: "It won't work. The form must be pure, either slapstick or drama; you cannot mix them, otherwise one element of your story will fail." … I said that the transition from slapstick to sentiment was a matter of feeling and discretion in arranging sequences.[6]

Chaplin's care in "arranging sequences" characteristically meant a dual-focus narrative, one branch a relatively loose assemblage of knockabout sequences, the other providing a developing narrative. *The Kid*, for example, draws its major story arc from reformist ideologies of child dependency. An unwed working-class mother abandons her baby; years later, now a successful opera singer, she commits to charitable aid for the children of the poor. Yet interleaved with these scenes – and constituting the bulk of the film's running time – are a series of more slapstick-oriented situations involving the tramp's relation with the abandoned child.

The Kid remains unusual within Chaplin's feature-length filmography for its rigorous separation of elements (the little fellow does not really participate in the sentimental plot until the film's final moments, when the woman welcomes both her long-lost son and the tramp into her home). Chaplin's subsequent tramp features more successfully harmonize the alternation of slapstick and sentimental narrative by focalizing both around the little fellow. *The Gold Rush* (1925), for example, interpolates knockabout sequences of the tramp's quest for gold within a romantic narrative of the tramp's unrequited love for good-time girl Georgia (Georgia Hale). The film's comedic tone is carefully modulated across the two lines: to the former belongs a number of comic scenes revolving around bodily appetite, such as the famous sequence in which the starving tramp dines on a boot; to the latter corresponds the more pathos-oriented pantomime of the dance of the bread rolls, when the lonely tramp dreams of impressing Georgia over dinner. This exact formal structure would continue into his subsequent two features – in *The Circus* (1928), which interleaves a sentimental romance with slapstick sequences of the tramp's work in the big ring, as well as in *City Lights* (1931), where the tramp's romantic scenes with the blind flower girl (Virginia Cherrill) alternate with more straightforwardly comedic scenes featuring a drunken millionaire (Harry Myers).

Chaplin also used his features to redefine the parameters of comic creativity. As Henry Jenkins has shown, the tradition of vaudeville and music hall comedy from which slapstick derived prioritized the *performer* as the chief creative force, emphasizing the individual comic actor's ability to "stop the show."[7] What one sees in Chaplin, by contrast, is an attempt to relocate comic creativity so that it was not only his virtuosity as a performer that was at issue, but also his behind-the-camera artistry as a filmmaker. This endeavor to authorize his identity as more than "just" a body pushed him in a number of directions. It led him autocratically to appropriate almost all major creative functions on his films: from early on, Chaplin customarily starred in, directed, wrote, edited, produced, and even – beginning with *City Lights* – composed scores for all his pictures. It also accounts for his decision to follow up the triumph of *The Kid* with *A Woman of Paris* (1923), a film that was not only not a slapstick comedy, but in which Chaplin appeared merely in an unheralded bit part – a double erasure of the body, that is, whereby Chaplin's artistry was located entirely outside the orbit of comic performance. Chaplin's desire to be recognized as a serious artist was expressed in *A Woman of Paris* through a style of sophisticated storytelling predicated on ironic understatement and implication, earning him plaudits for what one critic described as a "revolutionary event" in the history of film aesthetics (and which proved a major influence on the developing style of Ernst Lubitsch).[8]

Politics

It is clear, however, that a turning point in Chaplin's career is reached some time following *City Lights*, after which Chaplin would begin his second reinvention of slapstick – not, as earlier, to inscribe physical comedy in a continuum with high art, but now to seize upon slapstick's popular energies as a basis for socialist political engagement, a shift in strategies that would carry through to his penultimate movie, *A King in New York* (1957). Chaplin's interest in socialist politics can perhaps be dated to the start of his friendship with Upton Sinclair in 1918; but the particular form that his recalibration of comedy began to take in the 1930s had more proximate motivation in a fourteen-month world tour following *City Lights*' release. His firsthand witnessing of the global effects of the depression, together with meetings with Gandhi, H. G. Wells, and many others, seemingly persuaded him to turn to political commentary, as detailed in his subsequent account of that tour, *A Comedian Sees the World* (1933).

Yet Chaplin's project in transitioning toward a more politically engaged mode of comedy was complicated in relation to another transition: namely, the industry-wide conversion to sound, largely complete by 1929. Chaplin was famously resistant to the advent of sound (which he declared was "ruining the great beauty of silence") and, uniquely among Hollywood directors, made little concession to the new technology for his initial sound productions.[9] His first sound-era film, *City Lights*, thus amounted to what film scholar Michel Chion has described as a "manifesto in defense of the art of silent film," in which the soundtrack is used to provide musical accompaniment and sound effects only but with no audible dialogue.[10] His next, *Modern Times* (1936), included sporadic moments of dialogue – perhaps most famously at the end of the film, when Chaplin's tramp sings a nonsense song – but was still essentially a silent film. It was also Chaplin's most concerted effort to date to engage comedy as a platform for social commentary. Depicting a lowly worker (the little fellow) deranged by the pressures of working an assembly line, *Modern Times* gave stark, social realist inflection to themes of class inequality that Chaplin's previous films had engaged in a more sentimental mode. Aware that his political opinions might alienate some of his audience, Chaplin gave his film contradictory descriptions at the time: in one instance, he spoke of it openly as a "satire on the factory system," in another more evasively as "a comedy picture with no endeavor to comment … [on] political affairs."[11] Thus, while the film gave unusually stark visual expression to the economic realities of Depression-era America, *Modern Times* also used comedy to render its political commitments slippery. Symptomatic is a scene in which the tramp picks up a red flag that has fallen from a truck and, waving it and shouting to gain the driver's attention, finds that he is inadvertently leading a demonstration of striking workers. The depiction of a workers' march constitutes an acknowledgment of labor radicalism rarely encountered in classical Hollywood cinema, but the tramp's comically unintended relation to it arguably fudges the issue – which explains why the film's bid for social significance could be overlooked by a number of critics who saw in *Modern Times* simply rough-and-ready farce.

His next film would admit of no such ambiguities. Prompted in part by the resemblance between his tramp character and Adolf Hitler, Chaplin now began to develop ideas for a satire of the German Führer that would use dialogue in a sustained way to deliver what the *New York Times* described as "certain politico-sociological messages."[12] Although isolationist sentiment in the US more or less ensured damaging political fallout from such a project, Chaplin's desire to take a political stance overrode any hesitancy, resulting in the most controversial film of his career, *The Great Dictator* (1940). In order to resolve the dilemmas that synchronized dialogue posed for his pantomime-based comedy, Chaplin opted here to play dual roles, the paranoid dictator Adenoid Hynkel and a nameless Jewish barber, loosely based on the tramp. (As Chaplin explained in his autobiography, the former permitted him to indulge in nonsense dialogue and the other to exercise his pantomimic talents. "As Hitler I could harangue the crowds in jargon and talk all I wanted to. And as the tramp I could remain more or less silent.")[13] But the doubling does more than allow Chaplin to hedge his abandonment of silence; it also becomes a structural principle for his transition to unambiguously political speech. Hynkel's speech at a rally near the beginning of the film – a hate-spewing screed whose parodic "German" continues the vein of nonsense singing that ends *Modern Times* – is thus answered by another speech at the close when, in an infamous scene, the Jewish barber takes Hynkel's place to deliver a pacifist message of hope. A couple of sentences from this four-minute monologue can convey the tone:

> Let us fight for a new world, a decent world that will give men a chance to work, that will give you the future and old age and security. ... Let us fight to free the world, to do away with national barriers, do away with greed, with hate and intolerance.

Chaplin was proud of that speech, which he would be called upon to recite in Washington during FDR's third-term inauguration festivities in 1941; but its legacy would prove a difficult one, both for Chaplin's subsequent films and for his life as a public figure. In respect to the former, the climactic scene of *The Great Dictator* stands as a harbinger of what would become a formidable schism in the filmmaker's subsequent work, a rigid separation dividing speech from slapstick. Purged of comedy, Chaplin's speech would prove unable to transcend seriousness (resulting in the oft-remarked political speechifying of his subsequent films such as *Monsieur Verdoux* [1946]), while his comedy, purged of speech, found itself consigned to the wordless realm of pantomime (as in the stage routines, both dreamed and real, in *Limelight* [1952], his semi-autobiographical film about an aging clown). In respect to the latter, Chaplin's unambiguous expression of progressive politics in *The Great Dictator* gave him the confidence to pursue more openly political activity off-screen, fueling the hostilities of the FBI, which had opened a file on Chaplin as early as 1922. During the war years, Chaplin delivered addresses on behalf of several Communist Party-affiliated organizations, including Russian War Relief and the National Council of American-Soviet Friendship. After the war, Chaplin's reputation swiftly imploded under the pressure of a redbaiting slander campaign orchestrated by the FBI and the Justice Department to engineer Chaplin's deportation under charges of "moral turpitude," forcing him into exile in 1953.

***

Chaplin made two more films, both shot at the Pinewood Studios in England. The first, *A King in New York* (1957) continued the more autobiographical turn of *Limelight*, this time in the form of a political satire about a deposed king who falls under the suspicions of the House Subcommittee on Un-American Activities. The second, *A Countess from Hong Kong* (1967), marked Chaplin's return to the sophisticated comedy of manners of *A Woman of Paris*, although this time he was faced with unanimous disdain for what were now perceived as his old-fashioned themes and technique. Only once, in 1972, did he return to the US – five years before his death – to receive an honorary Oscar for his "incalculable effect in making motion pictures the art form of the century." The passage of time, in dating both his style and his politics, ensured that Chaplin's legacy could finally be flattened out as "incalculable" and readmitted to Hollywood's romanticized past. Since then, his achievements have been largely occluded in popular memory by his most iconic creation; Chaplin the filmmaker is obscured by Charlot the tramp. What might rather be remembered is how Chaplin, in making it possible for popular comic traditions to register as both art and politics, thereby gave voice to the better angels of cinematic mass culture.

Biography

Born in London in 1889, Charles Spencer Chaplin turned to the stage as a youth, finding success in comic sketches for music hall impresario Fred Karno. During a US tour, Chaplin signed with the Keystone Film Company where he developed a bowler-hatted "tramp" character that became an icon of twentieth-century popular culture. The most acclaimed performer-director of the silent and early-sound eras, Chaplin nonetheless attracted the suspicions of the US government for his political views and was eventually deported in 1953. He lived most of his remaining life in Switzerland, dying in 1977 on Christmas Day.

Notes

1 George Bernard Shaw, quoted in Richard Schickel, *Richard Schickel on Film: Encounters – Critical and Personal – with Movies Immortals.* New York: William Morrow, 1989, p. 17.

2 Charlie Chaplin, *My Autobiography.* London: Penguin, 1964, p. 146.

3 Minnie Maddern Fiske, "The Art of Charles Chaplin," *Harper's Weekly,* May 6, 1916, in Richard Schickel, ed., *The Essential Chaplin: Perspectives*

on the Life and Art of the Great Comedian. Chicago, Ill.: Ivan R. Dee, 2006, p. 98.

4 Delluc quoted in Jacques Rancière, *Aisthesis: Scenes from the Aesthetic Regime of Art*, trans. Zakir Paul. London: Verso, 2013, p. 195.

5 For a fuller account of Chaplin's approach to feature construction, see Steve Neale and Frank Krutnik, "Hollywood, Comedy, and the Case of Silent Slapstick," in Neale and Krutnik, *Popular Film and Television Comedy.* London: Routledge, 1990, pp. 96–131, from which a number of my following points derive.

6 Chaplin, *My Autobiography*, p. 233.

7 Jenkins, Henry. *What Made Pistachio Nuts? Early Sound Comedy and the Vaudeville Aesthetic.* New York: Columbia University Press, 1992, pp. 63–71.

8 Carr, Harry. "Will Charlie Kick Off His Old Shoes?" *Motion Picture Magazine*, December 1923: 28–29, 86, quoted in Lea Jacobs, *The Decline of Sentiment: American Film in the 1920s.* Berkeley, Cal.: University of California Press, 2008, p. 96.

9 Gladys Hall, "Charlie Chaplin Attacks the Talkies," *Motion Picture Magazine*, May 1929, 29, quoted in Kenneth S. Lynn, *Charlie Chaplin and His Times.* London: Aurum Press, 1997, p. 321.

10 Michel Chion, *Film, A Sound Art*, trans. Claudia Gorbman. New York: Columbia University Press, 2009, p. 22.

11 Chaplin quoted in Joan Mellen, *Modern Times.* London: BFI, 2006, pp. 27–28.

12 *New York Times*, February 16, 1937, IX.1, quoted in Charles Maland, *Chaplin and American Culture: The Evolution of a Star Image.* Princeton, NJ: Princeton University Press, 1989, p. 165.

13 Chaplin, *My Autobiography*, p. 387.

Filmography

Twenty Minutes of Love (1914) possibly directed by Joseph Maddern
Caught in the Rain (1914)
Mabel's Married Life (1914) possibly directed by Mack Sennett
Laughing Gas (1914)
The Property Man (1914)
The Face on the Bar Room Floor (1914)
Recreation (1914)
The Masquerader (1914)
His New Profession (1914)
The Rounders (1914)
The New Janitor (1914)
Those Love Pangs (1914)
Dough and Dynamite (1914)
Gentlemen of Nerve (1914)

His Musical Career (1914)
His Trysting Place (1914)
Getting Acquainted (1914)
His Prehistoric Past (1914)
His New Job (1915)
A Night Out (1915)
The Champion (1915)
In the Park (1915)
A Jitney Elopement (1915)
The Tramp (1915)
By the Sea (1915)
Work (1915)
A Woman (1915)
The Bank (1915)
Shanghaied (1915)
A Night in the Show (1915)
Burlesque on Carmen (1916)
Police (1916)
The Floorwalker (1916)
The Fireman (1916)
The Vagabond (1916)
One A.M. (1916)
The Count (1916)
The Pawnshop (1916)
Behind the Screen (1916)
The Rink (1916)
Easy Street (1917)
The Cure (1917)
The Immigrant (1917)
The Adventurer (1917)
A Dog's Life (1918)
The Bond (1918)
Shoulder Arms (1918)
Sunnyside (1919)
A Day's Pleasure (1919)
The Kid (1921)
The Idle Class (1921)
Pay Day (1922)
A Woman of Paris (1923)
The Gold Rush (1925)
The Circus (1928)
City Lights (1931)

Modern Times (1936)
The Great Dictator (1940)
Monsieur Verdoux (1946)
Limelight (1952)
A King in New York (1957)
A Countess from Hong Kong (1967)

Further reading

Robinson, David. Chaplin: His Life and Art. New York: McGraw-Hill, 1985.
Schickel, Richard, ed. The Essential Chaplin: Perspectives on the Life and Art of the Great Comedian. Chicago: Ivan R. Dee, 2006.

CECIL B. DEMILLE

By Kristian Moen

One of the most financially successful and publicly visible Hollywood filmmakers, Cecil B. DeMille was a central figure in Hollywood for the span of his forty-year career as a director. Although making films in a range of genres, including marital comedies, melodramas, Westerns and historical films, he is best known as the director of epic films with religious subjects, including The King of Kings (1927), The Sign of the Cross (1932), Samson and Delilah (1949) and two versions of The Ten Commandments (1923 and 1956). His public persona was associated with the role of showman, presenting films on the popular radio show "Lux Radio Theatre" and appearing within trailers and advertisements for his own films. He also was associated with an image of authority and influence within Hollywood, aiming to produce "the archetypal statement of American cultural history"[1] with Land of Liberty for the 1939 New York World's Fair, establishing a reputation as a dictatorial and controlling director and producer, and prominently promoting conservative politics.

DeMille's early films sometimes self-consciously aimed to push the boundaries of cinema as a culturally valued and socially engaged form of expression. The Cheat (1915), for example, used highly expressive mise-en-scène and lighting for expressive and visually arresting purposes. In her review of the film, the French author Colette remarked, "In Paris this week, a movie theater has become an art school. ... Every evening, writers, painters, composers, and dramatists come and come again to sit, contemplate and comment, in low voices, like pupils."[2] As well as this attention to the possibilities of film aesthetics, DeMille's films also sought cultural prestige through other means, such as casting a major opera star, Geraldine Farrar, in the lead role of *Carmen* (1915) and experimenting with cinema's capacity to depict subjectivity and psychology in *The Whispering Chorus* (1918). At the same time, DeMille's films from this period developed narratives with a striking social topicality. In a series of films featuring women enticed by the wonders of consumer culture, such as *The Cheat*, *The Golden Chance* (1916) and *Don't Change Your Husband* (1919), DeMille engaged with issues of ethnicity, class and gender roles. This was often coupled with lavish *mise-en-scène*, elaborating on cinema as a site of visual enticement and consumer pleasure. While often utilizing a moralistic tone to present the apparent transgression of women into realms of consumerist desire and fantasy, these films also offered images of female independence and sexuality as sources of wonder, intrigue and spectacle. In a string of such films, one of the silent era's most prominent stars, Gloria Swanson, played roles that anticipated the "flapper" of the 1920s, demonstrating an independent, consumerist and sexual character while wearing the latest fashions.

For some of his most prominent films in the 1920s and 1930s, DeMille transitioned from these modern fantasies to adopt a more epic scope. Rather than a radical change in his approach to cinema, the epic films foregrounded the spectacular images that had hovered in the background of his earlier films' sumptuous design or fantasy interludes. Not entirely abandoning an overt commentary on contemporary life, films such as *The Ten Commandments* (1923) and *The King of Kings* entwined modern stories and urban landscapes with overt moral and religious implications.

Within the form of the epic, as well as other genres, DeMille's films from the mid-1920s onwards often presented narratives about nation building or the formation of civilization. He described his religious trilogy's themes as: "*The Ten Commandments* is the giving of the law, *The King of Kings* is the interpretation of the law, and *The Sign of the Cross* is the preservation of the law."[3] Later films also engaged with these concerns, showing the introduction of "civilization" brought about through expansionism (*The Plainsman* [1937] and *North West Mounted Police* [1940]), new technologies of transportation and trade (*Union Pacific* [1939] and *Reap the Wild Wind* [1942]) and divine power (*Samson and Delilah* and *The Ten Commandments* [1956]). These films depict a threatened or nomadic civilization, one that needs a law and a leader to solidify it in order to overcome its sinfulness or to establish its strength. Through this theme melodramatic situations were often inflected with religious connotations by including images of suffering or martyrdom, as in the self-sacrifice of Buttons the Clown in *The Greatest Show on Earth* or Samson's destruction of the temple in *Samson and Delilah*, which leads to him giving himself over to the will of God. Self-sacrifice also takes the form of characters dying to help establish a new beginning for a social group (*Cleopatra* [1934] and *Union Pacific*), characters being cast out in order for society to continue (*The Plainsman* and *North West Mounted Police*) or characters setting aside their personal happiness in order to help institute law (*Unconquered* [1947] and *The Ten Commandments*). Interlinked with this theme is a recurring concern with freedom from the control of others but submission to larger religious and national forms; films including *Unconquered* and *The Ten Commandments* show how characters who are enslaved can become free through the power of duty and faith. Through tropes of genre, myth and religion, DeMille's films envisioned cinema as a site through which certain ideas of religious law, civilization and freedom could be presented as emotionally resonant narratives.

Historical settings provided a space not only for the articulation of such themes, but also for lavish *mise-en-scène* coupled with images of sensuality and violence. A film like *Samson and Delilah* – where Samson is shown as a paragon of masculine desire and strength – offers a particularly overt example of this comingling, but it is evident also in a range of other films, with the characters of Poppea (in the *Sign of the Cross*) and Cleopatra shown in revealing costumes or their counterparts, Marcus and Antony, parading their physical power. The modern circus milieu of *The Greatest Show on Earth* likewise gives opportunity for both male and female performers to publicly display their bodies as sensual and athletic spectacles. Such displays of the body took shape in DeMille's films through two recurring motifs: the bath and the whip. Scenes of women bathing became something of a specialty, from the display of fashionable and expensive modern bathrooms in early silent films to the famous scene of Poppea bathing in asses' milk in *Sign of the Cross*. Even in less ostentatious or salacious ways, the image of bathing is found in multiple DeMille films, as in the scene early in *The Ten Commandments* (1956) where women are bathing before discovering Moses in the bulrushes. Scenes of characters being whipped – a violent corollary to the sensual bodily display of bathing – also recur, as with Abigail (Paulette Goddard) being whipped by her slave-owner in *Unconquered*, Joshua being whipped in *The Ten Commandments* and Delilah's whipping of Samson. Even when not used as an opportunity to display the body, the skills that characters have with the whip, as displayed by Calamity Jane (Jean Arthur) in *The Plainsman* and Marcus (Fredric March) in *Sign of the Cross*, become a signifier of sexuality and violence.

Animals provide another recurring spectacular trope in DeMille's films. One of the most well-known scenes from a DeMille film is of the encounter between Mary (Gloria Swanson) and a lion in *Male and Female* (1919). Wild animals are seen in other contexts, such as the underwater attack of a giant squid in the climactic scenes of *Reap the Wild Wind* and Samson's fight against a lion in *Samson and Delilah*. Often absurd or excessive, in these scenes the images of a thrilling and threatening wildness being tamed (or killed) presents a melodramatic trope where animals allude to repressed desires and character conflicts, made spectacularly and thrillingly visible. Drawing further upon tropes of melodrama, as well as the Western, the display of animality extends to the depiction of people. In several films, native characters are represented as quasi-human (though sometimes sympathetic) obstacles to the growth of civilization. Women also play a role as potentially disruptive to civilization, threatening social stability with their apparent inability to control desires and emotions. In many of DeMille's films, a female character transgresses certain duties and laws, and become an impediment to civilization.

While the films directed by DeMille became less stylistically adventurous later in his career, they did engage with the storytelling potentials and sensorial appeals of new film technologies. In addition to the aesthetic innovations in lighting on display in his early films, he used scenes of two-strip Technicolor in *The King of Kings*, experimented with sound in *Dynamite* (1929), highlighted the visual impact of colour through the vivid red coats of the Mounties in his first three-strip Technicolor film, *North West Mounted Police*, and used extraordinary trick photography and special effects in many films, particularly in elaborate scenes of action and epic grandeur. In a somewhat reflexive fashion, this fascination with technology was evident also within narratives themselves: many of DeMille's films thematized and celebrated technological advancement. For example, *Union Pacific* is about building the transcontinental railroad, with a character at one point remarking: "Impossible? They said it was impossible for Moses to cross the Red Sea!"; in *Reap the Wild Wind*, one character's desire to captain a new steam ship leads to his eventual downfall; in both *The Plainsman* and *North West Mounted Police*, new technologies of weaponry (the rapid firing gun and the Gatling gun, respectively) fall into enemy hands and must be regained; and in *The Story of Dr. Wassell* (1944), the

19

main character devotes years to developing a new medicine. Technology in these films often resonates with American power and enterprise, but the novel introduction of new forms of military strength (in *Cleopatra*) and city-building (in *The Ten Commandments* (1956)) extend this interest in technological power into more distant pasts. Through such depictions of the central importance of technology, DeMille interweaves his civilization-building narratives with a vision of modern enterprise.

DeMille's later films include voice-overs or other forms of overt narration, in which DeMille sometimes takes the role of storyteller, educator and orator. This reaches its apogee in *The Ten Commandments* (1956), where he appears from behind a stage curtain to introduce the film. He explains:

> The theme of this picture is whether man ought to be ruled by God's law or whether they ought to be ruled by the whims of a dictator like Rameses. Are men the property of the state, or are they free souls under God? This same battle continues throughout the world today.

He describes how, "Our intention was not to create a story, but to be worthy of the divinely inspired story created 3,000 years ago, the five books of Moses." These opening moments capture several recurring features of DeMille's films: his roles as showman and educator, his attempts to draw moral value and contemporary resonance from film, and his vision of cinema as an extension of religious meaning. Accompanied by portentous music, the scene of him introducing *The Ten Commandments* fades into an image of a mountain set against a red sky and the Paramount lettering and circle of stars appear overtop the mountain. But it is not the actual logo that is shown: it is Mount Sinai, where Moses will receive his divine inspiration and power later in the film. The words "A Cecil B. DeMille Production" appear underneath. Displacing the Paramount logo with an image of immense religious significance – one that is also a central site of the film's narrative and spectacle – casts the film studio in a new light as a place that produces religious meaning and value, that hands down morality and faith. The filmmaker similarly takes on this divine power, both introducing the religious meaning of the film and appearing overtop Mount Sinai/ Paramount. The opening of *The Ten Commandments* emblematizes how DeMille's films offered one of cinema's most powerful examples of religious and societal meanings entwined with Hollywood narrative and spectacle.

Biography

Cecil B. DeMille (b. 1881 – d. 1959) was a key industry figure for most of his forty-year career. After working in theatre, he began making films in Hollywood in 1915. His early films, which included genre films, melodramas and sophisticated modern comedies, skilfully and cannily handled filmic storytelling, socially relevant subject matter and spectacular appeal. In the 1920s, his films increasingly emphasized spectacle and epic production values. After directing populist historical melodramas in the latter 1930s and 1940s, he returned to making large-scale epic films at the end of his career, to great financial success.

Notes

1 Allen W. Palmer, "Cecil B. DeMille Writes America's History for the 1939 World's Fair", *Film History*, vol. 5, no. 1, 1993, p. 37.
2 Colette, "Cinema: The Cheat", in Richard Abel (ed.) *French Film Theory and Criticism: A History/Anthology, 1907–1939*, Volume I, Princeton, NJ, Princeton University Press, pp. 128–29, 128.
3 George C. Pratt, "Forty-five Years of Picture Making: An Interview with Cecil B. DeMille", *Film History*, vol. 4, 1989, pp. 133–45, 139.

Filmography

The Squaw Man (1914)
Brewster's Millions (1914) co-directed with Oscar Apfel
The Master Mind (1914) co-directed with Oscar Apfel
The Only Son (1914) co-directed with Oscar Apfel
The Man on the Box (1914) co-directed with Oscar Apfel and Wilfred Buckland
The Virginian (1914)
The Call of the North (1914)
What's His Name (1914)
The Man from Home (1914)
Rose of the Rancho (1914)
The Ghost Breaker (1914) co-directed with Oscar Apfel
The Girl of the Golden West (1915)
The Warrens of Virginia (1915)
The Unafraid (1915)
The Captive (1915)
The Wild Goose Chase (1915)
The Arab (1915)
Chimmie Fadden (1915)

Kindling (1915)
Carmen (1915)
Chimmie Fadden Out West (1915)
The Cheat (1915)
The Golden Chance (1916)
Temptation (1916)
The Trail of the Lonesome Pine (1916)
The Heart of Nora Flynn (1916)
Maria Rosa (1916)
The Dream Girl (1916)
Joan the Woman (1917)
A Romance of the Redwoods (1917)
The Little American (1917)
The Woman God Forgot (1917)
The Devil Stone (1917)
The Whispering Chorus (1918)
Old Wives for New (1918)
We Can't Have Everything (1918)
Till I Come Back to You (1918)
The Squaw Man (1918)
Don't Change Your Husband (1919)
For Better, For Worse (1919)
Male and Female (1919)
Why Change Your Wife? (1920)
Something to Think About (1920)
Forbidden Fruit (1921)
The Affairs of Anatol (1921)
Fool's Paradise (1921)
Saturday Night (1922)
Manslaughter (1922)
Adam's Rib (1923)
The Ten Commandments (1923)
Triumph (1924)
Feet of Clay (1924)
The Golden Bed (1925)
The Road to Yesterday (1925)
The Volga Boatman (1926)
The King of Kings (1927)
The Godless Girl (1929)
Dynamite (1929)
Madam Satan (1930)
The Squaw Man (1931)

The Sign of the Cross (1932)
This Day and Age (1933)
Four Frightened People (1934)
Cleopatra (1934)
The Crusades (1935)
The Plainsman (1937)
The Buccaneer (1938)
Union Pacific (1939)
North West Mounted Police (1940)
Reap the Wild Wind (1942)
The Story of Dr. Wassell (1944)
Unconquered (1947)
Samson and Delilah (1949)
The Greatest Show on Earth (1952)
The Ten Commandments (1956)

Further reading

Birchard, Robert S. *Cecil B. DeMille's Hollywood*. Lexington, KY: The University Press of Kentucky, 2004.

DeMille, Cecil B. *The Autobiography of Cecil B. DeMille* (ed.) Donald Hane. London: W. H. Allen, 1960.

Higashi, Sumiko. *Cecil B. DeMille: A Guide to References and Resources*, Boston: G. K. Hall, 1985.

———. *Cecil B. DeMille and American Culture: The Silent Era*. Berkeley: University of California Press, 1994.

Jacobs, Lea. "Belasco, DeMille and the Development of Lasky Lighting", *Film History* 5.4 (1993): 405–18.

Louvish, Simon. *Cecil B. DeMille and the Golden Calf*. London: Faber and Faber, 2007.

Orrison, Katherine. *Written in Stone: Making Cecile B. DeMille's Epic, The Ten Commandments*. Lanham: Vestal Press, 1999.

D. W. GRIFFITH

By Kristian Moen

D. W. Griffith was a pivotal figure in American cinema. His most influential and well-known films were made during the period in which cinema became consolidated as an institution with the feature length narrative film as its dominant form and Hollywood at its centre. Griffith played a central role in these changes, directing hugely popular films such as *The Birth of a Nation* (1915) and *Way Down East* (1920), alongside films more closely associated with aesthetic ambition such as *Intolerance* (1916) and *Broken Blossoms* (1920). Entwining emotionally powerful narratives with artistic and moral pretensions, Griffith's films set forth a vision of cinema's potential. His work was often concerned with anxieties over perceived threats to the stability of families, gender roles and moral values. Within these conservative imaginings, which sometimes used crude and simplistic stereotypes, Griffith would also develop complex visions of familial tensions, shifting social roles, and historical, national and regional identities.

Griffith began his filmmaking career at Biograph where he directed more than 400 one-reel films between 1908 and 1913. These short films were diverse, including action films, costume pictures, urban melodramas, social problem films and adaptations of poems. They were often extraordinary in the concentrated intensity with which they used film's formal features to both tell engaging and coherent stories and develop dense networks of meaning and emotion. *The Country Doctor* (1909), for example, concerns the decision a doctor makes to attend to a neighbour's ill child while leaving his own ill child alone with her mother. Returning home, he discovers that his child has died. In order to give some kind of meaning to this heartrending subject, the film's introductory intertitle is overtly moralistic and religious: 'A story of the temporal deeds that reap spiritual reward.' But the way in which the film unfolds is more complex. The film begins with a long shot of the rural setting, the camera slowly panning over the landscape and coming to rest upon an image of the doctor, his wife and their daughter walking together in front of their home. The final shot of the film begins at this same point but does not show the family. It then pans in the opposite direction of the film's first shot, over the landscape towards the rural village within the countryside. Through the filmic gesture of the moving camera, a haunting and multifaceted repetition links these opening and closing scenes, providing a moment of rest so that we might reflect upon the tragic event we have just witnessed, connecting the family to a larger community and natural world, and suggesting a circularity of both narrative and life. While distinctive, *The Country Doctor* is indicative of the ways in which Griffith invested film aesthetics with a concentrated poetic force.

This could sometimes lead to overt symbolism such as characters illuminated by light in order to allegorically demonstrate their moral qualities or tableaux of reconstituted families bringing a story to a neat narrative close. But the implications of film form were often multi-faceted. *Ramona* (1910), another early Biograph film, uses images of landscape to shape meaning. The film tells the love story of Ramona (Mary Pickford) and Alessandro (Henry B. Walthall), and the suffering that they encounter due to, as the introductory intertitle informs us, 'the White Man's Injustice to the Indian'. At a key turning point, Alessandro's village is attacked by soldiers, shown through a visually stunning extreme long shot. Alessandro appears in the foreground, crying out in anger and helplessness. This view is returned to shortly after as Alessandro stands atop the hill surveying the destruction. With his back to the camera, he raises his arms and pulls them around his head in a gesture of despair, and then turns and walks slowly offscreen. Aligning the audience with Alessandro's viewpoint, the scenes vividly establish an understanding of the character's experience. The scene also has a powerful moral impact, underpinned by the sense in which a geographical fidelity – earlier noted in an intertitle – resonates with the history that the film aims to show. As the film draws to a conclusion, Alessandro's death is set against similar views of the landscape, establishing a symbolic link to his home that is freighted with the irony of his displacement. The depiction of landscape, alongside expressive framing and performance, powerfully invokes cinema's capacity to create emotional and moral impact.

Editing is perhaps the most celebrated formal feature of Griffith's Biograph films, functioning as a device of dramatic and moral potential in extraordinarily intense and extended ways. One of the more well-known narrative structures shows the threat of an invasion, ranging from revolutionaries at the door of a palace in *The Oath and the Man* (1910) to thieves trying to rob a train station in *The Girl and Her Trust* (1912). This kind of scenario becomes an opportunity to display not only the emotive trope of innocence, family and property under threat, but also the entwining of multiple lines of action – the villains, the rescuers and the potential victims – for thrilling narrative effect. Parallel editing could also be used to create thematic connections. *A Corner in Wheat* (1909) is a well-known example of this, editing together scenes of a farmer sowing seeds, people waiting for bread and a frenzied stock market in order to show interconnections and contrasts in social and economic life. Such uses of cinema, where multiple meanings and feelings could be shaped through film form, had implications for film's cultural and social role. Tom Gunning has lucidly analysed Griffith's 'narrator system' which

> fulfilled a number of desiderata of the film industry during this period: narrative coherence, an emulation of the psychology

found in other socially respectable narrative forms (such as drama and the novel), and the creation of a moral rhetoric for film.[1]

Through film form, Griffith became a storyteller by shaping meanings, embellishing the tale and inviting an emotional response. After leaving Biograph, Griffith relocated to Hollywood. The films he directed began to take on an increased length, running into several reels. This allowed for an enlarged scope of narrative development, leading to the most well-known and financially successful Griffith film, *Birth of a Nation*. The film engages with a particularly resonant historical subject, the American civil war and the Reconstruction Era, in ways that foregrounded film's entwining of melodramatic storytelling with rhetorical impact. The first part of the film focuses on the events leading up to the war and the war itself, showing its devastation through a series of powerful tableaux of the dead and wounded upon the battlefield. The second section shifts attention to a racist historical refiguration, presenting freed slaves as villainous and subhuman, and celebrating the early history of the Ku Klux Klan. Using dynamic editing and emotionally charged material, the film couples small town domesticity with scenes of battle, historical accounts with melodramatic excesses. One of the most well-known scenes from the film is the assassination of Abraham Lincoln at Ford's Theatre, which cuts between John Wilkes Booth, Lincoln, a stage performance and its audience. Alongside such bravura reconstructions, the film also includes extended scenes of parallel editing with a different kind of aim, showing imperiled and virtuous white characters being attacked by freed slaves. Here, the formal acuity is closely interwoven with lurid and violent subject matter. The kind of authority that Griffith would present in terms of historical validity – as in the intertitle claiming that the scene in Ford's theatre is based upon a careful historical reconstruction – became a means to bolster a larger ideological and political project: 'like history written with lightning' was Woodrow Wilson's apocryphal response. Griffith's next film, *Intolerance* (1916), was concerned with an even more expansive idea of cinema's potential. The film interweaves stories of Jesus, Babylon, the Saint Bartholomew's Day Massacre and contemporary life. Its innovative formal design extends earlier uses of parallel editing to present an expansive thematic conception, moving rapidly through space and time. Through recurring images of writing, forms of the written word and allegorical figurations of storytelling, *Intolerance* self-consciously situated film as a new form of moral education, narrative engagement and artistic expression.

Both *Birth of a Nation* and *Intolerance* used allegorical figures and simplistic stereotypes. However, this does not mean that these and other Griffith films were exclusively concerned with abstractions – they also created sympathetic, conflicted and complex characters. For example, in one of Griffith's first multi-reel films, *Judith of Bethulia* (1914), the main character shifts from duty and self-abasement to masquerade and desire to honour and guilt. The complexity is brought forth as she is set alongside characters embodying more basic emotional tenors and narrative functions. Scenes of the main character alone – or even abstracted from the diegetic world – provide an opportunity to vividly present intensity of emotion, displayed directly to the audience. *The Avenging Conscience* (1914), another early multi-reel film, extends this fascination with character depth through metaphorically charged close-ups, vision scenes and haunting super-impositions. A range of cinematic tropes is used to show the main character's frustrations, animality, anxiety and guilt. Whether inviting audience identification, empathy or simply fascination, these con-structions of character evoked qualities associated with culturally valued theatrical and literary forms. Like earlier Biograph films that aligned themselves with poetry, *Avenging Conscience* linked itself to the writings of Edgar Allan Poe through recurring allusions and direct quotations. Described shortly after its release by the poet and film theorist Vachel Lindsay as 'trac[ing] the innermost psychology'[2] of its main character and having 'the photographic texture which may be said to be an authentic equivalent of [Poe's] prose',[3] the film was seen to use cinema as a psychological art.

At the same time, a melodramatic imperative could take hold of Griffith's films. In *Broken Blossoms*, Lucy (Lillian Gish) is trapped within a cruel parody of home life with her abusive father. Lucy's desperation is shown through lingering close-ups of her face, images of her delicately handling personal mementos and scenes of her hesi-tant fondness for a local shopkeeper, Cheng Huan (Richard Barthel-mess). The film adds layers to this complexity through aspects such as the authorial commentary of its intertitles, dreamlike sequences, complex shifts in viewpoint and striking scenes of Cheng's alienation in the Limehouse district. When Lucy's father discovers that she has been given a place to stay by Cheng, he drags her back to their mis-erable home. Taking refuge from his fury by hiding in a closet, Lucy's terror is presented in a series of close-ups of her entrapment as her father hacks through the door with an axe. This scene – and the violence that follows – provides a brutal climax to the film, contrast-ing starkly with the subtlety of imagery and emotion that preceded it.

Broken Blossoms draws upon typical strategies of melodrama: 'a broad category of moving pictures', Linda Williams writes, 'that move us to pathos for protagonists beset by forces more powerful than they and who are perceived as victims.'[4] As a highly flexible expressive mode, melodrama allows for the presentation of both sensational and restrained emotionalism. *The Greatest Question* (1919), released shortly before *Broken Blossoms*, has a markedly similar climactic scene of entrapment where Nellie Jarvis (Lillian Gish) takes refuge in an attic room. Less subtle in its narrative rationale and emotional tone, the film's complexity is developed through a subplot about a mother whose son dies at war. This culminates in an extraordinary vision scene in a graveyard where the recently deceased son reappears for both his mother and his father. Such an elaboration of melodramatic storytelling coupled with overt religious overtones is indicative of the ways in which Griffith's films elaborated on multiple potentials of cinema, entwining moralism with narrative impact while proffering religious values, poetic expressions and social meanings.

Ranging from spectacular scope to lyricism, from social argument to formal experimentation, Griffith's multifaceted approach to cinema would anticipate and influence an enormous range of films. The treatment of many of the subjects in Griffith's films is rooted within a complex amalgamation of certain trends in American culture around the turn of the century, aspirations regarding film's potential role and Griffith's own worldview. While this can sometimes lend them the air of historical curiosities, the subjects themselves – circulating around how identities are formed through place and history, negotiated through social change and developed through familial and inter-generational conflicts – continue to be deeply resonant. Coupled with an approach to cinema that sought to elevate both its cultural status and its aesthetic potential, in sometimes astonishing and sometimes alarming ways, Griffith's films continue to enthral.

Biography

D. W. Griffith (b. 1875 – d. 1948) began his career in theatre, and started making films at Biograph in 1908. Directing over 400 single-reel films, he turned to longer works in the mid-1910s. Films such as *The Birth of a Nation* (1915) and *Intolerance* (1916) consolidated his reputation as one of Hollywood's most ambitious and grandiose film-makers. His later films continued to rely on cinema's rhetorical, melo-dramatic and spectacular appeals, though his prominence in Hollywood declined.

Notes

1 Tom Gunning, *D. W. Griffith and the Origins of American Narrative Film*, Urbana and Chicago: University of Illinois Press, 1993, p. 291.
2 Vachel Lindsay, *The Art of the Moving Picture* (1915), New York: Random House, 2000, p. 91.
3 Ibid., pp. 93–94.
4 Linda Williams, 'Melodrama Revised' in *Refiguring American Film Genres*, edited by Nick Browne, Berkeley: University of California Press, 1998, p. 42.

Filmography

Judith of Bethulia (1914)
The Avenging Conscience (1914)
The Birth of a Nation (1915)
Intolerance (1916)
Hearts of the World (1918)
The Great Love (1918)
The Greatest Thing in Life (1918)
A Romance of Happy Valley (1919)
The Girl Who Stayed at Home (1919)
True Heart Susie (1919)
Scarlet Days (1919)
The Greatest Question (1919)
Broken Blossoms (1920)
The Idol Dancer (1920)
The Love Flower (1920)
Way Down East (1920)
Dream Street (1921)
Orphans of the Storm (1922)
One Exciting Night (1922)
The White Rose (1923)
America (1924)
Isn't Life Wonderful (1924)
Sally of the Sawdust (1925)
That Royle Girl (1925)
The Sorrows of Satan (1927)
Drums of Love (1928)
The Battle of the Sexes (1928)
Lady of the Pavements (1929)
Abraham Lincoln (1930)
The Struggle (1931)

Further reading

Allen, Michael. *Family Secrets: The Feature Films of D. W. Griffith*. London: BFI, 1999.

Geduld, Harry M., ed. *Focus on D. W. Griffith*. Englewood Cliffs, NJ: Prentice-Hall, Inc., 1971.

Hansen, Miriam. *Babel and Babylon: Spectatorship in American Silent Film*. Cambridge: Harvard University Press, 1993.

Mayer, David. *Stagestruck Filmmaker: D. W. Griffith & The American Theatre*. Iowa City: University of Iowa Press, 2009.

Pearson, Roberta E. *Eloquent Gestures: The Transformation of Performance Style in the Griffith Biography Films*. Berkeley: University of California Press, 1992.

Rogin, Michael. "'The Sword Became a Flashing Vision": D. W. Griffith's *Birth of a Nation*'. *Representations* 9 (Winter 1985): 150–95.

Simmon, Scott. *The Films of D. W. Griffith*. Cambridge: Cambridge University Press, 1993.

Stokes, Melvyn. *D. W. Griffith's The Birth of a Nation: 'A History of the Most Controversial Motion Picture of All Time'*. Oxford: Oxford University Press, 2007.

Usai, Paolo Cherchi, ed. *The Griffith Project*. 12 vol. London: British Film Institute, 1999–2008.

Williams, Linda. *Playing the Race Card: Melodramas of Black and White from Uncle Tom to O. J. Simpson*. Princeton, NJ: Princeton University Press, 2001.

OSCAR MICHEAUX

By Shane Brown

How does one go about discussing a man's life and work when relatively little is known about either? Patrick McGilligan opens his biography of Oscar Micheaux, America's first black filmmaker, by telling his readers that it is not clear how to pronounce the director's name, or even the correct spelling of it. He goes on to say "it is unclear how many times Micheaux was married, or whether he fathered any children; arguable how much of a fortune he amassed, then squandered; uncertain how many times he went bankrupt, or was arrested".[1] To add to this, of the over forty films that Micheaux directed, only around fifteen are known to survive today. Of those a dozen are sound films, leaving just three key films from the more celebrated silent period.

Viewers of Micheaux's sound films might well question his inclusion in this volume. Indeed J. Ronald Green writes that "almost everyone has initial problems taking seriously much of Oscar Micheaux's sound-era film work" in large part due to their "technically awkward" aspects.[2] The sound films certainly suffer from a lack of budget, amateurish acting, static action, and inferior sound recording. To a certain degree, however, these features are all part of their charm and, often, power. Micheaux's career as director involved an inventive, entrepreneurial approach.

Micheaux's first film as director was *The Homesteader*, released in 1919 and based on his own 1917 novel of the same name. That novel was Micheaux's third and, in common with many of his cinematic and prose works, *The Homesteader* contained a number of elements that were semi-autobiographical. With its mix of professional, semi-professional and amateur actors, meagre budget and run-ins with the censors, *The Homesteader* prefigured Micheaux's subsequent directorial career. While *The Homesteader* is a lost film, the director's second, *Within Our Gates* (1920) survives, giving us the first chance to sample Micheaux's earlier works.

Within Our Gates has been viewed as Micheaux's response or riposte to D. W. Griffith's *The Birth of a Nation* (1915). The lengthy flashback section in the second half of the film appears to be his attempt to tell the *real* story of African-Americans, climaxing with the attempted rape of a young black woman by an older white man (in contrast to the notorious scene in *Birth of a Nation*). Much of the film consists of well-intentioned melodrama, concerning itself with attempts to find funding for a school for African-American children in Mississippi. While the acting is undistinguished, Evelyn Preer as Sylvia, the teacher at the heart of the story, shines throughout, most notably in the aforementioned flashback sequence. This flashback tells the story of Sylvia as a teenager and how her father, Landry, is accused of murdering his (white) boss. Forced to flee their homes, the family hide in the nearby forest, although they are eventually found and the mother and father are lynched. Meanwhile, Sylvia is cornered in a cabin (possibly her former home) by the brother of the man her father is accused of murdering. He attempts to rape her, only stopping when he notices a scar on her breast, identifying her as his own daughter from a previous relationship or sexual encounter. Unknown to Sylvia, it is subsequently her biological father who pays for her education.

While much of the film suffers from some of the "technical awkwardness" described by Green, the climax of the flashback is a remarkable achievement for Micheaux, directing just his second film and essentially learning his trade as he went along. The attempted rape of Sylvia is inter-cut with images of her parents' lynching, the latter taking on something of a dream-like quality due to unconventional camera angles, and blurred focus. Rather than show the lynching itself, Micheaux uses brief shots of the top of the makeshift gallows, the rope being pulled across the beam as the bodies are raised and, later, the rope being cut. Despite being made and released a full year before the 1921 American premiere of *The Cabinet of Dr Caligari* (Robert Wiene, 1920), these shots are strikingly similar to those associated with German Expressionism and are eerily similar in both style and composition to shots in Dreyer's *Vampyr* (1932). Micheaux does not stop with the shots of the gallows. As the attempted rape scene intensifies, he inter-cuts it with images of the bonfire on which Sylvia's parents will be burned by the lynchers. This harrowing sequence has rightly been hailed as one of Micheaux's greatest achievements, and it is hardly surprising that it fell foul of censorship.

The sole surviving print (discovered in Spain) is around a whole reel shorter than the original prior to cuts. While the intertitles had to be translated back into English from the Spanish, this has not obscured the cutting dark humour that often features in Micheaux's films. The opening intertitle reads: "At the opening of our drama, we find our characters in the North, where the prejudices and hatreds of the South do not exist – though this does not prevent the occasional lynching of a Negro." Such bitter humour resurfaces during the flashback when Sylvia's kid brother tries to run away from the lynchers and is shot at by the attackers. As he falls to the floor, the viewer is led to believe he is dead; a few seconds later he gets up and runs to a nearby horse, galloping away having fooled the men that are about to kill his parents.

Another recurring feature of Micheaux's work and, to some extent, life was his willingness to criticise his own race, something that caused criticisms from those around him. In the flashback in *Within Our Gates* we meet Efram, a servant of the man that Sylvia's father is accused of killing. Efram is the only witness to the killing and quickly runs into town to spread the news that Landry (Sylvia's father) has killed his boss. The intertitles describe Efram as an "incorrigible tattletale". He steals alcohol from his boss, and views himself as the "white man's friend". Efram represents a distinct racial stereotype, different to those perpetuated in *The Birth of a Nation* (D. W. Griffith, 1915) but nonetheless culturally powerful. Such characterisation – the articulation of negative racial types – proves uneasy for critics given Micheaux's prominence as an African-American filmmaker in this period. In his novel *The Homesteader*, Micheaux condemns some

African-Americans as "very ignorant and vicious".[3] While Micheaux was quite clearly not willing to reduce matters to a simplistic opposition of race and value, using a caricature such as Efram to make his point brought with it substantial criticism, not least from those who worked for him. According to Patrick McGilligan's biography, Carlton Moss, who acted in some of Micheaux's films during the early sound era, stopped working for the director because of his attitudes toward both black America and to filming. He remembers Micheaux remarking that some African-Americans wanted "ease, privilege and luxury without any great effort on their part" and, on another occasion: "That's the trouble with colored people, they always want someone giving them something."[4] Micheaux himself was quick to defend his films and the characters within them. In 1924 he wrote, "I have always tried to make my photoplays present the truth, to lay before the race a cross section of its own life, to view the colored heart from close range."[5]

After *Within Our Gates,* Micheaux directed a now lost boxing-themed film, *The Brute.* His next, *The Symbol of the Unconquered* (1920), is much more in line with the majority of Micheaux films from the era. It deals with the racial violence of lynching, the complications and misunderstandings experienced by those of mixed race, and the Ku Klux Klan. The sole surviving print, found in Belgium, appears to be incomplete despite a running time of around 75 minutes (presumably the print was struck after the censors had made their cuts). The film is certainly more polished and accomplished cinematically, but it lacks the punch and grit of *Within our Gates,* that film's grittiness replaced by a sentimentality and light humour that sits awkwardly with the serious subject matter.

Micheaux was remarkably prolific over the next period, writing and directing a wide range of films, all of which are now lost. His next film after *The Symbol of the Unconquered* was *The Gunsaulus Mystery* (1921), based on a real life murder case that would also form the basis for a later Micheaux film, *Murder in Harlem* (1935). *The Dungeon* (1922) found the writer/director exploring the idea of dreams as some form of premonition, a theme that recurs in many of his works. *A Son of Satan* (1924) is described as a "quasi-comedy about a haunted house taken over by a Ku Klux Klan-type organization",[6] and, perhaps most tantalising, there is *Deceit* (1923), a lost film about an African-American director and his problems with the film censorship board.

Micheaux himself experienced problems to some degree with censorship on virtually all of his films. *Body and Soul* (1925) saw the director having to take drastic action when the film was banned outright by the New York censors who claimed it was "sacrilegious, immoral, and would tend to incite crime". The censors objected primarily to the protagonist being a minister who was also a murderer, thief and heavy drinker. According to the preface attached to the George Eastman House restoration of the film, Micheaux changed the film's narrative and themes drastically in response, most notably by changing the character of the minister into an ex-convict *pretending* to be a minister. He even added an "it was all a dream" ending to the film to pacify the censors concerns, a device that sat uneasily with the film's content. Eventually four reels were excised from the film, bringing its length down from nine reels to just five, although the Eastman House print restores some of the censored footage bringing its length back to eight reels. However, even in this version the minister remains a disguise.

Body and Soul is probably the greatest of all of Micheaux's extant films, and this is in no small part due to the presence of Paul Robeson in the dual role of the fake minister and his good brother. In this, his first film, Robeson exudes charm and charisma, particularly in the larger role of the minister. His acting is remarkably natural, underlining how long Robeson was overlooked by the industry – it would be a further eight years before he was cast in a Hollywood film, and he would take only nine acting roles in mainstream films during his career. The casting of Robeson must have been quite a coup for Micheaux, who was used for the most part to casting his films using semi-professionals and amateurs. Robeson, meanwhile, had recently starred in two successful stage productions including a revival of *The Emperor Jones* the previous year.

Body and Soul includes features (both thematic and technical) found in the director's previous films, not least his penchant for including characters that were far from positive representations of African-Americans, most notably in this case the hard-drinking, gambling murdering fake-minister. Bowser and Spence write that "many of Micheaux's critics were successful professionals of 'respectable' taste and manners who wanted their own self-image to be heard, seen and understood. They wished to distance themselves ... from the drunken, dice-throwing lore that black skin (as some would have it) signalled to the world."[7] Micheaux, meanwhile, seemed more interested in making his films both entertaining and truthful.

Body and Soul is more technically accomplished than his previous film and the later examples that survive. The acting is more professional (aided and abetted by Robeson's presence), and the cinematography and editing is more fluent. Despite this, the film is still unmistakably Micheaux. The editing may be more fluent, but he uses a familiar stylistic device of cross-cutting back and forth from one scene to another in order to underline that two actions are happening simultaneously. This is not parallel editing in the traditional sense where the director cuts between two events that eventually combine in a single place. Micheaux's use of the technique is devoid of the suspense element that most viewers are used to. To modern viewers, therefore, Micheaux's technique can appear to be crude or even confusing as it seems to lack a purpose unlike, for example, the cross-cutting between the attempted rape of Sylvia and the lynching of her parents in *Within Our Gates*.

Micheaux continued to direct for another two decades, with some periods more prolific than others, often related to financial difficulties. For example in 1932 alone he made four films, but none between 1940 and 1947. The remaining extant films in the Oscar Micheaux filmography are all sound films, despite the fact that he would make a number of silent films after *Body and Soul*. Of his sound films, approximately half survive. The sound films do not have the same impact as Micheaux's silent work. The coming of sound caused yet more restraints on Micheaux's already tight budgets, and this showed in his work. While many of Hollywood's early sound films were static and awkward as a result of technical limitations, within the studios these obstacles had been largely overcome by 1930. By contrast, Micheaux's independent films from the late 1930s seem stiff and amateurish. While some of the sound films found the director driving home a powerful message in the manner of his earlier work, others included an array of musical numbers suggesting that he was veering towards entertainment. This is not to say that Micheaux's ambition ever left him, with his final film *The Betrayal* (1947) originally running at around three and a half hours in length.

Oscar Micheaux never made a Hollywood film, but eventually one of the first great independent filmmakers was honoured by Hollywood. In 1986, the Directors Guild of America honoured him with a Golden Jubilee Special Award for Lifetime Achievement and, in 1987, he was given a star on Hollywood's Walk of Fame. Since prints of Micheaux's work began to resurface in the 1970s and 1980s, the director has achieved a great deal of academic attention, and a number of biographies have also been published. With all of his films in the public domain, Micheaux's surviving films continue to be released by small independent labels.

Biography

Oscar Micheaux was born on January 2, 1884 in Metropolis, Illinois, one of thirteen children. In 1913 he published the first of his seven novels, *The Conquest*, with his second, *The Homesteader*, being published five years later. *The Homesteader* would provide the basis for his first film in 1919. Over the next thirty years, Micheaux would write and direct over forty independent films, often based on his own experiences and/or novels. He died of heart failure on March 25, 1951.

Notes

1 Patrick McGilligan, *The Great and Only Oscar Micheaux: The Life of America's First Black Filmmaker*, New York: Harper Collins, 2007, p. 1.
2 J. Ronald Green, "Sophistication under Construction: Oscar Micheaux's Infamous Sound Films", *Framework: The Journal of Cinema and Media*, Volume 51, Number 1, Spring 2010, p. 151.
3 Oscar Micheaux, *The Homesteader*, College Park: McGrath, 1969, p. 59.
4 McGilligan, pp. 266–67.
5 Oscar Micheaux, quoted in Paul Bowser and Louise Spence, "Oscar Micheaux's Body and Soul and the Burden of Representation", *Cinema Journal*, Volume 39, Number 3, Spring 2000, p. 7.
6 McGilligan, p. 202.
7 Paul Bowser, Jane Marie Gaines and Charles Musser (eds). *Oscar Micheaux and his Circle: African-American Filmmaking and Race Cinema of the Silent Era*. Bloomington: Indiana University Press, 2001, p. 6.

Filmography

The Homesteader (1919)★ (lost films are marked with an asterisk)
Within Our Gates (1920)
The Brute (1920)★
The Symbol of the Unconquered (1920)
The Gunsaulus Mystery (1921)★
The Dungeon (1922)★
The Virgin of Seminole (1922)★
Jasper Landry's Will (1923)★
A Fool's Errand (1923)★
Deceit (1923)★
Birthright (1924)★
A Son of Satan (1924)★
The House Behind the Cedars (1925)★

Marcus Garland (1925)★
The Devil's Disciple (1925)★
Body and Soul (1925)
The Conjure Woman (1926)★
The Spider's Web (1927)★
The Millionaire (1927)★
Thirty Years Later (1928)★
The Broken Violin (1928)★
The Wages of Sin (1929)★
When Men Betray (1929)★
Easy Street (1930)★
A Daughter of the Congo (1930)★
The Exile (1931)
Darktown Revue (1931) short
Veiled Aristocrats (1932)
Harlem After Midnight (1932)★
Ten Minutes to Live (1932)
The Girl from Chicago (1932)
The Phantom of Kenwood (1933)★
Murder in Harlem (1935)
Temptation (1937)★
Underworld (1937)
Swing! (1938)
God's Stepchildren (1938)
Birthright (1938)
Lying Lips (1939)
The Notorious Elinor Lee (1940)
The Betrayal (1947)★

Further reading

Bowser, Paul, Jane Marie Gaines and Charles Musser, eds. *Oscar Micheaux and his Circle: African-American Filmmaking and Race Cinema of the Silent Era*. Bloomington: Indiana University Press, 2001.

Green, J. Ronald. *Straight Lick: The Cinema of Oscar Micheaux*. Bloomington: Indiana University Press, 2000.

McGilligan, Patrick. *The Great and Only Oscar Micheaux: The Life of America's First Black Filmmaker*. New York: Harper Collins, 2007.

KING VIDOR

By Alice Maurice

King Vidor's life reads like a history of Hollywood cinema. He arrived in Hollywood as the consolidation of the studio system was just beginning, and his career was to some degree coterminous with it. Surviving the transition from silents to sound, and from the relative freedom of independent filmmaking to the strictures of the studio system, Vidor successfully navigated the shifting fortunes of the director in Hollywood – in terms of status, power, and creative control – between the 1920s and the 1950s.

Vidor seemed born to the role. His filmmaking life began at age 19, when he and a friend took a homemade camera made out of cardboard to the shore during the Galveston hurricane. The resulting actuality ran all over Texas and beyond. A few years later, when Vidor arrived in Hollywood, D. W. Griffith was shooting *Intolerance* (1916), and the feature film era was in full swing.[1] He soon found himself in the thick of things, rising to the top of his field in the 1920s. He established himself as a feature filmmaker by making three films with the independent production company Brentwood films (funded by a group of doctors and dentists impressed with Vidor's work). The first of these was *The Turn in the Road* (1919), a Christian Science-themed film that did very well at the box office and drew the attention of the bigger studios. After making these first films and then working under Thomas Ince's tutelage at "Inceville," Vidor tried to follow in Ince's footsteps by building his own studio, "Vidor Village." But the financial pressures were too great as independent production faced more and more obstacles in the early '20s, and Vidor Village went under after only two years. Vidor returned to making films for the most successful producers of the time – Ince, Metro, and Goldwyn.[2]

With the rise of the feature film in the teens, the director's role became more defined and valued in film production, and the best directors were being identified and sought after. Some directors even became "stars," or names that could help sell a film to the public. While some directors who came before Vidor were able to capitalize on their own reputations and seize more power – either by founding their own studios (like Griffith or Thomas Ince) or by taking on producing or quasi-executive roles within studios (like Cecil B. DeMille at Famous Players-Lasky) – Vidor came a bit too late to the party to follow these blueprints.[3] The mergers of studios and theater chains ramped up in the 1920s, laying the groundwork for the consolidation of the studio system and the rationalization of the production process that would centralize power in the hands of producers. Vidor wound up making pictures for Goldwyn on the eve of its merger with Metro, and thus he landed with MGM when it formed in 1924. There he would stay, for the most part, on a series of short-term contracts, with occasional work for other studios and forays into independent producing. Vidor would make over twenty films with MGM over the course of twenty-two years, until things ended badly in 1946, when clashes with David O. Selznick during the filming of *Duel in the Sun* led him to walk off the set.[4]

The incident with Selznick notwithstanding, studio heads reportedly saw Vidor as a more tractable and efficient director than some of his contemporaries.[5] He was not, however, a mere "company man." He was keenly aware of the fact that the studio system siphoned power away from the director, limiting creative control over the work as well as the director's ability to share in the profits. Seeing the need for collective action, he spearheaded the formation of the Screen Director's Guild (what we now know as the Directors' Guild of America) in 1936 and served as its first president. Throughout his career, Vidor was interested in the idea of directors' cooperatives, and as Raymond Durgnat and Scott Simmon recount in their biography, he came close to founding one in 1937. After making some unsuccessful films for Paramount and encountering too much producer interference (in the person of Sam Goldwyn) on *Stella Dallas* (1937), Vidor worked on a plan for a cooperative in which four directors would earn small salaries but take large percentages of the films' profits. That plan ultimately fell apart; inspired by some other directors' efforts to band together, he tried again in the mid 1940s after his break with MGM, but without success.[6] Like many of the best Hollywood directors of the studio era, Vidor sometimes strained at the bit, but opportunities to make films with a greater degree of freedom were few and far between. After MGM, he found his way to Warner Brothers to direct another big picture, the adaptation of Ayn Rand's *The Fountainhead* (1949).

Although Vidor had a long studio-era career, making films until the late 1950s, his signature style is best represented by his silent films, which allowed him to achieve what he called "silent music"[7] – the rhythm of images building to a scenic crescendo that, for Vidor, showcased cinema at its best. In some ways, he identified with the same late nineteenth-century preoccupations and sensibilities that animated Griffith's filmmaking. In the early days of MGM, when Irving Thalberg (with whom Vidor would have a productive relationship) asked him what sorts of movies he wanted to make, Vidor offered a trio of possible subjects that seemed to come straight from the turn-of-the-century: war, wheat, and steel. But if his ideas harkened back to the nineteenth century, his style was forward-looking, and his films were typically concerned with ordinary people navigating the shifting currents of modern life. The result of that conversation with Thalberg was *The Big Parade* (1925). Focusing on World War I from the perspective of the average soldier, *The Big Parade* fundamentally changed the way war movies were made; its style would be imitated for decades to come. Made for $250,000, the film grossed over 15 million, putting MGM "on the map," as Vidor put it, and establishing him as an elite director.[8]

While other top directors of the silent era failed to make the transition to sound, Vidor thrived. Although he lamented the limitations that sound brought with it, calling the format a return to the "nailed-down tripod of the early days,"[9] he was one of the first directors to take advantage of sound and to see its potential. In 1929, Vidor fought for and made *Hallelujah!*, a film featuring musical numbers and an all-Black cast. This film created a template for what Rick Altman calls the folk musical, an important sub-genre of the American film musical (a genre which of course had yet to be consolidated in 1929).[10] Vidor's films would continue to wind their way through a peculiarly American brand of folk wisdom, quasi-philosophical inquiry, and abortive economic critique. With that dream of a "war, wheat, and steel" trilogy still in the background, Vidor saw many of his best films as part of the same story cycle. He thought of the protagonist of *Our Daily Bread* (1934) – the cash-strapped city dweller who goes back to the land – as the main character from *The Crowd* (1928), several years down the road in his journey.[11] These and other Vidor films deal directly or indirectly with social class and American capitalism, but their politics are hard to pin down. As a result, his films often faced criticism from both the Left and the Right. For Vidor, individual striving trumped any clear-cut political message or social critique.

Film scholars have generally associated Vidor with melodrama, but this is a bit of a stretch at times. He certainly made a number of rural and domestic dramas, but his best films fall outside of the realm of moral certainty and Manichean dualism that tends to define the genre. In his study of American melodrama, Robert Lang groups Vidor with Griffith and Minnelli as makers of films that dramatize the inherent contradictions of patriarchy. Yet even he must force *The Crowd* into this taxonomy by calling it "a melodrama that resists being one."[12] There are no clear villains, and the film's expressionistic style and observational frankness highlight the complexity of forces shaping the protagonist's life. For Lang, the battle between desire and repression defines melodrama, and certainly many Vidor films, regardless of genre, seem to hinge on that battle. Because they focus on thwarted desire and often feature strong female leads, Vidor's films have been taken up by feminist film criticism, serving as key texts in debates about the relationship between gender and genre. *Stella Dallas*, in particular, has figured prominently in discussions of how class and gender identity are mediated by consumerism and mass culture in classic studio-era maternal melodramas. Vidor's films have prompted larger questions about the role Hollywood films play in reconciling (or revealing) the irreconcilable differences at the heart of American capitalism.

Reading his films in terms of the tension between freedom and constraint turns out to be more productive than genre as an organizing principle. In this sense, Miriam Hansen's important essay on *The Crowd* offers a particularly useful model for understanding Vidor's films. Hansen discusses *The Crowd* in terms of ambivalence, in the context of Siegfried Kracauer's theory of the "mass ornament." Despite its seeming optimistic individualism at the level of plot, she argues, *The Crowd*'s style repeatedly undercuts that individualism, creating ominous images of the masses and patterns of repetition that suggest the mechanization and dehumanization that accompany consumer capitalism.[13] MGM released the film with two alternate endings, from which the exhibitor could choose – a "happy ending" and, as Vidor puts it, a "realistic ending."[14] The latter is the famous ending, and one of the most memorable in film history: the last shot pulls out from our hero at a vaudeville show to a wide shot of the audience laughing, rocking back and forth with disturbing, mechanical sameness. If we are to believe Vidor, this ending was meant to be realistic but not pessimistic – a happy, if "resigned" ending of a man resigned to be one of the crowd. But it is hard not to read the final shot as a critique. The sheer excess of the shot destabilizes simple closure, not only by undercutting the "happy" ending, but also, as Hansen point out, by offering a disturbing mirror image for the audience – a reflexive portrait of the consumption of mass culture.

This sort of ambivalence or tension – where style seems to undercut or trump conventional storytelling – crops up across Vidor's body of work. There is a point in almost every King Vidor film when straightforward, conventional Hollywood style gives way to ecstatic filmmaking. The Depression-era feature *Our Daily Bread*, a film made independently and representative of a labor of love for Vidor, offers perhaps the most obvious example of this pattern. The story of downtrodden city dwellers who move to a farm and set about creating a collective, the film carries on with little tension and no surprises until a drought hits. The last ten minutes of the film chart the digging of an irrigation ditch, and suddenly, we are in a different filmic dimension altogether. A rhythmic study of physical movement in which all the laborers' bodies are part of one great mechanism, the film illustrates the laborers working in sensual communion with the earth.[15] As the water flows through the channel, irrigating the land, it seems to have the same effect on the spectator – who wakes up, alive to the physical reality the film depicts. In their freest moments, Vidor's films seek to bind realism and rhythm – a poetic documentary-like urge to follow the workings of nature, the energies of the body, or just the ebb and flow of everyday life.

In 1921, the fan magazine *Photoplay* ran an article titled "What is a Director?" At the time, the answer was still not entirely clear. Among the many responses came one from a young King Vidor: "A director is the channel through which a picture reaches the screen."[16] This statement seems telling for a filmmaker who survived in Hollywood for so many years. Vidor's artistry flows through his body of work, diverted by, but also defined by, the conventions and constraints of the studio system. His best films and best moments show off his keen film sense. Whether sound or silent, they tend to exceed the boundaries of conventional filmmaking to create visual music.

Biography

King Vidor was born in Galveston, Texas, in 1894. He made his first short film at age 19 and went on to direct nearly sixty feature films over the next forty years. He was nominated for the Academy Award for Best Director five times, and in 1979, he received an honorary Academy Award for "his incomparable achievements as a cinematic creator and innovator."

Notes

1 King Vidor, *A Tree is a Tree*, Hollywood: Samuel French, 1953, pp. 67–69.
2 Raymond Durgnat and Scott Simmon, *King Vidor, American*, Berkeley: University of California Press, 1988, pp. 19–58.
3 Richard Koszarski, *An Evening's Entertainment: The Age of the Silent Feature Picture, 1915–1928*, History of the American Cinema, vol. 3, Berkeley: University of California Press, 1994.
4 Durgnat and Simmon, pp. 235–55.

5 Koszarski, *An Evening's Entertainment*, pp. 232–34.
6 Durgnat and Simmon, pp. 172–73, 236.
7 Vidor, *A Tree is a Tree*, p. 116.
8 Joel Greenberg, "War, Wheat, and Steel," *Sight and Sound* 37, Autumn 1968: 193.
9 Vidor, *A Tree is a Tree*, p. 181.
10 See Rick Altman, *The American Film Musical*, Bloomington: Indiana University Press, 1988, pp. 272–316.
11 Vidor, *A Tree is a Tree*, pp. 220–29.
12 Robert Lang, *American Film Melodrama*, Princeton, NJ: Princeton University Press, 1989, p. 113.
13 Miriam Hansen, "Ambivalences of the Mass Ornament: King Vidor's *The Crowd*," *Qui Parle: Literature, Philosophy, Visual Arts, History* 5, no. 2, 1992: 102–19.
14 Vidor, *A Tree is a Tree*, p. 152.
15 Vidor shot this sequence without sound, using a metronome and a bass drum to set the beat, as he did in his silent filmmaking. See *A Tree is a Tree*, p. 225. See also Durgnat and Simmon, pp. 157–59.
16 "What is a Director?" *Photoplay*, August 1921: 154. Also cited in Brownlow, *The Parade's Gone By*, p. 68.

Filmography

Galveston Hurricane (1913)
Military Parade in Houston (1914)
In Tow (1914)
Bud's Recruit (1918)
The Chocolate of the Gang (1918)
The Lost Lie (1918)
Tad's Swimming Hole (1918)
Marrying Off Dad (1918)
The Preacher's Son (1918)
Thief or Angel (1918)
The Accusing Toe (1918)
The Rebellion (1918)
I'm a Man (1918)
The Turn in the Road (1919)
Better Times (1919)
The Other Half (1919)
Poor Relations (1919)
The Family Honor (1920)
The Jack-Knife Man (1920)
The Sky Pilot (1921)
Love Never Dies (1921)

The Real Adventure (1922)
Dusk to Dawn (1922)
Conquering the Woman (1922)
Peg o' My Heart (1922)
The Woman of Bronze (1923)
Three Wise Fools (1923)
Wild Oranges (1924)
Happiness (1924)
Wine of Youth (1924)
His Hour (1924)
The Wife of the Centaur (1924)
Proud Flesh (1925)
The Big Parade (1925)
La Bohème (1926)
Bardelys the Magnificent (1926)
The Crowd (1928)
The Patsy (1928)
Show People (1928)
Hallelujah! (1929)
Not So Dumb (1930)
Billy the Kid (1930)
Street Scene (1931)
The Champ (1931)
Bird of Paradise (1932)
Cynara (1932)
The Stranger's Return (1933)
Our Daily Bread (1934)
The Wedding Night (1935)
So Red the Rose (1935)
The Texas Rangers (1936)
Stella Dallas (1937)
The Citadel (1938)
Northwest Passage (1940)
Comrade X (1940)
H.M. Pulham, Esq. (1941)
An American Romance (1944)
Duel in the Sun (1946)
A Miracle Can Happen (1948)
The Fountainhead (1949)
Beyond the Forest (1949)
Lightning Strikes Twice (1951)
Japanese War Bride (1952)

Ruby Gentry (1952)
Man Without a Star (1955)
War and Peace (1956)
Solomon and Sheba (1959)
Truth and Illusion (1964)
The Metaphor (1980)

Further reading

Brownlow, Kevin. *The Parade's Gone By*. New York: Knopf, 1968.
—. "King Vidor." *Film* 34 (Winter 1962): 19–28.
Kaplan, E. Ann. "The Case of the Missing Mother: Maternal Issues in Vidor's *Stella Dallas*." *Feminism and Film*. Ed. Ann Kaplan. Oxford: Oxford University Press, 2000.
Maurice, Alice. "'Cinema at Its Source': Synchronizing Race and Sound in the Early Talkies." *Camera Obscura* 17.1 (2002): 31–72.
Mulvey, Laura. "Afterthoughts on 'Visual Pleasure and Narrative Cinema' Inspired by King Vidor's *Duel in the Sun* (1946)." *Framework* 15 (1981): 12–15.
Vidor, King. *King Vidor on Filmmaking*. New York: McKay, 1972.
Williams, Linda. "Something Else Besides a Mother: *Stella Dallas* and the Maternal Melodrama." *Cinema Journal* 24.1 (1984): 2–27.

LOIS WEBER

By Shelley Stamp

Considered one of the 'three great minds' in early Hollywood, alongside Griffith and DeMille, Lois Weber is not as well-known as her famous contemporaries, long ensconced as the 'fathers' of American cinema. Yet Weber's career has much to tell us about opportunities available during the industry's initial development and the way those opportunities narrowed, particularly for women, with the emergence of the studio system. Of all the women active in the first decades of moviemaking, Weber produced the most sustained and substantial body of work, writing and directing more than forty features and hundreds of shorts for close to thirty years. In fact, Weber's career traces the very genealogy of modern Hollywood.

After establishing her reputation in New York, writing, directing and starring in films at Edwin S. Porter's Rex Company, Weber arrived in Los Angeles in 1913, just as film production companies began to coalesce there. With Rex now absorbed into Universal Pictures, Weber began working within the emergent studio system, co-directing the Rex brand with her husband, Phillips Smalley. She served as Mayor of the sprawling new Universal City complex, eventually becoming the studio's top director, and the first woman inducted into the Motion Picture Directors' Association in 1916. An early advocate for the craft of screenwriting and a proponent of using trained actors in films, Weber was among the first filmmakers associated with quality feature filmmaking. Leaving Universal to form her own production company in 1917, Weber joined other high-profile directors striking out on their own in the postwar years. If lucrative distribution contracts with First National and Paramount signaled the initial promise of independent outfits like Lois Weber Productions, those prospects were short lived. Weber's company, along with so many other independents, soon fell victim to vertical integration as leverage consolidated within a few mighty studios in the early 1920s. Struggling to find work later in the decade, Weber found herself in a profession that had become increasingly 'masculinized', as Karen Ward Mahar has demonstrated.[1] Where once Weber's feminine decorum had enhanced Hollywood's cachet, by the Jazz Age it had become a liability. Where she had once commanded tremendous respect on any set, by the end of her career she found that men were unaccustomed – and sometimes unwilling – to work under a female director. Still, Weber remained active after most of her generation had retired. She continued to seek writing and directing projects in the sound era, making a final film, her only sound feature, in 1934.

Weber is best-known for the films she made on key social issues while at Universal in the mid-1910s. If Griffith and DeMille sought to establish cinema's prestige by drawing on literary, dramatic and historical material already well-established in highbrow culture, Weber took an opposite tack. She seized on the new medium's capacity to animate critical issues of the day. Cinema, she said, was a 'voiceless language', able to engage viewers in the era's most troubling questions. Likening her films to a newspaper's 'editorial page', she aimed to 'deliver a message to the world'.[2] And that she did. She tackled subjects like urban poverty and women's wage equity in *Shoes*, drug addiction and narcotics trafficking in *Hop, the Devil's Brew*, the crusade to abolish capital punishment and police brutality in *The People vs. John Doe*, and the campaign to legalize birth control in *Where Are My Children?* and *The Hand That Rocks the Cradle*. Though she fought censorship battles on many of these titles, Weber developed a reputation as a thoughtful, socially engaged filmmaker. One observer noted that she could 'deal successfully with subjects which other directors would not dare to touch for fear of condemnation'.[3] Although she vowed to abandon such 'heavy dinners' when she left Universal to form Lois Weber Productions, Weber remained a trenchant critic of social norms. Her later films on bourgeois marriage and domesticity, notably *Too Wise Wives, What Do Men Want?* and *The Blot*, provoke fundamental questions about capitalism, changing sexual mores, traditional family structures and a rising culture of consumption.

Female protagonists were central to Weber's films from the very beginning, whether the struggling wives, daughters and mothers she played in her Rex shorts, memorable characters like Portia and Fenella in adapted works such as *The Merchant of Venice* and *The Dumb Girl of Portici*, women struggling with poverty, addiction and social justice in her Universal features, married women and single working women jointly navigating modern sexual mores in the postwar years, or performers juggling fame, glamour, and commodification in the Jazz Age. With female characters at their center, Weber's scripts also grappled with issues close to women – not only marriage and domesticity, but also sexual violence, abusive relationships, contraception, wage equity, prostitution, unplanned pregnancy, and the sexual double standard. What is more, her social problem films made it clear that *every* issue, from capital punishment to urban poverty to addiction, not only affected women but necessitated women's engagement to enact social change. Each of these issues was framed through the singular experience of a female character, whether an impoverished, over-worked shop girl in *Shoes*, an opium addict in *Hop, the Devil's Brew*, an anti-death penalty crusader in *The People vs. John Doe*, or an advocate of legal birth control in *The Hand That Rocks the Cradle*.

If Weber understood cinema's cultural impact, she also grasped its visual impact as a storytelling medium. Collaborating with pioneering cinematographers such as Arthur C. Miller, Dal Clawson and Allen Siegler, Weber employed dissolves and superimpositions, matte shots and choreographed camera movements, sophisticated lighting techniques, and location shooting both indoors and out, producing some of the more subtle cinematic effects of the era. From her Rex days onwards, Weber was noted for fine visual storytelling, especially her capacity to render interior psychology cinematically. Working during an era when the role of the film director was just becoming understood, Weber articulated a commanding vision, saying 'a real director should be absolute. He [*sic*] alone knows the effects he wants to produce' and insisting that 'the work of a picture director, worthy of the name, is creative'.[4] A performer herself, Weber also devoted considerable attention to the craft of acting, becoming an early advocate of using trained performers in the movies and later experimenting with shooting films in narrative sequence so that actors could build 'characterizations' more holistically. Weber was also instrumental in the professionalization of directing through her work on the first director's committee at the fledgling Academy of Motion Picture Arts and Sciences in the late 1920s.

Unlike other prominent directors of her time, Weber wrote or adapted virtually all of her screenplays. In fact, she considered screenwriting one of the primary expressions of her creativity, claiming, 'I don't remember when I did not write.'[5] As she rose to prominence at Rex, Weber urged fellow scenarists to move beyond formulaic plots and compulsory happy endings. Moviegoers not only wanted more sophisticated fare, she maintained, they deserved it. Weber was active in the industry's first professional organization, the Photoplay Author's League, after it formed in 1914, having protested publicly when women were excluded from early meetings. Women would, of course, go on to dominate screenwriting in the next decade and Weber played a key role in mentoring writers such as Frances Marion, Jeanie Macpherson and Lenore Coffee early in their careers. Later she would note with evident pride that 'many of the girls who are now famous in the writing field' were 'under my care'.[6] Helping to promote a culture of amateur screenwriting, Weber also served on the Advisory Council for the Palmer Photoplay Corporation, the largest and most respected correspondence school for aspiring screenwriters, most of whom were women. She sponsored a screenwriting contest at Lois Weber Productions, and wrote a series of syndicated newspaper columns in 1921 offering advice and information on many aspects of the movie business.

Weber was also well known for mentoring female performers. Several of the actresses she directed at Universal went on to successful directing careers of their own, among them Cleo Madison, Elsie Jane Wilson, Lule Warrenton and Dorothy Davenport Reid. And several leading actresses were either 'discovered' by Weber or developed significantly under her tutelage, including Mary MacLaren, Mildred Harris Chaplin, Claire Windsor and Billie Dove. Weber thus developed a reputation as a 'star maker', able to fashion young starlets into full-blown celebrities. However complimentary, the 'star maker' epithet downplayed Weber's considerable investment in writing mature female roles for these actresses and directing some of their best performances. Critics noticed, for instance, that Weber's scripts allowed Dove to 'break the mold of the sweet young heroines' she had played in the past. If other directors had 'never let her do anything else but look lovely', Weber grasped Dove's 'vast emotional possibilities' as a performer.[7] Later in life Dove remembered Weber as 'the best director I ever had'.[8] Weber's commitment to training aspiring actresses is also evident in her early and ongoing involvement with the Girls' Studio Club, a residence for young women hoping to enter the movie business. By organizing guest speakers and studio tours for club residents, Weber demonstrated her keen interest in fostering the success of young women in an industry better known, even then, for exploiting them.

Beyond Hollywood, Weber maintained close associations with women's clubs, the premiere activist organizations for middle-class women of her era, acting as a visible embodiment of female leadership in the film industry. She addressed the Los Angeles chapter of the Federated Clubwomen of America several times on matters such as improving motion picture quality and the safety of young women who emigrated to Los Angeles looking for movie work, inviting a group of clubwomen to tour Universal City in early 1917.[9] Weber embarked on a national speaking tour in 1921, addressing clubwomen around the country on the subject of 'Woman's Influence in the Photoplay World', as well as more contentious topics such as 'Moving Picture Censorship' and 'The Sunday Blue Laws'.[10] Later in the decade she would be invited to address the Southern California Women's Press Club and the Women's University Club of Los Angeles. As Hollywood's ambassador, Weber became a visible index of feminine propriety behind the scenes at a time when clubwomen were stepping up calls for greater regulation of motion picture content.

Renowned for her films, Weber also became one of the first celebrity filmmakers, famous in a way that virtually no other director was at the time. Featured as one of *Sunset Magazine*'s 'Interesting Westerners' in 1914, Weber was profiled in several other general interest monthlies throughout the 1910s and 20s. Movie fan magazines also cast the filmmaker as a star, furnishing readers with intimate glimpses of her home life with first husband Phillips Smalley and her second husband Harry Gantz; visiting her 'on the lot'; and touring state-of-the-art facilities she had erected at her own studio. Weber's relationship with Smalley was a central facet of her fame early on. The couple's working partnership often featured as a model for ideas about companionate marriage emerging in American culture; and it became a way of packaging Weber's image as a professional woman working in a field many considered man's domain.

Despite the optimistic tone of such early publicity, Weber became increasingly critical of the film industry's treatment of women on-

and off-screen. Returning from a trip to Europe in 1922, she announced her plan to create a new feminine 'screen type' to counter the flappers and vamps who clouded Hollywood's imagination – 'cute little dolls dressed up in clothes that they do not know how to wear'. In contrast, Weber proposed the 'womanly woman' who possessed 'brains and character', and was, above all, 'able to act'. She had been inspired, she said, by European actresses, women whose primary attributes were not beauty or glamour, but depth of personality and range of dramatic talent.[11] This effort is evident in three of Weber's later films – *The Marriage Clause*, *Sensation Seekers* and *The Angel of Broadway* – each of which features a remarkably reflexive meditation on the industry's glamour culture and a leading female role designed to challenge conventional female types. Even as these films helped revive her reputation, Weber spoke publicly about the difficulties she faced as a woman directing in Hollywood and the increased control exercised by studios now run like corporations. If her early publicity had promoted the unique opportunities available to women in the fledgling movie business, by the end of her career, Weber was becoming known as Hollywood's 'only' female filmmaker, a distinction that celebrated her achievements even as it marginalized them. Weber became the exception that proved the rule.

For a filmmaker so renowned and distinguished in early Hollywood, Weber is remarkably unknown. Even before she directed her last production in 1934, Weber was being written out of Hollywood history, cast aside in the first chronicles of American moviemaking that focused exclusively on pioneering male figures and valued women's contributions only as stars. Scores of women like Weber, essential to early Hollywood as directors, screenwriters, producers, journalists and studio executives, were forgotten in an early rush to 'masculinize', and thus legitimate, the newly powerful industry.

Biography

Florence Lois Weber was born in Allegheny, Pennsylvania, in 1879, the middle daughter of George Weber, an upholsterer and decorator, and Mary Matilda Weber (née Snaman) whose father and grandfather were Christian ministers. Trained as a pianist and singer, Weber joined a touring theater group where she met actor and stage manager Phillips Smalley, whom she married in 1904. The couple divorced in 1922 and in 1926 Weber married her second husband, Captain Harry Gantz, an aviator and wealthy citrus grower. She died in Los Angeles in 1939 at age 60, five years after directing her last picture.

Notes

1 Karen Ward Mahar, *Women Filmmakers in Early Hollywood*, Baltimore, MD: Johns Hopkins University Press, 2008, pp. 154–60.
2 'The Smalleys Have a Message to the World', *Universal Weekly*, 10 April 1915, p. 17; and *Moving Picture World*, 9 August 1913, p. 640.
3 Marjorie Howard, '"Even As You and I," A Drama of Souls at Bay', *Moving Picture Weekly*, 14 April 1917, p. 18.
4 Mlle. Chic, 'The Greatest Woman Director in the World', *Moving Picture Weekly*, 20 May 1916, pp. 24–25.
5 Fritzi Remont, 'The Lady Behind the Lens', *Motion Picture Magazine*, May 1918, p. 60.
6 Ibid.
7 Katherine Lipke, 'Marriage First With Her', *Los Angeles Times*, 15 August 1926, C19; and Alma Whitaker, 'Billie Dove is Grateful for Big Chance at Success', *Los Angeles Times*, 20 February 1927, C17.
8 Quoted in William M. Drew, *At the Center of the Frame: Leading Ladies of the Twenties and Thirties*, New York: Vestal Press, 1999, p. 32.
9 *Photoplay*, September 1913, p. 73; and 'Lois Weber Club Women's Hostess', *Moving Picture Weekly*, 7 January 1917, n.p., env. 2518, Robinson Locke Collection, New York Public Library for the Performing Arts.
10 'Nationally Known Club Woman Endorses Lois Weber's Photoplays', *Hollywood Informer*, 18 March 1921, p. 19.
11 William Foster Elliot, 'Exit Flapper, Enter Woman: Lois Weber Describes Next Screen Type', *Los Angeles Times*, 6 August 1922, III, 25.

Filmography

The Merchant of Venice (1914) also screenplay adaptation and lead role
The Traitor (1914)
False Colors (1914) also screenplay and lead role
Hypocrites (1915) also screenplay
It's No Laughing Matter (1915) also screenplay
Sunshine Molly (1915) also screenplay adaptation and lead role
Captain Courtesy (1915) also screenplay adaptation
Betty in Search of a Thrill (1915)
Scandal (1915) also screenplay and lead role
Jewel (1915) also screenplay adaptation
Hop, the Devil's Brew (1916) also screenplay and lead role
The Flirt (1916) also screenplay adaptation
The Dumb Girl of Portici (1916) also screenplay adaptation
John Needham's Double (1916)
Where Are My Children? (1916) also screenplay
The Eye of God (1916) also screenplay and onscreen role
Shoes (1916) also screenplay adaptation

Idle Wives (1916) also screenplay adaptation, also lead role
Saving the Family Name (1916) also screenplay
Wanted – A Home (1916) also screenplay
The People vs. John Doe (1916) also screenplay
The Mysterious Mrs. M. (1917) also screenplay adaptation
Even as You and I (1917)
The Hand That Rocks the Cradle (1917) also screenplay and lead role
The Price of a Good Time (1917) also screenplay
The Doctor and the Woman (1918) also screenplay adaptation
For Husbands Only (1918) also screenplay adaptation
Borrowed Clothes (1918) also screenplay adaptation
When a Girl Loves (1919) also screenplay
A Midnight Romance (1919) also screenplay adaptation
Mary Regan (1919) also screenplay adaptation
Home (1919) also screenplay
Forbidden (1919) also screenplay adaptation
To Please One Woman (1920) also screenplay
What's Worth While? (1921) also screenplay
Too Wise Wives (1921) also screenplay
The Blot (1921) also screenplay
What Do Men Want? (1921) also screenplay
A Chapter in Her Life (1923) also co-writer with Doris Schroeder
The Marriage Clause (1926) also screenplay adaptation
Sensation Seekers (1927) also screenplay
The Angel of Broadway (1927)
White Heat (1934) also screenplay

Further reading

Cooper, Mark Garrett. *Universal Women: Filmmaking and Institutional Change in Early Hollywood*. Urbana: University of Illinois Press, 2010.

Mahar, Karen Ward. *Women Filmmakers in Early Hollywood*. Baltimore, MD: Johns Hopkins University Press, 2008.

Norden, Martin F, ed. *Lois Weber: Interviews*. Jackson: University Press of Mississippi, 2014.

Parchesky, Jennifer. 'Lois Weber's *The Blot*: Rewriting Melodrama, Reproducing the Middle Class.' *Cinema Journal* 39.1 (1999): 23–53.

Slater, Thomas. 'Transcending Boundaries: Lois Weber and the Discourse Over Women's Roles in the Teens and Twenties.' *Quarterly Review of Film and Video* 18.3 (2001): 257–71.

Slide, Anthony. *Lois Weber: The Director Who Lost Her Way in History.* Westport, CT: Greenwood Press, 1996.

Stamp, Shelley. *Lois Weber in Early Hollywood.* Berkeley: University of California Press, 2015.

Weber, Lois. 'How I Became a Motion Picture Director.' 1915. Rpt. in *Red Velvet Seat: Women's Writing on the First Fifty Years of Cinema.* Ed. Antonia Lant. London and New York: Verso, 2006, pp. 658–60.

—. 'A Dream in Realization.' 1917. Rpt. in *Hollywood Directors, 1914–1940.* Ed. Richard Koszarski. Oxford: Oxford University Press, 1976, pp. 50–53.

CLASSICAL HOLLYWOOD

ROBERT ALDRICH

By Christopher Kelly

It is perhaps little surprise that director Robert Aldrich remained underappreciated during his lifetime. A master of tapping into dark undercurrents of feeling in the tawdriest-seeming of genre pictures, Aldrich turned out his greatest works – *Kiss Me Deadly* (1955), *The Big Knife* (1955), *What Ever Happened to Baby Jane?* (1962), and *Hush … Hush, Sweet Charlotte* (1964) – in an era when the popular culture still insisted upon stodgy distinctions between "A" and "B" pictures; between high-minded, star-studded works like David Lean's *Lawrence of Arabia* (1962) or George Stevens' *Giant* (1958) that all but begged to be taken seriously, and the considerably lower-budgeted efforts that pushed against the restrictions of the Hays Code and tried to show audiences a down-and-dirty good time. Aldrich's fellow directors seemed to understand Aldrich's talents, yet he never earned recognition from the larger Academy of Motion Pictures Arts and Sciences. Mainstream critics, meanwhile, were prone to shrug off the filmmaker altogether. Reviewing *What Ever Happened to Baby Jane* in *The New York Times*, Bosley Crowther wrote: "The feeble attempts that Mr. Aldrich has made to suggest the irony of two once idolized and wealthy females living in such depravity and the pathos of their deep-seated envy having brought them to this, wash out very quickly under the flood of sheer grotesquerie."[1]

What *is* surprising, though, is that in the three-plus decades since his death, Aldrich has never been "re-discovered" in the manner of many of his early "B"-movie counterparts, such as Jacques Tourneur (*Cat People, Out of the Past*) or Abraham Polonsky (*Body and Soul*, on which Aldrich served as assistant director). Aldrich's films continue to be referenced elsewhere in the popular culture – witness, most famously, the glowing briefcase in Quentin Tarantino's *Pulp Fiction* (1994), which tips its hat to the nuclear device in *Kiss Me Deadly*. His films have also inspired numerous sequels and remakes, including a made-for-television version of *What Ever Happened To Baby Jane?*

(1991) starring real-life sisters Vanessa and Lynn Redgrave, and a remake of *The Longest Yard* featuring comic Adam Sandler in the Burt Reynolds role. Yet Aldrich is rarely mentioned as one of the first filmmakers to successfully bridge the divide from the studio system to our modern, auteur-focused era; nor is he remembered as one of those artists – like Sam Peckinpah (*The Wild Bunch*) or Arthur Penn (*Bonnie and Clyde*) – whose expressive use of genre stories and on-screen violence helped to revolutionize the American film industry in the late 1960s. Little wonder, indeed, that one of the few critical studies on the director to be published is titled: *What Ever Happened to Robert Aldrich?*

Born in 1918 to a privileged Rhode Island family – his grandfather was United States Senator Nelson Adrich; his cousin was Nelson Rockefeller – Robert Aldrich was expected to work for the family-owned Chase Bank. But while studying economics at the University of Virginia, he experienced his first taste of show business, booking jazz and dance bands on campus. In 1941, a family friend helped him secure a job at RKO Studios, and he dropped out of college and moved to Los Angeles. He cut his teeth as an assistant director for the likes of Jean Renoir (on 1945's *The Southerner*), William Wellman (on 1948's *The Story of G.I. Joe*), and Charlie Chaplin (on 1952's *Limelight*). According to Tony Williams, his most formative experience was a two-year apprenticeship at Enterprise Studios, where he worked closely with directors such as Polonsky, Robert Rossen and Joseph Losey, and actors such as John Garfield. The studio, which only lasted a few years, sought to "make films criticizing the state of American society and hoping for radical change in much the same manner as the Group Theatre and the developing wave of new playwrights such as Tennessee Williams and Arthur Miller."[2] (Adrich was never made a victim of the Hollywood Blacklist, or called to testify before the House Committee on UnAmerican Activities, like many of his Enterprise colleagues – which the director himself ascribed to being "just fortunate."[3]) Aldrich's earliest films include a sentimental sports drama called *Big Leaguer* (1953) and a pair of entertaining, if minor, Westerns starring Burt Lancaster, *Apache* (1954) and *Vera Cruz* (1954), both made for United Artists.

Yet even as he rose up through the studio system, there were early signs that Aldrich was a talent ahead of his time. For one thing, he was steadfast in his auterist conviction that all films could have "a style that expresses my personality, my behavior patterns."[4] For another, he sought to finance and produce his own films, long before the likes of John Cassavetes popularized the notion of "American independent filmmaking." In 1955, he formed his own production company, called Associates and Aldrich. For a brief stretch in the late 1960s and early 1970s, he even owned his own studio, though – as with Francis Ford Coppola and his Zoetrope Studios – a series of box-office failures forced him to sell it.

Aldrich's ambition may have been a double-edged sword, at least in terms of his own legacy; any filmmaker who works as frequently as Aldrich did, on both self-generated and studio-generated projects, is going to be tricky to pin down thematically, and is likely to turn out his share of misfires. But his dual 1955 triumphs, *The Big Knife* and *Kiss Me Deadly*, go a long way toward illuminating Aldrich's sensibilities. A pair of uncommonly urgent crime thrillers, fueled by a sense of paranoia about and outrage towards "the system," these films hint at far greater perversions to come in the director's canon. *The Big Knife*, from the Clifford Odets play, is the more conventional of the two: a famous Hollywood movie star (Jack Palance) desperate to break free from his studio contract squares off against his blackmailing studio boss (Rod Steiger). But with its tight framing and rat-a-tat pacing, the film generates an unease that runs deeper than even the blackest of *film noirs*. In Aldrich's vision, everybody's got the goods on everybody else, and the only means of escape seems to be the wholesale auction of one's soul. As Tony Williams has noted, the tensions within *The Big Knife* would recur throughout Aldrich's career. "Using the legacy of Clifford Odets, Aldrich developed a cinema that would clash by day and night with the delusionary mechanisms of a system he was a part of and attempted to change," Williams writes.[5]

Even more impressive – and shockingly grim – is *Kiss Me Deadly*, a low-budget detective thriller that, in its exceedingly strange way, ends up becoming an uncommonly telling portrait of American nuclear age anxiety. Based on one of Mickey Spillane's Mike Hammer novels, the film follows a detective (Ralph Meeker) who picks up a hitchhiker (Cloris Leachman) who has escaped from a mental asylum. When the hitchhiker ends up dead, the detective tries to figure out what happened – a mystery at the center of which is a box that everyone is trying to get their hands on. Moving with remarkable speed, and using canted angles and stark, melodramatic music, Aldrich registers the increasingly bizarre twists of the story with a matter-of-fact detachment, so that this detective story turns, almost imperceptibly, into a nightmarish science-fiction thriller about how the government, industry and technology are all conspiring to destroy American society. When that box is finally opened, in the film's famed final sequence, all of the characters' (and 1950s-era audience's) worst fears are realized;

this time, the complete compromise of a man's soul comes with a side of nuclear annihilation.

Some critics argue that Aldrich never exceeded the work he did in the mid-1950s, which also included the Joan Crawford melodrama *Autumn Leaves* (1956), for which Aldrich won the Best Director prize at the Berlin International Film Festival, and the excellent *Attack* (1956), a tense morality drama about a World War II Lieutenant who challenges his commanding officer, starring Eddie Albert and Jack Palance. "Did overbearing producers and more restrictive censorship push Aldrich into a disciplined and even ironic evocation of brutality? Did the cheerfulness of the fifties allow such glittering darkness to slip through?" asked David Thomson, in *The New Biographical Dictionary of Film*.[6] Thomson went on to suggest that that Aldrich's feverish work pace, averaging about a movie a year, was ultimately a kind of undoing. "[S]o often his energy went astray."[7]

Box office, too, may have been an issue: Neither *The Big Knife* nor *Kiss Me Deadly* were commercial successes, forcing Aldrich to take studio jobs "so I could make some money to put back into my own company."[8] Alas, many of those studio pictures – Westerns such as *Ten Seconds to Hell* (1959), *The Last Sunset* (1961), and *4 for Texas* (1963); the Biblical epic *Sodom and Gomorrah* (1962) – were mostly forgettable, impersonal efforts. Meanwhile, his two greatest box-office successes of the 1960s – *The Flight of the Phoenix* (1965), about the survivors of a plane crash in the Sahara trying to build a new plane to fly themselves to safety, and *The Dirty Dozen* (1967), about a ragtag team of convicted murderers recruited for a dangerous World War II killing mission – are both the sort of lumbering Hollywood epics that Aldrich's earlier pictures seemed to be railing against.

Still, the filmmaker never received the full credit he deserved for *What Ever Happened to Baby Jane, Hush … Hush, Sweet Charlotte*, and *The Killing of Sister George* (1968), which form a kind of unofficial trilogy. Thomson has dismissed these films as "horribly calculated, smirking exploitations of sub-Gothic emotional horror."[9] But such criticisms fail to acknowledge the formal invention of these films, which deftly skirt the line between horror and melodrama, unintentional camp and knowing comedy. These criticisms also misunderstand the proto-feminist themes of these films, each of which is about women pushed to the margins of society and steadily coming undone. *Baby Jane* tells the story of a pair of rivalrous sisters and onetime celebrities (Bette Davis and Joan Crawford), now living together and decaying, mentally and physically, in a sprawling mansion. *Hush … Hush, Sweet Charlotte* again stars Davis, this time as an aging spinster trying to maintain her sanity as a poor cousin (Olivia De Havilland, a role which Crawford was originally cast to play) schemes to steal her fortune. *The Killing of Sister George* is about a television actress (Beryl Reid), in love with a younger woman (Susannah York), who learns that she is about to be killed off the popular soap opera in which she stars. In each of these films, Aldrich employs exaggerated make-up and borderline-grotesque close-ups of his leading ladies; indeed, he seems to take perhaps a little too much camp-comic pleasure in the notion of female hysteria. The visual cruelty, however, is counterbalanced by an uncommon attention to his female characters' interior lives. As David Greven has noted, in these films the "levels of pain and the pathos are palpable. They emanate from the suffering of the socially cast-off characters as well as the real, genuine loss of the film's stars' own youth and marquee-power."[10] Greven, who considers these films as part of what he calls the "woman's horror" genre, also notes that these films "reclaim bodies and identities that fall outside of their normative dictates. Along with their more questionable maneuvers of making their stars' aging bodies something of a freakshow entertainment, the films establish, maintain, and evince sympathy for their female protagonists, however wildly off-putting, erratic, or unkempt they may be."[11] It is worth noting, too, that *The Killing of Sister George* was one of the first Hollywood films to explore lesbian subject matter and portray gay female sex – another point where the perennially dismissed Robert Aldrich was years ahead of his time.

In 1968, flush from the profits of *The Dirty Dozen* – the biggest box office hit of 1967 – Aldrich realized a longstanding dream of buying his own studio. The goal, according to Arnold and Miller, was to produce between eight and sixteen films over the following five years. Whether because he ended up being spread too thin professionally – or merely suffered a lousy spell of luck – the four films produced under the Aldrich Studios banner were all commercial failures. The best of them, *The Killing of Sister George*, was slapped with a restrictive X rating by the then recently formed MPAA; even though Aldrich agreed to cut the film's sex scene for its release in a number of cities, the film's commercial prospects were doomed. The other three Aldrich Studios films are among Aldrich's weakest: *The Legend of Lylah Clare* (1968); *Too Late the Hero* (1970); and *The Grissom Gang* (1971). Whatever chance for Hollywood immortality he might have had as his own mogul was lost – Aldrich was soon forced to sell the studio and again take a series of for-hire jobs.

Aldrich's final decade is not without achievement: *Ulzana's Raid* (1972), about a Calvary team (led by Bruce Davison and Burt

Lancaster) chasing after a violent Apache war chief (Joaquín Martínez), is an unusually somber Western, which gradually reveals the ostensible heroes to be as corrupted as the purported bad guys; although overlong, sentimental and riddled with gay and African-American stereotypes, *The Longest Yard* (1974) – about a team of inmates who challenge their sadistic wardens to a football game – is nonetheless another of Aldrich's vigorous critiques of Establishment politics and corporate culture, a spiritual sequel of sorts of *The Big Knife*. Yet more often Aldrich's work in the 1970s was lurching and crass, and the director's auterist fingerprints were nowhere to be found. Could the same sneakily satiric artist who made *Kiss Me Deadly* really be responsible for the rudderless Mel Brooks-knock-off *The Frisco Kid* (1979), about a Polish rabbi (Gene Wilder) and his adventures in the Old West? Other low points include *Hustle* (1975), a thriller starring a spectacularly mismatched Burt Reynolds and Catherine Deneuve, and *The Choirboys* (1977), a crime drama based on a Joseph Wambaugh novel.

Aldrich obviously felt the need to keep working, explaining to an interviewer – in the aftermath of having to sell Aldrich Studios – "You get on a bottle of whiskey for about six months, and then you've got to get back to work. How? You cut your price and then you take pictures you wouldn't have taken before."[12] Alas, this dreary stretch of last films may be part of the reason why Aldrich was so quickly forgotten – and has yet to be resurrected – by the critical establishment. His final effort, ... *All the Marbles* (1981), is an all-but-forgotten sports comedy about a female wrestling tag team (Vicki Frederick and Laurene Landon) and their oddball manager (Peter Falk). Alternately shamelessly titillating (at one point, the women are inexplicably entered into a mud wrestling competition) and oddly affecting, it contains just enough glimmers of the old Aldrich – and his preoccupations with crushing patriarchal systems and the women who won't bear to be contained by them – to make one wonder if he might yet have had another masterpiece or two in him.

Biography

Born in 1918 to a well-heeled Rhode Island family, Aldrich was twice nominated for the Directors Guild of America prize, for *What Ever Happened to Baby Jane?* and *The Dirty Dozen*. Aldrich began a production company (Associates and Aldrich) in 1955, and even helmed his own studio (Aldrich Studios), though both efforts were relatively short lived. The director died in 1983, at age 65, of kidney failure.

Notes

1 Crowther, Bosley. Review of *What Ever Happened to Baby Jane*. *The New York Times*, November 7, 1962.
2 Williams, Tony. *Body and Soul: The Cinematic Vision of Robert Aldrich*. Landham, MD: Scarecrow Press, 2004, p. 48.
3 Miller, Eugene and Arnold, Edwin T. (eds.). *Robert Aldrich: Interviews (Conversations with Filmmakers Series)*. Jackson: University Press of Mississippi, 2004, p. 112.
4 Miller and Arnold, p. 7.
5 Williams, p. 25.
6 Thomson, David. *The New Biographical Dictionary of Film*. New York: Knopf, 1994, p. 7.
7 Ibid., p. 8.
8 Miller and Arnold, p. 13.
9 Thomson, p. 7.
10 Greven, David. "Sisters and other strangers: *What Ever Happened to Baby Jane?*" *Jump Cut: A Review of Contemporary Media*, No. 55, Fall 2013. Access at: http://www.ejumpcut.org/currentissue/grevenWmHorror/2.html.
11 Ibid.
12 Miller and Arnold, p. xi.

Filmography

Big Leaguer (1953)
World for Ransom (1954)
Apache (1954)
Vera Cruz (1954)
The Big Knife (1955)
Kiss Me Deadly (1955)
Attack (1956)
Autumn Leaves (1956)
The Garment Jungle (1957) uncredited, replaced by director Vincent Sherman
Ten Seconds to Hell (1959)
The Angry Hills (1959)
The Last Sunset (1961)
Sodom and Gomorrah (1962)
What Ever Happened to Baby Jane? (1962)
4 for Texas (1963)
Hush … Hush, Sweet Charlotte (1964)
The Flight of the Phoenix (1965)
The Dirty Dozen (1967)
The Legend of Lylah Clare (1968)

The Killing of Sister George (1968)
The Greatest Mother of Them All (1969) short
Too Late the Hero (1970)
The Grissom Gang (1971)
Ulzana's Raid (1972)
Emperor of the North (1973)
The Longest Yard (1974)
Hustle (1975)
Twilight's Last Gleaming (1977)
The Choirboys (1977)
The Frisco Kid (1979)
... All the Marbles (1981)

Further reading

Miller, Eugene and Arnold, Edwin T. (eds). *Robert Aldrich: Interviews (Conversations With Filmmakers Series)*. Jackson: University Press of Mississippi, 2004.

Perrine, Toni. *Films and the Nuclear Age: Representing Cultural Anxiety*. New York: Routledge, 1997.

Silver, Alain and Ursini, James. *What Ever Happened to Robert Aldrich: His Life and Films*. New York: Limelight Editions, 1995.

Williams, Tony. *Body and Soul: The Cinematic Vision of Robert Aldrich*. Lanham, MD: Scarecrow Press, 2004.

DOROTHY ARZNER

By Eylem Atakav

When asked whether there was any pressure over the ending of her film *Honor Among Lovers* (1931) – in which Claudette Colbert's married character embarks on an ocean voyage with a man who is not her husband – Arzner responded:

> No, there was no pressure regarding the script, I had very little interference with my pictures. Sometimes there were differences in casting, sets, or costumes, but usually I had my way. You see I was not dependent on the movies for my living, so I was always ready to give the picture over to some other director if I couldn't make it the way I saw it. Right or wrong, I believe this was why I sustained so long – twenty years.[1]

Dorothy Arzner was the only woman to sustain a directorial career through the height of the Hollywood studio system. Bridging silent and sound eras, Arzner worked variously as director, editor and screenwriter. She collaborated with many of the major female stars of the day, overseeing the anxieties around Clara Bow's first sound film and showcasing Katherine Hepburn's developing independent woman persona in the actress' second film *Christopher Strong* (1933).

Arzner's film work repeatedly foregrounded communities of women while her professional practice was grounded in female collaboration, an aspect of her working life drawn out by Judith Mayne in her 1994 study *Directed by Dorothy Arzner*. Mayne writes:

> It has always been tempting to attribute some of Arzner's success as a star-maker to her affinity with women stars. Arzner and [Marion] Morgan's collaboration suggests a more precise basis to that affinity, one based on female creativity as manifested in dance and fashion, on the one hand, and film, on the other.[2]

These elements – female performers in strong roles, female communities of one kind or another, dance and fashion as substantive and meaningful elements of the film world – would recur as important elements across Arzner's work. The striking styling of Hepburn in *Christopher Strong* as a masculinized aviatrix frames the famous scene in which she is seen wearing an extraordinary shimmering gown (designed by Howard Greer) for a costume party in which she appears as a moth complete with antennae. In both feminine and non-traditional costumes Hepburn's costumes evoke a powerful female nonconformity.

With seventeen feature films credited over her fifteen years as a director, Arzner has proven a fascinating figure for scholars interested in women's often neglected contribution to Hollywood history. Arzner's films too have received scholarly attention, particularly during the 1970s as part of a larger feminist reappraisal of classical Hollywood. Indeed, as Jane Gaines notes "feminist film theory produced a strangely split discourse resulting in two 'Dorothys': the 'textual Arzner' and the highly visible image of Dorothy Arzner."[3] The image of Arzner on set became a familiar marker of authoritative female agency in studies of classic Hollywood eager to identify female creative figures. Mayne's study brought the director's lesbian identity – frequently alluded to via images of Arzner's butch styling, yet repressed as a topic for discussion – into dialogue with her body of work. Writers such as Theresa Geller would also link Arzner's unconventional characterizations to her lesbianism, drawing out the emphasis on women's relationships with one another in films such as *The Wild Party* (1929), *Working Girls* (1931) and *Dance, Girl, Dance* (1940).[4]

In common with many Hollywood directors of the time, Arzner was a career professional, tackling less prestigious production roles and lobbying for a chance to direct on the basis of her performance as editor and writer. As an insider holding her own in an industry that typically excluded women from high-status directorial roles Arzner has unsurprisingly attracted attention. Interviews in which Arzner comments on or looks back on her career suggest an acute under-standing of the precariousness of the industry and her place within in it, as well as a reluctance to accept a simplified account of her role. Ironically, reflecting on her work for Paramount, and on women in the workplace, she later recalled in an interview by Gerald Peary and Karyn Kay: "No one gave me trouble because I was a woman. Men were more helpful than women."[5] As this remark suggests, the retro-spective casting of Arzner as feminist pioneer can involve overlooking the challenges of her location within the film industry of the day, a simplification that Mayne manages to avoid. Nonetheless the appeal of Arzner's films for feminist scholarship is clear. Mayne characterizes her as "the great exception" to the norms of classical Hollywood, explain-ing how 1970s feminist writing cast her as an "overtly proto-feminist director".[6]

Following the four silent feature films she made for Paramount, *Fashions for Women* (1927), *Ten Modern Commandments* (1927), *Get Your Man* (1927) and *Manhattan Cocktail* (1928) (which featured synchro-nized music but no dialogue), Arzner made the transition to sound with *The Wild Party*, Paramount's first sound feature. With Clara Bow as its protagonist, the film was marketed as the "'It' girl's talkie debut'.[7] *The Wild Party* received both critical acclaim and box-office success. Bow plays Stella, a popular student in school who risks her reputation to help fellow-student Helen (Shirley O'Hara). In Kendhal Cruver's words, *The Wild Party* shows women in college as "mostly biding their time until marriage".[8] The contradiction between images of privileged young women who "lounge around in negligees, filing their nails and discussing men"[9] and the opportunities for education and advancement that the college represents is intriguing. Indeed the discourses of women's freedom in the film are very much to do with sexuality (for which "wildness" stands in) rather than education. Stella's developing romance with a teacher James Gilmore (Fredric March) who expresses disappointment at her antics, and her loyalty to Helen form the central threads of the narrative. Cruver assesses *The Wild Party* in the context of the decade, as "an awkward, but entertaining portrait of the naiveté and spirit of the flapper girl and the excitement and pitfalls of the increasingly fast-paced society rushing around her".[10] Bow's flapper wildness was central to the marketing of the film, her character succumbing to the conventions of romance only after numerous misunderstandings.

Although many of Arzner's films present stereotypical Hollywood conventions regarding the depiction of women, critics such as Mayne finds in Arzner's work "a sense of women's independence and a stylistic vision to go with it".[11] In *Working Girls*, for example, Arzner moves away from the good girl/bad girl dichotomy so prevalent at the time. *Christopher Strong* has been extensively discussed within feminist film studies, in large part due its bold female protagonist, Lady Cynthia Darrington (Katherine Hepburn), a figure who serves to subvert patriarchal ideology in terms of her actions and her appearance. The film's aristocratic milieu is one in which the preservation of an appearance of propriety is at odds with the desires of individuals. "A woman over twenty-one who has never had a love affair," Darrington's aviatrix presents an icon of female independence. Sexuality is figured as a threat, not only in the familiar ways in which Hollywood cinema constructs female desire as dangerous to men but because Cynthia's involvement with the MP disrupts her confidence. As Geller writes, "Her love affair with Christopher Strong is ultimately her undoing and she dies in a suicide plane crash, pregnant with his child."[12] The film's discourse on monogamy and the suppression of the feminine in the film helped establish critical credentials for Arzner as a proto-feminist auteur. Yet, Arzner's own response to Christopher complicates issues around feminist reclamation of her authorship:

> ... I was more interested in Christopher Strong, played by Cohn Clive, than in any of the women characters. He was a man 'on the cross'. He loved his wife, and he fell in love with the aviatrix. He was on the rack. I was really more sympathetic with him, but no one seemed to pick up on that. Of course, not too many women are sympathetic about the torture the situation might give to a man of upright character.[13]

Disconcerting with respect to feminist claims, this remark is read by Gaines as repudiating any impulse to "automatic auteurism", who adds that "transgression in one arena doesn't necessarily mean transgression in another".[14]

This said, a number of Arzner's films have proven immensely fruitful for feminist theorists and historians, among them *Craig's Wife*

(1936) and *Dance, Girl, Dance* (1940). Although not a commercial success on original release, *Dance, Girl, Dance* would become Arzner's best known film. It focuses on the meaning and significance of women's performance, using dance as an avenue for women's self-expression and financial independence. The film's representation of sexual, racial and class differences have been extensively discussed in both scholarly work and reviews. As Geller states, this is a consistent theme in Arzner's films, "the contrast of social paths for women, usually embodied in two central but opposed characters, and the class distinctions that underlie this opposition".[15] A pivotal scene is that in which Judy (Maureen O'Hara), a ballerina playing stooge to friend Bubbles' (Lucille Ball) more popular/sexualized dance act speaks back to the jeering audience. In a scene often taken as a commentary on the dynamics of woman as sexual spectacle in the cinema, Judy lectures the crowd on their behaviour, appealing to a sense of the moral superiority of women over male hecklers who use the theatre as a means to fend off their insecurities. Judy scathingly remarks that their wives and sweethearts (just like the female performers) are not fooled by this act: "I'm sure they see through you just like we do!"

Judy's speech has been understood as a moment of turning the tables on a tradition of American entertainment in which woman serves above all as spectacle. Arzner's final feature *First Comes Courage* (1943) has also been read as offering an alternative to patriarchal narratives that affirm male dominance and female subordination. For Diane Carson, *First Comes Courage* showcases Arzner's exceptional cinematic contribution: strong, complex women who resist, even defy, stereotypical characterization.[16] The film atypically celebrates the independent central woman, Nicole Larsen (Merle Oberon), by letting her narrate her own story. While the contemporaneous *Casablanca* (Curtiz, 1943) was lauded for its celebration of a man who gets involved in the resistance movement, similar wartime heroism was featured in *First Comes Courage*, yet the film received no Oscar nominations. Instead, the film was seen to valorize "a self-determined, strong-willed woman at the center of personal and political intrigue".[17]

Considering the persistent inequality of opportunity within certain key authorial roles in Hollywood, Arzner's case underlines the urgent need to take note of – even to celebrate – women filmmakers and women's cinema. Feminist scholars have highlighted both the marginalization of women filmmakers and the problematic insistence of diverse auteur theories on 'virility' as a marker of directorial quality. Both factors frame interest in Arzner. Over her career Dorothy Arzner produced, in Judith Mayne's words, "a body of work that consistently challenges many of our assumptions about the necessary limitations of Hollywood cinema".[18] Her films, with their smart use of fashion and design, central interest in strong women and female communities, suggest the rich possibilities as well as the limits of Hollywood cinema.

Biography

Dorothy Arzner (1897–1979) grew up in Hollywood, California, where her father, Louis Arzner, owned a restaurant famous amongst actors and filmmakers. She studied medicine at the University of Southern California. Her work in the film industry began with a position typing scripts for the Famous Players-Lasky Corporation (later Paramount). She worked as a cutter and editor at Realart Studio. She stopped directing features in 1943 though continued working over the following three decades, making Women's Army Corps training films and commercials for Pepsi. In the 1960s and 1970s, she taught screenwriting and directing at UCLA Film School until her death.

Notes

1 Karyn Kay and Gerald Peary, 'Interview with Dorothy Arzner' http://agnesfilms.com/interviews-with-female-filmmakers/interview-with-dorothy-arzner/. This interview also appeared in *Women and the Cinema*, eds. Karyn Kay and Gerald Peary, New York: E.P. Dutton, 1977. The interview first appeared in *Cinema*, no. 34 (1974).

2 Judith Mayne, *Directed by Arzner*, Bloomington and Indianapolis: Indiana University Press, 1994, p. 44.

3 Jane Gaines, 'Dorothy Arzner's Trousers', http://www.ejumpcut.org/archive/onlinessays/JC37folder/ArznersTrousers.html Originally published in *Jump Cut*, no. 37, July 1992, pp. 88–98.

4 Geller, Theresa L., *Senses of Cinema*, Issue 26, May 2006. 'Dorothy Arzner.' http://sensesofcinema.com/2003/great-directors/arzner/.

5 Gerald Peary and Karyn Kay. 'Interview with Dorothy Arzner,' in Claire Johnston (ed.), *The Work of Dorothy Arzner: Towards a Feminist Cinema*. London; British Film Institute, 1975, p. 23.

6 Mayne, op. cit., p. 1.

7 See http://www.cinema.ucla.edu/events/2003-05-31/directed-dorothy-arzner-tour.

8 Kendahl Cruver, 'The Wild Party', *Senses of Cinema*, Issue 33, October 2004, http://sensesofcinema.com/2004/cteq/wild_party/

9 Ibid.

10 Ibid.

11 Mayne, op. cit., p. 1.

12 Geller, *op. cit.*
13 Karyn Kay and Gerald Peary, 1977, p. 163.
14 Gaines, op. cit.
15 Geller, op. cit.
16 Diane Carson, 'First Comes Courage', *Quarterly Review of Film and Video*, Vol. 27, No. 5, 2010, pp. 375–76.
17 Ibid., p. 376.
18 Mayne, op. cit., p. 1.

Filmography

Get Your Man (1927)
The Wild Party (1929)
Fashions for Women (1927)
Ten Modern Commandments (1927)
Manhattan Cocktail (1928)
Anybody's Woman (1930)
Sarah and Son (1930)
Working Girls (1931)
Honor Among Lovers (1931)
Merrily We Go to Hell (1932)
Christopher Strong (1933)
Nana (1934)
Craig's Wife (1936)
The Bride Wore Red (1937)
Dance, Girl, Dance (1940)
First Comes Courage (1943)

Further reading

Bryant, Sara. 'Dorothy Arzner's Talkies: Gender, Technologies of Voice, and the Modernist Sensorium', *Modern Fiction Studies*, Vol. 59, No. 2, 2013, pp. 346–72.

Durham, C. A. 'Missing masculinity or Cherchez L'Homme: Re-reading Dorothy Arzner's *Christopher Strong*', *Quarterly Review of Film and Video*, Vol. 18, No. 1, 2001, pp. 63–70.

Ehrenstein, D. 'Working Girls', *Quarterly Review of Film and Video*, Vol. 27, No. 5, 2010, pp. 371–73.

Field, A. N. 'Dorothy Arzner', in Jane Gaines, Radha Vatsal, and Monica Dall'Asta (eds). *Women Film Pioneers Project*. Center for Digital Research and Scholarship. New York, NY: Columbia University Libraries, 2013. https://wfpp.cdrs.columbia.edu/pioneer/ccp-dorothy-arzner/

Kay, K. and Gerald, P. *Women and the Cinema: A Critical Anthology.* New York: Dutton, 1977.

Mayne, J. 'Lesbian Looks: Dorothy Arzner and Female Authorship' in Bad Object-Choices (eds). *How Do I Look?: Queer Film and Video,* Seattle, Bay Press, 1991, pp. 103–43.

FRANK CAPRA

By Elizabeth Rawitsch

Although it has been over fifty years since Frank Capra retired from directing, his movies tenaciously remain part of American culture. From *It Happened One Night* (1934) to *Mr. Smith Goes to Washington* (1939) to *It's a Wonderful Life* (1946), Capra's films continue to be celebrated for repeatedly foregrounding American iconography and uniquely championing American ideology. Indeed, when faced with the task of summarizing Capra's life and career upon his death on September 3, 1991, "American" was the adjective that newspaper obituaries most frequently used.[1] But Capra's style, like his contemporary Alfred Hitchcock's, had also garnered its own adjective—two adjectives, in fact: Capraesque and Capracorn, although the latter was also frequently used as a noun.

Both constructions of Capra's authorial signature—Capraesque and Capracorn—hint at a problem that Robert Sklar and Vito Zagarrio first observed in 1992: namely that Capra's name "has become an instantly recognizable signifier, loosely defined but clearly understood, standing for a particular strain of national self-conception."[2] It is precisely that "loose"—and often conflicting—definition of what "a Capra film" means that makes this classical Hollywood icon such an intriguing case study, one who ultimately calls into question the boundaries of authorship, classical Hollywood, and national identity itself.

Although Capra has long been recognized as an important figure in the 1930s studio system—one who helped Columbia Pictures rise from Poverty Row to "major-minor" status—the issue of whether or not he qualifies as an auteur has long been debated and never resolved. As Zagarrio has noted, the director's name rarely appeared in *Cahiers du Cinéma* during its heyday; in a retrospective symposium on *la politique des auteurs*, Jean-Louis Comolli conceded that Capra was a director for whom "the battle still has to be fought."[3] There are a number of possible explanations for this disinterest: that his commercial success somehow precluded critical success or claims of artistry; that the quality of his filmmaking supposedly declined from the late 1940s; and that his output for most of the 1950s was primarily in television (the Bell Laboratory Science series from 1956–58), a medium in which *Cahiers* was uninterested. John Raeburn even speculated that the innate Americanness of Capra's films simply did not translate into French: "Much of the world of a Mr. Deeds or a Mr. Smith or a John Doe was simply culturally unavailable to non-Americans."[4] Additionally, while the impetus of the auteur movement was largely to "rescue" neglected and overlooked talents,[5] Capra had received considerable recognition from the Academy of Motion Picture Arts and Sciences, including three Oscars for Best Director—a record beaten only by John Ford. Simply put, Capra did not need "rescuing"; he was already a celebrated figure within the industry.

When Andrew Sarris published his hierarchical ranking of Hollywood directors in *The American Cinema* he, unlike the *Cahiers* critics, included Capra, but he relegated the director to the second-tier "Far Side of Paradise" rather than including him in the vaunted "Pantheon."[6] Although Sarris declared that "Capra is a genuine *auteur*, and there is no mistaking his point of view," he also found fragmentation in Capra's personal vision, specifically in *Lost Horizon* (1937), a film about primarily British travelers who discover a utopian society deep in the Tibetan mountains—a departure for a filmmaker whose output was supposedly all-American. "At that point," Sarris declared, "Capra stopped the world and got off."[7]

While one debate around Capra and authorship centers on the criteria for meeting auteur status, a second debate has interrogated whether or not Capra is even the individual responsible for the thematic consistency of the films that have been attributed to him. Capra was, to some degree, an exceptional figure within the studio system, a semi-autonomous producer-director with relative freedom to choose his own projects at Columbia.[8] In his autobiography *The Name Above the Title*, Capra repeatedly advocated what he called the "one man, one film" approach to filmmaking ("in art it is 'one man, one painting—one statue—one book—one film'") and vehemently argued that he himself was a practitioner firmly committed to this method: "Regardless of the origin of a film idea—I made it mine; regardless of differences with studio heads, screenwriters, or actors—the thought, heart, and substance of a film were mine."[9]

Yet Capra also typified the collaborative working characteristic of the studio system.[10] He repeatedly worked with screenwriter Robert Riskin, cinematographer Joseph Walker, editor Slavko Vorkapich, composer Dmitri Tiomkin, and set designer Stephen Gossoon, as outlined in Joseph McBride's biography *Frank Capra: The Catastrophe of Success*. Denying the myth of authorship while at the same time building a case for Riskin as the genius behind Capra, McBride declared *The Name Above the Title* to be "largely a work of fiction," a self-mythologizing display of egotism wherein Capra willfully and maliciously revised his personal history to deny credit to his closest collaborators, many of whom could not contradict his version of events because Capra had been blessed with the good fortune to outlive them.[11] (Indeed Capra lists a whopping twenty-nine deceased "fellow riders" of cinema's magic carpet in his autobiography's dedication.) Whereas Capra's autobiography sought to construct the director as a Horatio Alger–style hero, the biography sought to construct him as an egomaniacal villain.

Whoever was responsible for Capra's authorial signature—and whether that signature should in fact be called Capraesque, Riskinesque, Capriskin, or something else entirely—the films are understood to document the fight between an idealistic "little guy" and a corrupt system—a trademark first identified by Capra himself, who asserted that the message of his films was:

> A simple honest man, driven into a corner by predatory sophisticates, can, if he will, reach deep down into his God-given resources and come up with the necessary handfuls of courage, wit, and love to triumph over his environment. [...] It was the rebellious cry of the individual against being trampled to an ort by massiveness—mass production, mass education, mass politics, mass wealth, mass conformity.[12]

For example, in *Mr. Smith Goes to Washington*, Jefferson Smith (James Stewart) gradually comes to take a stand against corrupt newspaper magnate Jim Taylor, who is threatening to use a federal deficiency bill for his own personal profit. Left with no weapons but his voice and the democratic process, Senator Smith stages a one-man, twenty-three-hour filibuster. Lost causes are "the only causes worth fighting for," he declares in a hoarse whisper, and his words reach the heart of Joseph Paine, the corrupt senior senator who confesses his complicity in the graft scheme when Smith finally collapses from exhaustion.

Mr. Smith is packed full of both American iconography (the Capitol dome, the Lincoln Memorial, the Declaration of Independence) and American folk music ("The Star-Spangled Banner," "Yankee Doodle," "My Country 'Tis of Thee"), presenting Americana on both visual and aural levels. And this kind of iconography is not exclusive to

Mr. Smith.[13] Grant's Tomb is a site of pilgrimage (and the inspiration of a speech that references Lincoln) in *Mr. Deeds Goes to Town*. In *It's a Wonderful Life* there is a portrait of Woodrow Wilson in George Bailey's father's office, and the Bailey house itself boasts a portrait of Lincoln. An early draft of *Wonderful Life* had even set the film's heavenly opening in Founding Father "Ben Franklin's Office and Workshop."[14] The characters and plots of Capra's films repeatedly foreground iconography that celebrates American history—history that all citizens could supposedly claim as their own regardless of their place of birth.[15]

"Capraesque" therefore encapsulated a belief in the underdog, a spirit of unshakable optimism, and a commitment to "love thy neighbor," all firmly grounded in American history and folklore: catholic without being Catholic, populist without being Populist. The degree to which it veered into saccharine sentimentality pushed it into the realm of "Capracorn," into naivety and an implied bygone sort of Americanness, one that was nostalgic for an earlier period of American history, one that possibly never existed. Yet this defining pattern in Capra's *oeuvre* is primarily supported by films from only a small segment of Capra's lengthy career: *It Happened One Night, Mr. Deeds Goes to Town, You Can't Take It With You, Mr. Smith Goes to Washington, Meet John Doe*, and *It's a Wonderful Life*. So it is worth emphasizing that Capra did not just make films in the studio system. He also had a collaborative star-director system of production with comedian Harry Langdon during the silent era, worked as an "in-house independent" producer-director at Warner Bros., served in the extremely hierarchical U.S. Army, had his own production company Liberty Films, worked as a television producer, and directed films for star-led production companies. Capra's engagement with themes of American identity varied throughout his career and across these systems of production.

Capra did not just thematize American ideology by drawing upon exclusively American reference points. He also engaged with the broader world. In *It's a Wonderful Life*, for example, George Bailey (James Stewart, again) repeatedly fantasizes about places beyond America's borders: Tahiti, where, as he tells young Mary Hatch, coconuts come from; Arabia, for which he would need a suitcase big enough for 1,001 nights; South America, where he hopes to board a cruise ship after his brother returns from college; Europe, where he wants to serve during the war, and so on. But George never actually sets foot in any of these places. He is repeatedly confronted with a choice between the domestic obligations of his hometown and the exotic allure of the foreign. He always chooses his family and America, always privileges the community above his personal desires. In the end, the compromise is that the exotic can be domesticated; George cannot go to the Caribbean for his honeymoon, but his wife and friends can temporarily decorate his new home with travel posters advertising luxury cruise liners to the South Seas. Small-town America can contain all the adventure that George needs.

These various aspects of Frank Capra (studio director, rogue independent, fairy tale hero, egomaniacal liar) and of Capra's films (Capraesque, Capracorn, nationalistic, global in scope) raise a number of interesting questions about the precise nature of authorship within the studio system, about where the boundaries of classical Hollywood are drawn, and about the construction of national identity. While Capra remains one of the most iconic figures in film history, he also remains one of the most elusive.

Biography

Frank Capra was born on May 18, 1897 in Bisacquino, Sicily, and immigrated to America at the age of six. He graduated from Throop Polytechnic Institute (later the California Institute of Technology) with a degree in chemical engineering in 1918. Working his way up the Hollywood career ladder from film cutter to gag man to director, Capra was eventually nominated for six Oscars for Best Director and won three (for *It Happened One Night*, *Mr. Deeds Goes to Town*, and *You Can't Take It With You*). He was president of the Academy of Motion Picture Arts and Sciences (1935–39) and the Directors Guild of America (1939–41, 1960–61). In 1982, he received the American Film Institute's Life Achievement Award. Capra died of a heart attack in La Quinta, California, on September 3, 1991.

Notes

1 See, for example, Bob Thomas, "Capra Gifted With Outsider's Special Vision of the American Psyche," *Associated Press*, 3 September 1991; Jim Bawden, "All-American Moviemaker Frank Capra: 1897–1991: They Don't Make 'Em Like This Today," *Toronto Star*, 4 September 1991, p. B1; Peter B. Flint, "Frank Capra, Whose Films Helped America Keep Faith in Itself, Is Dead at 94," *The New York Times*, 4 September 1991, p. B10.

2 Robert Sklar and Vito Zagarrio, "Introduction," in *Frank Capra: Authorship and the Studio System*, eds. Robert Sklar and Vito Zagarrio, pp. 1–9 (Philadelphia: Temple University Press, 1998), p. 1.

3 See Jean-Louis Comolli, Jean-André Fieschi, Gérard Guégan, Michel Mardore, Claude Ollier, and André Téchiné, "Twenty Years On: A

Discussion about American Cinema and the *Politique des Auteurs*," in *Cahiers du Cinéma, 1960–1968: New Wave, New Cinema, Reevaluating Hollywood*, ed. Jim Hillier (Cambridge: Harvard University Press, 1986), p. 205. Originally published in French as "Vingt ans après: le cinema américain et la politique des auteurs," *Cahiers du cinéma* 172 (November 1965).

4 John Raeburn, "Introduction," in *Frank Capra: The Man and His Films*, eds. Richard Glatzer and John Raeburn (Ann Arbor: University of Michigan Press, 1975), p. viii.

5 See, for example, Andrew Sarris's discussion of this trend in "Notes on the Auteur Theory in 1962," *Film Culture* 29 (Winter 1962/1963): pp. 1–8.

6 Andrew Sarris, *The American Cinema: Directors and Directions 1929–1968* (New York: Da Capo, 1968), pp. 87–88.

7 Ibid.

8 See Thomas Schatz, *The Genius of the System: Hollywood Filmmaking in the Studio Era* (London: Simon and Schuster, 1988), p. 5.

9 Capra, *The Name Above the Title: An Autobiography* (New York: De Capo, 1997), pp. 34, 185.

10 See Thomas Schatz, "Anatomy of a House Director: Capra, Cohn, and Columbia in the 1930s," in *Frank Capra: The Man and His Films*, eds. Richard Glatzer and John Raeburn, pp. 10–36 (Ann Arbor: University of Michigan Press, 1995).

11 McBride, *Frank Capra: The Catastrophe of Success* (London: Faber and Faber, 1992), p. 648.

12 Capra, *The Name Above the Title*, p. 186.

13 Ian Scott, "Populism, Pragmatism, and Political Reinvention: The Presidential Motif in the Films of Frank Capra," in *Hollywood's White House: The American Presidency in Film and History*, eds. Peter C. Rollins and John E. O'Connor (Lexington: University Press of Kentucky, 2003), pp. 180–92.

14 See the 20 March 1946 estimating script of *It's a Wonderful Life*, excerpted in Jeanine Basinger, *The It's a Wonderful Life Book* (London: Pavillion, 1987), p. 325.

15 The inverse of this trend is Capra's repeated negative iconographic use of Napoleon. For example Henry Potter has several statues of the French emperor in his home and office in *Wonderful Life*, and Mary Matthews calls her husband "Nappy" sometimes ("when I get a little too big for my britches," Grant says) in *State of the Union* (1948).

Filmography

Fultah Fisher's Boarding House (1922)
The Strong Man (1926)
Long Pants (1927)
For the Love of Mike (1927)
That Certain Thing (1928)
So This Is Love (1928)
The Matinee Idol (1928)

The Way of the Strong (1928)
Say It With Sables (1928)
The Power of the Press (1928)
Submarine (1928)
The Younger Generation (1929)
The Donovan Affair (1929)
Flight (1929)
Ladies of Leisure (1929)
Rain or Shine (1930)
Dirigible (1931)
The Miracle Woman (1931)
Platinum Blonde (1931)
Forbidden (1932)
American Madness (1932)
The Bitter Tea of General Yen (1933)
Lady for a Day (1933)
It Happened One Night (1934)
Broadway Bill (1934)
Mr. Deeds Goes to Town (1936)
Lost Horizon (1937)
You Can't Take It With You (1938)
Mr. Smith Goes to Washington (1939)
Meet John Doe (1941)
Arsenic and Old Lace (1944)
Prelude to War (1942)
The Nazis Strike (1943)
Divide and Conquer (1943)
The Battle of Britain (1943)
Know Your Ally Britain (1943)
The Battle of Russia (1943)
Army-Navy Screen Magazine (1943–45) 50 issues
The Negro Soldier (1944)
Tunisian Victory (1944)
The Battle of China (1944)
War Comes to America (1945)
Your Job in Germany (1945)
Two Down and One to Go! (1945)
Know Your Enemy: Japan (1945)
Here Is Germany (1945)
Our Job in Japan (1946)
It's a Wonderful Life (1946)
State of the Union (1948)

Riding High (1950)
Here Comes the Groom (1951)
Our Mr. Sun (1956)
Hemo the Magnificent (1957)
The Strange Case of the Cosmic Rays (1957)
The Unchained Goddess (1958)
A Hole in the Head (1959)
Pocketful of Miracles (1961)

Further reading

Bowman, Barbara. *Master Space: Film Images of Capra, Lubitsch, Sternberg, and Wyler.* New York: Greenwood, 1992.

Carney, Ray. *American Vision: The Films of Frank Capra.* Hanover: Wesleyan University Press/University Press of New England, 1986.

Cavallero, Jonathan. *Hollywood's Italian American Filmmakers: Capra, Scorsese, Savoca, Coppola, and Tarantino.* Chicago: University of Illinois Press, 2011.

Girgus, Sam B. *Hollywood Renaissance: The Cinema of Democracy in the Era of Ford, Capra, and Kazan.* Cambridge: Cambridge University Press, 1998.

Lourdeaux, Lee. *Italian and Irish Filmmakers in America: Ford, Capra, Coppola, and Scorsese.* Philadelphia: Temple, 1990.

Maland, Charles J. *Frank Capra.* New York: Twayne, 1980.

McBride, Joseph. *Frank Capra: The Catastrophe of Success.* London: Faber and Faber, 1992.

Poague, Leland A. *Another Frank Capra.* Cambridge: Cambridge University Press, 1994.

——. *The Cinema of Frank Capra: An Approach to Film Comedy.* New York: A. S. Barnes and Co., 1975.

Rawitsch, Elizabeth. *Frank Capra's Eastern Horizons: American Identity and the Cinema of International Relations, 1922–1961.* London: I.B. Tauris, 2014.

Scherle, Victor and William Turner Levy. *The Complete Films of Frank Capra.* New York: Citadel Press, 1977.

Smoodin, Eric. *Regarding Frank Capra: Audience, Celebrity and American Film Studies, 1930–1960.* Durham: Duke University Press, 2004.

Willis, Donald C. *The Films of Frank Capra.* Metuchen, NJ: Scarecrow Press, 1974.

Wolfe, Charles. *Frank Capra: A Guide to References and Resources.* Boston: G. K. Hall, 1987.

GEORGE CUKOR

By Martha P. Nochimson

Born in 1899 in New York City to a middle class Jewish immigrant family that expected him to become a lawyer, George Cukor is a perplexing subject of inquiry. He was a first-rate Hollywood craftsman, the kind of denizen of Old Hollywood that current critics tend to either write off as a hack or seek to redeem as a covert interrogator of mainstream values. But the evidence suggests that Cukor was neither a hack nor a subversive. And his interviews give no hints that we ought to search harder for such evidence. Cukor was a passionate director, but he was not in the business of expressing his own ideas. He mined the scripts that were assigned to him for *their* ideas, and the emotional range of their characters. Some critics have tried to trace in his filmography the theme of the outsider, because Cukor was gay. (Though he never publicly spoke of his sexuality, his sexual orientation was common knowledge in the industry and has since become common public knowledge.) Called a "woman's director," a designation that served partially as code for his sexuality, Cukor frequently insisted that he gave his all to making actors and actresses alike look and act their best onscreen. His assertion is convincing. When he was assigned blockbuster actresses, like Greta Garbo, he made them shine, but when he was assigned charismatic actors, like Cary Grant, he worked very well with them too. As for finding an auteuristic "Cukor theme" or preoccupation, since he never wrote his own scripts and almost always worked with scripts adapted from novels and plays that came equipped with their own world views, it is only reasonable to understand Cukor as a filmmaker who could artfully bridge the gap between the language of print literature and of the stage on one hand, and the language of cinema on the other.

In other words, Cukor was a star *metteur en scène*. It would be ideal to discuss all of his productions to demonstrate how proficient he was in the art of translation, since his virtuosity becomes visible only on examination of his individual films, but that is beyond the present scope. However, close consideration of several of Cukor's films will serve to illuminate the rest of his filmography. In *David Copperfield* (1935), Cukor's first big success, he intelligently harnesses the glorious comedy and tragedy of Dickens' characters, and the warmth of family life that the scriptwriters channeled from the novel. He coaxes winning performances out of the inimitable Edna May Oliver as Aunt Betsy Trotwood, whose good heart keeps her from being a prisoner of her own absurdly strict standards of decorum; the irrepressible W. C. Fields as Wilkins Micawber; Lennox Pawle as Aunt Betsy's child-man friend named Mr. Dick; and the amazingly beautiful child actor, Freddie Bartholomew, as the young David. The story follows Dickens' story of the orphaned Copperfield as he traverses England, to escape the Murdstones, his over-controlling, loveless guardians. And ultimately, he reaches a happy manhood thanks to the better angels of Victorian England. But if there are ideas in this film about social repression, they are Dickens' and those mandated by Hollywood conventions, not Cukor's.

Nonetheless, it is Cukor who artfully models the domestic spaces through light and shadow and two and three shots that convey the special affection among Copperfield and those who love him, as well as the torment inflicted on Copperfield by the characters who mean no one any good. Cukor buttresses that vision with striking visual evocations of the script's conservative themes about the perils of straying beyond ordinary domestic limits. One of the most startling of these cautionary images occurs early in the film when Copperfield is playing at the beach with Emily (Fay Chaldecott), a friend whose exuberance will eventually destroy her. Cukor foreshadows that fate, as he frames Emily and David at play. He shows Emily running suddenly out to the end of a pier, shocking David with the energy with which she throws her arms up to embrace the endless possibilities represented by the sea and the horizon. At first, Cukor frames her in a long shot. But suddenly he cuts to a low angle shot that places Emily against the open sky, the gulls flying wildly, screaming around her, and, just as suddenly, cuts to a high angle down shot in which he shows us her small body juxtaposed perilously against the foaming waves of the sea. In Hollywood fashion, Cukor's subtle prefiguration of the potential problem of Emily's wild streak is so full of her exuberant energy that it distracts us from thinking too hard about the construction of a society in which human desire to go beyond its narrow limits is a dangerous indulgence.

Cukor's handling of Marguerite in *Camille* (1936) is an equally impressive demonstration of his mastery of the Old Hollywood approach to storytelling. In this film, Cukor renders a ravishingly romantic picture of patriarchy and the power of money embedded by Alexandre Dumas Fils into his novel and play about the doomed romance between Marguerite "Camille" Gautier (Greta Garbo), a legendary courtesan, and a nobleman named Armand Duval (Robert Taylor). The fatal consumption that Camille acquires through the unhealthy life she lives as a woman for hire is transformed by Cukor into something much closer to a charming aspect of fragile femininity. We are told that she is dying but never confronted with the fearfulness, ugliness, and dark mysteries of leaving life. Garbo's Marguerite is soulfully gorgeous even as she expires in Armand's arms when the film ends. At this moment, death leaves the realm of the biological to become a metaphor for the power that can rid their love of the stain with which her profession and his disobedience to his father in loving her has besmirched. Marguerite dies without even a troubled exhalation of breath, bathed in light as Armand disappears from the screen, his head falling in despair on her bosom below the level of the film frame. Now she belongs to the audience. The camera grants us the exhilaration of the final possession of this screen goddess as darkness envelops her so beautifully that just before the screen goes to black, there is a moment in which Garbo's peaceful, still face seems to exude light from her astonishing cheekbones. No one "spoke" Hollywood's language of romantic fantasy better than Cukor.

In *Keeper of the Flame* (1942), Cukor worked from a script based on an anti-Fascist book of the same name by Australian author I. A. R. Wylie, aka Ida Alexa Ross Wylie. It rivets the audience by dramatizing the emotional and erotic relationship between its protagonists, Christine Forrest (Katharine Hepburn) and Steven O'Malley (Spencer Tracy). Since the scriptwriters followed the book's author in fusing the relationship between this charismatic pair with a dedicated anti-Fascist philosophy, Cukor did too. The film's backstory is that Christine is the widow of Robert Forrest, an American hero. Having discovered Forrest's intention to use his celebrity to destroy democracy in a quest for personal power, Christine realizes that it is up to her to save the country from its idol. When he sets out in a storm to meet his lieutenants and put his plans into action, she chooses not to give him a warning about a hazardous bridge, which collapses, killing him instantly. The film documents the aftermath of her courageous choice, as O'Malley, a newspaper reporter who initially reveres Forrest, pries the truth out of a reluctant Christine.

Keeper of the Flame begins in a public space rather than the kind of private enclave in which Cukor and Hollywood were always so much more comfortable. We, as audience members, are out in the rain with the hordes of reporters and "little people" who mill around mourning Robert Forrest. But little by little, Cukor shepherds O'Malley and the audience inside Christine's exclusive, enclosed world. In O'Malley's first meeting with Christine she is dressed in a simple white gown in her darkened mansion, becoming for him and for us a queen. But this is a noble lady who is doomed to sacrifice herself to keep the flame of freedom alive, with the help of O'Malley, her knight in shining armor. Throughout the story, Christine thinks of nothing but love of country, bringing down upon herself the wrath of Forrest's vengeful henchmen, Clive Kerndon (Richard Wharf), who kills her in a vain attempt to keep Forrest's evil plans alive. After Christine is shot by Kerndon, she is elevated from queen to saint. Although dead in body, Christine is resurrected by O'Malley's articles about her that substitute her truth for her husband's lies. Interestingly, Cukor renders Christine more powerful as a dead saint than she might have been as a live heroine, a happy ending to this frightening drama that Cukor's direction punches home. Instead of cautioning us that American Fascism is possible, it soothes us with a fairy tale assurance that the good forces in the United States will never let that happen. A soporific happy ending was his way because it was Hollywood's way.

How far Cukor was able to stretch his craft and yet remain within the parameters drawn by the studio system became obvious as the 1940s became the 1950s and the studios had to open up to new European ideas about filmmaking. *Adam's Rib* (1949) is full of disturbing ideas, and French New Wave film craft that was making its way into the United States. But Cukor makes us entirely comfortable with such techniques as he translates to the screen ideas that emanated from the script written by Garson Kanin and Ruth Gordon. *Adam's Rib* is structured as if it were a series of fragmentary playlets, which sequentially reveal the trials and tribulations of Amanda and Adam Bonner (Katharine Hepburn and Spencer Tracy) a married pair of lawyers who find themselves on opposing sides of the same case. If the New Wave directors effectively broke the illusion of film though fragmentation, the playlet form in this film only *seems* to do so. Similarly at a thematic level, although Amanda and Adam *seem* to take on women's status as second-class citizens, *Adam's Rib* effectively maintains the customary Hollywood gender line. The Bonner marriage appears to break on the rocks of Amanda's feminist struggle to convince the jury to acquit Doris Attinger (Judy Holiday), a woman who has shot at both her husband and his mistress, whom Amanda characterizes as a desperate wife and mother defending her home, and Adam characterizes as a criminal. But by closure there is barely a trace of their previous enmity, as Adam takes Amanda to bed. Filtered through Cukor's charm and style, the Kanin/Gordon script reassures America that everything is all right with our gender relations.

As in *Keeper of the Flame*, Amanda and Adam inhabit a special space of privilege and beauty while the crowds of New Yorkers outside their sphere live in congested, unattractive surroundings. But here,

Cukor flirts with the slightly over exposed image shot in "available light" and the documentary style of the New Wave and Neo-Realism, aesthetics that challenged the controlled lighting and sound stage shooting favored by the studio system. Cukor adopted these new practices in a number of films of this period, notably *Born Yesterday*, *Pat and Mike*, *It Should Happen to You*, and *The Marrying Kind*. He is extremely creative in his use of the documentary style in *Adam's Rib*, but this too only appears to defy studio practice. For example, there is a seeming verismo in the scene in which Amanda interviews Doris in preparation for the trial. The room is stark, as it would be in the jail where Doris is being held, the lighting is flat as it would be in such a room, but at the same time, Cukor recuperates the scene for Hollywood through an elegant use of an unmoving camera and a formal frame-within-frame composition of the interview room and ante-room beyond. Empty space was another hallmark of the New Wave and Neo-Realists, allowing the new crop of European filmmakers to plunge the audience into the unknown. Cukor, however, makes empty space a completely comfortable known entity, for example in a scene in which he holds the camera on the empty Bonner bedroom while Amanda and Adam disappear into their off screen dressing rooms and their voices restore normality by amusingly cutting across the unpopulated space. Once the trial is over, Adam takes sexual charge of his wife. And as all returns to normal, Cukor moves back toward the older Hollywood visual style of artfully crafted, artificial beauty.

With *A Star is Born* (1954), Cukor made his first color film, and it is a testimony to his ability to immediately respond to the needs of Hollywood. Despite his lack of experience with color, his use of it is subtle, and stunningly effective. In fact, in this foundational behind-the-cameras tale of a Hollywood couple in which her career takes off as his slides into oblivion, Cukor seems to discover his virtuosity anew. He draws from Judy Garland, as rising star Vicki Lester, the performance of her life, fluid, nuanced, and unmarred by her trademark, mannered ingénue gestures. From James Mason, as descending star Norman Maine, Cukor extracts a performance almost superhuman in its brilliance, as an artist veering between drunken self-loathing and passionate, hopeful love for Vicki. If any film proves Cukor's contention that he gave equally to male and female actors, it is this, his last hurrah as a director at the top of his form.

Cukor continued to direct until 1981, two years before his death, but his work was increasingly unsatisfying to him and to his audiences. He was suited for the studio system in its heyday, which gave him well-defined conventional limits within which to work, and unthreatening themes about love, loss, and what they wore. If we attend to *Sylvia Scarlett* (1935), adapted from a novel by Sir Compton Mackenzie, *The Early Life and Adventures of Sylvia Scarlett* (1918), Cukor's one abysmal failure during his early days as a director, it can tell us much about Cukor's relationship to that system. In *Sylvia Scarlett*, Sylvia (Katharine Hepburn) masquerades as a boy, Sylvester, to protect her con-man father, who is in trouble with the law, with Hepburn giving a gender bending performance that might have unsettled the binaries of male and female. But despite the possibilities for something different, this film was, in execution, such a debacle that Cukor offered to make it up to producer Pandro Berman by directing another movie for him for free, an offer Berman refused because he could not face working with Cukor again.

Unlike Cukor's other films of the early period, *Sylvia Scarlett* is plagued by one bad decision after another. Cukor balks at every chance to give Sylvia/Sylvester a moment of fun in her adventures in cross-dressing. By contrast, Cary Grant as con-man Jimmy Monkley, a somewhat distasteful supporting character, inappropriately shines as a figure of fascination and delight from the first moment we see him on screen, in a foggy night on board a ship, wearing a trench coat and slouch hat, a sliver of light illuminating his face in the darkness. This sexy "foreign intrigue" image fights relentlessly with Monkley's role in the film as a darkly clownish, freewheeling cynic. Monkley is an imp of the perverse, hilariously laughing at the pain of others. Introducing this antic schemer as if he were Devlin, the dashing federal agent Grant would play in Hitchcock's *Notorious*, is a remarkable instance of Cukor using the worst image possible for the telling of this particular story, much as it may have propelled Grant toward a position in the Hollywood pantheon.

What possessed Cukor during this strangely misbegotten endeavor? Arguably, at that point in his career, *Sylvia Scarlett* came too close to forcing him to speak of forbidden subjects in what was then a thoroughly homophobic America. However, by the time he made his last film, *Rich and Famous* (1981), he was ready to take advantage of the new social permission to venture into previously taboo territory. The film is poorly written, and unimaginatively shot, but it is much more daring in its gender construction than anything Cukor had previously done. It concerns the long-term, highly competitive friendship of two novelists, Merry Noel Blake (Candice Bergen) a crassly commercial success, and Liz Hamilton (Jacqueline Bisset), whose equally famous books are less profitable but more critically esteemed. The film is a remake of *Old Acquaintance* (Dir. Vincent Sherman, 1943), starring

Bette Davis and Miriam Hopkins, in which there is a barely discernible lesbian subtext. *Rich and Famous,* however, ends with a pretty bold New Year's Eve embrace between Liz and Merry in front of a blazing fireplace, suggesting a society in which heterosexual love is so plagued by emotionally crippling materialism that the two women are each other's best option. However, the major scene of queer eroticism occurs earlier when Liz, in a carefree moment, allows a male prostitute to seduce her. Jim (Matt Lattanzi) is so clearly coded as a gay sex object that Liz seems to be a surrogate for Cukor. Hardly a moment of piercing insight into the life of a gay man, it is, however, uniquely in the canon of Cukor's oeuvre, a moment in which the director visualizes his personal desire.

For most of his career, George Cukor spoke only the language of mainstream Hollywood that assures us that death is magic and the war between the sexes is a delightfully choreographed dance, untouched by non-negotiable conflicts or grey areas in the structure of sexuality. To the last, Cukor was so much a creature of the industry that it was only when it let down its guard, that he did too, permitting the new freedom take him to the brink of reflecting on his own desires and his own experience of a complexly gendered universe.

Biography

George Cukor was born in 1899 in New York City to a Jewish immigrant family. He attained success and fame in Hollywood as a "woman's" director, but that was only a code phrase for "gay." His career spanned fifty-one years, from 1930 to 1981, during which time he was responsible for shepherding numerous Hollywood classics, including *Dinner at Eight; Camille; Gaslight; Adam's Rib;* and *A Star is Born.* Cukor made only modest strides in the direction of depicting a wider range of sexualities, but his last film, *Rich and Famous,* opened up a vivid subtext of gay and lesbian desire.

Filmography

Grumpy (1930)
The Virtuous Sin (1930)
The Royal Family of Broadway (1930)
Tarnished Lady (1931)
Girls About Town (1931)
What Price Hollywood (1932)
A Bill of Divorcement (1932)

One Hour With You (1932) uncredited
Une heure près de toi (1932) uncredited
Rockabye (1932)
The Animal Kingdom (1932) uncredited
Our Betters (1933)
Dinner at Eight (1933)
Little Women (1933)
Manhattan Melodrama (1934) uncredited
David Copperfield (1935)
No More Ladies (1935)
Sylvia Scarlett (1935)
Romeo and Juliet (1936)
Camille (1936)
I Met My Love Again (1938) uncredited
The Adventures of Tom Sawyer (1938) uncredited
Holiday (1938)
Zaza (1938)
The Women (1939)
Gone with the Wind (1939) uncredited
Susan and God (1940)
The Philadelphia Story (1940)
A Woman's Face (1941)
Two-Faced Woman (1941)
Her Cardboard Lover (1942)
Keeper of the Flame (1942)
Gaslight (1944)
Winged Victory (1944)
I'll Be Seeing You (1944) uncredited
Desire Me (1947) uncredited
A Double Life (1947)
Edward, My Son (1948)
Adam's Rib (1949)
A Life of Her Own (1950)
Born Yesterday (1950)
The Model and the Marriage Broker (1951)
The Marrying Kind (1951)
Pat and Mike (1952)
The Actress (1953)
It Should Happen to You (1954)
A Star is Born (1954)
Bhowani Junction (1956)
Lust For Life (1956) uncredited

Les Girls (1957)
Wild is the Wind (1957)
Hot Spell (1958) uncredited
Heller in Pink Tights (1960)
Song Without End (1960) uncredited
Let's Make Love (1960)
The Chapman Report (1962)
My Fair Lady (1962)
Justine (1969)
Travels With My Aunt (1972)
Love Among the Ruins TV (1975)
The Blue Bird (1976)
The Corn is Green TV (1979)
Rich and Famous (1981)

Further reading

Bernardoni, James. *George Cukor: A Critical Study and Filmography.* Jefferson, NC: McFarland, 1985.

Clarens, Carlos. *George Cukor.* London: Secker and Warburg for the British Film Institute, 1976.

Lambert, Gavin. *On Cukor.* Ed. Robert Trachtenberg. New York: Rizzoli, 2000.

Levy, Emanuel. *George Cukor, Master of Elegance: Hollywood's Legendary Director and His Stars.* New York: Morrow, 1994.

Long, Robert Emmet, ed. *George Cukor: Interviews.* Jackson: University Press of Mississippi, 2001.

McGilligan, Patrick. *George Cukor, a Double Life: Biography of the Gentleman Director.* New York: St. Martin's Press, 1991.

MICHAEL CURTIZ

By Ina Rae Hark

Michael Curtiz was the model studio director during that system's heyday in the 1930s and 1940s. After establishing himself in Europe in 1912, Curtiz came to Hollywood under contract to Warner Bros. in 1926 and remained there for the next twenty-five years. His prodigious output averaged more than three feature films a year in genres ranging from swashbucklers to musical biopics, from Westerns to film noir, from melodrama to horror. His most notable achievements, concentrated in the decade 1935 to 1945, formed two clusters. He made eight historical dramas starring Errol Flynn, five featuring English adventurers (*Captain Blood*, *The Charge of the Light Brigade*, *The Adventures of Robin Hood*, *The Private Lives of Elizabeth and Essex*, and *The Sea Hawk*) and three casting Flynn as an American in the Old West (*Dodge City*, *Virginia City*, and *Santa Fe Trail*). He also continued with the sorts of films the studio had assigned him upon his arrival: crime pictures ranging from classic whodunits to the careers of working class criminals, women's pictures about crimes of passion, and political thrillers. Belonging tangentially to this latter grouping, although in the end *sui generis*, is his undisputed masterpiece, *Casablanca* (1942).

On set, Curtiz was a perfectionist and a taskmaster. His methods injured extras in the flood scenes of *Noah's Ark* (1928) and horses in the eponymous charge in *The Charge of the Light Brigade* (1936). He frequently referred to actors as "bums," finding them lazy and undisciplined in comparison to his own tireless immersion in his craft. (They, in turn, mocked his thick accent and malapropisms on set.) He micromanaged, involved himself in casting even small parts, and fired cameramen in mid-picture. This made him unpopular with performers and crew alike but often elevated their work in the most routine films. Many a Warner Bros. contract player first revealed star potential in a Curtiz feature: Flynn and Olivia de Havilland in *Captain Blood* (1935), Bette Davis in *The Cabin in the Cotton* (1932), John Garfield in *Four Daughters* (1938), and Doris Day in *Romance on the High Seas* (1948). Eleven performances he directed received Oscar nominations and two won: James Cagney for *Yankee Doodle Dandy* (1942) and Joan Crawford for *Mildred Pierce* (1945).

The typical Curtiz picture depended less on compelling plot or clever dialogue than on the emotions of the characters and the director's distinctive visual style. Sidney Rosenzweig notes that the latter featured

> high crane shots to establish a story's environment; unusual camera angles and complex compositions in which characters are often framed by physical objects; much camera movement; subjective shots, in which the camera becomes the character's eye; and high contrast lighting with pools of shadows.[1]

A Curtiz film, Peter Wollen asserts, impresses with its energy and "obsessive attention to detail."[2] Thematically, Curtiz returned throughout his career to projects in which characters had to deal with injustice, oppression, entrapment, displacement and exile.

Born Manó Kertész Kaminer in 1886 to a Jewish family in Budapest, Hungary, he began his artistic life under the name Mihály Kertész. Beginning as both a stage actor and director, he involved himself in the fledgling Hungarian film industry from its inception. After going to Denmark for six months to apprentice with the Nordisk film company in 1913, he returned home to become one of the most prolific Hungarian directors until the industry was nationalized in 1919. A similarly productive period occurred during his time with the Sascha Company in Vienna. Two biblical epics he made with the company, *Sodom und Gomorrha* (1922) and *Die Sklavenkönigen* (*The Slave Queen*, 1924), caught the attention of the Warners, who were planning a version of the story of Noah's Ark. They offered him a contract in 1926. When he worked outside Hungary, Kertész had sometimes been billed under the first name Michael or the last name Courtice. Arriving in Hollywood with sixty-four films to his credit, he became Michael Curtiz for the rest of his career.

The studio delayed *Noah's Ark* until 1928, and Curtiz's first directorial assignment was instead *The Third Degree* (1926), a melodrama starring Dolores Costello as a woman whose lover is forced by police brutality to confess to a murder of which Costello's long-lost mother is actually guilty. Six other women's pictures with Costello followed during the late 20s. Curtiz's early 30s output was a grab bag of genres of the day, including horror movies – most notably *Mystery of the Wax Museum* (1932) – and the proletarian social problem films in which the Warners specialized. But other directors made the studio's signature successes of this period, whether gangster films such as William Wellman's *The Public Enemy* (1931) or the Lloyd Bacon/ Busby Berkeley backstage musical *42nd Street* (1933).

This is not to say that Curtiz's films of the early thirties are atypical or inferior to those that followed. For instance the prison picture *20,000 Years in Sing Sing* (1932) explored themes of social alienation, redemption and sacrifice within sets that provided a visual correlative. A brash, egotistical and defiant crook (Spencer Tracy), much celebrated in the newspapers, loses the attitude and gains a sense of honor under the strict but just correctional regime of Warden Long (Arthur Byron). He ends up taking the rap for a killing perpetrated by his girl friend (Bette Davis), telling her to forget about trying to clear him and to start over with a "square guy" as he awaits execution. With its bars, railings and limited sources of exterior illumination, the Sing Sing sets allowed for much Expressionist play of light and shadow, always a Curtiz signature. The film's multileveled common spaces, packed with inmates, display his predilection for dynamic action scenes involving large crowds. A failed prison break utilizes all these visuals to great effect. At the same time, Curtiz knew that talents like Tracy and Davis required no stylistic flourishes; he shot many of their scenes in close-up with a still camera, letting their performances carry the story. *20,000 Years in Sing Sing* in all these respects prefigures the director's finest crime film, *Angels with Dirty Faces* (1938).

Curtiz got his chance to define a studio genre (and used it to rise into the top directorial ranks) when the success of United Artists' *The Count of Monte Cristo* (1934), starring Robert Donat, and directed by Rowland V. Lee, convinced Warners to enter into the historical adventure-romance cycle. The studio owned the rights to Rafael Sabatini's novel *Captain Blood* and committed a large budget to a film version to star Donat, with Curtiz directing. When Donat dropped out late in the game, director and studio gambled their considerable investment on the relatively unknown contract players Flynn and de Havilland. The gamble paid off in a major financial and critical success.

Captain Blood, along with *The Adventures of Robin Hood* and *The Sea Hawk*, represent the best of the Curtiz-Flynn costume dramas; they also foreground and codify persistent traits of the Curtizian cinema. In all three a tyrant monarch threatens the freedom of ordinary Englishmen; the protagonist, caught up in this oppressive rule, loses his comfortable status. He and a band of diverse but dedicated rebels turn outlaw until the tyrant is defeated. Along the way a woman who is the ward of the tyrant or one of his lackeys falls in love with the protagonist and embraces his cause. After escaping slavery or imprisonment but before prevailing against the oppressor, the Flynn character and his comrades carve out a place of safety (such as pirate vessels or the wilds of Sherwood Forest) that protects them but also stresses their liminal, outlaw/exile status. Boats for Curtiz represent the ambiguities of safety and danger, community and banishment, heroism and outlawry. This preoccupation is evident not only in his swashbucklers but also in films as disparate as *Noah's Ark*, *The Sea Wolf* (1941), *Passage to Marseille* (1944), and *The Breaking Point* (1950).

Curtiz contrasts the spaces of tyranny and rebellion visually as well. Tyrants occupy cavernous, high-ceilinged rooms in palaces, colonial outposts, or kangaroo courts that furnishings and inhabitants do not come close to filling. Activities within these spaces are stiff and formal. Rebel home bases, by contrast, are crowded and intimate, with people and the camera in continual motion. Again, pirate ships epitomize these spaces. With multiple decks, rigging to be climbed, anchors hoisted and ropes to swing from, they bustle with energy. The sea battle set pieces in *Captain Blood* and *The Sea Hawk* dial up this kinetic potential exponentially.

Tyranny only falls when outlaw energy upsets its formality. *Sea Hawk's* Geoffrey Thorpe (also played by Flynn) prefigures his duel with a traitorous minister within Queen Elizabeth's court by sending in a pet monkey to run roughshod. Peter Blood becomes the governor of Jamaica to replace the man who enslaved him and pursued him and his men after their escape. In the grandest battle of them all, Robin Hood and his men (disguised as monks) infiltrate Prince John's (Claude Rains) illegitimate coronation and an all out melee ensues. Action ebbs and flows around the one-on-one swordfight between Robin and Sir Guy of Gisbourne (Basil Rathbone). Recurrent images from these triumphs of liberating chaos over inflexible order include giant silhouettes shadowing the walls, furniture overturned, candles bisected, staircases ascended and descended and piles of weapons or treasures thrown together in heaps.

Due to increasing conflict between the two men, Curtiz severed his professional relationship with Flynn after 1941, a parting that allowed Curtiz to direct A-pictures of more generic variety. First and foremost was *Casablanca*. Everything about the film provided opportunities for Curtiz to play to his strengths. Humphrey Bogart's Rick is a characteristic Curtizian exile and the other displaced persons who gather every night at his Café Americain function like the motley, diverse groups who gather around Flynn's outlawed freedom fighters. The night that threatens their precarious existence drips with fog, and a probing searchlight casts crosshatched shadows into interior spaces. This high contrast lighting works well to render Ingrid Bergman's Ilsa a lustrous beauty but it also symbolizes the Nazi danger in this area of colonial France where the Nazis technically have no authority. For once, the tyranny Curtiz portrays occurs not in centuries past but is alive in the present, its defeat by no means assured. The cast (other than Bogart and Dooley Wilson as Sam) consists almost entirely of European émigrés who, like their director, came from countries that were at the time either occupied or threatened by Hitler.

Scenes in the club display again how the director's visuals can create both energy and camaraderie in the depiction of crowded rooms. In a famous scene, German troops sit at a large table, singing songs in praise of the Fatherland. The camera looks over Rick's shoulder from behind as he stands on a balcony. The next shot pans the patrons sitting at the bar, including some Nazi sympathizers who join in. The bartenders and others remain silent, and the camera rests on Capt. Louis Renault (Claude Rains), likewise silent and disapproving. Curtiz then cuts to a reverse shot of the balcony where Victor Laszlo (Paul Henreid) comes up behind Rick, Laszlo's face showing displeasure. Laszlo starts down the stairs and the camera picks him up as he strides to the bandstand, telling the musicians to strike up the Marseillaise. Two intercut close-ups show the bandleader looking for Rick's approval and him providing it. The sequence then proceeds primarily in long shot, cutting between Laszlo at the bandstand, a view of the rest of those at tables from the point-of-view of the female singer-guitarist, and the perspective from behind the bar. Strategic close-ups come between the three long-shot perspectives. We see the Germans trying to drown out the singing of the anthem and failing; the quasi-collaborator Yvonne (Madeleine Lebeau) in tears, singing it loudly and ending with "Vive la France"; and two adjacent extreme close-ups of a defiant Victor and a rapt Ilsa. Clearly *this* is the man she fell in love with.

This sequence emphasizes how *Casablanca's* famous romantic triangle and its somewhat unexpected resolution adhere to a pattern that characterizes many of Curtiz's films. He often portrayed a charismatic but reckless (and potentially dangerous) protagonist whom the heroine loves. However, this man realizes that he is not the best match for the woman and sacrifices their relationship – and often his life – so that she can settle down with a duller but more admirable man. Rick is not the cynical loner looking out only for himself that he pretends to be but neither is he the idealistic leader of men such as Peter Blood or Robin Hood. Although his staff displays unwavering loyalty and affection, his way of fighting tyranny is to go off on his own, accompanied at the last minute by fellow cynic-with-a-heart Louis. Rick telling Ilsa that she must leave with Laszlo echoes romantic resolutions worked out among characters played by Flynn, de Havilland and Patric Knowles in *Charge of the Light Brigade*; and John Garfield, Priscilla Lane and Jeffrey Lynn in *Four Daughters* (1938). Variations on the theme have *Mildred Pierce* suggesting that Mildred should give her first husband Bert (Bruce Bennett), a "good and gentle" man (if unexciting and a poor provider), a second chance after her involvement with caddish Monty Baragon (Zachary Scott). And Rocky Sullivan's (James Cagney) pretending to die a coward serves to steer the neighborhood boys' hero worship away from the mercurial gangster and to make them more receptive to the pieties offered by Father Connolly (Pat O'Brien) in *Angels with Dirty Faces*.

Several other Curtiz classics followed *Casablanca*. Later in 1942 came *Yankee Doodle Dandy*, the biography with music of patriotic Broadway composer and performer George M. Cohan. The high octane star turn by Cagney, who abandoned his gangster portrayals to return to his song-and-dance-man roots, provided a level of kinetic energy Curtiz needed whole armies or armadas to generate in other films. Cagney's propulsive tap dancing imbued musical numbers with athleticism as exciting as Flynn and Rathbone's fencing matches.

In 1945 *Mildred Pierce* wrapped James M. Cain's novel about ambition, greed, betrayal and filial ingratitude in a *noir* murder mystery that benefited from Curtiz's myriad expressionistic devices: the murdered Baragon falls right into the camera, after which the camera picks up the magnificently broad-shouldered Mildred (Joan Crawford) striding in mink along a seaside landscape shrouded in shadow, glistening with rain and fog, and penetrated by searchlights. Characters' large silhouettes make their usual appearances. As in *The Third Degree* and *20,000 Years in Sing Sing*, both Mildred and Bert make false confessions to shield their spoiled daughter Veda (Ann Blyth), although Mildred is pragmatic enough to try to frame her weasely business partner Wally (Jack Carson) for the crime first.

In quite another mode, Curtiz filmed the classic family comedy *Life with Father* in 1947, but even here there are traces of tyranny: Victorian patriarch Clarence Day's fiscal stringency toward his wife and children leads them to various acts of rebellion, which culminate in his finally being hauled off to the baptismal font. Since the baptism occurs at his wife's behest, the action is symbolic of a better-ruled household to come.

Despite his earlier successes, Curtiz's relationship with Warner Bros. began to deteriorate in 1946, when fraught negotiations for a contract renewal took place. Combined with the pressures on Warners as the studio system itself began to collapse, mutual disaffection grew until the director and the studio finally parted company in 1953. Even though on his own, Curtiz's versatility and dependable craftsmanship left him with plenty of projects. Curtiz worked regularly up until 1961, a year before he died at 75 after a four-year struggle with cancer. His experience with historical material led to seven Westerns or other period pieces; five films continued the string of musicals or biographies of musicians that had stemmed from the success of *Yankee Doodle Dandy*.

Nevertheless, the studio system was crucial to what made the best Curtiz films work. None of his later films rises to the level of his prior achievements, although the pleasant holiday musical *White Christmas* (1954) has remained a December staple on television. His reputation has likewise suffered because he worked within that system for so long. Curtiz's death coincided with the rise of the auteur theory, which valued directors as the authors of Hollywood's significant films, but only if they strained against the system to express an individual creative vision. Because he made so many films for the same studio for so many years, auteurists discounted Curtiz as a mere cog in the studio machine, classifying his direction as more effect than cause. To the more polite he was the workhorse of Warners; to the less polite, he was a studio hack. Leading American auteur critic Andrew Sarris damned Curtiz's films with faint praise as "lightly likable," dubbed him an "amiable technician" who "faithfully served the studio's contract players," and said that *Casablanca* was "the happiest of happy accidents, and the most decisive exception to the auteur theory."[3]

This judgment has been challenged more recently[4] as has the validity of the auteur theory in the first place. Curtiz's films do demonstrate the same themes, character types, and stylistic flourishes. It is impossible to say for sure whether they were Curtiz's own preoccupations or familiar elements of the Warners' brand for which he was a consistent conduit. What is certain is that "directed by Michael Curtiz" summons up many Hollywood classics filled with indelible images and performances that became still recognizable précis of their actors' star personae. *Casablanca* is their pinnacle, and it is no accident.

Biography

Michael Curtiz was born December 24, 1886, in Budapest, Hungary. He began working as an actor and director in the theatre but by 1912 was directing films in Hungary and later Austria. He came to Hollywood in 1926 as a contract director for Warner Bros. and remained with them until 1953. After parting ways with the studio, he directed films for eight more years and then died of cancer in Los Angeles on April 11, 1962.

Notes

1 Sidney Rosenzweig, Casablanca *and Other Major Films of Michael Curtiz,* Ann Arbor, MI, UMI Research Press, pp. 6–7.
2 Peter Wollen, "The auteur theory: Michael Curtiz and *Casablanca,*" in David A. Gerstner and Janet Staiger (eds.) *Authorship and Film* (AFI Film Readers), New York and London, Routledge, 2003, p. 66.
3 Andrew Sarris, "The American Cinema," *Film Culture,* no. 28 (1963), pp. 35–36.
4 See Wollen.

Filmography

Today and Tomorrow (Hungary, 1912)
My Husband's Getting Married (Hungary, 1913)

The Last Bohemian (Hungary, 1913)
Captive Souls (Hungary, 1913)
Bánk Bán (Hungary, 1914)
Prisoner of the Night (Hungary, 1914)
The Borrowed Babies (Hungary, 1914)
Golddigger (Hungary, 1914)
The Princess in a Nightrobe (Hungary, 1914)
One Who Is Loved by Two (Hungary, 1915)
The Exile (Hungary, 1915)
Seven of Spades (Hungary, 1916)
The Wolf (Hungary, 1916)
Mr. Doctor (Hungary, 1916)
The Medic (Hungary, 1916)
The Strength of the Fatherland (Hungary, 1916)
The Karthauzer (Hungary, 1916)
The Black Rainbow (Hungary, 1916)
Master Zoard (Hungary, 1917)
Tavasz a télben (Hungary, 1917)
The Fishing Bell (Hungary, 1917)
A Penny's History (Hungary, 1917)
The Last Dawn (Hungary, 1917)
Az ezredes (Hungary, 1917)
Secret of St. Job Forest (Hungary, 1917)
Nobody's Son (Hungary, 1917)
Jean the Tenant (Hungary, 1917)
Earth's Man (Hungary, 1917)
Peace's Road (Hungary, 1917)
The Charlatan (Hungary, 1917)
Tatárjárás (Hungary, 1917)
The Red Samson (1917)
Magic Waltz (Hungary, 1918)
Lulu (Hungary, 1918)
Lu, the Coquette (Hungary, 1918)
Júdás (Hungary, 1918)
The Devil (Hungary, 1918)
A víg özvegy (Hungary, 1918)
A skorpió I. (Hungary, 1918)
Alraune (Hungary, 1918)
The Ugly Boy (Hungary, 1918)
99 (Hungary, 1918)
The Sunflower Woman (Hungary, 1918)

Jön az öcsém (Hungary, 1919) short
Liliom (Hungary, 1919)
Die Dame mit dem schwarzen Handschuh (Austria, 1919)
Boccaccio (Austria, 1920)
Der Stern von Damaskus (Austria, 1920)
Die Gottesgeisel (Austria, 1920)
Mrs. Tutti Frutti (Austria, 1921)
Good and Evil (Austria, 1921)
Mrs. Dane's Confession (Austria, 1921)
Labyrinth of Horror (Austria, 1921)
Sodom und Gomorrha (Austria, 1922)
Der junge Medardus (Austria, 1923)
Die Lawine (Austria, 1923)
Nameless (Austria, 1923)
General Babka (Austria, 1924)
Ein Spiel ums Leben (Austria, 1924)
Harun al Raschid (Austria, 1924)
Die Sklavenkönigin (Austria, 1924)
Das Spielzeug von Paris (Austria, 1925)
Fiaker Nr. 13 (Austria, 1926)
Der goldene Schmetterling (Austria, 1926)
The Third Degree (1926)
A Million Bid (1927)
The Desired Woman (1927)
Good Time Charley (1927)
Tenderloin (1928)
Noah's Ark (1928)
Glad Rag Doll (1929)
Madonna of Avenue A (1929)
The Gamblers (1929)
Hearts in Exile (1929)
Mammy (1930)
Under a Texas Moon (1930)
The Matrimonial Bed (1930)
Bright Lights (1930)
River's End (1930)
A Soldier's Plaything (1930)
Dämon des Meeres (1931)
God's Gift to Women (1931)
The Mad Genius (1931)
The Woman from Monte Carlo (1932)

Alias the Doctor (1932)
The Strange Love of Molly Louvain (1932)
Doctor X (1932)
The Cabin in the Cotton (1932)
20,000 Years in Sing Sing (1932)
Mystery of the Wax Museum (1932)
The Keyhole (1933)
Private Detective 62 (1933)
Goodbye Again (1933)
The Kennel Murder Case (1933)
Female (1933)
Mandalay (1934)
Jimmy the Gent (1934)
The Key (1934)
British Agent (1934)
Black Fury (1935)
The Case of the Curious Bride (1935)
Front Page Woman (1935)
Little Big Shot (1935)
Captain Blood (1935)
The Walking Dead (1936)
The Charge of the Light Brigade (1936)
Stolen Holiday (1937)
Mountain Justice (1937)
Kid Galahad (1937)
The Perfect Specimen (1937)
Gold Is Where You Find It (1938)
The Adventures of Robin Hood (1938)
Four's a Crowd (1938)
Four Daughters (1938)
Angels with Dirty Faces (1938)
Dodge City (1939)
Sons of Liberty (1939) short
Daughters Courageous (1939)
The Private Lives of Elizabeth and Essex (1939)
Four Wives (1939)
Virginia City (1940)
The Sea Hawk (1940)
Santa Fe Trail (1940)
The Sea Wolf (1941)
Dive Bomber (1941)

Captains of the Clouds (1942)
Yankee Doodle Dandy (1942)
Casablanca (1942)
Mission to Moscow (1943)
This Is the Army (1943)
Passage to Marseille (1944)
Janie (1944)
Roughly Speaking (1945)
Mildred Pierce (1945)
Night and Day (1946)
Life with Father (1947)
The Unsuspected (1947)
Romance on the High Seas (1948)
My Dream Is Yours (1949)
Flamingo Road (1949)
The Lady Takes a Sailor (1949)
Young Man with a Horn (1950)
Bright Leaf (1950)
The Breaking Point (1950)
Force of Arms (1951)
Jim Thorpe – All-American (1951)
I'll See You in My Dreams (1951)
The Story of Will Rogers (1952)
The Jazz Singer (1952)
Trouble Along the Way (1953)
The Boy from Oklahoma (1954)
The Egyptian (1954)
White Christmas (1954)
We're No Angels (1955)
The Scarlet Hour (1956)
The Vagabond King (1956)
The Best Things in Life Are Free (1956)
The Helen Morgan Story (1957)
The Proud Rebel (1958)
King Creole (1958)
The Hangman (1959)
The Man in the Net (1959)
A Breath of Scandal (1960)
Francis of Assisi (1961)
The Adventures of Huckleberry Finn (1960)
The Comancheros (1961)

Further reading

Canham, Kingsley. *The Hollywood Professionals Volume 1: Michael Curtiz, Raoul Walsh, Henry Hathaway.* London: Tantivy, 1980.

Hark, Ina Rae. "The Visual Politics of *The Adventures of Robin Hood.*" *Journal of Popular Culture* 5.1 (1976), 3–17.

Leggett, Paul. "The Noble Cynic: Michael Curtiz." *Focus on Film* 23 (Winter 1975), 15–19.

Robertson, James C. *The* Casablanca *Man: The Cinema of Michael Curtiz.* London: Routledge, 1993.

JOHN FORD

By Zoran Samardzija

John Ford is one of the most iconic directors of the Classical Hollywood era, one whose influence on American cinema is impossible to overstate. His career as director begins in 1917 (an era when the visual grammar of the feature length film codifies) and concludes in 1966 (the year before works like *The Graduate* and *Bonnie and Clyde* inaugurated what is now known as New Hollywood). Though most associated with the Western genre, John Ford created masterpieces in multiple genres, and he is comparable only to Howard Hawks in the range of his filmography. Also like Hawks, Ford mastered the "invisible style" that defines the Classical Hollywood era. As the often repeated story goes, Orson Welles claims to have watched *Stagecoach* (1939) forty times in preparation for directing *Citizen Kane* (1941) because he felt it was a perfect textbook for filmmaking. Throughout his career Ford has shown an interest in wide ranging themes such as mythologizing American history with *Young Mr. Lincoln* (1939); the ethics and politics of community and family with his adaptation of *The Grapes of Wrath* (1940) and his masterpiece *How Green Was My Valley* (1941); and militarism and honor with *The Long Gray Line* (1955). Though it is impossible to offer a comprehensive synthesis of his career and themes, two aspects of his career merit the most consideration: his attempts to represent Ireland and his Irish heritage and his evolving approach to the Western, the genre whose foundational myths he helped popularize and eventually reject.

Ford's representations of Ireland are conflicted and alternate between idealized fantasy and attempts to confront its contentious political history. While Irish characters appear throughout his works, *The Informer* (1935) is his first aesthetically significant attempt to examine his heritage on screen. As Joseph McBride observes in his biography, "The increasingly personal nature of Ford's work in the mid-30s was manifested in his growing preoccupation with Irish subject matter."[1] Adapted from a novel by Ford's cousin, Liam O'Flaherty, *The Informer* is set in Dublin during the Irish War of Independence. Because of its depressing subject matter, Ford had trouble finding financing despite his popularity as director. Most studios rejected it before RKO agreed to fund it with a small budget. The film tells the story of Gypo who has been kicked out of the Irish Republic Army for not murdering a British soldier. Poor, hungry, and angry, Gypo informs on his friend Frankie in the IRA in order to collect the reward. Visually, the film remains one of Ford's most impressive works. Collaborating with cinematographer Joseph H. August, Ford creates a vision of Dublin that is shrouded in fog, light, and shadow. The expressionistic style mirrors the psychological torment and guilt that Gypo feels for betraying his friend for a small sum of money. In the film's final scene, Gypo stumbles into a church after being shot by members of the IRA. He sees Frankie's mother praying and begs for forgiveness. While such an ending may seem improbable and sentimental today, it reflects Ford's sincere interest in the theme of redemption, which he will return to in multiple works including his Westerns and his most popular Irish film, *The Quiet Man* (1952).

Before returning to Ireland to film *The Quiet Man*, John Ford loosely adapted three plays from Irish American playwright Eugene O' Neill in the form of *The Long Voyage Home* (1940), a film shot in a similar expressionistic style to *The Informer* by the great cinematographer Gregg Toland. *The Quiet Man* remains, however, his most popular and iconic vision of Ireland, which he presents as an idealized utopia. An unabashed fantasy shot in beautiful Technicolor and set in the fictional town of Innisfree, the film is a romantic comedy about the redemption of John Wayne's character, Sean Thornton. Sean returns to Innisfree after living in America as a boxer. After accidentally killing his opponent in the ring he refuses to fight ever again. The film's idealization of the Irish countryside is apparent from the beginning. Upon seeing Maureen O'Hara's character, Mary Kate Danaher, herding sheep Sean tells the town's matchmaker, "Hey is that real? She can't be." Soon they are married. After a series of plot complications involving Mary Kate's brother refusing to hand over her dowry, Sean must again learn to fight and engages in a lengthy and slapstick fist-fight with her brother. By the end of the film, he is able to overcome his guilt for killing someone in the ring.

Ford would return to Ireland one last time for the anthology film *The Rising of the Moon* (1957), which he made in hopes of sparking film production in Ireland. While it was not a financial success like *The Quiet Man* and is not well remembered today, the three stories show the range of Ford's interest in Ireland. Two of the stories are light-hearted and populate the Irish countryside with drunken benevolent characters stumbling through comedic scenarios. "1921," the final story, though, represents a slight return to the visual expressionism of *The Informer* and *The Long Voyage Home*. While its plot is absurdist and often funny—fake nuns help Sean Curran escape execution by the British—it is reminder that however much Ford tries to create a fantasy version of Ireland its real and traumatic history keeps piercing the veil.

Though Ford had a more personal connection to his Irish films, he is best remembered for his innovations with the Western. In fact, a large portion of Ford's early silent films were Westerns, most of which are lost or exist only in partial prints. However, what does survive shows how Ford creates the foundational myths and genre tropes of the Classical Western he would deconstruct late in his career. *Bucking Broadway* (1917), discovered and restored in 2003, is a fascinating example of a Western that has yet to settle on its most iconic imagery such as stagecoaches, Native Americans, or border towns at the edge of civilization. It is set in the present and concludes with the peculiar image of cowboys on horseback riding down the streets of New York full of cars—an image that oddly foreshadows Sam Peckinpah's "late" Westerns fifty years later where cowboys on horseback are rendered outmoded by capitalist progress.

Ford's most significant silent Western is *The Iron Horse* (1924). An epic and sentimental ode to the idea of manifest destiny and traveling westward, it establishes each of the Western tropes that later populate the genre in its classical phase. Set in the aftermath of the Civil War, the film features legendary gunfighters like Wild Bill Hickok, saloons, judges, and border towns. Unfortunately, the racism inherent in the idea of manifest destiny also structures the story. The Native Americans are barely characterized and are presented as an obstacle to the building of the railroad and the vision of progress of its white characters, including a dignified Abraham Lincoln who is dramatized as unifying the country from East to West. To be fair, *The Iron Horse* does contain several fascinating scenes of multi-ethnic laborers building train tracks, showing that the white fantasy of manifest destiny required an *other* to become a reality.

While he directs one more silent Western, *3 Bad Men* (1926), Ford does not return to the genre until his masterpiece, *Stagecoach* (1939). With the advent of sound, major studios produced fewer Westerns per year. They became more commonly associated with serials and B-studios. Republic Pictures, for example, released dozens of Westerns in the 1930s with stars such as Gene Autry, Roy Rogers, and even a young John Wayne. Consequently, Ford's choice of casting Wayne as the lead in *Stagecoach* led to some difficulty securing funding as producers wanted more seasoned and recognizable stars. Ford's instincts, however, were correct as the film was successful and helped turn John Wayne into a cultural icon and one of the most popular actors in Hollywood for more than thirty years. It is not difficult to understand why, as Wayne's first appearance as The Ringo Kid is one of the most visually stunning character entries in the cinema history. He shouts, "hold it" as the camera aggressively moves into a close-up of his sweaty face.

Stagecoach—which alternates between expressionistic interiors of saloons and stagecoach stops and landscapes like Monument Valley—serves as the visual template for the twelve Westerns Ford would make after WWII, seven of which star John Wayne. In addition to Wayne, Ford loved working with actors multiple times, such as Ward Bond and Henry Fonda, who were often called The John Ford Stock Company. That said, while less triumphant than *The Iron Horse* about the idea of manifest destiny, *Stagecoach* is still more straightforward than Ford's later Westerns in its handling of the foundational myths of the genre. Ford will increasingly question masculine heroics and dramatize racism toward Native Americans and African Americans. For example, his masterful "cavalry trilogy"—*Fort Apache* (1948), *She Wore A Yellow Ribbon* (1949), and *Rio Grande* (1950)—is remarkable in its depiction of the personal loses and sacrifices associated with military service. The trilogy also represents Native Americans more sympathetically, prefiguring Ford's final Western, *Cheyenne Autumn* (1964) whose subject is the mistreatment of the Cheyenne tribe.

Ford's greatest post-WWII Westerns, however, are *The Searchers* (1956) and *The Man Who Shot Liberty Valance* (1962). In the former, John Wayne portrays Ethan Edwards, a former Confederate soldier who engages in an obsessive and vengeful quest to find his brother's daughter, Debbie, who is kidnapped after a Comanche attack on his family. Rather than presenting it as a heroic quest for justice, Ford gives *The Searchers* a melancholy and tragic tone. Wayne's character is a racist whose vision of the world is represented in ambivalent terms, both as outmoded and also somewhat necessary to find his niece.

In the iconic final shot, a long-take shows Ethan delivering Debbie to the family of a local ranch. As the camera moves inside the home, Ethan is framed in darkness around the doorway as he walks off into the distance. A wipe into complete darkness and the end credits figuratively closes the door on Ethan who no longer has a purpose in the world. In the context of the Western and John Wayne's onscreen persona, this self-conscious image casts doubt on his heroism.

Ford directed three more Westerns prior to his final Western masterpiece, *The Man Who Shot Liberty Valance* (1962). Of those, *Sergeant Rutledge* (1960) is the most stunning. Ford regular Woody Strode stars as an African American cavalry sergeant falsely accused of raping and murdering a white woman. The film is remarkable for its time for how it calls attention to racism against African Americans while demonstrating their military service.

But it is *The Man Who Shot Liberty Valance* that most subverts the myths of the Western. Similar to the later "revisionist Westerns" of Sam Peckinpah and Robert Altman, Ford's film offers a meta-commentary on the Western genre and questions how myths are created. James Stewart's character, Ransom Stoddard, becomes a U.S. Senator because of the legend that he shot and killed the notorious gunfighter Liberty Valance. In truth it was John Wayne's character, Tom Doniphon, who shot him and yet dies poor and forgotten. After confessing the truth to the newspaper reporter, Stoddard asks whether the reporter will print the real story. He is told: "this is the West sir, when the legend becomes fact, print the legend." Rather than validating the myths and noble lies of the frontier (as Ford does in his first major Western, *The Iron Horse*) *The Man Who Shot Liberty Valance* ends with a resigned melancholy, a knowledge that history is founded upon lies and distortions of facts.

Ford's visions of Ireland and the Western are not the entirety of his career but they are a useful beginning to understanding one of the most iconic directors of the Classical Hollywood era. Though he created masterpieces in many genres, his relationship to the Western is the most significant since it most clearly illustrates the evolution of his aesthetic—a youthful idealism about American history that becomes weary and resigned. His final work, the grim *7 Women* (1966), completes this transformation and can be read as Ford's last address to his audience. It tells the story of a cynical, secular female doctor and seven Christian missionary women in China who are confronted by bandits. The doctor, portrayed by Anne Bancroft who critics have read as a stand-in for Ford himself, enslaves herself to save the other women. In the end she poisons herself and her captor but not before uttering "So long ya bastard!" Those are Ford's final words on American history and the myth of the ever-expanding frontier.

Biography

John Ford was born in 1894 in Maine to Irish parents. After moving to California he began working in Hollywood in 1914 as an assistant to his older brother Francis. In 1917 he directed his first silent films. Sadly, most of his silent films are lost or exist only in fragments. For the next fifty years, he directed over 140 shorts, features, television episodes, and documentaries. While best remembered for his Westerns and films about Ireland, Ford's filmography spans multiple genres, styles, and themes.

Notes

1 Joseph McBride. *Searching For John Ford: A Life*. St. Martin's Press, 2001, p. 214.

Filmography

The Tornado (1917)
The Trail of Hate (1917)
The Scrapper (1917)
The Soul Herder (1917)
Cheyenne's Pal (1917)
Straight Shooting (1917)
The Secret Man (1917)
A Marked Man (1917)
Bucking Broadway (1917)
The Phantom Riders (1918)
Wild Women (1918)
Thieves' Gold (1918)
The Scarlet Drop (1918)
Hell Bent (1918)
A Woman's Fool (1918)
The Craving (1918)
Three Mounted Men (1918)
Roped (1919)
The Fighting Brothers (1919)
A Fight for Love (1919)

Rustlers (1919)
Bare Fists (1919)
Gun Law (1919)
The Gun Packer (1919)
By Indian Post (1919)
Riders of Vengeance (1919)
The Last Outlaw (1919)
The Outcasts of Poker Flat (1919)
Ace of the Saddle (1919)
Rider of the Law (1919)
A Gun Fightin' Gentleman (1919)
Marked Men (1919)
The Prince of Avenue A (1920)
The Girl in Number 29 (1920)
Hitchin' Posts (1920)
Just Pals (1920)
The Big Punch (1921)
The Freeze-Out (1921)
The Wallop (1921)
Desperate Trails (1921)
Action (1921)
Sure Fire (1921)
Jackie (1921)
Little Miss Smiles (1922)
Silver Wings (1922)
The Village Blacksmith (1922)
The Face on the Bar-Room Floor (1923)
Three Jumps Ahead (1923)
Cameo Kirby (1923)
North of Hudson Bay (1923)
Hoodman Blind (1923)
The Iron Horse (1924)
Hearts of Oak (1924)
Lightnin' (1925)
Kentucky Pride (1925)
Thank You (1925)
The Fighting Heart (1925)
The Shamrock Handicap (1926)
3 Bad Men (1926)
The Blue Eagle (1926)
Upstream (1927)

Mother Machree (1928)
Four Sons (1928)
Hangman's House (1928)
Napoleon's Barber (1928)
Riley the Cop (1928)
Strong Boy (1929)
The Black Watch (1929)
Salute (1929)
Men Without Women (1930)
Born Reckless (1930)
Up the River (1930)
Seas Beneath (1931)
The Brat (1931)
Arrowsmith (1931)
Air Mail (1932)
Flesh (1932)
Pilgrimage (1933)
Doctor Bull (1933)
The Lost Patrol (1934)
The World Moves On (1934)
Judge Priest (1934)
The Whole Town's Talking (1935)
The Informer (1935)
Steamboat Round the Bend (1935)
The Prisoner of Shark Island (1936)
Mary of Scotland (1936)
The Plough and the Stars (1936)
Wee Willie Winkie (1937)
The Hurricane (1937)
Four Men and a Prayer (1938)
Submarine Patrol (1938)
Stagecoach (1939)
Young Mr. Lincoln (1939)
Drums Along the Mohawk (1939)
The Grapes of Wrath (1940)
The Long Voyage Home (1940)
Tobacco Road (1941)
How Green Was My Valley (1941)
Sex Hygiene (1942) co-directed with Otto Brower
The Battle of Midway (1942)
Torpedo Squadron (1942)

We Sail at Midnight (1943) co-directed with Julian Spiro
How to Operate Behind Enemy Lines (1943)
German Industrial Manpower (1943)
December 7th (1943)
They Were Expendable (1945)
My Darling Clementine (1946)
The Fugitive (1947)
3 Godfathers (1948)
Fort Apache (1948)
She Wore a Yellow Ribbon (1949)
When Willie Comes Marching Home (1950)
Wagon Master (1950)
Rio Grande (1950)
This Is Korea! (1951)
The Quiet Man (1952)
What Price Glory (1952)
The Sun Shines Bright (1953)
Mogambo (1953)
The Long Gray Line (1955)
Mister Roberts (1955)
"Bamboo Cross" (1955) TV episode of *Jane Wyman Presents The Fireside Theatre*
"Rookie of the Year" (1955) TV episode of *Screen Directors Playhouse*
The Searchers (1956)
The Wings of Eagles (1957)
The Rising of the Moon (1957)
Gideon of Scotland Yard (1958)
The Last Hurrah (1958)
Korea (1959)
The Horse Soldiers (1959)
Sergeant Rutledge (1960)
"The Colter Craven Story" (1960) TV episode of *Wagon Train*
Two Rode Together (1961)
The Man Who Shot Liberty Valance (1962)
"Flashing Spikes" (1962) TV episode of *Alcoa Premiere*
"The Civil War" (1962) segment of *How the West Was Won*
Donovan's Reef (1963)
Cheyenne Autumn (1964)
7 Women (1966)
Chesty: A Tribute to a Legend (1976) completed in 1970

Further reading

Buscombe, Edward. *The Searchers* (BFI Film Classics). London: British Film Institute, 2008.

Crosson, Sean and Rod Stoneman, eds. *The Quiet Man ... And Beyond: Reflection on a Classic Film, John Ford and Ireland*. Dublin: The Liffey Press, 2009.

Eckstein, Arthur M. and Peter Lehman, eds. The Searchers: *Essays and Reflections on John Ford's Classic Western*. Detroit: Wayne State University Press, 2004.

Eyman, Scott. *Print The Legend: The Life and Times of John Ford*. Baltimore: John Hopkins University Press, 2001.

Grant, Barry Keith. *John Ford's* Stagecoach. (Cambridge Film Handbooks). Cambridge: Cambridge University Press, 2002.

Kalinak, Kathryn. *How The West Was Sung: Music in the Westerns of John Ford*. Berkeley: University of California Press, 2007.

Peary, Gerald, ed. *John Ford: Interviews*. (Conversations With Filmmakers Series). Jackson: University Press of Mississippi, 2001.

McBride, Joseph. *Searching For John Ford*. New York: St. Martin's Press, 2001.

Studlar, Gaylyn and Matthew Bernstein, eds. *John Ford Made Westerns: Filming the Legend in the Sound Era*. Bloomington: Indiana University Press, 2001.

SAMUEL FULLER

By Steve Neale

Samuel Fuller is usually characterised as a primitive maverick whose tabloid training and pulp sensibility found direct articulation in a series of movies aimed at the denizens of suburban drive-ins and subsequent-run cinemas located in the sleaziest areas of post-war city centres. There are elements of truth in this. Fuller was trained as a journalist. He did write pulp fiction. And many of his films were second features. But this by no means tells the whole story. As Lisa Dombrowski points out, Luc Moullet, one of Fuller's earliest champions, characterised Fuller as an 'intelligent primitive' whose ignorance of the protocols of filmmaking and whose 'reliance on his own instincts' enabled him 'to produce a vision of life more spontaneous and real than rule-bound classical cinema.'[1] As she also points out, those who followed in Moullet's footsteps, among them Andrew

Sarris and Manny Farber, did so too. While these notions persist, Fuller had been writing stories and scripts for major as well as minor Hollywood companies since 1936. And as Dombrowski demonstrates, while a number of Fuller's films stretched, ignored or deliberately transgressed the rules of classical cinema, others, most notably *Hell and High Water* (1954) and *House of Bamboo* (1955), which were produced by Twentieth-Century Fox, and *Merrill's Marauders* (1962), which was produced for distribution by Warner Bros., were marked as much by their classical construction and style as they were by their bigger budgets, imaginative staging, and complex set-pieces.

These stagings and set-pieces, among them the fluent orchestrations of movement in and around the submarine in *Hell and High Water*, the chase on and around the Ferris wheel in *House of Bamboo*, and the climactic combat sequence in *Merrill's Marauders*, were among Fuller's finest achievements. They could not have been produced without careful and conscious planning. Nor could the idiosyncratic sequences in some of the equally idiosyncratic films he produced himself. As Dombrowski points out, Fuller often charted the plot lines of his films on a blackboard, marking out points of exposition, the introduction of characters, sequences of romance, and sequences of action. The results were often deliberately unusual, stressing conflict and contradiction and marked by abrupt shifts in style and tone, jarring juxtapositions of humour and violence, and unstable combinations of didacticism, sentiment and irony, all underpinned by a style based on lengthy master shots (some of them unusually elaborate), interspersed with occasional cut-ins or interspersed with or linked by flurries of rapid editing.

Many of these stylistic characteristics were evident in the very first scene in Fuller's very first film, *I Shot Jesse James* (1949), which begins not just in the midst of a bank robbery, but with a set of tension-filled close-ups of unidentified men followed by a master shot revealing the robbery under way. A further set of close-ups articulate the wordless action until one of the tellers sets off the alarm, at which point a cut to the master shot is followed by a series of rapidly edited cuts as members of the gang are spurred into action and head for the door. A further cut takes us to a moving exterior master shot, which begins to track right as the gang escapes. Interrupted by a shot of the tellers in the bank, the master shot continues as members of the gang, now framed in high-angle medium long-shot, make good their escape on horseback while exchanging gunshots with one of the tellers. The teller is killed. Following another cut, the camera tracks in to show that the stolen money has been dropped and now litters the street. A newspaper report of these events is superimposed on the shot, which is followed by a montage of Jesse (Reed Hadley) and Robert Ford (John Ireland) making their escape.

Typical of Fuller is the film's focus on Ford rather than on Jesse and the fact that the story is based on actual events. Typical too is Ford's obsessive nature and outsider status, qualities that also characterise O'Meara (Rod Steiger) in *Run of the Arrow* (1957), Tolly Devlin (Cliff Robertson) in *Underworld U.S.A.* (1961), Johnny Barrett (Peter Breck) in *Shock Corridor* (1963), and James Addison Reavis (Vincent Price) in *The Baron of Arizona* (1950). Following *I Shot Jesse James*, *The Baron of Arizona* was the second of three films Fuller directed for Lippert Productions, a company specialising in the production and distribution of B films and more ambitious second features. *The Baron of Arizona* was less flamboyant in style than Fuller's earlier films. Its unpredictable narrative line and its indeterminate generic status were, however, features characteristic of a number of Fuller's later films, among them *Park Row* (1952), *Verboten!* (1959) and *The Naked Kiss* (1964).

Set in Korea and drawing on Fuller's experiences as a soldier in World War II, *The Steel Helmet* (1951) was the first of Fuller's combat films. In addition to opening with one of Fuller's most arresting images – a close-up of a helmet with bullet hole that rises unexpectedly to reveal that the GI wearing it is somehow still alive – *The Steel Helmet* focuses on the paradoxes and preoccupations of being a soldier (staying alive, staying dry, trying to eat and sleep). It also contains two remarkably frank discussions of racism in the U.S. as a captured Korean Communist engages in conversation, first with a black U.S. medic then with a Nisei soldier. If Fuller was always pro-American, he was also consistently and overtly anti-racist, as is evident not just in *The Steel Helmet*, but in *House of Bamboo*, *Run of the Arrow*, *Verboten!*, *The Crimson Kimono* (1959), *Shock Corridor* (1963), *The Big Red One* (1980) and *White Dog* (1982) too.

It was the success of *The Steel Helmet* that led to a contract with Fox, the production of *Fixed Bayonets* (1951), another Korean combat film, and the subsequent production of *Pickup on South Street* (1953), *Hell and High Water* and *House of Bamboo*. These last two films were the most expensive productions Fuller ever worked on, and *Hell and High Water* in particular performed well at the box-office. However, having had some of his own scripts rejected, and having already had a taste of independence by producing, scripting and directing *Park Row* (1952), his paean to the world of late nineteenth-century New York journalism and a film chock full of vivid characters, elaborate takes, master shots, and trademark cut-in close-ups, Fuller left Fox and set up Globe Enterprises in order to produce his own films. His first Globe production was *Run of the Arrow*, a film about an ex-Confederate who joins the Sioux at the end of the Civil War and his second was *China Gate* (1957), the story of a young Eurasian woman who helps a group of French Foreign Legionnaires destroy a Communist ammunition dump in Vietnam. His third Globe production was *Forty Guns* (1957), another of Fuller's idiosyncratic Westerns and arguably his most flamboyant 1950s film.

Like *China Gate*, *Forty Guns* was filmed in black-and-white and CinemaScope. Overstuffed with plotlines and in danger of sacrificing narrative clarity in favour of localised effects and unpredictable juxtapositions of tone, *Forty Guns* begins with a high angle shot of Jessica Drummond (Barbara Stanwyck) and her men galloping past the brothers Bonnell, who are riding in a buckboard in the opposite direction. The buckboard is forced to halt as a heady combination of high and low angle framings articulate this initial encounter; the effect is of an immensely powerful kinetic force overwhelming an unwittingly immobilised object. By the end of the film, these positions have been reversed as a relentless Griff Bonnell (Barry Sullivan) puts a stop not only to Jessica's power, but also to the life of her delinquent brother Brockie (John Ericson), whom he calmly shoots at the end of the final walkdown (shot in ever more extreme widescreen close-ups) even though Jessica is standing in front of him and thus is shot herself. Along the way, Wes Bonnell (Gene Barry) is killed at his wedding by Brockie and mourned by his widow Louvenia (Eve Brent) in the space of two adjacent scenes; the first involves a disorienting flurry of moving two-shot close-ups as Wes falls to the ground clutching his bride, the second a single take that begins with Louvenia standing alone on a hillside, tracks left to a mourner singing at Wes's grave, then back to Louvenia before cutting to the film's next scene.

Forty Guns was followed by *Verboten!*, *The Crimson Kimono* and *Underworld U.S.A. Verboten!* was distributed by RKO, the others by Columbia. By this time, the market for low-budget features aimed at adult rather than teenage audiences was on the decline and Fuller's attempts to appeal to the adult market by augmenting the sensational aspects of his films courted the ire of the Production Code Administration. Produced independently and thus bereft of support from the Hollywood majors, scenes such as the deliberate running over of a young girl on a bicycle, the immolation of an underworld boss, and the suicide of a corrupt police chief, all in *Underworld U.S.A.*, had to be carefully constructed to imply rather than to show violence. However, as effective as scenes like these eventually were, they were not enough to attract bookings in numbers sufficient to keep Globe afloat. As a consequence, Fuller went freelance, directing *Merrill's Marauders*, then writing, producing and directing *Shock Corridor* and *The Naked Kiss* for Fromkess-Firks Productions.

Shock Corridor and *The Naked Kiss* were Fuller's most extreme films. Combining elements of disorientation, sensation and shock, they were stuffed full of extraordinary sequences and provocative devices. *Shock Corridor* focuses on a journalist called Johnny who gets himself admitted to an asylum in order to track down the murderer of an inmate and win himself a Pulitzer Prize. Along the way he is attacked by nymphomaniacs, shares quarters with a homicidal opera singer, and interviews a nuclear scientist who behaves like a child, a Korean War veteran who thinks he is a Confederate General, and, most outrageous of all, an African-American who puts on a Ku Klux Klan hood and whips up a race riot. Toward the end of the film, Johnny begins to lose his mind. Signalled by a rumble of thunder on the soundtrack and a drop of rain falling into the palm of Johnny's hand as he sits in the asylum corridor, Fuller cuts to a shot of the self-same Johnny standing in the corridor in pouring rain, then to a close-up of Johnny filmed from below against a torrent of water, then to colour footage of a waterfall (the third of three colour sequences in the film) before returning to the set-up with which the sequence begins.

If this is one of the most inventive mixes of objective and subjective filmmaking ever put on screen in a narrative film, the opening images of *The Naked Kiss* are almost equally arresting. A woman lunges toward the hand-held camera brandishing a handbag. A hand-held reverse shot shows a man reeling away. As the sequence continues the woman's wig falls off, revealing that she is bald, while the dialogue reveals that she is a prostitute and that the man is a client who has refused to pay her for her services. Having beaten him to the ground, the woman takes the money she is owed, kicks him out the door, and puts her wig back on. She then decides to leave town and head off to Grantville, where, prompted by her love of children, she hopes to lead a better life working in an orthopaedic hospital. Along the way, the woman, Kelly (Constance Towers) finds herself drawn to the possibility of love and marriage to Grant (Michael Dante), a wealthy local benefactor. However, she questions her impressions of Grant in the midst of a kiss in a later sequence. The sequence is suffused with idealised romantic imagery. Yet the filming of the kiss and Kelly's reaction to it convey that something is wrong; her sense that Grant is in fact a sinister figure is later confirmed when she discovers a young girl in Grant's house, realises that he is guilty of child abuse, and beats him to death. Presented elliptically, the precise nature of these events had to be deduced. In 1964, two years prior to the abandonment of the Production Code, Fuller was simply unable to be more explicit (though as was the case with so many Hollywood directors, it was precisely because of these constraints that he was forced to be so inventive).

The Naked Kiss was the last film Fuller was able to produce, direct and edit himself. Following a number of abortive projects (and work on the television series *Iron Horse*), his next film, *Shark!* (1969), was taken out of his hands and edited by others, as indeed were most of his later films, many of which were produced in Europe. His pet project, *The Big Red One*, a paean to the infantry regiment in which he fought in World War II, was heavily cut (though restored for release on DVD after his death), and *White Dog* was accused of racism (of all things) and never released in the U.S. (though it too was eventually made available on DVD). Fuller moved to France, directed two further films, then moved back to California where he eventually died.

Biography

The son of Jewish immigrants, Fuller was born in Worcester, Massachusetts on 12 August 1912. He worked as a journalist and wrote novels and screenplays prior to the outbreak of World War Two, when he joined the U.S. army. Heavily decorated, he returned to the U.S. and began directing and producing films in 1949. He died on 30 October 1997.

Notes

1 Dombrowski, Lisa. *The Films of Samuel Fuller: 'If You Die, I'll Kill You!'*. Middletown, CT: Wesleyan University, 2008, pp. 7–8.

Filmography

I Shot Jesse James (1949)
The Baron of Arizona (1950)
The Steel Helmet (1951)
Fixed Bayonets (1951)
Park Row (1952)
Pickup on South Street (1953)

Hell and High Water (1954)
House of Bamboo (1955)
Run of the Arrow (1956)
China Gate (1957)
Forty Guns (1957)
Verboten! (1959)
The Crimson Kimono (1959)
Underworld U.S.A. (1961)
Merrill's Marauders (1962)
Shock Corridor (1963)
The Naked Kiss (1964)
Shark! (1969) also released as *Caine* and *Man-Eater*
Dead Pigeon on Beethoven Street (1972)
The Big Red One (1980)
White Dog (1982)
Thieves After Dark (1984)
Street No Return (1989)

Further reading

Fuller, Samuel. *A Third Face: My Tale of Writing, Fighting, and Film-making*. New York: Knopf, 2002.
Hardy, Phil. *Samuel Fuller*. London: Studio Vista, 1970.
Will, David and Peter Wollen, eds. *Samuel Fuller*. Edinburgh: Edinburgh Film Festival, 1969.

HOWARD HAWKS

By Yvonne Tasker

The long and prolific career of Howard Hawks spans almost fifty years of Hollywood history, extending from his work in the silent period through to his final film *Rio Lobo* released in 1970. Hawks worked in and across an extraordinary range of Hollywood genres directing and producing comedies, Westerns, war, epic, gangster, and science-fiction films. Movies such as *Scarface* (1932), *Bringing Up Baby* (1938), *Only Angels Have Wings* (1939), *His Girl Friday* (1940), *To Have and Have Not* (1943), *The Big Sleep* (1946), *Red River* (1948) and *Rio Bravo* (1959) have been routinely and thoughtfully analysed within film studies. Indeed Hawks' work as a whole has been celebrated by cinephiles for decades, subject to the veneration of auteur critics such as Jacques Rivette, whose 1953 essay "The Genius of Howard Hawks" celebrated an oeuvre that he claimed "epitomizes the highest qualities of the American cinema".[1] Hawks' films exemplify an American genre cinema that has fascinated scholars both European and American not for flaunting Hollywood conventions but for drawing out their richness and complexity.

According to Rivette, Hawks "is the only American director who knows how to draw a *moral*". While this is surely an example of the sort of evaluative overstatement for which some *Cahiers du Cinema* critics were notorious, the observation underlines what has been a recurrent (and rather contradictory) theme in writings on Hawks: that his films are both exemplary pieces of Hollywood genre cinema and that they are distinguished in some way, marking them out as extraordinary within the genre system. As Robin Wood summarises, writing in 1968 of *Rio Bravo*, "Hawks is at his most completely personal and individual when his work is most firmly traditional."[2] For these critics of the 1950s and 1960s then, Hawks signals a fascination with Hollywood cinema as a mode of filmmaking that is both rule-bound (genres, conventions) and capable of rich expression in the manipulation of these rules. To some extent, thinking now about the films of Howard Hawks means looking past the veneration of earlier decades.

Cinephile admiration for Hawks was far from unanimous in these decades, with some finding the veneration of a quintessentially Hollywood filmmaker problematic or distasteful. More nuanced debates evolved around whether Hawks' film work represented a bleak or an optimistic view of the themes he consistently addressed. Given the scope of his work, critics have often divided Hawks' films into two broad categories – the action films and the comedies – mapping the overlapping thematic concerns of the films in this way. Thus Robin Wood writes: "If the adventure films place high value on the sense of responsibility, the comedies derive much of their tension and intensity from the fascination exerted by irresponsibility."[3] In both groups can be seen a preoccupation with the gendered codes of behaviour – the professionalism of the male group so central to action, the rules of heterosexual courtship contrasted to bonds between men – that structure American society and cinema.

It is unsurprising that a director so firmly associated with action should be so insistently concerned with themes of male strength, responsibility and dependence. In the Western *Red River* John Wayne's relentless, embittered rancher is eventually challenged by his surrogate son, a rebellious and distinctively gentler Matt Garth played by Montgomery Clift. Their intense bond turns to contest before ultimately being resolved via the intervention of a woman and – of course – a fight. *Red River*'s epic backstory of driving cattle North gives a dramatic scale to the intimate tensions and rivalries played out between the central characters – the 360-degree panning shot that precedes the cattle drive and the stampede scenes later in the film revolve around the interplay of spectacular landscape and the figures within it. The increasingly tyrannical character of Wayne's Thomas Dunson pre-figures his more complex and famous role in John Ford's *The Searchers* (1956), underlining his range as an actor.

In *Rio Bravo* Wayne's Sheriff John T. Chance redeems Dean Martin's drunken Dude by not only trusting, but placing responsibility on him. The extraordinary opening scene of *Rio Bravo* unfolds without dialogue as Dude's degradation and resentment of Chance, Joe Burdette's villainy and Chance's physical and moral authority is played out via gesture, camerawork and music. In this sequence although Wayne is knocked out (by Dude) he re-emerges, bloodied, to utter the film's first line of dialogue, arresting Burdette. Meanwhile, Dude, who we see fallen low and beaten, ends the scene by assuming authority of his own: he takes guns from Burdette's men and backs up Chance. These reversals and the melodramatic quality of the scene set up *Rio Bravo*'s powerful dynamic of male dependence and loyalty, themes evident throughout Hawks' action films.

Hawks is known primarily as a director of action, with the male group central to this body of work. Westerns and war films more generally of course couple a fundamental sense of dependence and reliance on others with the individualism that defines the heroic male of Hollywood cinema. Hawks' first sound feature, *The Dawn Patrol* (1930) turns on the tensions within a military unit. (A major box-office success, the film would be remade in 1938. Directed by Edmund Goulding the later film cannibalised Hawks' spectacular flight footage.) Flying aces Richard Barthelmess and Douglas Fairbanks Jr. exist in an antagonistic relationship with their commanding officer, resenting his seeming willingness to send untrained pilots to their deaths; when Barthelmess must himself take on the role he comes to understand the costs of command, ultimately undertaking a suicidal mission to avoid condemning his friend and comrade to death in action. The mutual dependence of men and the presence of death in war movies – scenarios in which survival of the individual depends on the group (and vice versa) – underpins the moral code of duty that has come to be associated with Hawks films. This sense of duty and responsibility extends beyond the war film to the action/adventure scenarios of films such as *Only Angels Have Wings* (focused on an aviation company), Westerns such as *Red River* and *Rio Bravo*, and the noir crime worlds of *To Have and Have Not* or *The Big Sleep.*

The intensity of *Only Angels Have Wings* stems not from military operations, but the characters' professionalism and desire to prove their worth. (The figure of Bat, haunted by a cowardly act, is crucial.) And as Robert B. Ray observes, while *Angels* is not a war movie, it features many of the motifs that would become associated with the genre: an isolated male group, stoicism, teams built of diverse individuals and so on.[4] Cary Grant's stoicism in the face of loss (and his inability to directly ask Jean Arthur's Bonnie to remain with him) exemplifies the Hawksian hero, drawing out a nuanced performance from a star associated primarily with comedy at that point. (Hawks had already made the landmark comedy *Bringing Up Baby* with Grant the previous year).

Writing of the comedies, Victor Perkins observes that: 'Most of all Hawks likes to upset the relationship between the sexes.'[5] Hawks' comedies thrive on the anarchic potential of societal rules, whether gender roles (as Perkins alludes to) or a more general sense of the requirements of propriety being upturned, reversed and otherwise complicated. Hawks' *Bringing Up Baby*, a box office failure that subsequently acquired a status as classic film, rehearses a delirious comic scenario around the hapless scientist David Huxley (Cary Grant) who the aristocratic Susan Vance (Katherine Hepburn) sets out to snare. Perkins writes that the film's hero "is completely dominated by women" from his fiancée Alice who insists on duty before pleasure to Susan who puts her own desires before everything. Huxley progressively but inexorably loses his dignity, intellectual and physical, as he is drawn into Susan's anarchic world, ultimately falling for her (or perhaps simply giving in to her). For Perkins: "In this chaotic world language aids confusion, not comprehension,"[6] a contrast to the sparse use of dialogue in Hawks' adventure films.

While Susan is the source of energy and disruption in *Bringing Up Baby*, ensuring that David's world collapses around him, Rosalind Russell's newsman Hildy Johnson in *His Girl Friday* is forceful, fast-talking and professionally formidable. Playing the film as a comedy of remarriage rather than the male scenario in the play (*The Front Page*) from which it was adapted, *His Girl Friday* revels in Grant and Russell's verbal sparring and sets a hectic pace. Again Hawks works with Grant, here a savvy editor seeking reconciliation with Hildy as both romantic interest and ace reporter. *I Was a Male War Bride* (1949) stages this scenario of "women on top" in a post-war setting with

Cary Grant (again) undergoing indignities as GI bride to Lieutenant Catherine Gates (Ann Sheridan). Grant is once more the foil in *Monkey Business* (1952) in which he and wife Ginger Rogers accidentally take a drug created by a monkey, regressing to a youthful state. If *Monkey Business* arguably reinforces gender norms – Rogers becomes a "shy virgin"[7] while Grant pursues more adult desires – Hawks comedies more often exploit the disruptive consequences of powerful female protagonists as played out via Hildy Johnson's glee in rediscovering her professional talents as a journalist. Jane Russell's Dorothy Shaw in *Gentlemen Prefer Blondes* (1953), a smart-talking foil to Marilyn Monroe's diamond-focused Lorelei Lee, plays the aggressive woman to the point of parody, not least in the gymnasium number in which Olympic athletes form the chorus.

Mark Shivas characterises this female power somewhat romantically: "Men may fight the wars, fly the planes, rule the West, catch the animals, but it's the girls who wear the trousers in the world of Howard Hawks."[8] The cross-dressing imagery stems perhaps from the memorable images of Grant in female clothes in both *Bringing Up Baby* and *I Was a Male War Bride*. If this implies a strict delineation – conventional in classical and contemporary Hollywood movies – between male action and sexualised female power, Hawks' films are more nuanced and intense in their construction of the couple amidst action. Thus the assertive woman has frequently been noted as a feature of Hawks' adventure films with Lauren Bacall in *To Have and Have Not*, Joanne Dru in *Red River* or Angie Dickinson in *Rio Bravo* challenging the male hero/love interest. When asked about his use of romantic scenarios in which women are "aggressive", Hawks remarks:

> It's just a method of thinking and it becomes attractive because they don't act like a heroine or a hero. They're just kind of normal people. I call it honesty and it allows you to make a scene that's a little different.[9]

Ray suggests that a common mistake in the extensive scholarship on Hawks is to read his films as simple scenarios of the male group. Instead, he argues, Hawks' "groups were very special, capable of accommodating individualism without devouring it, relying as much on personal acts of heroism as on teamwork".[10] We might also argue that this quality shapes Hawks' ability to integrate women into the action of his films in quite particular ways. In her 1971 essay "The Hawksian Woman" Naomi Wise summarises the director's atypical approach to female characterisation, particularly in the adventure films, a Hollywood genre that tends to assign women a role of innocent and ineffectual (or active but bad, a transgression signalled most often by sexuality). She writes:

> In most of Hawks' adventure films, women play consequential roles; in fact, the heroines are, if anything superior to the heroes. The good girl and bad girl are fused into a single, heroic heroine, who is both sexual and valuable.[11]

Wise captures something of the qualities that make Hawks' films atypical. Their preoccupation with male groups, and their ability to incorporate challenging women underline the extent to which Hawks' films are distinct from many of the Hollywood films we might compare them to. In his 1962 analysis of *Rio Bravo* Robin Wood compares the boldness of Feathers (Dickinson) to Ford's work: "The respect Ford accords his heroines is an artificial thing, tainted by an insufferable condescension and at bottom not clearly distinguishable from contempt. ... Feathers is the equal of any man – while remaining unequivocally a woman."[12]

In Hawks' adventure films the responsibility of the hero – so much to the fore in thematic and narrative terms – is primarily to himself and the group of which he forms a part, not to the wider society. For Robin Wood this quality renders Hawks' work contemporary rather than nostalgic – the men (and women) fight for each other rather than for an abstracted society ("We look back nostalgically to the heroes of Ford, but we feel the heroes of *Rio Bravo* as our contemporaries."[13]) It is this that facilitates a sense of Hawks' modernity so often remarked upon by critics – Henri Langlois enthuses over Hawks as a "modern man," one "ahead of his time"[14] – since the values for which heroes such as those in *Only Angels Have Wings* or *Rio Bravo* strive are intimate and personal rather than social or ideological. Whether comedies such as *Bringing Up Baby* or adventures such as *The Big Sleep* or *Hatari!* (1962), Hawks' films appealed so strongly to the auteur critics of the post-war years not only for their striking thematic continuity but for their evocation of the tensions and connections that bind together individuals with those they love and/or those with whom they work.

Biography

Howard Hawks was born in 1896 in Indiana. He began in the industry working with props during the teens, and served as a scriptwriter during the early 1920s before getting the chance to direct. Through his career he would continue to write, sometimes un-credited. He died in 1977 in California.

Notes

1 Jacques Rivette, "The Genius of Howard Hawks" in Jim Hillier and Peter Wollen (eds) *Howard Hawks: American Artist*. London: BFI, 1996, p. 28.
2 Robin Wood, "Rio Bravo" in *Howard Hawks: American Artist*, p. 89.
3 Robin Wood, *Howard Hawks*, London: BFI, 1981, p. 68.
4 Robert B. Ray "Classic Hollywood's Holding Pattern" (originally 1985) in *Howard Hawks: American Artist*, pp. 190–99.
5 Victor Perkins, "Hawks' Comedies" (originally 1962) in *Howard Hawks: American Artist*, p. 69.
6 Ibid., p. 70.
7 Ibid., p. 21.
8 Mark Shivas, "Blondes" *Movie* 1962, p. 23.
9 In *Howard Hawks: American Artist*, p. 56.
10 Robert B. Ray, "Classic Hollywood's Holding Pattern: The Combat Films of World War II" in *Howard Hawks: American Artist*, pp. 190–91.
11 Naomi Wise, "The Hawksian Woman", (originally 1971) in *Howard Hawks: American Artist*, pp. 112–13.
12 Robin Wood, "Rio Bravo", *Movie* 1962, p. 25.
13 Ibid., p. 26.
14 Henri Langlois, "The Modernity of Howard Hawks" (1963) in *Howard Hawks: American Artist*. p. 72.

Filmography

The Road to Glory (1926)
Fig Leaves (1926)
The Cradle Snatchers (1927)
Paid to Love (1927)
A Girl in Every Port (1928)
Fazil (1928)
The Air Circus (1928)
Trent's Last Case (1929)
The Dawn Patrol (1930)
The Criminal Code (1931)
Scarface (1932)
The Crowd Roars (1932)
Tiger Shark (1932)
Today We Live (1933)
Viva Villa! (1934)
Twentieth Century (1934)
Barbary Coast (1935)

Ceiling Zero (1936)
The Road to Glory (1936)
Come and Get It (1936)
Bringing Up Baby (1938)
Only Angels Have Wings (1939)
His Girl Friday (1940)
Sergeant York (1941)
Ball of Fire (1942)
Air Force (1943)
To Have and Have Not (1943)
The Big Sleep (1946)
Red River (1948)
A Song is Born (1948)
I Was a Male War Bride (1949)
The Thing (1951)
The Big Sky (1952)
Monkey Business (1952)
Gentlemen Prefer Blondes (1953)
Land of the Pharaohs (1955)
Rio Bravo (1959)
Hatari! (1962)
Man's Favorite Sport? (1964)
Red Line 7000 (1965)
El Dorado (1967)
Rio Lobo (1970)

Further reading

Hillier, Jim and Peter Wollen (eds). *Howard Hawks: American Artist*. London: BFI, 1996.

McBride, Joseph. *Hawks on Hawks*. Berkeley: University of California Press, 1982.

Wood, Robin. *Howard Hawks*, London: British Film Institute, 1981 (revised ed.).

ALFRED HITCHCOCK

By Alan Nadel

As *Psycho*'s (1960) opening credits appear, the camera, high above Phoenix, Arizona, slowly approaches a high-rise hotel, until, in a series of dissolves, we reach an unspecified upper floor. Penetrating a window, we see a post-coital couple: Marion (Janet Leigh) sitting on the bed, in underskirt and bra, and, standing, Sam (John Gavin), bare-chested. This sequence is telling in relation to the structure of *Psycho*, the preoccupations of Hitchcock's Hollywood years and indeed his entire cinematic opus.

If Sam and Marion have had sex, we see just as much of this cou-pling as American cinema allowed: his flesh, not hers; only one person on the bed. In the censored world of American film[1] what the audience could see impacted every aspect of production. Appro-priately, Sam and Marion talk about seeing each other, a task as dif-ficult for them as actually showing their liaison is for Hitchcock. Subverting Hollywood plot conventions, Hitchcock will make the solution to the two problems mutually exclusive: the event that allows us to "see" Marion will prevent Sam from ever doing so again, in that the shower murder that exposes Marion also eliminates her. When Norman Bates (Anthony Perkins), looking through a peep-hole, sees Marion prepare for her fatal shower, the light pouring onto his eyeball replicates light spreading from a movie projector onto a movie screen. Norman's eyeball thus receives – and represents – the scene Hitchcock cannot show. Immediately after the murder, an ultra-close-up of Marion's eyeball exchanges her dead eye for Nor-man's voyeuristic one in an alternative post-coital scene; subsequently the film shows little violence, forcing its audience to share Norman's implicitly cinematic imagination.

Because *Psycho* contributed to the dissolution of the Production Code, it perhaps helped precipitate Hitchcock's decline, in that his work reflected a genius struggling for the visual and narrative equiva-lent of what could not be shown. In the 1950s, at the height of his Hollywood years, Hitchcock could apply thirty years of experimenting with how to represent the tension between the interiority of psychol-ogy and the exteriority of suspense, delimited by the constraints on representation. Understanding Hitchcock's Hollywood opus, therefore, requires recognizing how a rigid and repressive period in American culture facilitated Hitchcock's most inventive work.

If *Psycho* (arguably) culminates that period, *Rope* (1948) (arguably) initiates it. It is fitting, then, that the opening of *Psycho* echoes the opening of *Rope*, which takes us through the window into a New York apartment just as two (implicitly) homosexual partners, Brandon (John Dall) and Phil (Farley Granger) murder their friend David (Dick Hogan). As in *Psycho*, the scene suggests both sexual climax and post-coital release.

119

These parallel sequences are inverted in the opening of *Rear Window* (1954), made exactly half way between *Rope* and *Psycho*. That film moves out from the window of a New York City apartment into the connected backyards of adjoining apartment buildings. Although the space is rife with sexuality—newlyweds, a dancer removing her bikini top and doing provocative exercises, a married couple sleeping on the fire escape, with one's head at the other's feet, as if positioned for oral sex—Jeff (Jimmy Stewart) contains in his imagination this space where these titillating alternatives constitute the transgressions not shown in *Rope* and *Psycho*: sex and murder. Whether we start by moving in or out of a window, Hitchcock, toying with the conventions of Classical Hollywood style (which work to obscure our awareness of the frame), foregrounds the frame by making the window a surrogate for the lens.

The allure of controlling what he could show initially brought Hitchcock to Hollywood, as he had no interest in films as photographs of people talking. Known for using back projection, even in films shot on location, Hitchcock wanted the visual to disorient rather than confirm what we were being told. Thus, in *The Man Who Knew Too Much* (1956), Ben and Jo McKenna are clearly in North Africa, while Doris Day and James Stewart often are not; Roger Thornhill (Cary Grant), in *North by Northwest* (1959), gets into a taxi in New York, but the cab drives Cary Grant through a projected version of that Manhattan. If these moments suggest the game Hitchcock had learned to play when making silent films, they also signify his relentless desire to be apart from the constraints of his surroundings.

If Hitchcock's work can be seen as exploring transactions with the alter ego, the transaction that brought him to Hollywood was a contract with the control-obsessed David O. Selznick, whom Hitchcock seems to acknowledge as his alter ego in *Rear Window*, making the murderous Thorwald (Raymond Burr) resemble Selznick; the joke is self-deprecatory, however, since Thorwald acts out Jeff's repressed desires. His transactions with Selznick, moreover, turned Hitchcock himself into the object of relentless transactions: renting Hitchcock to United Artists to direct *Foreign Correspondent* (1940), Selznick received three times as much as he paid Hitchcock. Until 1948, therefore, Hitchcock was at the mercy of several studios and largely limited to working with the performers they had under contract. Ironically, Hitchcock was lucky that the majority of films made while under contract to Selznick were not made for Selznick, a compulsive micromanager.

Hitchcock's first actual Selznick film, *Rebecca* (1940) was marked by a literalness of sensibility much more characteristic of the producer.

A gothic tale, *Rebecca* explores a second wife who is virtually observed by the deceased first wife. If *Rebecca* was the least Hitchcockian of the ten films made under contract to Selznick, the two Selznick actually produced, *The Paradine Case* (1947) and *Spellbound* (1945), were among the worst. In both cases, Hitchcock was saddled with Gregory Peck, about whom he was unenthusiastic and who was, especially in *The Paradine Case*, miscast. In the Selznick years, Hitchcock found himself oscillating chiefly between stories with morally and psychologically conflicted principals (*Suspicion* [1941], *Shadow of a Doubt* [1943], *Notorious* [1946]), and films with unambiguous heroes confronted by duplicity (*Foreign Correspondent*, *Saboteur* [1942], *Lifeboat* [1944]).

Despite his contractual and thematic oscillation, Hitchcock in this period still managed to experiment stylistically. In *Foreign Correspondent*, he effectively evoked an airplane crash-landing in the ocean, combining a cockpit set with back projection on tissue paper through which, at the right moment, a large tank of water was released. *Suspicion* played with the effect of cast shadows while *Saboteur* perfected an array of special effects, including the famous shot of the saboteur plunging backward from the top of the Statue of Liberty. *Spellbound's* dream sequences, designed by Salvador Dali, helped Hitchcock hone his representation of subjective reality, and *Lifeboat* allowed him to practice shooting on a very limited set, experience he would later exploit in *Dial M for Murder* (1954) and *Rear Window*.

In *Shadow of a Doubt,* his most accomplished film of the Selznick years, Hitchcock made the small town, and its sensibilities, integral to the narrative. Part of Hitchcock's personal affection for *Shadow of a Doubt* owed, almost certainly, to its being the first film in which he could present characters complexly implicated with one another and also with their locale. In the way that it integrates complex characters into a world of problematic physical and social circumstances, *Shadow of a Doubt* anticipates his best Hollywood films, starting with *Strangers on a Train* (1951). In that film, he combined the psychological dimension of *Spellbound* and *Shadow of a Doubt* with the domestic intensity of the latter film and with the pace of his thrillers. In addition, by setting Patricia Highsmith's novel in Washington, D.C., Hitchcock added historical and political dimensions missing from most of his pre-war films (and heavy-handedly present in his "patriotic" wartime productions).

Strangers on a Train created suspense by integrating domestic, national, and psychological narratives. It also built on Hitchcock's earlier visual experiments. His first post-Selznick-contract film, *Rope*, was shot to look as though it was made in a single take. In the process

Hitchcock undermined the effect of "limited omniscience" characteristic of the Hollywood style. Instead of obscuring the frame, he made it a relentless aspect of the viewing experience. The apparent absence of cuts precluded a cinematic space facilitated by continuity editing (the process of creating the illusion of totality by suturing together complementary views). Instead, the world appeared through a mobile peephole detached from any of the characters, so that the audience could not see that peephole as replicating one subjective point of view. Instead, the technique underscored the illusory premises on which Hollywood's typical, privileged perspective relied.

Hitchcock's first color film, *Rope*, allowed him an extended palette, as did *Under Capricorn* (1949), a period drama made in England. Like *Rope*, the film uses very long takes, although here they are cut together rather appearing to be continuous. The compositional skill learned through trial and (especially in *Under Capricorn*) error, helped Hitchcock manipulate the cumbersome 3-D cameras in navigating visually the constrained set of *Dial M for Murder*; his experiments also prepared him to construct the complex editing patterns in *Strangers on a Train*, which coordinate close-up and long shot, long takes and rapid cross-cutting.

Strangers on a Train ties together many of the elements—stylistic, thematic, and structural—that characterized the first thirty years of Hitchcock's career. The concept of "crisscross," wherein strangers avoid detection by committing murders for which the other would be the likely suspect, enabled Hitchcock, on a thematic level, to demonstrate the interdependence of transactions between good and evil, innocence and guilt, love and suspicion. When Bruno (Robert Walker), the psychotic, Oedipal son, who detests his wealthy father, offers to murder Guy's promiscuous wife so that Guy (Farley Granger), a clean-cut tennis star, may marry a Senator's daughter, he takes the discussion to be a contract. In this way, Bruno literalizes Guy's desires just as Thorwald, in *Rear Window*, literalizes Jeffries' desire to escape a confining relationship.

The framing and editing pull together the locations and dislocations, the crisscrossing and cross-cutting, the doubling and reciprocity, the loyalty and betrayal, and the normativity and deviance that, in composite, characterize Hitchcock's Hollywood films to that point. *Strangers on a Train*, therefore, is not just about doubles or alter egos, but about the transactions between them. The overtly envious and implicitly sexual regard of Bruno for Guy echoes the regard in *Shadow of a Doubt* of the young woman, Charlie (Theresa Wright) for her homicidal uncle, Charlie (Joseph Cotton). Similarly, Alexander's

(Claude Rains) love for his wife Alicia (Ingrid Bergman) in *Notorious* makes him, in some ways, a lover truer than her ostensibly true love, Devlin (Cary Grant), who coerces Alicia into marrying Alexander, in order to facilitate his own spying, and then subsequently betrays Alicia's liaison with him. Devlin's actions lead to Alicia's slow poisoning, from which she is saved by the ostensive villain, Alexander, who accepts almost certain death at the hands of his own espionage ring.

In another instance of this theme, *Rear Window*'s Jeff allows his love, Lisa (Grace Kelly) to fall into the deadly hands of his alter ego, Thorwald. The moment Thorwald captures her culminates with Lisa's inadvertently tipping off Thorwald to Jeff, producing the film's greatest moment of horror: Thorwald and Jeffries at last see eye-to-eye. In *Rear Window* Hitchcock matches this intricate psychological doubling/reversal with an equally complex interplay of interiors and motivations. Staged on one of the largest sets Paramount ever built, the world exterior to Jeff's apartment—simultaneously reflective of the surveillance state of McCarthyism, the heteronormativity of 1950s America, and that period's marked double-standard in gender relations—intrudes equally on Jeff's apartment and on his interior life. Hitchcock's masterful cinematic integration of the social, the psychological, and the spatial in *Rear Window* has led many critics to cite the film as epitomizing the use of continuity editing in constructing a cinematic narrative space.

Vertigo (1958), too, enacts tragic transactions with the dead, of which the central character, Scottie (Jimmy Stewart), becomes a repetitive facilitator, compelled to reproduce the very murder plot he was duped into enabling. Asked by Gavin Elster (Tom Helmore) to follow his deranged wife, Madelaine (Kim Novak), because Madeleine seems suicidally obsessed with her dead ancestor, Carlotta, Scottie not only falls in love with Madeleine but also helplessly watches her apparent suicide. In fact, Judy (Novak) was impersonating Madeleine to produce a narrative that would enable Elster to exchange the corpse of Madeleine for the figure Judy played in Madeleine's feigned suicide. Scottie, later discovering Judy, forces her to become the fictional Madeleine, in the same way that that fictional Madeleine appeared obsessed with becoming the fictional Carlotta. To complete this cycle of fictional exchanges, Scottie in effect kills the false Madeleine in the same way that Elster killed the actual one. Hitchcock constructs an elaborate visual pattern that reveals the circularity of social and psychic systems; using camera movements and editing patterns that emulate circling, plummeting, or bridging, the film repeatedly exchanges the object of love for the dead lover.

North by Northwest—in many ways a remake of *The 39 Steps* and *Saboteur*—develops a hero, Roger Thornhill (Cary Grant) who unwittingly encounters two versions of his own alter-ego. A suave advertising executive whose middle initial, "O," stands for nothing mirrors in his rivalry for Eve (Eva Marie Saint)—herself a double agent—the equally suave Vandamm (James Mason). Thornhill also inadvertently doubles George Kaplan, a fictitious double agent created by the CIA. Using fascinating God's-view shots and an epic sense of national space, Hitchcock relentlessly explores issues of scale that enable the instability of personal desire and the duplicity it proliferates to become indistinguishable from the gendered rivalry that informed Cold War politics.

Psycho concludes Hitchcock's exploration of spectral perversion that commenced with the peeping effect of *Rope*. Norman Bates, starting out as the logical extension of Jeff, in *Rear Window*, peeps at the verboten and, by virtue of that process—a process that identifies him with the movie audience—is converted from the spectator of the unshowable into the agent of the unwatchable. Norman effects the violence that Jeff and Lisa need to imagine in order to solidify their own relationship. Hitchcock's ultimate psychic transaction is not one in which Guy becomes Bruno, Jeff becomes Throwald, Judy becomes Madeleine (twice), or Thornhill becomes Kaplan, but rather one in which Norman, a surrogate for the film audience, becomes himself in the guise of his mother, the homicidal maniac.

For critics such as Robin Wood, *The Birds* (1963) and *Marnie* (1964) represent the culmination of this exploration of the perverse spectral psyche (for others the point at which it becomes subsumed by heavy-handed psychologizing).[2] In either case, a moment in *The Birds* exemplifies Hitchcock's insistence that films work to externalize the violence inherent in the spectator. In the restaurant under siege during the birds' assault on Bodega Bay, a hysterical mother, in close-up, her eyes looking directly into the camera, screams at Melanie (Tippi Hedren): "Who are you? What are you? Where did you come from? I think you're the cause of all this. I think you're evil!" This diatribe strongly suggests a rebuke to the spectator; in its need to see and its thirst for violence, the audience has exploited cinema in much the way Jeff exploited his rear window and Norman Bates his peephole.

Hitchcock's final Hollywood films—*Torn Curtain* (1966), *Topaz* (1969), *Frenzy* (1972), and *Family Plot* (1976)—manifest, some more successfully than others, a nostalgia for the themes of his earlier work. With the decline of the Production Code's heft and its replacement, in 1968, with a liberal rating system, Hitchcock's films had lost their ability to shock; with the need for nuance less apparent, these later films lack the sophistication, stylistic experimentation, and technical panache exemplified by films such as *Rear Window*. European films of the 1960s suggested that style was no longer a matter of negotiating, subverting, or coopting norms. Seeing Antonioni's *Blow-Up* (1966), Hitchcock exclaimed, "These Italian directors are a century ahead of me in terms of technique! What have I been doing all this time?"[3] What he had been doing was profoundly influencing a generation of European directors—as he would a later generation of American directors—who would go on to make films in the spirit of Hitchcock, sans the restrictive financial and social environment, in contestation with which Hitchcock produced his best work.

Biography

Hitchcock's biography is rather straightforward. Born in 1899 and educated in a trade school as a draftsman, he worked for a brief time in that trade while publishing short stories. By 21, he was working in the British film industry, starting out as a designer of titles for silent films. By volunteering to undertake any task available, he became versed in every aspect of film production; at age 26 he was promoted to director, and by the 1930s he had become one of England's leading filmmakers. Early in his career, he met Alma Reville who eventually became his assistant director, wife, and lifetime collaborator. In the 1940s he moved to Los Angeles and started making Hollywood films. In the 1950s, his hugely successful television series, every episode of which he personally introduced with brief, darkly humorous monologues, secured his wealth and established him as major international celebrity. When he died in 1980, he was still making films, but none after the early 1960s achieved the critical esteem or popularity of his earlier works.

Notes

1 Although the rating system does not replace the Production Code until 1968, the emergence of the rating system is a symptom of the Code's increasingly diminished heft between 1960 and 1968.
2 Critics who, for different reasons, place *The Birds* and *Marnie* within the trajectory of Hitchcock's canonical works include: Richard Allen (2007), Leslie Brill (1988), and Murray Pomerance (2004).
3 Quoted in Patrick McGilligan, *Alfred Hitchcock: A Life in Darkness and Light*. New York: Harper Collins, 2003, p. 681.

Filmography

The Pleasure Garden (1925)
The Mountain Eagle (1926)
The Lodger (1926)
The Ring (1927)
When Boys Leave Home (1927)
The Farmer's Wife (1928)
Easy Virtue (1928)
Champagne (1928)
The Manxman (1929)
Blackmail (1929)
The Shame of Mary Boyle (1929)
Murder! (1930)
The Skin Game (1931)
Mary (1931)
East of Shanghai (1931)
Number 17 (1932)
Strauss' Great Waltz (1934)
The Man Who Knew Too Much (1934)
The 39 Steps (1935)
Secret Agent (1936)
Sabotage (1936)
The Girl Was Young (1937)
The Lady Vanishes (1938)
Jamaica Inn (1939)
Rebecca (1940)
Foreign Correspondent (1940)
Mr. & Mrs. Smith (1941)
Suspicion (1941)
Saboteur (1942)
Shadow of a Doubt (1943)
Lifeboat (1944)
Spellbound (1945)
Notorious (1946)
The Paradine Case (1947)
Rope (1948)
Under Capricorn (1949)
Stage Fright (1950)
Strangers on a Train (1951)
I Confess (1953)
Dial M for Murder (1954)
Rear Window (1954)

To Catch a Thief (1955)
The Trouble with Harry (1955)
The Wrong Man (1956)
The Man Who Knew Too Much (1956)
Vertigo (1958)
North by Northwest (1959)
Psycho (1960)
The Birds (1963)
Marnie (1964)
Torn Curtain (1966)
Topaz (1969)
Frenzy (1972)
Family Plot (1976)

Further reading

Allen, Richard. *Hitchcock's Romantic Irony*. New York: Columbia UP, 2007.

Allen, Richard, and S. Ishii-Gonzales, eds. *Alfred Hitchcock Centenary Essays*. London: British Film Institute, 1999.

Brill, Leslie. *The Hitchcock Romance: Love and Irony in Hitchcock's Films*. Princeton: Princeton UP, 1988.

Corber, Robert J. *In the Name of National Security: Hitchcock, Homophobia, and the Political Construction of Gender in Postwar America*. Durham, NC: Duke UP, 1993.

Freedman, Jonathan, and Richard Millington, eds. *Hitchcock's America*. New York: Oxford UP, 1999.

Leff, Leonard J. *Hitchcock and Selznick: The Rich and Strange Collaboration of Alfred Hitchcock and David O. Selznick in Hollywood*. Berkeley: U California P, 1987.

McGilligan, Patrick. *Alfred Hitchcock: A Life in Darkness and Light*. New York: Harper Collins, 2003.

Modleski, Tania. *The Women Who Knew Too Much: Hitchcock and Feminist Theory*, 2nd edition. London: Routledge, 2005.

Pomerance, Murray. *An Eye for Hitchcock*. New Brunswick, NJ: Rutgers UP, 2004.

Spoto, Donald. *The Dark Side of Genius: The Life of Alfred Hitchcock*. Boston: Little Brown, 1983.

Truffaut, Francois, in collaboration with Helen G. Scott. *Hitchcock* (Revised Edition). New York: Simon and Schuster, 1985.

Wood, Robin. *Hitchcock's Films Revisited*. New York: Columbia UP, 1989.

ELIA KAZAN

By Cynthia Lucia

In the work of Elia Kazan, more than in that of any other American filmmaker of his era, the personal is unmistakably political and the political is powerfully personal—whether in terms of the stories he chose to tell, the characters he created, the performances he helped to shape, or the visual style he would come to develop. The same might also be said of Kazan himself, a Greek immigrant with artistic roots in the theater, and his own controversial political alliances—whether as a short-lived member of the American Communist Party in the 1930s during his Group Theater days or as, first, an unfriendly witness and then a friendly witness, who named eight former Party members during his 1952 HUAC testimony. Among the nineteen feature films he directed (and in some cases co-wrote and co-produced), from *A Tree Grows in Brooklyn* (1945) to *The Last Tycoon* (1976), many are well-known classics of the American cinema: *Boomerang!* and *Gentleman's Agreement* in 1947, *Pinky* (1949), *Panic in the Streets* (1950), *A Streetcar Named Desire* (1951), *Viva Zapata!* (1952), *Man on a Tightrope* (1953), *On the Waterfront* (1954), *East of Eden* (1955), *Baby Doll* (1956), *A Face in the Crowd* (1957), *Wild River* (1960), *Splendor in the Grass* (1961), and *America, America* (1963). His second feature, *The Sea of Grass* (1947), adapted from a Conrad Richter novel, and his final three: *The Arrangement* (1969), *The Visitors* (1972) and *The Last Tycoon*, although uneven in narrative, provide textured treatments of character, in keeping with his self-professed goal of "turn[ing] psychology into behavior."[1]

While the final three films lack the taut narrative structure of the earlier films, in these works the already accomplished Kazan struggles with themes of uncertainty, anxiety and regret—perhaps an expression of his own reflective position as a man in his sixties. As Haden Guest points out, the characters "suddenly become unmoored and unstable," and "find themselves grappling with life and career decisions that often directly echo those infamously made by Kazan himself," thus inviting autobiographical readings,[2] as earlier films like *Man on a Tightrope* and *On the Waterfront* more eminently do. Two of the final three take on even greater resonance when reflexive and autobiographical readings intersect. *The Arrangement*, adapted from Kazan's novel of the same title, contemplates the troubled relationship between a successful, Americanized son and his Greek immigrant father, while also exploring the complications of marriage, erotic attraction, and (in)fidelity in a privileged yet sterile upper middle class world.[3] Desire here, as in most of American culture, is mediated by the ubiquitous advertising industry, in which the protagonist, Eddie Andrews (Kirk Douglas) is a successful executive. Inexplicably initially, Eddie attempts suicide one morning as he drives to work on the freeway, violently veering his tiny sports car into a tractor-trailer in an adjacent lane. Much as in the critically acclaimed *A Face in the Crowd*, though in a very different register, *The Arrangement* examines media-made desire, acquisition and consumption as it penetrates, corrupts and numbs the human heart and spirit.

Most self-reflexively in terms of movies and movie making, *The Last Tycoon*—adapted from a portion of F. Scott Fitzgerald's final, unfinished novel—examines similar issues as played out in the life of Monroe Stahr (Robert De Niro), a staid yet fabulously successful 1930s Hollywood producer (in the novel based on Irving Thalberg), who is brought down by the older studio chief Pat Brady (Robert Mitchum), a character based on mogul Louis B. Mayer in the novel. Beyond Fitzgerald's narrative and its built-in reflexivity that charts the dealings of Old Hollywood powerbrokers, Kazan infuses multiple new layers of reflexivity relevant to the 1970s, as a "New Hollywood" was emerging. Kazan heightens the generational conflict between Brady and Stahr in his casting of De Niro—clearly associated with the New Hollywood through his work with director Martin Scorsese in *Mean Streets* (1973) and in *Taxi Driver* (released in February 1976, with *Tycoon* released in November 1976)—alongside Old Hollywood screen icons such as Mitchum, Dana Andrews and Ray Milland, as well as those perceived, perhaps, as transitional figures: Tony Curtis (playing an actor whose sexual performance anxiety with a younger wife marks him as one who wishes but cannot make a transition into the new) and French actress Jeanne Moreau (famously associated with the *Nouvelle Vague*, a movement so influential in the birth of a new Hollywood). Much like Stahr in the film, Kazan faced his own very difficult challenges—with pressures from producer Sam Spiegel, largely over the casting of De Niro whom Kazan supported, and with a rather intractable screenwriter in Harold Pinter. Such contention was not new to Kazan, who waged earlier battles over Production Code restrictions threatening *A Streetcar Named Desire*, *Baby Doll*, and *Splendor in the Grass*, in which he fiercely fought to retain sexual content that challenged the increasingly outmoded mores of the Code.[4] Kazan's experience on his final film, however, reinforced his determination that, "long before this, I'd made up my mind never to work in films again, that *The Last Tycoon* would be it."[5] The final image of the film, not present in the Pinter screenplay is, as Kazan admits, his dark, defeated farewell to the movies. Vanquished by Brady, Stahr walks along a deserted studio lot, entering an empty sound stage. "The gloom enveloped him and he disappeared. Forever—it seemed," as Kazan observes. "It was the end, the fade-out of the film I was making and the end for me and my time as a director ... it was a kind of death for me."[6]

During his early filmmaking career, in *Boomerang!*, *Gentleman's Agreement*, and *Pinky*—clearly political in content as true of other "social problem" films of the period—Kazan interrogates, respectively, a politically corrupt court system, as based on an actual 1924 murder case in Bridgeport, Connecticut; covert middle class anti-Semitism; and the complexities of racism and racial identity. Also overtly political are *Viva Zapata!*, a historically based study of the eponymous Mexican revolutionary, adapted from the John Steinbeck novel; *Man on a Tightrope*, a critique of the oppressive Stalinist regime in Czechoslovakia as played out in the lives of a circus master and his performers; *On the Waterfront*, an exposé of equally oppressive corruption within the longshoremen's union in Hoboken, New Jersey; and, much later, *The Visitors*, about crimes committed during the Vietnam War that haunt the present lives of its characters. *Tightrope*, *Waterfront* and *Visitors* also have their autobiographical implications—in all cases characters are pressured by larger political forces either to comply (*Tightrope*)—as Kazan felt he was pressured by the American Communist Party during his Group Theater days and, in refusing, was expelled—or to testify as Terry Malloy does against powerful union officials in *Waterfront* and as Bill Schmidt (James Woods) had in Vietnam against his fellow soldiers who raped and killed villagers, recalling the My Lai massacre. The specter of HUAC hovers over many Kazan films from the mid-1950s onward. Kazan claims that the eight individuals he named had previously been named by others and that he did so only after prior consultation with almost all of them. A much-debated subject, Kazan's HUAC testimony must and does factor into the more lengthy studies of his career.[7]

No less political in their content (if even indirectly so) are Kazan's exploration of gender and family relationships in *A Streetcar Named Desire*, *On the Waterfront*, *East of Eden*, *Baby Doll*, and *Splendor in the Grass*, all of which examine shifting power relationships in a post-war America undergoing and adjusting to alterations in attitude and ideology.[8] While *Waterfront*, *Eden* and *Splendor* take on bildungsroman themes from an articulated masculine perspective on one level—its protagonists struggle with what it means to become and be "a man"—the films, at the same time, critically interrogate the deform-ing, corrupting impact of longstanding patriarchal ideologies and institutions. In these films, as also in *Pinky*, the struggle and the strength of female characters emerge as equal, if not more important concerns in the narrative trajectories.[9] The complexities of gender relationships also infuse and sometimes eclipse more explicit political themes, as in *Wild River*, set in the 1930s and centered on the Ten-nessee Valley Authority (TVA) as part of FDR's New Deal—a film considered by some to be Kazan's most accomplished work, as critic Jonathan Rosenbaum argues, calling it "a masterful integration of the social with the personal, the romantic with the practical, the historical with the contemporary, the subjective with the objective, the local with the universal."[10] In it Montgomery Clift plays Chuck Glover, a TVA official charged with evicting an irascible old Ellen Garth (Jo Van Fleet) from her family homestead on an island soon to be flooded by the Authority. In a narrative that unflinchingly explores both the promise and the price of progress, Glover grows to respect Garth's desire for self-determination, while the film adds layers of contradiction when exploring Garth's relationship with the black employees who live and work on her land for low wages in circum-stances harkening back to slavery. Upon hiring these workers for wages equal to those of white workers, Glover faces the community's violent animosity, heightened when he falls somewhat uncertainly in love with Garth's widowed granddaughter Carol (Lee Remick), engaged to marry a local man she cares for but does not love. The delicacy of the love story, rife with ambivalence, characterizes the emotional complexity of all of Kazan's work, dating back to *A Tree Grows in Brooklyn*, in which a young girl who adores her alcoholic father observes, though doesn't always understand, the conflicting emotions her parents share—tinged in varying degrees with affection, disappointment, frustration, aspiration, and promises unfulfilled.

Such delicacy and ambivalence take on an added dimension in Kazan's close collaboration with gay playwright Tennessee Williams on *Streetcar* and *Baby Doll*, with gay screenwriter William Inge on *Splendor*, and with bi-sexual or gay actors James Dean on *Eden* and Clift on *Wild River*. Kazan's iconic long shot, deep focus framings of Marlon Brando in *Streetcar* as an object of erotic desire and of Dean in *Eden* as a hurt, vulnerable object of desire for his brother's girlfriend, lead Mark Harris to conclude that Kazan, "a wounded boy who looked with envy at men who seemed comfortable in their own bodies,"[11] was sensitive to "neurotic sexual uncertainty"—an uncer-tainty made palpable in Dean's and Clift's performances in *Eden* and

Wild River, especially.[12] In his shaping of character and of nuanced performances, Kazan created films that, in Harris's estimation, are "as close to a sympathetic midcentury conception of homosexual protagonists as any American director of the time cared or dared to go."[13] In more muted form, gender politics infuse Kazan's deeply autobiographical immigrant narrative, *America, America*, based on the life of his uncle, an Anatolian Greek who struggles to free himself and his family from the tyrannical Turks of the Ottoman Empire. He finds himself first in Constantinople (Istanbul after 1930) and eventually in the United States. During his journey the strikingly handsome Stavros (Stathis Giallelis) is torn between the Old World comfort his impending marriage to a young woman in Constantinople potentially will provide and the promise of New World liberation from the oppressions of government, family obligations, and favors owed. Choosing the latter, he willingly prostitutes himself to a wealthy married woman on board the ocean liner where he travels in crowded steerage, along with so many other hopeful immigrants. Acknowledging this story as his own, Kazan introduces himself in voiceover as the film opens: "My name is Elia Kazan. I am a Greek by blood, a Turk by birth, and an American because my uncle made a journey. This story was told me over the years by the old people in my family." He goes on to provide a brief history of Anatolia, as it was taken over by the Turks, and of the Greek and Armenian populations subjugated there. In its style and story, the film integrates so many of the oppositions Rosenbaum cites in his commentary on *Wild River*.

Although Kazan admits in his autobiography and in countless interviews that he understood very little about cinematography and editing when first transitioning into film from theater, he would go on to achieve visual mastery, primarily through deep focus long take shooting, inviting viewers to contemplate the multi-faceted, often contradictory ways in which characters interact with their surroundings and with each other—greatly enhanced by wide screen formats in *East of Eden*, *Wild River* and *Splendor in the Grass*, especially. Kazan's careful attention to all details of mise-en-scène, including camera placement and character positioning, not only captures the shifting power relationships among characters but also conveys so palpable a sense of place and space, inextricably defining characters as products of their environments and settings as extensions of character psychology, ambition and desire. Kazan's characters are products of their time and place and struggle both to recognize and understand that relationship—whether ultimately to find a place comfort to which they can adapt or a means by which they can escape or radically alter that relationship.

Biography

Born of Anatolian Greek parents as Elia Kazanjioglou in Istanbul, Elia Kazan (September 7, 1909–September 28, 2003) moved with his family as a young child first to Berlin and eventually to New York City, where his father established a successful rug business. Kazan's formative years were spent in the suburb of New Rochelle, after which he attended Yale Drama School, leading to his work with The Group Theater. There, as someone handy with tools, he became known as "Gadg" (short for "Gadget"), a nickname he didn't particularly like but one that lingered throughout his life. As an actor in the Group Theater during his early years, Kazan met directors Lee Strasberg, Harold Churlman, and playwright Clifford Odets, all of whom became influential collaborators in his later career as a stage and film director. Kazan directed critically acclaimed theatrical productions of works by Arthur Miller, Thornton Wilder, Tennessee Williams, and Eugene O'Neill—to name just a few. As co-founder of The Actor's Studio, introducing Stanislovskian-inspired Method Acting to the American stage and screen, Kazan earned high praise always as an "actor's director" and was responsible for nurturing actors who would become iconic figures, including Marlon Brando, James Dean, Warren Beatty, Kim Hunter, Eva Marie Saint and Lee Remick. A member of the American Communist Party in the 1930s, Kazan's HUAC testimony as a "friendly witness" would salvage his Hollywood directing career, yet it would come to haunt his accomplishments, as evident in the mixed response that greeted him in 1999 when, at the age of 90, he was awarded an Oscar for lifetime achievement. Kazan directed nineteen features, many among the most highly acclaimed in American film history. In addition to directing for stage and screen, Kazan also was a writer, with eight books to his credit, including novels and an imposing autobiography. He was married three times—to Molly Day Thatcher and actress/filmmaker Barbara Loden, both of whom predeceased him, and to Frances Rudge, to whom he was married from 1982 until his death. Among his five children, his son Nicolas is a screenwriter and his son Chris produced and was screenwriter of Kazan's 1972 film, *The Visitors*.

Notes

1 Jeff Young, *Kazan on Kazan,* New York and London: Faber and Faber, 1999, p. 15.
2 Haden Guest, "Late Kazan, or The Ambiguities," in *Kazan Revisited*, Lisa Dombrowski, ed. Middletown, Connecticut: Wesleyan University Press, 2011, p. 189.

3 Kazan was married three times, and, although never divorced, admitted in his autobiography to having had multiple affairs.

4 See also Elia Kazan, *Elia Kazan: A Life,* New York: Alfred A. Knopf, 1988; Jeff Young, *Kazan on Kazan*; Lucia, Cynthia, "Natalie Wood: Studio Stardom and Hollywood in Transition," in *The Wiley-Blackwell History of American Film, Volume III,* Oxford and Malden, MA: Wiley-Blackwell, 2012, pp. 38–45; and *A Streetcar Named Desire, Two Disc Special Edition.* (Dir. Elia Kazan, "Disc 2—Special Features." Warner Bros., 1993).

5 Elia Kazan, *Elia Kazan: A Life,* p. 781.

6 Ibid.

7 Young, pp. 327–45. See also Kazan's autobiography, *Elia Kazan: A Life,* pp. 444–85; Dan Georgakas, "Kazan, Kazan," *Cineaste,* Vol. XXXVI, No. 4; 2011, pp. 4–9.

8 Although *East of Eden,* loosely based on the John Steinbeck novel, is set in 1917–18 and *Splendor in the Grass* is set primarily in 1928–29, their themes resonate within the contemporaneous mid-1950s and early 1960s culture in which they, respectively, were made and released.

9 See Savannah Lee, "The Other Side of the Story: Elia Kazan as Director of Female Pain," in *Kazan Revisited,* Lisa Dombrowski, ed. Middletown, Connecticut: Wesleyan University Press, 2011, pp. 116–29.

10 Jonathan Rosenbaum, "Elia Kazan, Seen from 1973," in *Kazan Revisited,* Lisa Dombrowski, ed. Middletown, Connecticut: Wesleyan University Press, 2011, p. 35.

11 Mark Harris, "A Straight Director's Queer Eye: 1951–61," in *Kazan Revisited,* Lisa Dombrowski, ed. Middletown, Connecticut: Wesleyan University Press, 2011, p. 106.

12 Ibid., p. 110.

13 Ibid., p. 115.

Filmography

People of Cumberland (1937) short, assistant director

It's Up to You (1941) short

A Tree Grows in Brooklyn (1945)

The Sea of Grass (1947)

Boomerang! (1947)

Gentleman's Agreement (1947)

Pinky (1949)

Panic in the Streets (1950)

A Streetcar Named Desire (1951)

Viva Zapata! (1952)

Man on a Tightrope (1953)

On the Waterfront (1954)

East of Eden (1955) also producer

Baby Doll (1956) also producer
A Face in the Crowd (1957) also producer
Wild River (1960) also producer
Splendor in the Grass (1961) also producer
America, America (1963) also producer, screenwriter, and story author
The Arrangement (1969) also producer, screenwriter, and story author
The Visitors (1972)
The Last Tycoon (1976)

Further reading

Ciment, Michel. *Kazan on Kazan: Interviews with Michel Ciment.* London: British Film Institute, 1973.

Kazan, Elia. *Kazan on Directing.* New York: Vintage, 2010.

Murphy, Brenda. *Tennessee Williams and Elia Kazan: A Collaboration in the Theater.* New York and Cambridge: Cambridge University Press, 2006.

Neve, Brian. *Elia Kazan: The Cinema of an American Outsider.* London and New York: I.B. Tauris, 2008.

Schickel, Richard. *Elia Kazan: A Biography.* New York: Harper Collins Publishers, 2005.

FRITZ LANG

By Tim Bergfelder

Despite being half-Jewish and Austrian, few directors (perhaps with the exception of Erich von Stroheim and Josef von Sternberg) have come to epitomise the stereotype of 'the genial German director' as much as Fritz Lang: his aristocratic appearance replete with monocle, riding boots, and jodhpurs, and reputedly fully conforming to the idea of the autocratic and obsessive perfectionist who was admired and hated in equal measures. Throughout his life Lang cultivated this almost caricatured self-image (responding to a question from an interviewer as to how he liked his coffee with the retort: 'Black – like my soul'[1]). How much this pose reflected his real personality is open to debate. Patrick McGilligan's controversial 1997 biography, *Fritz Lang and the Nature of the Beast*,[2] paints an unflattering portrait of an inveterate self-publicist who covered his tracks to hide a sordid private life.

Irrespective of perceived or actual personal qualities, Lang is widely acknowledged as one of the most influential filmmakers of the twentieth century. His legacy has been marked by contradictions and ruptures, by aesthetic and ideological disagreements and preferences among his critics, but also by a remarkable uniqueness of vision and continuity of thematic and aesthetic concerns. By the time he arrived in Hollywood in the mid-1930s, Lang already enjoyed international fame after having made close to thirty films in Germany. Irrefutable classics of silent and early sound cinema such as *Destiny* (*Der müde Tod*), *Dr Mabuse*, *Die Nibelungen*, and *M* had established his reputation as a master craftsman, working at the cutting edge of film art, and proving especially inventive in the fields of production design, mise-en-scène, editing, and sound. His best-known film, *Metropolis*, on its first release a colossal financial failure, has subsequently almost transcended Lang's authorship to become an enduring emblem of modernity itself, its decontextualised imagery endlessly recycled to the present day in advertising, design, and popular culture. After having fled Nazi Germany, Lang moved to Hollywood, where, from the mid-1930s to the mid-1950s, he worked on a diverse range of genres, including Westerns, social dramas, musicals, and women's melodramas, although he is best remembered for his anti-Nazi propaganda pictures during World War II (*Man Hunt, Hangmen Also Die!*), and as one of the prime exponents of *film noir* (*The Woman in the Window, Scarlet Street, The Big Heat*). But although he managed to retain a considerable autonomy over his work, as in Germany, Lang's Hollywood career was erratic, shifting between hits and flops, and between prestige productions and inconsequential contract assignments.

Film historians have never ceased to compare the German and the American phase of Lang's career. Back in the 1950s, French critics championed the classicism of the Hollywood Lang, whose films were only rivalled by those of Alfred Hitchcock, a director often seen as Lang's competitor or successor.[3] In post-war Germany and in Britain, meanwhile, critics dismissed Lang's American films as a postscript to his superior modernist cinema of the 1920s (an assessment shared subsequently by the film historian Noël Burch). Beyond purely formal concerns, the two phases have also been demarcated with respect to their ideological meaning. Champions of Lang's Hollywood films have pointed to the progressive, socially reformist message in films such as *Fury* and *You Only Live Once*, the anti-Fascism of Lang's wartime films, and the implicit critique of Cold War society in Lang's films from the 1950s. On the other hand, since at least the late 1940s,[4] accusations have been levelled against Lang's German films for harbouring totalitarian, proto-Fascist, and anti-Semitic tendencies.

Whatever the merit of these interpretations, a schematic division ignores the continuities between Lang's Hollywood and German films, and more generally underestimates the permeability and reciprocity of cultural influences between America and Europe in the first half of the twentieth century. Although stereotyped as Germanic and even nationalist in outlook, Lang had embraced American modernity and popular culture since the early days of his career, and by his own admission was an eager consumer of US Westerns, newspapers, and comics. Even his most austere productions from the 1920s are at the core popular genre films, indebted to the conventions of science fiction (*Metropolis*), the spy thriller (*Spione*), the epic (*Die Nibelungen*), and the serial adventure (*Dr Mabuse*; *Die Spinnen*). Conversely, as scholars including Tom Gunning or Thomas Elsaesser have argued, many of Lang's American films remain indebted to modernist themes and principles. Joe McElhaney, drawing on Deleuze and Miriam Hansen's concept of 'vernacular modernism', has persuasively argued that the opposition between modernism and classicism in making sense of aesthetic trajectories such as Lang's is unproductive and that in fact his films encompass both.[5]

As with the man himself, while Lang's cinematic vision as a whole may elicit admiration, his films have also been characterised as cold and distant. While there is a streak of sardonic irony, genuine humour is absent from Lang's filmic universe, and few of his films are much concerned with the formation of the romantic couple. Farcically summarising Lang's main themes, an online article about Lang's work suggests a drinking game, where participants take a shot whenever a Fritz Lang film shows an angry mob or a woman in a nightgown.[6] As has been pointed out in many feminist critiques of Lang's noir films, but also in analyses of some of his Weimar classics, most notably *Metropolis*, Lang's gender politics are at best ambivalent. Male anxieties are his central concern, while women are frequently located in the Catholic dyad of innocent, saintly wife and *femme fatale* (the two Marias in *Metropolis* are in this respect archetypal).

In terms of social order, Lang's view of the world is if not explicitly misanthropic then at least oppressive and deterministic, with characters trapped in a malevolent system of surveillance and control they can neither influence nor escape, and a society that exists in constant fear of an imagined eruption of uncontrolled forces, unleashing chaos and anarchy. Lang's social universe is characterised by an interconnectedness of different media and lines of communication, hence the frequent references to communication technologies such as telephony and tele-graphy. Some scholars have interpreted this vision of a controlled world, enforced through media and communication networks, and fuelled by paranoia, as an expression of the director's ambivalence towards modernity, the latter's fascination and seduction being tempered with deep anxieties. Anton Kaes has pointed out that Lang's formative encounter with modernity had been the trauma of indus-trialised warfare during World War One, and that this experience is likely to have influenced Lang's worldview forever after.[7] Fate features prominently across Lang's oeuvre, but as Tom Gunning noted,

> Lang's destiny is not a metaphysical concept (...), but a material one, less a meaning than a structure (...). Destiny appears in Lang's films, not as a philosophy, but as a machine, whose mechanical nature in most of the films remains very literal (...) The machine in Lang does stand for something beyond itself. But, rather than a metaphor for a view of human nature or metaphysics, the machine is a metonymy, a fragment which stands for the whole systematic nature of the modern world which Lang sees as a complex determining destiny.[8]

This 'systematic nature of the modern world' corresponds with Lang's equally systematic approach towards visual style and narration. Across his career, there is a gradual development towards abstraction and reduction, a pared-down aesthetic that in Lang's American films becomes highly self-reflexive. Lang has often attracted criticism for the fact that his narratives (especially in his Hollywood films) were perfunctory, simplistic, and formulaic. But even though Lang used generic templates, he often subverted the expectations associated with those very conventions. For example, many of his Hollywood crime films lack what one might expect to be a necessary ingredient, namely suspense – the outcome of the story is often predictable from the start. Narrative strategies such as ruptures in continuity, often through ellipses, are a hallmark. Implausible or unmotivated plot twists and *deus ex machina* endings as in *Woman In The Window* or *Beyond A Reasonable Doubt* may feel preposterous, but serve their purpose pre-cisely for that very reason, namely by drawing attention to the machinations of the narration itself. As in the case of his con-temporary Bertolt Brecht (with whom he collaborated and fell out with on the production of *Hangmen Also Die!*[9]), Lang's aesthetic is anti-illusionist and deliberately attempts to distance, deceive, and even frustrate the viewer; also like Brecht, Lang was not interested in psychological realism or depth. His Hollywood heroes are anonymous everymen, which is reflected in Lang's casting choices, often featuring somewhat uncharismatic leading men such as Brian Donlevy, Walter Pidgeon, Glenn Ford, or Dana Andrews. When Lang on occasion used a star like Marlene Dietrich (as in *Rancho Notorious*), the discrepancy between fictional character and star persona became an intended effect of the casting.

Nor, again like Brecht, was Lang interested in representational realism. For the trained architect Lang, built space embodied primarily power relations and social hierarchies. This principle is most evident in Weimar films such as *Metropolis* or *Die Nibelungen*, but it continued to define Lang's approach to mise-en-scène in Hollywood. Unlike in Expressionism (a movement with which Lang is regularly associated, in most cases mistakenly, especially from the mid-1920s onwards) and unlike in the 1950s melodramas of Douglas Sirk, cinematic space, sets and props in Lang's films do not externalise interior psychological states, erotic desires or social aspirations of characters, instead they articulate a topography of social structures and visual regimes. For this reason there is not much of a focus in Lang's films on domesticity and the home, but on what Marc Augé[10] has referred to as 'non-spaces': hotels, offices, court rooms, jails, police headquarters. Natural landscapes do not hold much interest for Lang either. His Westerns (most prominently *The Return of Frank James*) substitute the panoramic vistas of open landscapes one usually finds in this genre with quite obvious rear projections. Laura Mulvey's observation on the latter technique suggests one of the reasons why it suited Lang's visual regime:

> Rear projection introduces a different kind of temporal duality: two diverse registration times are 'montaged' into a single image. While this is true for any photographic superimposition, the dramatic contrast between the 'document'-like nature of the projected images and the artificiality of the studio scene heightens the sense of temporal dislocation.[11]

Another significant element within Lang's visual vocabulary are signs, marks, and objects. Numerous scholars have identified the close-up, used almost like an insert shot, as one of the director's favourite visual tropes. Thomas Elsaesser has noted that close-ups in Lang's films often act as digressions and retarding elements to the narrative, opening up a space for the viewer that takes them outside of the fictional world of the film to a point of existential cognition:

> What is crucial is that the close-up in Lang's *mise-en-scène* does not simply regulate or conflate distance and proximity: it introduces a "beyond distance and proximity." In effect, it asks: who looks, and what looks back when one looks, and what happens in the gap of those moments of not knowing whether the look is a look or a blind look that sees through me? Lang's editing and framing, in other words, become identified with a non-returnable look, the equivalent of the blank stare, but now not the blank stare *in* the film, as much as the blank stare *of* the film.[12]

As the above examples indicate, Lang's visual and narrative strategies add up to a consistent and coherent aesthetic that is both resolutely non-realist, yet at the same time can give a deceptive impression of being 'constructed with a pure economy of storytelling in mind'.[13] At the same time, as the use and function of the close-up in Lang's films illustrates, there is a correspondence between the visual regime Lang creates and the paranoid social universe his films critique. As Elsaesser notes, 'the moments in Lang that unsettle vision are those of the watcher watched. This sense of being ambushed by another look is profoundly disturbing and disruptive.'[14] It may be no coincidence that Lang's unsettling (of) vision has once again been in the ascendancy in the past decade, as contemporary analogies to Lang's destiny machine have emerged: the war on terror, the NSA revelations, global economic crises, and renewed ideological polarisation are all developments that have created an oppressive climate of fear and a craving for social order that increasingly appears not so dissimilar to the anxieties during Lang's lifetime. Meanwhile some of the new forms of seeing and consuming images and social media have brought with them new technologies, such as satellites and GPS, that perpetuate on a global scale patterns of 'watching while being watched'. Refusing to simply affirm these regimes of surveillance, and rendering the processes through which they operate uncanny, albeit in relation to older technologies, Fritz Lang's films can still make a profound contribution to the concerns of today.

Biography

Friedrich Christian Anton Lang was born in Vienna in 1890. He studied architecture and fine art, before joining the Austrian army following the outbreak of World War One. Decorated for bravery, he was discharged after being injured at the Eastern Front, and began writing film screenplays for companies in Berlin. During the 1920s and early 1930s, he became one of German cinema's best-known directors, working for companies such as Ufa and Nero, and often collaborating with his then wife, the screenwriter Thea von Harbou (1888–1954). Following the Nazi takeover in 1933, Lang emigrated to the United States via France. In 1945, Lang was one of the co-founders of a short-lived film company, Diana Productions. In the late 1950s, Lang returned temporarily to Germany, where he directed his final films. He died in 1976 in Beverly Hills.

Notes

1 Barry Keith Grant, ed., *Fritz Lang: Interviews*, Jackson, University of Mississippi Press, 2003, p. 158.

2 Patrick McGilligan, *Fritz Lang and the Nature of the Beast*, London, Faber and Faber, 1997.

3 Thomas Elsaesser, 'Too Big and Too Close: Alfred Hitchcock and Fritz Lang' in S. Gottlieb and R. Allen (eds.), *The Hitchcock Annual Anthology*, London, Wallflower Press, 2009, pp. 211–35.

4 See, e.g., Siegfried Kracauer, *From Caligari to Hitler. A Psychological History of the German Film*, Princeton, Princeton Unversity Press, 1947; David J. Levin, *Richard Wagner, Fritz Lang, and the Nibelungen*, Princeton, Princeton University Press, 1999.

5 Joe McElhaney, *The Death of Classical Cinema: Hitchcock, Lang, Minnelli*, New York, SUNY Press, 2006.

6 Noel Murray, 'The Sprawling, Obsessive Career of Fritz Lang', *The Dissolve*, http://thedissolve.com/features/career-view/222-the-sprawling-obsessive-career-of-fritz-lang/

7 Anton Kaes, *Shell Shock. Weimar Culture and the Wounds of War*, Princeton, Princeton University Press, 2009, pp. 168–210.

8 Tom Gunning, *The Films of Fritz Lang*, London, BFI, 2000, p. 10.

9 Gerd Gemünden, 'Brecht in Hollywood: *Hangmen Also Die!* and the Anti-Nazi Film', in *The Drama Review*, 43:4 (Winter 1999), pp. 65–76.

10 Marc Augé, *Non-Places: An Introduction to Supermodernity*, London, Verso, 2009.

11 Laura Mulvey, 'A Clumsy Sublime', in *Film Quarterly*, 60:3 (Spring 2007), p. 3.

12 Elsaesser, 'Too Big and Too Close: Alfred Hitchcock and Fritz Lang' in S. Gottlieb and R. Allen (eds.), *The Hitchcock Annual Anthology*, London, Wallflower Press, 2009, p. 227.

13 Gunning, *The Films of Fritz Lang*, London, BFI, 2000, p. 409.

14 Elsaesser, 'Too Big and Too Close: Alfred Hitchcock and Fritz Lang' in S. Gottlieb and R. Allen (eds.), *The Hitchcock Annual Anthology*, London, Wallflower Press, 2009, p. 227.

Filmography

Halbblut (Germany, 1919) also screenplay
Der Herr der Liebe (Germany, 1919) also actor
Harakiri (Germany, 1919)
Die Spinnen. 2. Teil: Das Brilliantenschiff (Germany, 1920) also screenplay
Das wandernde Bild (Germany, 1920) also screenplay
Kämpfende Herzen (Germany, 1920) also screenplay
Der müde Tod (Germany, 1920) also screenplay and editing
Dr Mabuse, der Spieler. I: Der grosse Spieler. Ein Bild der Zeit (Germany, 1922) also screenplay
Dr Mabuse, der Spieler. II: Inferno. Ein Spiel von Menschen unserer Zeit (Germany, 1922) also screenplay
Die Nibelungen: 1. Teil: Siegfried (Germany, 1924) also screenplay
Die Nibelungen. 2. Teil: Kriemhilds Rache (Germany, 1924) also screenplay
Metropolis (Germany, 1926) also screenplay and editing
Spione (Germany, 1928) also screenplay and producer
Frau im Mond (Germany, 1929) also producer
M (1931) also screenplay
Das Testament des Dr Mabuse (Germany, 1933) also screenplay
Liliom (France, 1934)
Fury (1936) screenplay,
You Only Live Once (1937)
You and Me (1938) also producer
The Return of Frank James (1940)
Western Union (1941)
Man Hunt (1941)
Hangmen Also Die! (1943)
Ministry of Fear (1944)
The Woman in the Window (1944)
Scarlet Street (1945) also producer
Cloak and Dagger (1946)
Secret Beyond The Door (1948) also producer
House by The River (1950)
American Guerrilla in The Philippines (1950)
Rancho Notorious (1952)
Clash by Night (1952)
The Blue Gardenia (1953)
The Big Heat (1953)
Human Desire (1954)
Moonfleet (1955)
While the City Sleeps (1956)

Beyond a Reasonable Doubt (1956)
Der Tiger von Eschnapur (Germany, 1959) also screenplay
Das indische Grabmal (Germany, 1959) also screenplay
Die 1000 Augen des Dr Mabuse (Germany, 1960) also screenplay

Further reading

Bogdanovich, Peter. *Fritz Lang in America*. London: Studio Vista, 1967.
Eisner, Lotte H. *Fritz Lang*. London: Secker & Warburg, 1976.
Humphries, Reynold. *Fritz Lang: Genre and Representation in his American Films*. Baltimore: Johns Hopkins University Press, 1989.
Jenkins, Stephen. *Fritz Lang. The Image and the Look*. London: BFI, 1981.

JOSEPH LOSEY

By Christopher Weedman

Joseph Losey's transnational film career was shaped and, by the blacklisted American director's own admission, galvanized by the Communist witch hunts of the late 1940s and 1950s. The social dissident and political exile first gained recognition for his experimental stage direction of the Living Newspaper plays *Triple-A Plowed Under* and *Injunction Granted* for the Federal Theatre Project in New York in 1936. Losey's predilection for both avant-garde production design and left-wing social politics was established early in these two controversial plays, which sought to instruct the public about New Deal-era social issues. Eschewing Samuel Goldwyn's often-quoted advice, "Messages should be delivered by Western Union," Losey continued critiquing dominant American political ideology when he began working in Hollywood and directed his first feature, *The Boy with Green Hair* (1948), for RKO Pictures in 1948. This political commitment inflected all five features that the director made in Hollywood over the next three years, a thematic consistency that caught the attention of the House Un-American Activities Committee. After fleeing the United States in 1951 to escape testifying about his Communist associations, Losey relocated briefly to Italy and later Britain, where his exilic outsider perspective became increasingly astute and antagonistic against his host country. Such attitudes were particularly evident in his collaboration with British dramatist and screenwriter Harold Pinter on the acclaimed art-house films *The Servant* (1963), *Accident* (1967), and *The Go-Between* (1970).

Losey amassed one of the most fascinating and eclectic filmographies of any director working in the postwar period. Over the course of his thirty-six-year feature film career, Losey transformed his persona from a Hollywood director of *film noirs* and often didactic social melodramas into an aspiring European auteur of challenging and opaque art-house films. The latter boasted self-conscious direction with fluid camera movements and intricately designed *mise-en-scène*, which featured distorted compositions, reflections in mirrors and windows, and oppressive decor (often in collaboration with production designer Richard MacDonald) that typically foregrounded social class tension and character narcissism. These characteristics were seen prominently in *The Servant*, the film that solidified this transformation. Originally deemed unmarketable by its British co-financier and distributor, Elstree Distributors, the film became a surprise hit on the art-house film circuit after being well-received at the first New York Film Festival in September 1963. *The Servant*'s dark and sardonic tale of a sexually ambiguous manservant (Dirk Bogarde) usurping his aristocratic boss's (James Fox) role as master of their Chelsea townhouse resonated with Britain's young left-wing cinemagoers, whose derision of British institutions and stiff-upper-lip traditions rose to new heights after the resignation of Conservative Prime Minister Harold Macmillan during the aftermath of the Profumo Affair the same year.

Already a fringe filmmaker with a cult following that included both the French auteur critics of *Cahiers du Cinéma* (who devoted a special issue to his *oeuvre* in September 1960) and the editorial staff of the British film journal *Movie*, Losey became one of the most prominent European-based directors in the two decades following *The Servant*. The film's success enabled Losey the creative latitude to make more narratively and aesthetically challenging films such as the anti-war drama *King & Country* (1964) and the subsequent collaborations with Pinter, *Accident* and *The Go-Between*. These two domestic melodramas featured fragmented, non-linear narratives that were inspired by both high modernist literature and the French Left Bank films of Alain Resnais. Losey admitted that, by the time he made *The Servant*, he no longer possessed a desire to "make direct statements" or "to give solutions."[1] Instead, he proclaimed himself to have a:

> greater security with the medium, a greater sense of knowledge of the society I was dealing with, and far greater freedom than I

had ever had before. And also subjects of my choice. *The Servant, King and Country* and *Accident* were all scripts I wanted to do, and they were complete one way or another in themselves; they were entities, had their own style, from which one could develop a cinematic style.[2]

Revealing of his desire to be taken seriously as an artist, Losey's words are also tinged with a romantic air of an auteur director desiring to transcend his commercial origins.

Yet Losey never fit easily within the already problematic framework of auteur criticism. He was not a writer–director, and three of his most remarkable films were made in close collaboration with Pinter, the influential stage dramatist whose stature eclipsed that of Losey's. Losey was also later marginalized by some of the same auteur critics who championed his early Hollywood and British genre films like the *film noirs The Prowler* (1951), *Time Without Pity* (1957), and *The Criminal* (1960), as well as the science fiction-cum-juvenile delinquent film *The Damned* (1963, filmed in 1961). This backlash was in large part due to the fact that after he directed *Eve* (1962, a French-Italian sexual melodrama with Jeanne Moreau, which, like *The Damned*, was heavily recut by its producers) and *The Servant* he began distancing himself from genre films (the type of films typically exalted by auteur critics) and instead became increasingly associated with literary adaptations and art-house cinema (the type of films they often criticized). "With *Accident*, Losey has escaped the clutches of the cultists to fall into the hands of the snobs," Sarris declared in 1968. "Only time will tell if such fashion will be fatal to Losey's artistic personality."[3]

Losey was often derided by his fellow filmmakers on both sides of the Atlantic. Whereas many of his Hollywood contemporaries shunned him due to the blacklist, his British contemporaries gave him generally faint praise. He was viewed in Britain as a cynical foreigner, who became increasingly pretentious in his storytelling. "What he did with *The Prowler* was what the script demanded—and I really liked *Accident*," Karel Reisz commented. "Losey's peculiar sourness toward the English worked very well. But then he became a dandy."[4] Losey's American identity—and particularly, his past identity as a Hollywood director—also worked against him, since many critics refused to unequivocally accept Hollywood filmmakers as artists. When Losey went from making *film noirs* like *The Prowler* and *The Criminal* to art-house films like *Accident* and *Don Giovanni* (1979), an exuberant adaptation of Mozart's opera, the transition was probably interpreted by his detractors as the result of a director taking his collaboration with Pinter too seriously. Losey's surprise win of the *Palme d'Or* for *The Go-Between*, over Luchino Visconti's favored *Death in Venice* (1971), was likewise viewed by his critics as stemming from an awards jury desiring to please the cult surrounding Losey in France. (Few in Britain or the United States gave Losey's work the same level of adulation bestowed to him by French scholars, who compared him to Continental European art-house filmmakers such as Resnais, Visconti, and Michelangelo Antonioni.)

Despite this perceived dichotomy between European art and Hollywood commerce, the art-house films that Losey made in Britain and Continental Europe were never devoid of commercial interests. In fact, they exhibited a desire to bridge the gap between art-house and popular cinema in order to reach a wider audience. Whereas early films of the French New Wave such as Jean-Luc Godard's *Breathless* (1959) and François Truffaut's *The 400 Blows* (1959) rebelled against studio filmmaking, operated on low budgets, and were filmed on location with partially improvised screenplays, Losey's 1960s films such as *The Servant*, *King and Country*, and *Accident* were shot on moderate budgets, both in studios and on location. These films also had fully developed screenplays, employed large production crews, and featured British stars such as Bogarde, Tom Courtenay, and Stanley Baker. The success of *The Servant* paved the way for Losey's uneven foray into big-budget, Hollywood-financed British productions including the secret agent satire *Modesty Blaise* (1966, financed by Twentieth Century-Fox for $3 million); the Richard Burton-Elizabeth Taylor-Tennessee Williams vehicle *Boom!* (1968, financed by Universal Pictures for $4.5 million); and the psychological thriller *Secret Ceremony* (1968, financed by Universal for $3 million). All three films were ambitious attempts to fuse a European art-house aesthetic and narrative style with Hollywood polish and star power. However, despite Losey and Richard MacDonald's stunning op art visuals in *Modesty Blaise* and baroque sets in *Boom!* and *Secret Ceremony*, the underdeveloped scripts and the awkward casting of Hollywood and international stars such as Monica Vitti and Terence Stamp in *Modesty Blaise*; Burton and Taylor in *Boom!*; and Taylor, Mia Farrow, and Robert Mitchum in *Secret Ceremony* made the films play as art film kitsch. Interestingly, these films are in the twenty-first century being reclaimed by some cult film audiences for this reason, best illustrated by John Waters' enthusiasm for *Boom!*, which he hails as "the greatest failed art film ever made."[5]

Losey's working within "the system" should not, however, be interpreted as either selling out or pedestrian 1960s filmmaking. It is remarkable, in fact, that films this ambitious could be made within British cinema during this period. Britain's film industry, like much of the rest of Britain's economy, subsisted on American financing during the 1960s. Hollywood film companies invested in British filmmaking because of lower production costs and the Eady Levy subsidy, which helped subsidize the films of Hollywood companies as long as they boasted mostly British performers and production crews.[6] This attraction to Britain only escalated after the phenomena of the Beatles and the James Bond series, as well as the unexpected success of British films such as the Oscar-winning *Tom Jones* (Richardson, 1963) in the United States. These financial incentives, plus the cultural allure of Britain during the "Swinging Sixties," attracted an influx of international filmmakers to Britain, a group that ranged from Americans like John Huston, Stanley Kubrick, Richard Lester, and Sidney Lumet to Europeans like Truffaut, Michelangelo Antonioni, Roman Polanski, and Jerzy Skolimowski.

Losey's 1960s and early 1970s films rode this wave of American and international financing in Britain. *The Servant* was partially financed by Associated British Picture Corporation (ABPC) and distributed by Associated British Pathé (both partners with Warner-Pathé, Warner Brothers' British film division); *King and Country* was distributed by Warner-Pathé; *Modesty Blaise* was financed and distributed by Twentieth Century-Fox; *Boom!* and *Secret Ceremony* were both financed and distributed by Universal; the allegorical political thriller *Figures in a Landscape* (1970) was financed by Cinema Center Films (the theatrical film division of CBS Television) and distributed by Twentieth Century-Fox in the UK and National General Corporation in the US; and *The Go-Between* was co-financed by ABPC's new owner, EMI Film Productions and Metro-Goldwyn-Mayer, the latter of whom sold its US interests in the film to Columbia Pictures out of fear that it would be unmarketable.[7] Of Losey's films between 1963 and 1971, only *Accident* possessed no involvement from major American companies. This limited *Accident's* release, particularly in the United States where it reportedly did little business outside of New York.[8]

Not unlike the manservant in *The Servant*, who gains the confidence of his master in order to enter the house, Losey attempted to work within the British-Hollywood commercial system in order to get his films made and distributed. Yet, if Losey held any hope that the major companies would commit long term to financing films both artistic and commercial, such optimism dissipated by the early 1970s. American financing in British filmmaking began to dry up in the late 1960s, after many British films failed to find an audience in either Britain or the United States, including the period epic *Alfred the Great* (1969) and the musicals *Half a Sixpence* (1967) and *Goodbye Mr. Chips* (1969). The major companies still made a handful of films in Britain in the 1970s, but these were reserved mostly for large productions such as the Bond films, *Star Wars* (1977, shot at both Elstree and Shepperton Studios), *Superman* (1978, shot at Pinewood Studios), and works by profitable filmmakers such as Alfred Hitchcock (*Frenzy*, 1972) and Stanley Kubrick (A *Clockwork Orange*, 1971 and *Barry Lyndon*, 1975).

The moribund British cinema, along with the ever-escalating artistic ambitions of Losey and Pinter, also precipitated the demise of the Losey-Pinter collaboration. Both Losey and Pinter envisioned their planned adaptation of Marcel Proust's *À la recherche du temps perdu* as the artistic height of their cinematic careers. Pinter spent three months in early 1972 condensing all seven volumes of Proust's modernist French novel into a script for a single English language film. However, the estimated $5.5 million budget needed to film the screenplay as Losey and Pinter conceived it was cost prohibitive. Not only did Pinter and Losey desire to film all of the scenes in luxurious French locales like the Hôtel du Baron Élie de Rothschild and the Hôtel du Baron Alain de Rothschild, but Pinter's ambitious screenplay also called for 455 shots with an estimated running time of four hours, a length unheard of in British and Hollywood cinema at the time.[9] Losey and Pinter also planned to fill the cast with an all-star list of international performers, including Alan Bates or Alain Delon as Swann; Laurence Olivier or Marlon Brando as Charlus; and Julie Christie, Helen Mirren, or Susannah York as Odette.[10] A deal was discussed to make the film for television, but Losey was unable to persuade Pinter to allow the networks to split the film into separate parts.[11] These artistic mandates, as well as the large costs and running time, killed off any chances of making the film.

Losey continued striving to put together projects, yet such efforts were impeded by the fact that he was no longer considered bankable. After making the mixed to poorly received films *The Assassination of Trotsky* (1972), *A Doll's House* (1973), *Galileo* (1975), and *The Romantic Englishwoman* (1975), Losey went into tax exile in France in order to escape the escalating taxes in Britain in the mid-1970s. The director was faced with having to pay "83–87 per cent British tax on worldwide earnings over £20,000."[12] Losey continued working in Europe, but the high art subject matter and alienating narrative style of films like the Holocaust thriller *Mr. Klein* (1976) and the Italian opera *Don Giovanni* made it difficult for him to connect with a wider audience. Losey returned to Britain to direct the poorly received feminist drama *Steaming* (1985), which was released posthumously after his death in 1984.

Losey's career was marked by adversity and perseverance amidst a postwar filmmaking landscape that perceived him as both a political subversive and an industrial outsider. He mirrored his blacklisted contemporaries Jules Dassin and Cy Endfield by resurrecting his career in Europe, where he compiled an admittedly uneven, yet intermittently brilliant, filmography. Losey's films challenged both ideological and stylistic sensibilities. Renouncing films offering easy solutions, Losey came to feel that films "can only provide a stimulation which I think at its best is some sort of complete artistic statement, which therefore is form and emotion, which will stimulate the people seeing, hearing, absorbing it, to further thought and investigation."[13] In an era when many of his past Hollywood contemporaries like Elia Kazan, Nicholas Ray, Orson Welles, and Fred Zinnemann were either concluding their filmmaking careers or experiencing difficulties securing funding, Losey remained prolific and made a film almost annually until his death. If anything, his vision to bridge the gap between commerce and high art was, and to a large extent still is, before its time.

Biography

Joseph Losey was born in La Crosse, Wisconsin, in 1909. After directing experimental stage productions, industrial films, and short subjects in the United States in the 1930s and 1940s, Losey made his feature debut with *The Boy with Green Hair* in 1948. The left-wing political overtones of his Hollywood films raised the ire of the House Un-American Activities Committee and contributed to his backlisting in 1951. Losey resurrected his career in Britain, where he collaborated with writer Harold Pinter on the art-house films *The Servant* (1963), *Accident* (1967), and *The Go-Between* (1971). While often derided in Britain and the United States during his lifetime, Losey's films were revered in France, where he garnered the *Palme d'Or* for *The Go-Between* and the Grand Prize of the Jury for *Accident* at Cannes, and Best Film and Best Director for *Mr. Klein* (1976) at the César Awards. Losey died in London in 1984.

Notes

1 Tom Milne. *Losey on Losey*. Garden City, Doubleday, 1968, p. 48.
2 Ibid.

3 Andrew Sarris. *The American Cinema: Directors and Directions, 1929–1968.* New York, Da Capo, 1996, pp. 96–97.
4 David Caute. *Joseph Losey: A Revenge on Life.* New York, Oxford University Press, 1994, p. 466.
5 John Waters. "The Kindness of a Stranger." *The New York Times,* 19 November 2006, p. G20.
6 Robert Murphy. *Sixties British Cinema.* London, BFI, 1992, p. 257.
7 Caute, p. 264.
8 Caute, pp. 203–4; and Natasha Fraser-Cavassoni. *Sam Spiegel.* New York, Simon, 2003, pp. 275–76.
9 Caute, p. 338; and Paul Newland and Gavrik Losey. "An Involuntary Memory?: Joseph Losey, Harold Pinter, and Marcel Proust's *À la recherche du temps perdu,*" in *Sights Unseen: Unfinished British Films,* ed. Dan North. Newcastle, Cambridge Scholars, 2008, pp. 40–41.
10 Newland and Losey, p. 44.
11 Ibid., 44.
12 Caute, 387.
13 Milne, p. 42.

Filmography

Pete-Roleum and His Cousins (1939)
A Child Went Forth (1941)
Youth Gets a Break (1941)
A Gun in His Hand (1945)
The Boy with Green Hair (1948)
The Lawless (1950)
M (1951)
The Prowler (1951)
The Big Night (1951)
Stranger on the Prowl (Italy, 1952)
The Sleeping Tiger (UK, 1954)
A Man on the Beach (UK, 1955)
The Intimate Stranger (UK, 1956)
Time Without Pity (UK, 1957)
The Gypsy and the Gentleman (UK, 1958)
Blind Date (UK, 1959)
First on the Road (UK, 1959)
The Criminal (UK, 1960)
The Damned (UK, 1961) released in 1963
Eve (France/Italy, 1962)
The Servant (UK, 1963)
King & Country (UK, 1964)
Modesty Blaise (UK, 1966)

Accident (UK, 1967)
Boom! (UK, 1968)
Secret Ceremony (UK, 1968)
Figures in a Landscape (UK, 1970)
The Go-Between (UK, 1971)
The Assassination of Trotsky (Italy/France/UK, 1972)
A Doll's House (UK/France, 1973)
Galileo (1975)
The Romantic Englishwoman (UK/France, 1975)
Mr. Klein (France/Italy, 1976)
Roads to the South (France/Spain, 1978)
Don Giovanni (Italy/France/West Germany, 1979)
The Trout (France, 1982)
Steaming (UK, 1985)

Further reading

De Rham, Edith. *Joseph Losey*. London: André Deutsch, 1991.
Ciment, Michel. *Conversations with Losey*. New York: Methuen, 1985.
Gardner, Colin. *Joseph Losey*. Manchester: Manchester University Press, 2004.
Hirsch, Foster. *Joseph Losey*. Boston: Twayne, 1980.
Leahy, James. *The Cinema of Joseph Losey*. London: Zwemmer, 1967.
Palmer, James and Michael Riley. *The Films of Joseph Losey*. Cambridge: Cambridge University Press, 1993.
Sargeant, Amy. *The Servant*. London: BFI/Palgrave Macmillan, 2011.

ERNST LUBITSCH

By Steve Neale

Ernst Lubitsch is in some ways comparable to Alfred Hitchcock. Like Hitchcock, he was an émigré; like Hitchcock his name was known to the general public; and like Hitchcock he was director whose stylistic preoccupations – whose directorial 'touches' as they were called – were often discussed in contemporary reviews. These touches are usually characterised as moments of metaphor, wit and displacement, as marked directorial intrusions designed to generate irony and comedy and to represent otherwise censorable events, actions and thoughts. However, as William Paul points out in his book on Lubitsch, while retaining a number of these ingredients, Lubitsch's style and concerns changed over time, responding both to contemporary socio-political developments and to new stylistic trends.[1]

Lubitsch was born in Germany. He began his career in the cinema as a performer in comedies at the Bioscope film studios in Berlin. In 1916, he began writing and directing films, most of them drawing on ethnic Jewish humour, and in 1919 he directed *Carmen/Gypsy Blood*, which was a major international hit. *Carmen* was followed by *Die Austernprinzessin/The Oyster Princess* (also 1919) and a series of large-scale spectacles, among them *Madame Dubarry/Passion* (1919) and *Anna Boleyn/Deception* (1920). These films all focussed on libidinal desires and transgressions within a markedly hierarchical social order, and critics were impressed by how Lubitsch humanised these stories by interweaving lucid scenes of large-scale pageantry with telling details and intimate moments. In 1921 Lubitsch went to the U.S. to promote *Das Weib der Pharoah/The Loves of Pharoah* (1922). He returned to direct Mary Pickford in *Rosita* the following year and from that point on worked solely in Hollywood.

Lubitsch rapidly familiarised himself with Hollywood's stylistic norms, abandoning what Kristin Thompson has called the 'rough continuity' of contemporary European cinema with its 'diffuse lighting, aggressive sets, and pantomimic acting' and adapting himself to the protocols of continuity editing, three-point lighting, the designing of impressive but functional sets, and the cultivation of performance styles based on restraint.[2] In these as in other respects, he appears to have been influenced by *A Woman of Paris*, which was directed by Charlie Chaplin and released in 1923. In telling the story of a woman who misses her chance to marry and becomes the mistress of a Paris roué, *A Woman of Paris* was marked by nuance and irony, an avoidance of didacticism, and a lightness of comic touch, particularly in the Paris scenes, which were all perceived as refreshingly new. *The Marriage Circle* (1924), the first in a series of films that Lubitsch directed for Warner Bros., was released the following year. Though deriving from a problem play about adultery in an upper middle-class milieu, it was more consistently farcical in tone and structure than the play or Chaplin's film and as such was much more dependent on 'deliberate deception', 'the misapprehension of events' and the formalised patterning of motifs and repetitions, as Lea Jacobs has pointed out.[3] Nevertheless reviews of *The Marriage Circle* coupled the names of Lubitsch and Chaplin, helping to further the former's reputation and to mark the advent of a new kind of comedy and a new kind of style.

This style was based in part on what a reviewer in *Moving Picture World* called 'concentration', a trait evident in the way Lubitsch 'confines his scenes to the particular portion of the set in which the action occurs' and 'puts over his points with a minimum of footage, having his characters portray whole situations in a gesture, a look and even by absolute inaction'.[4] This style also displayed scrupulous adherence to the conventions of continuity editing, especially those involved in eye-line and spatial matching. When coupled with the knowledge built up as the story evolved, these convention enabled spectators not only to know who was looking at whom (or what) when cutting to and from glances, people and objects, but also to infer what they were thinking, and to further infer whether or not they were mistaken. In so doing, Lubitsch, who edited this and all his other films himself, not only controlled the flow of narrative knowledge, often marking this control by cutting away from the characters to shots of doors and other objects, but also drew attention to the importance of inference itself in the rule-bound milieux of the upper-middle and upper classes in which *The Marriage Circle* and its immediate successors, *Forbidden Paradise* (1924), *Lady Windermere's Fan* (1925) and *So This Is Paris* (1926), were set. In addition, while retaining a dominant comic tone, the frustrations and disappointments to which life in these milieux gave rise would often be marked by moments of melancholy, a trait evident in *The Student Prince in Old Heidelberg* (1927) and a number of Lubitsch's later films as well.

The coming of sound prompted the production of musicals in the late 1920s and early 1930s, and Lubitsch's first sound films were operettas. With their inherent artifice, their focus on romance, and their fanciful, hierarchical and class-bound settings (usually in equally fanciful European kingdoms), the conventions of operetta were used by Lubitsch to further explore the representation of libidinal desires and the restrictions placed upon them by etiquette, by other social norms and obligations, and by the differential class and gender status of the characters involved. These films included *The Love Parade* (1929), *Monte Carlo* (1930) and *The Smiling Lieutenant* (1931) as well as *One Hour With You* (1932) (a musical remake of *The Marriage Circle*, which was partially directed by George Cukor), all of them made at Paramount.

Films such as these were produced at a time when Hollywood was under pressure to develop its own code of censorship. A version of the code was introduced in 1930 and the application of its guidelines was refined during the course of the next four years. While Lubitsch's operettas, like his earlier comedies, were sometimes considered risqué, they were already heavily dependent on various forms of indirect representation. However, as the pressures on the code intensified, so too did these particular characteristics. Such strategies are particularly evident in *Trouble in Paradise* (1932) and *Design for Living* (1933), both of which were made at the height of the Great Depression and both of which exhibited a radically sceptical attitude to the worlds of business, wealth and commerce.

Marked by extensive montage sequences and passages of oblique narration built around clocks, doors, window, stairs and other elements of decor, *Trouble in Paradise* begins in Venice with an extensive elliptical sequence involving garbage and gondolas, prostitution and crime, the idle rich and those who service them, and the beginnings of an intense romantic relationship between two jewel thieves, Gaston (Herbert Marshall) and Lily (Miriam Hopkins), who fall in love as they pick each other's pockets. After moving to Paris, they are short of money. However, Gaston encounters Mariette Colet (Kay Francis), the wealthy heiress of a perfume company. He steals her purse, returns it to her, claims the reward, charms her into appointing him her secretary, then with the help of Lily, whom Mariette also hires, sets about stealing her jewellery. However, Gaston and Mariette (whose other-worldly generosity is strongly contrasted with the self-serving meanness of her company's board of directors) fall in love. Gaston delays the theft. But time is passing and Gaston is recognised by one of Mariette's male acquaintances as the thief who stole his wallet in Venice. A jealous Lily forces Gaston to break into Mariette's safe. Mariette catches them red-handed. But she allows them to escape with the contents of the safe and they renew their relationship by picking each other's pockets in the back of taxi.

Less dazzling in its use of montage and ellipsis than *Trouble in Paradise*, *Design for Living* is nevertheless marked by a similar preoccupation with triangular relationships. However, where *Trouble's* triangle involves a man and two women, *Design for Living* not only involves a woman and two men, but ends with the woman at the centre of a ménage à trois. Women had been at the centre of number of Lubitsch's earlier films and *Design for Living* was followed by *Angel* (1937) and *Bluebeard's Eighth Wife* (1938), both of which explored the discontents of marriage (and the failures, flaws and weaknesses of men) from the point of view of their female protagonists.

Angel and *Bluebeard's Eighth Wife* were the last films Lubitsch made at Paramount. They were followed by *Ninotchka* (1939) and *The Shop Around the Corner* (1940), which were both produced at MGM. The former starred Greta Garbo as a Soviet envoy who falls in love with a

French Count. The latter was a romantic comedy set in and around a leather-goods shop in Budapest. Here the effects of the Depression are still being felt. Having a job and hence a place among the workers in the shop is as important as finding a suitable partner. Desperation and disappointment are thus never far away, and this reality is made plain when the shop's owner discovers that his wife is having an affair with one of his employees, when he wrongly surmises that Kralik (James Stewart) is the employee in question and sacks him. Once reinstated, Kralik discovers that the woman with whom he has been in romantic correspondence is in fact Klara (Margaret Sullivan), an employee who has done nothing but criticise him since getting her job by questioning his judgement. Here, the intricate interplay of correct and incorrect inference, knowledge and judgement in a film that encompasses potential tragedy as well as romance and farce is supplemented not only by Lubitsch's trademark touches but also by the distinctive patterns, structures and metaphors evident in Samson Raphaelson's dialogue.

Raphaelson had been working with Lubitsch since the early 1930s. In *The Shop Around the Corner* his dialogue is peppered with striking rhythms, most of them based on repetitions and substitutions: 'Tell him I won't', 'I will'; 'Psychologically I'm very confused, but personally I don't feel bad at all'; and 'I just don't believe in mixing shoes with pleasure'. However, along with repetitions and substitutions of practically every other kind, this style of dialogue arguably reaches its peak in *To Be or Not to Be* (1942). Produced independently for release by United Artists, *To Be or Not to Be* centres on a troupe of Jewish actors in Nazi-occupied Poland. Beginning just before the occupation, it highlights the vanity of most of the actors as well as that of the Nazi hierarchy. (One of the film's most famous lines occurs when, in a rehearsal, an actor playing the Führer follows three scripted 'Heil Hitlers with an improvised 'Heil myself'). However, while the actors are only human (a point underlined by twice quoting Shylock's 'If you prick us do we not bleed' speech from *The Merchant of Venice*), the Nazi underlings are unthinking automatons and their senior representatives either cunning or bumbling egomaniacs. Further repetitions occur not only in the three separate performances of the soliloquy from *Hamlet* that begins with the words 'To be or not to be' (itself not only a repetitious line, but a repetitious signal for young male admirers of the lead actor's wife to leave the auditorium and rendezvous backstage), but in the recurrence of 'So they call me concentration camp Ehrhardt' and other distinctive lines. The substitutions include the actors playing Nazis both off stage as well as on, a Nazi professor who masquerades as a member of the Polish resistance, and lines of dialogue such as 'What you are I wouldn't eat' (as said by one Jewish actor to another) and 'Let me give you my opinion'. 'No'. 'Then let me give you my reaction: a laugh is nothing to be sneezed at'.

Increasingly dogged by ill-health, Lubitsch completed only two more films, *Heaven Can Wait* (1943) and *Cluny Brown* (1946), both of which were produced at Fox, and both of which were marked by longer takes and fewer flamboyant touches. *Heaven Can Wait* (his first and only film in colour) tells the story of Henry Van Cleve (Don Ameche), a man looking back over a life preoccupied with women, love and romance as he converses with the Devil on the assumption that he is likelier, now that he is dead, to enter Hell than Heaven. Although essentially a comedy, the interior shots of the Van Cleve house that begin and end the phases of Henry's life become imbued with a greater sense of loss as Henry begins to age, as the number of characters who disappear or die increases, and as the house itself becomes more and more empty. *Cluny Brown* focuses on the relationship between a young working-class woman and a European émigré, both of them outsiders in a rural British village where the former is a servant and the latter a guest in a country house. If the émigré's outsider status is marked by his accent and his occasional misunderstandings of upper-class etiquette, that of the young woman is marked by her love of plumbing, which scandalises her fiancé and his family, bringing an end to the possibility of a conventional lower-middle class marriage and prompting them both to leave. Ending up in New York, they are finally depicted in montage as a happily married couple who are able to flourish far away from the rule-bound norms that govern life and love in Britain and Europe.

For over twenty years, Lubitsch was widely regarded as one of the world's greatest directors. Allusions to his style can be found in the work of Leo McCarey, Yasujiro Ozu and Billy Wilder, and tributes to his films include the 1983 remake of *To Be or Not to Be* and *You've Got Mail* (1998), a remake of *The Shop Around the Corner*. For some, Lubitsch's style is largely a matter of sexual innuendo, exemplified by the cutaway to a gondola going under a bridge while a romantic couple demonstrate their mutual attraction in *Trouble in Paradise*, or by the shot of a woman entering an officer's apartment at night followed by a shot of the same woman leaving the following morning in *The Smiling Lieutenant*. If that were all though, Lubitsch and his films could easily be seen as ingenious, possibly salacious, but above all old-fashioned exemplars of outmoded mores and systems of censorship. However, there is much more to Lubitsch than that. His is a style governed not by sexual metaphors but by patterns of repetition and substitution. Hence the substitution involved in the gondola sequence in *Trouble in Paradise*; hence the repetition involved in the framing of the woman's visit in *The Smiling Lieutenant*; hence the repeated lines of dialogue in *To Be or Not to Be*; and hence the substitution of Pepi (William Tracy) for Vadas (Joseph Schildkraut) and Rudy (Charles Smith) for Pepi during the course of *The Shop Around the Corner*.

Biography

The son of prosperous Jewish tailor, Lubitsch was born in Berlin in 1892. He began his career as a performer in cabaret and music hall before becoming involved in the making of films. The success of his German films led him to Hollywood, where he enjoyed fame, praise and considerable artistic autonomy for over twenty years. After several bouts of ill-health, he died of a heart attack in 1947.

Notes

1 William Paul, *Ernst Lubitsch's American Comedy*, New York: Columbia University Press, 1983.
2 Kristin Thompson, *Herr Lubitsch Goes to Hollywood: German and American Film after World War I*, Amsterdam: Amsterdam University Press, 2005, p. 107.
3 Lea Jacobs, *The Decline of Sentiment: American Film in the 1920s*, Berkeley: University of California Press, 2008, p. 106.
4 Charles S. Sewell, "The Marriage Circle," *Motion Picture World*, February 16, 1924, p. 581.

Filmography

Carmen / Gypsy Blood (1916)
Die Austernprinzessin / The Oyster Princess (1919)
Madame Dubarry / Passion (1919)
Anna Boleyn / Deception (1920)
Das Weib der Pharoah / The Loves of Pharoah (1922)
Rosita (1923)
The Marriage Circle (1924)
Three Women (1924)
Forbidden Paradise (1924)
Kiss Me Again (1925)
Lady Windermere's Fan (1925)
So This Is Paris (1926)

The Student Prince in Old Heidelberg (1927)
The Patriot (1928)
Eternal Love (1929)
The Love Parade (1929)
Paramount on Parade (co-dir.) (1930)
Monte Carlo (1930)
The Smiling Lieutenant (1931)
The Man I Killed/Broken Lullaby (1932)
One Hour with You (1932)
Trouble in Paradise (1932)
If I Had a Million (1932) one episode
Design for Living (1933)
The Merry Widow (1934)
Angel (1937)
Bluebeard's Eighth Wife (1938)
Ninotchka (1939)
The Shop Around the Corner (1940)
That Uncertain Feeling (1941)
To Be or Not to Be (1942)
Heaven Can Wait (1943)
Cluny Brown (1946)
That Lady in Ermine (1948) completed by Otto Preminger

Further reading

Eyman, Scott. *Ernst Lubitsch: Laughter in Paradise*. Baltimore: Johns Hopkins University Press, 1993.
Paul, Robert. *Ernst Lubitsch's American Comedy*. New York: Columbia University Press, 1983.
Thompson, Kristin. *Herr Lubitsch Goes to Hollywood: German and American Film after World War I*. Amsterdam: Amsterdam University Press, 2005.

IDA LUPINO

By Shelley Cobb

The only woman to have a substantial directorial output in 1950s Hollywood, and, alongside Dorothy Arzner, one of the two female directors to have an extended career during the Studio Era, Ida Lupino was a director, writer, producer of film, as well as a television director in later life. However, it is for the films she made for the production company co-founded with husband Collier Young that she is usually remembered. An independent studio, The Filmmakers made low-budget films with up-and-coming talent and provocative themes. Lupino's films all feature characters struggling against their own limits and, more importantly, the limits of society in 1950s America.

Lupino began her Hollywood career in 1933 as an actress contracted with Paramount. Throughout the thirties she built a career on screen that reached its heights after she signed to Warner Bros in 1940 and starred in films like *High Sierra* (Raoul Walsh, 1941), and *Ladies in Retirement* (Charles Vidor, 1941). She continued to act throughout the 1940s for Warner Bros in a range of films, playing Emily Brontë in *Devotion* (Curtis Bernhardt, 1946) and a femme fatale in *Road House* (Jean Negulesco, 1948). Wheeler Winston Dixon suggests that during these years Lupino nursed her ambitions to be a director, while biographer William Donati notes that two directors in particular influenced Lupino's move into directing and the kinds of films she made: Dorothy Arzner, whom Lupino greatly admired but whose career ended when she lost her contract with Columbia in 1943 (no woman directed a film in Hollywood again until Lupino's directorial debut, *Not Wanted*, in 1949); and Roberto Rossellini, who complained to Lupino at a party for his *Rome Open City* (1945) that 'In Hollywood movies, the star is going crazy ... when are you going to make pictures about ordinary people, in ordinary situations?'.[1]

Not Wanted opens on Sally Kelton walking aimlessly through the city when she happens upon a baby carriage outside a shop. Sally picks up the baby and walks away until the mother appears screaming for her baby. Sally, in a dazed voice, says, "but he's my baby ... " Thrown in a cell, she wonders aloud, "How did I get here?" and her story unfolds in flashback. Nagged by her mother, who doesn't want Sally "to slave around the kitchen for the rest of your life like I have", she seeks independence at a local lounge and falls in love with a tra-velling singer-piano player whom she follows to the city. Drew, a wounded war veteran, courts Sally and just as she appears to be falling for him, she discovers she is pregnant by the singer. In a home for unwed mothers, she gives the baby up for adoption, changing her mind too late. In the present, the baby's mother decides not to press charges. Free, but distraught, Sally runs away aimlessly, followed by Drew who has tracked her down. He collapses; Sally turns around, and they fall into each other's arms.

Elmer Clifton is credited with directing *Not Wanted* but fell ill 72 hours after production began and Lupino took over. Like all of The

Filmmakers' productions, the budget was small ($154,000) and it was shot quickly (less than thirty days). The original screenplay, *Bad Company* – written by Malvin Wald and Paul Jarrico, was rejected twice by the PCA. Scholars such as Diane Waldman have examined the changes to the original script, Lupino's negotiations with the PCA for approval, and the significant differences between the approved script and the final film.[2] The evidence suggests that Lupino made revisions that shifted the emphasis, as Dan Georgakas puts it, 'from a seduction/quasirape scenario to one in which the man is a louse but not a predator and the female is less a victim than a sexually active woman caught in tragic circumstances'.[3] It was Lupino too who changed the title to one that seems to encompass both the pregnancy and Sally. Due to budget constraints, much of the film was shot on location, subsequently a signature of Lupino's realist style. Researching *Not Wanted*, she met unwed mothers in homes, experiences that she discussed with Eleanor Roosevelt on the first lady's regular radio program. Though she did not take directorial credit, advertisements read 'Ida Lupino's *Not Wanted*' and the film established her interest in ordinary people in ordinary situations. The film grossed a million dollars, raising interest in Lupino as a director.

Lupino's first official direction credit was *Never Fear* (1939), the story of Carol, a dancer and choreographer who is disabled by polio and struggles with her rehabilitation. Some have suggested the film is autobiographical (Lupino was infected with polio during her early days in Hollywood). However, as Ronnie Scheib suggests it is really, 'a "reverse" autobiography … [for] the story of a dancer who could not become a choreographer – read actress who could not become a director'.[4] At the beginning of the film, Carol and partner/fiancé Guy are a dance team on the cusp of success. When Carol is told that she is unlikely to dance again and must enter a residential institute for therapy, she falls into despair. Guy stays nearby, working as a salesman, but Carol rejects his renewed proposal of marriage, insisting that he find a new dance partner. Guy returns to dancing, while Carol makes enough of a recovery to walk with a cane; though they both flirt with other romantic partners, when Carol walks out of the institute, she finds Guy waiting for her. Based on a true story and shot on location at the Santa Monica Kabat-Kaiser Institute, a key montage sequence takes place in the institute's facilities. Voices of her doctor, Guy, and a fellow patient accompany shots of Carol doing strengthening and balancing exercises; the camera often focuses on her feet, clad in white socks and sneakers, her tentative movements emphasized by her baggy trousers. Her body is most definitely on display, 'to-be-looked-at', but it is active in its struggle against inactivity; it is a film about 'being a woman' but specifically about the 'difficulty of accepting a mutilated, dependent intersubjective version of womanhood'.[5] Carol's illness and suffering seem to fit the common 'affliction' narrative of the 'woman's film', but the film does not end with Carol's martyrdom or tragic death. Nor is it a heroic ending; there is no indication that Carol will turn her experience into something greater than her own survival and happiness – dreams of fame have been left behind for more ordinary hopes for her future.

Released two years later, *Hard, Fast and Beautiful* (1951) tells the story of a young woman turned successful tennis star. Guided by her mother's ambitions from her first match, Florence ultimately wins Wimbledon and the US Championship only to retire at the end of the film, choosing to walk away from the money and fame and into her fiancé's arms, much to her mother's dismay. Florence retires when she learns that her mother has accepted financial favors, in the process risking Florence's amateur status and inciting the other players' disdain. The film received mixed reviews. On one hand, a social commentary on corruption in amateur sport, like many sports films it utilizes on-location shooting and clips from existing tournament footage. On the other hand, it is a melodrama of mother-daughter relations that intimately explores the mother's hopes for a better life for her daughter. Unlike the sacrificial Stella Dallas, however, Milly, the controlling 'stage-mother', receives her comeuppance when her daughter hands her the Championship trophy (sarcastically remarking, "You've earned it") before walking away with her fiancé. And yet, as Mandy Merck suggests, Florence's 'happy ending' does not really balance out Milly's destruction.[6] Milly's ambition for her daughter is a result of her own entrapment in a traditional post-war marriage, and Florence's decision to end her career and, apparently, pursue domesticity, reads more ambivalently in light of this knowledge.

In between *Never Fear* and *Hard, Fast and Beautiful*, Lupino wrote and directed *Outrage* (1950), a film that 'tackled the volatile issue of rape at a time when the word *rape* was not acceptable for use in newspapers'.[7] In the film, Ann, a recently engaged bookkeeper, stays late at work and on her way home is followed by war veteran who had made previous advances toward her. He rapes Ann who, unable to deal with the guilt and shame, runs away to California, finding solace working on an elderly couple's farm under the care of the local pastor. At a barn dance, a young man's advances cause Ann to recall the rape; she fends the man off with a wrench, nearly killing him. In court, the pastor pleads for leniency for both Ann and her rapist, citing the traumatic effects of sexual assault and the experience of war as a reason for therapy rather than incarceration. The film ends with Ann on a bus back to her parents and her waiting fiancé. The liberal humanist message implicit in the narrative did not sit well with feminists of the 1970s nor is it any easier today to accept the parity of the rapist's pursuit and attack and Ann's instinctual defense against unwanted advances. Nonetheless Ann exemplifies Lupino's women in her struggle against the social and legal limits of the post-war era. Whether experiencing unwed motherhood, physical disability, traditional marriage or the aftermath of sexual assault, the social exclusion and censure of women in Lupino's first four films and the ambivalent ways they attempt to escape those traps offer space for feminist readings. Moreover, the social critique offered in these films remain resolutely anti-utopian in their gender politics.

Lupino's two final films for The Filmmakers shift away from the limits of post-war society on women in order to focus on crises of masculinity. *The Hitch-Hiker* (1953) has no significant female characters. Lauren Rabinovitz argues, 'while this film does not actively critique gender roles, it does unsettle, and foreground the alienation of, rigidly defined gender roles'.[8] The film begins with two men in a car headed for a weekend fishing trip, temporarily escaping their domestic responsibilities. Following radio reports of a killer on the loose, they pick up a hitch-hiker, Meyers, who is revealed to be the killer. The men become hostages in a bid to escape the police. Based on a true story, *The Hitch-Hiker* seems like a solid B-movie thriller in which two ordinary men must test their masculinity in the face of death. Meyers forces them to take him to the Mexico border, taunting them that at least one might have escaped if they shared his everyman-for-himself attitude. And yet, their trip, their 'first time away from the wife and kids since the war' suggests a desire to look out for themselves first, to rebel against 1950s society, if only on a small scale.

The Bigamist (1953) continues this examination of post-war masculinity, fusing the conventions of film noir and the domestic melodrama. The title tells us Harry Graham's crime; when he and wife Eve apply to adopt a child, it is only a matter of time before the investigating social worker finds out. When Harry is caught with his second wife, Phyllis, taking care of their child, the tale is told in flashback: a salesman of no particular talent or intelligence, whose business success depends on one woman and his happiness on another, Harry is not unlike many other noir protagonists. The film offers no convenient femme fatale. Both Eve and Phyllis are sympathetic, even as Eve initially appears to be cast as a symbolically castrating career woman. In striking contrast to narrative norms that construct marriage as the concluding reward of melodrama, marriage here is a grind for all. Dissatisfied with Eve early on, Harry's romantic courtship of Phyllis doesn't last after she becomes pregnant and they marry – the crying baby and post-partum illness get in the way. In the final courtroom scene, the marriages are dissolved but the judge does not sentence Harry, leaving it for the wives to decide who will take him back. Neither sheds a tear, though Phyllis leaves and Eve stays as the cops lead out Harry. 'Such a lack of narrative closure', argues Ellen Seiter, 'may be a necessary component of narratives that are so potentially subversive of the ideology of the nuclear family'.[9] Lupino played the part of Phyllis, making her the first woman to direct herself in a feature. However, the film was not received well, several critics disparagingly calling it a soap opera. The Filmmakers attempted to distribute the film themselves, but it never reached a wide audience.

In 1954 The Filmmakers released their last film, for which Lupino received no formal credit. Possibly for financial reasons as much as creative ones, Lupino started television acting in 1953 and, as she would have it, fell into directing television a few years later. She continued as both an actress and a director throughout the 'Golden Age' of television, directing for shows such as *Gilligan's Island* and *Bewitched*. Her skill with masculine narratives of action is evinced by her direction of episodes of *The Fugitive*, *The Virginian*, *Have Gun Will Travel* and *Twilight Zone*. In 1966, she directed her final feature film *The Trouble with Angels* (1966), the story of two teenage girls sent to a convent school. Lupino complained about a lack of creative control over the film, but compared to other 'nun films' released around that time – *The Sound of Music* (1965) and *The Singing Nun* (1966) – *Angels* emphasizes the female space of the convent, largely leaving the masculine institution of the church outside of the young Mary's trajectory toward taking orders. Played by teen star Haley Mills, Mary's connection with the Mother Superior (Rosalind Russell) suggests the homosocial space as one removed from the patriarchal pressures of society outside the convent. The film had a respectable box office take, but Lupino returned to directing television, which she did until 1968. Her last television appearance was in 1978.

Biography

Ida Lupino was born in London on February 4, 1918. Her father came from a long line of Italian theatre performers, and was a well-known revue comedian during the 1910s and 20s; her mother was a musical comedy actress. While accompanying her mother on an audition, she landed her first starring role, at fourteen, as a young ingénue in the British film *Her First Affaire* (1932). After starring in five British films, she was contracted by Paramount in 1933 and became a US citizen in 1948. Married three times – to actor Louis Hayward in 1938; to producer Collier Young in 1948; and to actor Howard Duff in 1951, with whom she had a daughter, Bridget – she died following a stroke in Los Angeles at the age of 77 on August 3, 1995.

Notes

1 William Donati. *Ida Lupino: A Biography*. Lexington: University Press of Kentucky, 1996, p.146.
2 Annette Kuhn (ed.) *Queen of the 'B's: Ida Lupino Behind the Camera*. Bradford: Flicks Books, 1995, pp. 13–29.
3 Dan Georgakas. "Ida Lupino: Doing It Her Way." *Cineaste* 25.3 (June 2005): 33.
4 Kuhn, p. 55.
5 Scheib in Kuhn, p. 54.
6 Kuhn, p. 83.
7 Georgakas, p. 34.
8 Kuhn, p. 98.
9 Kuhn, p. 116.

Filmography

Not Wanted (1949) uncredited
Never Fear (1949)
Outrage (1950)
Hard, Fast and Beautiful (1951)
The Hitch-Hiker (1953)
The Bigamist (1953)
The Trouble with Angels (1966)

Further reading

Donati, William. *Ida Lupino: A Biography*. Lexington: University Press of Kentucky, 1996.
Dixon, Wheeler Winston, "Ida Lupino." *Senses of Cinema*, Great Directors Issue 50 (April 2009).
Georgakas, Dan. "Ida Lupino: Doing It Her Way." *Cineaste* 25.3 (June 2005): 32–6.

Hastie, Amelie. *The Bigamst: BFI Film Classics*. London: BFI, 2009.

Kuhn, Annette, ed. *Queen of the 'B's: Ida Lupino Behind the Camera*. Bradford: Flicks Books, 1995.

Lupino, Ida and Mary Ann Anderson. *Ida Lupino: Beyond the Camera*. Albany: Bear Manor Media, 2011.

Scheib, Ronnie. "Ida Lupino: Auteuress." *Film Comment* 16.1 (1980).

ANTHONY MANN

By Jeanine Basinger

Anthony Mann's movie career (1941–64) is a prime example with which to understand the history of the director's role in Hollywood. His career represents an individual's ability to define and maintain a personal style of movie-making within the Hollywood factory system. He succeeded in three distinctly different business and creative eras: 1) the peak of the studio system; 2) the years of transition in which the system collapsed; and 3) the emergence of a new international model of movie production. Over two decades, Mann successfully faced significant changes in social attitudes, business practices, leadership and technological developments that directly affected his role as director.

Anthony Mann arrived in Hollywood in 1941, a time in which the average American attended the movies on a weekly basis. The studio system was at its peak, and Mann was able to benefit from its positives: state-of-the-art production equipment; highly skilled support in all craft areas; movie star development programs; strong advertising, distribution and exhibition; a culturally sophisticated influx of European directors who fled Nazism; and large sums of available money. For a fledgling movie director, the Hollywood studio system was a film school of sorts, as it provided newcomers with mentorship, opportunities to observe and learn, and low-budget first-time directorial venues such as previews, shorts, screen tests, and B-level features. The years 1939–41 are often cited as an ideal time for young directors, the Director's Guild having organized and asserted the right to "first cut" of any motion picture. Thus, Mann's arrival was well-timed to benefit his education and growth.

In 1941, Mann was hired by Paramount Pictures and apprenticed to the great comedy director, Preston Sturges, who was planning and preparing *Sullivan's Travels* (a 1942 release). After Sturges's mentorship of Mann (which gave him an uncredited Assistant Directorship on the film) he was immediately assigned his first feature, a Paramount B-film,

Dr. Broadway (1942), which meant he would direct his first movie *inside* the establishment, at a high level, and fully prepared for the responsibility. He knew how to overcome the negatives of *Dr. Broadway* (a small, restricted budget; inexperienced leading actors; a short shooting schedule of only twenty days; and an underdeveloped 67-minute script) by making full use of the system's positives. These include: a working crew of Paramount professionals, in particular, cinematographer Theodor Sparkuhl, an experienced German expatriate who had photographed, among others, Renoir's *La Chienne* [France, 1931]; experienced supporting actors J. Carrol Naish and Eduardo Ciannelli; excellent equipment; access to Paramount's sets and wardrobe collections; a solid storyline (based on an idea by Borden Chase); and, above all, a minimum of supervision in the B-unit, which gave him freedom to create.

Mann turned *Dr. Broadway* into an entertaining movie with style and pace, using it to explore four cinematic devices that would become important in the definition of his later work: swish pans, the specific use of background settings, the meaningful placement of objects in the frame, and the manipulation of composition. *Dr. Broadway* proved Mann could direct successful features, but shortly after its completion, Paramount dissolved its B-film production unit. Instead of remaining as a large studio "house" director, Mann became a freelancer. Having gained the benefits to be had from the system, he embarked upon a less restricted career, which can be separated into specific periods: his early years of practice and learning, from 1942 to 1947; his emergence as a visual artist with a personal style (1947–50); his importance to the definition of the adult Western (1950–60); and his final years (1960–67).

After the completion of *Dr. Broadway* in 1942 until his breakthrough year of 1947, Mann directed an additional nine movies: five low-budget musicals and four minor atmospheric dramas. On the one hand, he presented light entertainment (*Moonlight in Havana*, 1942; *Nobody's Darling*, 1943; *My Best Gal*, 1944; *Sing Your Way Home*, 1945; and *Bamboo Blonde*, 1946) and on the other he addressed fears and subtexts (*Strangers in the Night*, 1944; *The Great Flamarion*, 1945; *Two O'Clock Courage*, 1945; and *Strange Impersonation*, 1946). These years of varied practice largely coincide with the years of US involvement in World War II (1941–45), so that Mann was faced with production shortages, absences of skilled co-workers who had been called into service, increased censorship related to home-front morale, and ceilings on material usage and budgetary expenditures. He was forced to master all areas of filmmaking, compensate for diminished production values, create with the minimum, and in particular, learn how to visually *suggest* for his audience. Since he was also directing films for a wartime audience undergoing stress, he developed a keen awareness of "directing" audiences as well as actors. These early years illustrate how one could become a successful movie director in the old studio system, and more importantly, how one had the opportunity to become a *good* director. Mann, unlike some others, made the most of his low-budget, varied opportunities to practice his craft and learn from experts. It is the difference between learning a trade and becoming an artist. He began to define cinema on his own terms, a crucial element in the success and endurance of a director's ability to put a personal stamp on studio manufactured work.

By 1947, Mann had completed films for studios both large (Paramount, Universal) and small (Republic, RKO). In 1947, after making a final film for RKO (*Desperate*) he moved away from studio production toward independent filmmaking. When Mann had arrived in 1941, the "ideal" studio system already had growing problems: labor troubles, socialist and communist lobbying, governmental investigations regarding theater chains and block-booking practices, and censorship pressures, as well as the impending war in Europe and the Far East, which threatened international markets. The war muted or postponed most of these issues, but in the postwar years, governmental decisions regarding theatre ownership and block-booking began the demise of studio power and control. Concurrently, Mann began his move away from these studio problems into an independent scene where he was afforded even greater creative freedom. His next two years (1947–49) were the second phase of his growth, from which he emerged as a unique visual artist. He joined Eagle-Lion (a company newly formed by a merger of the poverty-row Producer's Releasing Corporation and the powerful J. Arthur Rank Organization from England). It was an important step for Mann. At Eagle-Lion cinematic experimentation was encouraged. Mann was given larger budgets, fully-developed scripts with longer running times, and most important of all, a new collaborator, John Alton, a superb cinematographer who played brilliantly with light and shadow, and who responded well to Mann's desire for cinematic experimentation. Alton was a major influence on Mann. Together they created exciting, visually beautiful examples of a type of film that latter-day French critics would dub "film noir" (*T-Men*, 1947; *Raw Deal*, 1948; and *Reign of Terror*, 1949.) Noir was a formal style that united various genres (crime movies, women's films, melodramas, detective stories, murder mysteries, etc.) with cinematic creativity. The movies had a dark mood, a dark look and a dark attitude that appealed to audiences who had come through a depression followed by a long and difficult world war, which culminated in the invention of a weapon of mass destruction. Mann became a master of lighting contrasts, the use of shadows, manipulation of cinematic space, claustrophobic framing, camera movements both restrictive and free-flowing, and arrhythmic editing. He became a teller of violent stories about flawed heroes who did not earn the traditional happy ending.

The success of his noir films, particularly *T-Men*, brought Mann wider critical attention, taking him back into the studios. In 1949, he was invited to the prestigious MGM to direct. His first three movies showed his ability to maintain his own personal style and yet adjust to Hollywood's postwar desire to embrace new attitudes of social awareness: *Border Incident* (about the exploitation of Mexican farm workers), *Side Street* (a story of how the American dream can die for an ordinary young couple) and *Devil's Doorway* (an honest portrait of the plight of Native Americans in United States history).

In the Hollywood of the 1950s, the decade during which the former studio system would dissolve and disappear, Mann's eclectic experience directing a total of nineteen movies in nine years under differing conditions prepared him to not only survive, but succeed even further. In addition to no longer having monopolistic control of both manufacturing and selling their product, studios would face the influx of large numbers of foreign films (previously available largely only in urban areas), the House Un-American Activities Committee investigations which divided co-workers and destroyed talent, creating an atmosphere of suspicion and mistrust, and the ever-growing threat of television, which kept audiences at home. Hollywood fought back by introducing new technical effects (widescreen, 3D, and stereophonic sound); by changing to more realistic acting modes, such as "the Method," which created a new type of movie star; and by developing more mature, darker and violent stories that challenged censorship rules. None of these new developments would be difficult for Mann, who had moved forward out of studio apprenticeship, adjusting to every challenge change had brought him along the way.

In 1950, Mann was asked by Universal Pictures to replace director Fritz Lang on a Western to star James Stewart, *Winchester '73*. Mann was the right man in the right place at the right time. In a Western, his mastery of space could be applied to the entire out of doors, and he had already directed two, *Devil's Doorway* and the noirish *The Furies* (earlier in 1950). His pairing with Stewart led to outstanding work and growth for both of them. Together they would complete a total of eight films, five of which were ground-breaking Westerns:

Winchester '73, *The Naked Spur*, *Bend of the River*, *The Far Country* and *The Man From Laramie*. These films were highly successful, providing movie-goers with a contrast to the television Westerns of the era, being less simplistic, less heroic, and much more violent. Mann became a major force in the creation of the "adult Western" of the 1950s, in which the hero was flawed, as capable of violence and treachery as the villain. By the end of the 1950s, Mann was an A-list director whose directorial skills were adaptable to any genre, all production modes, and the story needs of the transitional era.

As Mann began his final career phase (1960–67), the power of the former studio system had been significantly diminished. Having never relied totally on the establishment, Mann was ready to step out onto an international stage, leaving Hollywood behind. He began working on an epic scale, directing movies that would appeal to foreign markets, and which would make use of a roster of international movie stars such as Italy's Sophia Loren, embrace the wide screen, and inspire audiences to leave their homes to go to the movie theater for cinematic spectacle. *El Cid*, *The Fall of the Roman Empire* and *The Heroes of Telemark* were shot on locations in Spain, Italy and Norway. They reflected the "new" Hollywood in which projects were no longer shot mostly on sound stages in California, and which were internationally financed.

A summary of Mann's directorial career reveals an historical triumph: he had gained the best from the old in training, moved away to more independent freedom when ready, and abandoned the past as times changed. By moving from studio to studio, from independent to independent, from genre to genre, he had received support and input from an impressive group of collaborators. He had shifted from light-hearted films to melodramas to noir crime and Westerns and onward. He was a thorough professional, a reliable director, but also a consummate artist. He survived changes in censorship, distribution and exhibition, developments in technology, and the collapse of the system that nurtured his growth. He had also developed a personal cinematic style in both form *and* content. The Mann films favored a simple story with a minimum of dialogue and a maximum of opportunities to "speak" with the camera. His preferred narrative concerned a flawed hero undergoing some kind of conflict (internal or external) that would be manifested in a physical journey. His formal style was based on his manipulation of composition, but he also mastered editing, lighting, camera movement, and the use of interior space for specific meanings, as well as use of an entire real landscape. Mann fused three levels of storytelling: the literal plot, which could be appreciated by any filmgoer; the psychological involvement in it by the hero, which would be reflected in the landscape or interiors surrounding him; and the emotional response inspired by the narrative for both hero and audience, which was a summation of plot, landscape, performance, response and cinematic technique. Referring to Mann's final Western (*Man of the West* with Gary Cooper), Jean-Luc Godard described it as "both course and discourse." Mann's films were always pure entertainment for a general audience, but they were also the highest level of cinematic achievement. He had defined for himself what movies were, and his sense that the visual story, with its use of cinematic devices for specific meanings, made him modern and prepared him to be the focus in the 1960s of the emerging "auteur theory," which would make directors into gods. The "auteur theory" was an idea that asked a simple question: within the commercial system, or in the collaborative world of filmmaking, could individual artists (of any type, be it director, producer, star, writer, designer, etc.) put a personal stamp on work that was being manufactured under studio control for a mass audience? In setting out to search for the answer, auteurists felt the best group to examine would be directors, since they were the most responsible for what ultimately appeared on the screen in all categories. Anthony Mann was a perfect candidate with which to test the case, perhaps better than any other.

However, Mann's sudden death at the age of sixty in 1967 removed him from major consideration by auteurists, because he was not available for their retrospectives, interviews and conversations. Although his work inspired maximum respect, he did not receive the analysis and coverage that some of his contemporaries did. It is not hard to speculate that as movies turned increasingly to independent production, Mann's career would have continued to flourish, and since he had been an early director in the emerging field of television in the late 1930s in New York, it is also easy to imagine he could have become the first great television visualist. Had Mann lived another decade, his could be the complete story of Hollywood directorial style.

Mann's final film, *A Dandy in Aspic*, was a spy thriller, shot in Berlin, which presented a shrewd combination of former Mann strengths: crime and melodrama, use of outdoor spaces, movie star power, slight story enhanced by style, and an international setting. Tragically, Mann died of a heart attack during the making of the movie, which was finished by its star, Laurence Harvey.

Biography

Anthony Mann was born Emile Anton Bundsman in San Diego, California, on June 30, 1906. For many years, his biographical background was shrouded in mystery, anecdote and misinformation. The child of intellectuals who were part of the Theosophical movement, Mann was exposed at an early age to art and culture. He participated in theater, both as actor and director, under the name of Anton Bundsman. After working as a director in both summer stock and on Broadway, Mann began his first connection with Hollywood in 1936 when David O. Selznick's company hired him to help Kay Brown scout actresses for the leading role in the planned production of *Gone with the Wind*. He also became a pre-war employee of early NBC Television in New York where he directed short-form narratives and documentaries.

In 1941 Mann relocated to Hollywood, arriving with directorial experience in theater, movie screen tests, and emerging television. Within a short period of time, he renamed himself "Anthony Mann" and began his successful film directing career.

Anthony Mann died of a heart attack on April 29, 1967 at the age of sixty.

Filmography

Dr. Broadway (1942)
Moonlight in Havana (1942)
Nobody's Darling (1943)
My Best Gal (1944)
Strangers in the Night (1944)
The Great Flamarion (1945)
Two O'Clock Courage (1945)
Sing Your Way Home (1945)
Strange Impersonation (1946)
The Bamboo Blonde (1946)
Desperate (1947)
Railroaded (1947)
T-Men (1947)
Raw Deal (1948)
He Walked By Night (1948)
Reign of Terror, aka *The Black Book* (1949)
Border Incident (1949)
Side Street (1949)
Devil's Doorway (1950)
The Furies (1950)

Winchester '73 (1950)
The Tall Target, (1951)
Bend of the River (1952)
The Naked Spur (1953)
Thunder Bay (1953)
The Glenn Miller Story (1954)
The Far Country (1955)
Strategic Air Command (1955)
The Man From Laramie (1955)
The Last Frontier, aka *The Savage Wilderness* (1955)
Serenade (1956)
Men in War (1957)
The Tin Star (1957)
God's Little Acre (1958)
Man of the West (1958)
Cimarron (1960)
El Cid (1961)
The Fall of the Roman Empire (1964)
The Heroes of Telemark (1965)
A Dandy in Aspic (1968)

Further reading

Alvarez, Max. *The Crime Films of Anthony Mann*, Jackson: University of Mississippi Press, 2014.

Basinger, Jeanine. *Anthony Mann*, Boston, MA: Twayne Publishers, 1979.

Basinger, Jeanine. *Anthony Mann, New and Expanded Edition*, Middletown, CT: Wesleyan University Press, 2007.

Darby, William. *Anthony Mann, The Film Career*, New York: McFarland and Company, 2009.

Kitses, Jim. *Horizons West*, Bloomington: Indiana University Press, 1970.

Missiaen, Pierre. *Anthony Mann*, Paris: Editions Universitaires, 1964.

VINCENTE MINNELLI

By Steven Cohan

Except for three films he directed toward the end of his career, Vincente Minnelli worked exclusively at Metro-Goldwyn-Mayer, making two pictures a year on average. As one of the primary directors in the acclaimed and profitable Arthur Freed production unit at MGM,

Minnelli joined a cohort of regular collaborators (performers, writers, set dressers and scenic designers, costumers, cinematographers, editors, music composers and arrangers) in what amounted to a repertory company. The stability of his collaboration with so many other creative artists working behind and in front of the camera under his direction, all at the top of their respective games, enabled his body of work to take on its distinctive visual style. The long tenure at MGM, moreover, enabled Minnelli to work repeatedly in the studio's major genres—musicals, melodramas, and comedies; to direct major stars such as Judy Garland, Fred Astaire, Gene Kelly, Spencer Tracy, Kirk Douglas, Frank Sinatra, and Shirley MacLaine, from whom he drew nuanced performances; and to be MGM's choice for directing prestigious properties, such as hit plays like *Brigadoon* (1954), *Kismet* (1955), and *Tea and Sympathy* (1956), and best sellers such as *Father of the Bride* (1950), *Lust for Life* (1956) and *Some Came Running* (1958).

Critically, Minnelli is now acclaimed for his masterful composition of shots and breathtaking, even innovative sense of color and visual design. When preparing a film, Minnelli drew for research and inspiration on his seeming exhaustive collection of notebooks containing magazine clippings, articles, photographs, and sketches. Although the Culver City studio was run as a hierarchical factory, Minnelli was freer than most other directors at MGM to disregard the protocols governing the various art and craft departments within that hierarchy. For example, Cedric Gibbons, MGM's longtime head of art direction, reportedly did not get along with Minnelli but still routinely deferred to the director whenever the latter broke with the art department's policies regarding, say, a plan for a bolder than usual color palette for a set design.

Likewise, Minnelli was freer than most of his MGM colleagues to ride a boom for filming of certain shots. This apparatus was expensive and difficult to maneuver, so it was ordinarily restricted to special uses; however, no one at MGM apparently questioned Minnelli whenever he requested a boom. His moving camera from on high—as when it sweeps back at the end of the "'S Wonderful" musical sequence in *An American in Paris* (1951) to observe a bird's eye view of the street below, with Gene Kelly finishing the number at one side of the frame and Georges Guétary at the other—became a Minnelli trademark. Just as characteristically, in the famous ball scene of *Madame Bovary* (1949), Minnelli's camera moves in circles around the room along with Emma Bovary (Jennifer Jones) and Rudolf (Louis Jourdan) as their waltzing gains in momentum, underscoring her sense of intoxication. At one point, Minnelli cuts to her blurred perspective of the chandeliers as they seem to move in dizzying circles above her head. Then, as Emma says she cannot breathe and is going to faint, one window after another behind the moving couple is smashed by a servant to let in air. Also intercut with this frenzied scene, in an adjoining room Emma's tipsy husband (Van Heflin) noisily knocks over a tray of drinking glasses as he stumbles toward the ballroom in search of her. Minnelli's camerawork and editing work together to evoke the passion and fatality overwhelming Emma while visualizing the narcissism in her overwrought imagination. The oscillation between Minnelli's proximity to and distance from Emma functions as the cinematic correlative for Flaubert's irony in the source novel.

Minnelli's fascination with every element of *mise-en-scène* (composition, color, set design, props) is not surprising given his professional background prior to turning to motion pictures. He started out in Chicago as a window dresser for the Marshall Field department store and was soon hired by the Balaban and Katz movie theatre chain to supervise costumes for their stage shows. Transferred to New York by that chain's owners, he ended up being responsible for both sets and costumes at Radio City Music Hall until Broadway lured him away to create revues and musicals. Despite Minnelli's unhappy and frustrating first effort in Hollywood at Paramount in 1937, the producer Arthur Freed convinced Minnelli to give motion pictures another try at MGM three years later. At first Minnelli helped out on several productions, learning the picture business from the ground up and making uncredited contributions to Freed musicals that were in trouble. The producer then assigned him to his first solo directing project, *Cabin in the Sky* (1943), an all African American musical with Lena Horne and Ethel Waters. The success of that risky endeavor led to Minnelli's first major directorial assignment, *Meet Me in St. Louis* (1944), where he began his short but important personal and professional relationship with Judy Garland. Married in 1945 (and divorced in 1951), the couple worked together on *The Clock* (1945) and *The Pirate* (1948) and Minnelli directed Garland's musical numbers in *Ziegfeld Follies* (1945) and *Til the Clouds Roll By* (1946).

More than just another vehicle for Garland, *Meet Me in St. Louis* is a landmark film and certainly among Minnelli's greatest. Simply put, it crystallized the integrated film musical as it came to be identified with MGM and the Arthur Freed unit, nicknamed the studio's "Royal Family." For with *Meet Me in St. Louis* Minnelli perfected an aesthetic of integration based on the seamlessness with which numbers and narrative flow into and out of each other in terms of their emotional coloration, visual design, and performance style so that the twin elements of a musical, narrative and number, are of apiece stylistically. For instance, "The Trolley Song" sung by Garland never seems like the intrusion on the narrative that it actually is; even though the number goes nowhere plot-wise, it heightens yet still shares the emotional texture of the scenes preceding and following it. The Halloween sequence, which comes immediately after "The Trolley Song," is not a number but plays like one due to how Minnelli stages, lights, and films the costumed children in their holiday ritual of "killing" neighbors with bags of flour and then celebrating before a roaring bonfire.

Minnelli was temperamentally well suited to the musical genre since he rarely displays a keen interest in tight narrative plotting but instead finds most compelling, as the building blocks of narrative, larger-than-life moments of intense emotions—precisely what musical numbers typically express. His musicals after *Meet Me in St. Louis*—*Yolanda and the Thief* (1945), *The Pirate*, and *An American in Paris*—take this tendency even further. Indeed, it is no stretch to say that these three later films musicalize the earlier film's Halloween sequence while enhancing its sense of exciting unworldliness. These musicals feature elaborate dream or daydream musical numbers incorporating dance with an eye-popping, otherworldly décor suggesting the overwhelming of an ordinary, unsatisfying world by fantasy; playing out on this landscape, the films draw their narratives from a longing for something more than the real world offers.

The ballet in *An American in Paris*, the most well-known example, essentially replays the film's romance plot but filters it through the heightened emotional imagery enabled by a dreamer's perspective. Playing an American painter living in postwar Paris, Gene Kelly reflects on his unhappy romance with Leslie Caron and the ballet is his daydream, a fantasy dramatizing his feelings about love, art, and Paris. Divided into segments according to the musical arrangement of the Gershwin suite, the color palette, set designs, and costumes are modeled on Impressionist and Post-Impressionist artists who, stimulating the Kelly character's imagination as a painter, personify the reason he came to Paris: Dufy, Renoir, Rousseau, Van Gogh, Toulouse-Lautrec. Logically, the dream ballet has no causal effect on the plot, since the long number also ends with Kelly again losing Caron—at once his omnipresent muse and elusive lover throughout the ballet. Yet, the film's formal structure implies some kind of integrative relation of the ballet with the narrative, at least psychologically and intuitively: immediately after the ballet's conclusion, Caron leaves her fiancé and returns to Kelly. *An American in Paris* ends with their embrace.

The Minnelli musical following *An American in Paris* is different yet as great an achievement. *The Band Wagon* (1953), Minnelli's sole backstage musical, self-reflexively comments on the genre and on his own artistry, too. It is formally structured according to the oppositions of popular entertainment and elitist art, hoofing and ballet, an old pro and young star—in short, differences personified for the narrative and the choreography by Fred Astaire and Cyd Charisse. Its formal momentum, moreover, pushes toward what amounts to a plotless mini-revue in the final forty-five minutes or so, with one number after another representing the show featuring those two stars. Before then, the musical is more plot heavy, going backstage to dramatize how a Broadway musical meant to entertain gets derailed by arty pretensions on the part of its director (Jack Buchanan). He strives to give "a nice little musical comedy" greater heft and stature as high art. He thus builds up the show's allusions to the Faust legend with complicated, unworkable stage machinery, elaborate special effects that drag down or stop cold the dancing, busy and distracting sets, and overly elaborate balletic choreography until, when the show moves to New Haven for its out of town tryout, this bloated production lays an egg. Thereafter, Astaire sells his collection of nineteenth century and modernist French paintings to refinance the show and takes over at the helm, stripping away the layers of stuffy, pretentious artifice to reveal the purer entertainment beneath. The finale to this revised and enlivened show, "The Girl Hunt Ballet," works much as the fantasy numbers do in other Minnelli musicals. An affectionate send-up of hardboiled detective fiction, this ballet stands out as the successful reformulation of what had earlier bombed in New Haven due to that first version's arty pretensions and clutter.

Given its endorsement of popular entertainment over high art, it is tempting to view *The Band Wagon* as Minnelli's rebuttal to high-brow reviewers who unfavorably compared *An American in Paris* with the British art house hit, *The Red Shoes* (1948). And with the pointed contrast between the good and bad versions of a stage musical in *The Band Wagon*, Minnelli may also have been having some fun twitting his own public persona as a director more interested in cinematic style than anything else. After all, in "The Girl Hunt Ballet" Minnelli successfully and subtly deploys every mechanical device (such as smoke machines) and choreographic tropes (such as ballet lifts) that had been mishandled and critiqued in that tryout run as phony "high art."

An American in Paris and *The Band Wagon* are just a few of the numerous films Minnelli made about artists and their struggles with creativity. *The Bad and the Beautiful* (1952) explores the obsessions of a filmmaker (Kirk Douglas) modeled on producer David O. Selznick.

Lust for Life is a biography of tormented painter Vincent Van Gogh (Douglas again). *Some Came Running* revolves around a novelist (Frank Sinatra) suffering from writer's block who returns to his home town after many years away. These films, moreover, exemplify Minnelli's accomplishment in a genre other than the musical, namely, melodrama. In fact, after *An American in Paris* and *The Band Wagon* and with the exception of *Gigi* (1958), his finest films during the fifties were melodramas.

With Hollywood's move to widescreen processes in the 1950s, Minnelli's melodramas in CinemaScope—*The Cobweb* (1955), *Lust for Life*, *Tea and Sympathy*, *Some Came Running*, *Home from the Hill* (1960)—display an extraordinary command of visual depth in the screen's new and, in the hands of many other directors, often unwieldy rectangular shape. If anything epitomizes the sophisticated yet well-crafted Minnelli style in these films, it is his subtle attention to detail in both the foreground and background of the framed cinematic image. Oftentimes the image seems supersaturated with visual information in terms of its dense materiality and bold coloring, and either one does not know where to look first or the eye is instantly drawn to a seemingly irrelevant point inside the frame. In the climax of *Some Came Running*, Shirley MacLaine's former lover crazily waves a revolver as he stalks her and Sinatra, and behind these three figures making their way through crowds, the lurid, streaking colors of the carnival setting bleed through the frame to create the scene's hallucinatory effect, its prediction of the violence just moments away. More subtly, earlier in the film the heavily decorated kitchen set of schoolteacher Martha Hyer's (Gwen French) house, which represents her hideaway from passion, visually fills up the frame comfortably yet somewhat *too* fully, implying a critique of the bourgeois life that Sinatra craves yet distrusts in falling for her. Due to Minnelli's carefully deliberated sense of detail, either scene can be considered a master class in how a melodrama works through color, music, lighting, and props as well as action.

Minnelli's melodramas, finally, are thematically compelling for their progressive treatment of gender, a recurring concern that situates his films in their postwar cultural contexts. *Tea and Sympathy*, *The Cobweb*, and *Home from the Hill* feature young men struggling against the machismo belittling their more boyish, sensitive, and hence deviant expressions of masculinity. A well-known scene in *Tea and Sympathy* shows John Kerr, suspected by peers and teachers of being *too* different, asking his more "manly" roommate to show him how to walk like a man. The scene enacts the very performative basis of a masculine norm—it is something one *learns* as opposed to something one *is*, raising the possibility of alternate masculinities. In other melodramas, Minnelli pushes the virile personae of stars such as Kirk Douglas, Frank Sinatra, and Robert Mitchum to their breaking points, bringing out the self-destructiveness arising from the cultural mandate that men must conform to an emotionless and hard masculinity.

Minnelli pursues this theme in his musicals and comedies, too. "The Girl Hunt Ballet" uses Astaire's slender yet lithe body to send up the hard-boiled detective, much as Gene Kelly's more muscular yet very flashy itinerant actor in *The Pirate* impersonates (and sends up, too) a swashbuckling outlaw in order to impress Judy Garland. In *Designing Woman* (1957), Minnelli's best comedy about gender relations, choreographer Jack Cole, with a physique much like Astaire's, plays an effeminate dance director whose heterosexuality is suspect, even though he has photos of his wife and children to prove he is straight. In the finale, a rowdy brawl between mobsters and theatre-folk in an alley, Cole makes use of his physical prowess as a dancer to end the fight single-handedly and with great finesse, while a beaten Gregory Peck looks on, helpless and awestruck.

Designing Woman endorses a view of alternate masculinities but it also typifies the extent to which, in almost all Minnelli's films, ambiguous portrayals of sexuality are thematically expressed as—some may prefer to say, displaced onto—plots raising questions about gender conformity and nonconformity. For this reason Minnelli's body of work has received a great deal of attention for its queer subtexts. Several factors intersect to warrant such interest on the part of Minnelli scholars. First, censorship restrictions on representations of homosexuality were rigorously enforced during his tenure at MGM, and the elimination or softening of controversial subject matter often resulted in an overcoding of gender issues with resonances of sexual dissidence or alternate expressions of desire. Second, Minnelli's deliberated and frequently excessive or exaggerated visual style, dominated by his interest in décor, costuming, and color, lends itself to camp appreciation of his imagery, and the same has to be said for his thematic preoccupation with gender as a performance. Third, a historical source for that camp reception can be traced to the director's own background as part of the sexually liberal New York theater set of the thirties, and later as a member of the Freed unit, where many if not most of the people working there were gay, lesbian, or bisexual. Fourth, whether Minnelli himself was straight, gay, or bisexual has remained an open question for his biographers; this very ambiguity, however, suggests a queer authorial sensibility radiating through his films, which continues to move and speak to gay audiences today.

Whatever sense one makes of its personal impact on Minnelli, the studio system and MGM in particular provided him with the best working conditions for his talents and tastes, enabling him to explore his creativity as a director fully and happily. By the same token, following his Academy Award for directing *Gigi*, the studio system that had fostered Minnelli's creativity was in the process of being dismantled. His films after *Home from the Hill* became increasingly more lackluster due to a combination of factors: in addition to the turmoil at MGM as it downsized, there is apparent disinterest in some projects on his part, severe miscasting of some lead players, and an obvious loss of editorial control. His final film project enabled him to fulfill a longtime goal of finally directing in a film his beloved daughter with Judy Garland, Liza Minnelli, who at that time was a major Oscar-winning star in her own right. However, *A Matter of Time* (1976) was taken out of his hands and butchered by the producer to the point of incoherence before its unsuccessful release, marking a sad coda to an otherwise distinguished career.

Biography

Vincente Minnelli was born on February 28, 1903 in Chicago, Illinois, to theatrical parents. During his childhood, the family moved to Delaware, Ohio, where he was schooled and showed a talent for art. After high school graduation, he moved to Chicago and New York City, before settling in Los Angeles in 1940. For most of his career as a film director he worked at MGM. He died on July 25, 1986.

Filmography

Strike Up the Band (1940) uncredited
Babes on Broadway (1941) uncredited
Panama Hattie (1942) uncredited
Cabin in the Sky (1943)
I Dood It (1943)
Meet Me in St. Louis (1944)
The Clock (1945)
Ziegfeld Follies (1945) several musical sequences
Yolanda and the Thief (1945)
Undercurrent (1946)
Til the Clouds Roll By (1946) uncredited
The Pirate (1948)
Madame Bovary, (1949)

Father of the Bride (1950)
Father's Little Dividend (1951)
An American in Paris (1951)
Lovely to Look At (1952) uncredited
The Bad and the Beautiful (1952)
The Story of Three Loves (1953) "Mademoiselle" segment
The Band Wagon (1953)
The Long, Long Trailer (1953)
Brigadoon (1954)
The Cobweb (1955)
Kismet (1955)
Lust for Life (1956)
Tea and Sympathy (1956)
Designing Woman (1957)
The Seventh Sin (1957) uncredited
Gigi (1958)
The Reluctant Debutante (1958)
Some Came Running (1958)
Home from the Hill (1960)
Bells Are Ringing (1960)
The Four Horsemen of the Apocalypse (1962)
Two Weeks in Another Town (1962)
The Courtship of Eddie's Father (1963)
Goodbye Charlie (1964)
The Sandpiper (1965)
On a Clear Day You Can See Forever (1970)
A Matter of Time (1976)

Further reading

Griffin, Mark. *A Hundred More Hidden Things: The Life and Films of Vincente Minnelli*. New York: DaCapo Press, 2010.

Harvey, Stephen. *Directed by Vincente Minnelli*. New York: Harper and Row, 1989.

Knox, Donald. *The Magic Factory: How MGM Made* An American in Paris. New York: Praeger, 1973.

McElhaney, Joe, ed. *Vincente Minnelli: The Art of Entertainment*. Detroit: Wayne State University Press, 2009.

Naremore, James. *The Films of Vincente Minnelli*. New York: Cambridge University Press, 1993.

Tinkcom, Matthew. *Working Like a Homosexual: Camp, Capital, Cinema*. Durham, NC: Duke University Press, 2002.

MAX OPHÜLS

By *Walter Metz*

There is a stunning scene in the middle of Max Ophüls' *Letter from an Unknown Woman* (1948) in which a lothario, Stefan Brand (Louis Jourdan), woos one of many lovers, Lisa Berndle (Joan Fontaine). He brings her to a restaurant where a machine operated by the proprietor rotates backdrops next to a table inside a fake train car, such that it appears the diners are speeding through the European landscape. Brand explains that this way, they can see all of Europe—from the beaches of Spain to the wintery Alps—while enjoying their dinner, and without moving. The film is narrated in flashback by Lisa via a letter she has written to an aged Brand, whose insatiable lust has caused him to forget her (twice!). After his mute manservant indicates that only he could be such a cad as to forget the darling Lisa, Brand leaves to surely die in the duel with Lisa's husband. *Letter from an Unknown Woman* offers a meta-cinematic meditation on the relationship between Eros and Thanatos, between love and death.

Part of a tetralogy of late 1940s Hollywood films by German exile filmmaker Max Ophüls, *Letter from an Unknown Woman* laments the destruction of Europe at the hands of the Nazis. The irony of Ophüls' American films is that they depict a European world that can only exist in the Hollywood cinema, as the real version lay in rubble. To return to *Letter from an Unknown Woman* at our moment in time serves two useful purposes. First, we can understand how important Ophüls is to contemporary American cinema.

In his triumphant film, *The Grand Budapest Hotel* (2014), Wes Anderson indicates that his script was "inspired by the writings of Stefan Zweig". The work of a nearly forgotten Austrian writer who committed suicide in Brazil in 1942 lamenting the Nazi destruction of European civilization is an odd choice for the quirky American comedian Anderson. And yet, via Zweig, *The Grand Budapest Hotel* features the same thematic obsessions as an Ophüls film—the human sexual drive for connection is set amidst the destruction of Europe. The hotel in Anderson's film is filled with sex-obsessed patrons, oblivious to the Nazi destruction of their world.

Letter From an Unknown Woman was based on a 1922 novella by Zweig, an Austrian writer who was part of a group of Viennese intellectuals obsessed with sex and death, including Sigmund Freud and Arthur Schnitzler, the latter of whom was the source for Ophüls' crowning achievement, the 1950 European art film, *La Ronde*, in which a series of ten sexual encounters connect a lowly prostitute to a prince, again set in a fantasy studio holding at bay the fact that the Europe depicted in reality lay in ashes.

Despite the glorious box office failures of all four of his American films, Ophüls has had a profound effect on contemporary Hollywood filmmaking. Paul Thomas Anderson, director of such films as *There Will Be Blood* (2007) and *The Master* (2012) comments lovingly on the moving camera on the commentary track of the Criterion Collection's release of *The Earrings of Madame de ...* (1953), one of Ophüls' French art films. Stanley Kubrick, whose favourite film was reportedly another French art film *Le Plaisir* (1952), emulated Ophüls' roaming camera in films ranging from *Paths of Glory* (1957) to *The Shining* (1980). Kubrick explained that Ophüls' camera "went through every wall and every floor". In his final work, *Eyes Wide Shut* (1999), Kubrick exposes not only the aesthetic debt to Ophüls, but also a thematic one. Adapting Arthur Schnitzler's *Traumnovelle* (1926), Kubrick's film adapts Ophüls' depiction of morally decayed Vienna as a trance-like New York City, shot on a soundstage in England. *Eyes Wide Shut* is the *La Ronde* of the post-Cold War era.

Secondly, and more interesting for the vicissitudes of the study of film, a return to Max Ophüls' *Letter from an Unknown Woman* provides an opportunity for re-assessing the psychological importance of the twentieth century's most important art form for a twenty-first century future. In the 1980s, feminist film criticism rightfully and necessarily shifted the study of film away from a Romantic, auteurist celebration of the greatness of male film artists toward a genre-based understanding of how film engages in a complex representation of the human subject's desires. The melodramas of Max Ophüls, particularly the American ones, such as *Caught* (1949), *The Reckless Moment* (1949), and especially *Letter from an Unknown Woman* served as the perfect nexus for academic feminism's project. Built on a radical re-reading of Sigmund Freud via Jacques Lacan, Ophüls was understood as activating cinema as a desiring machine, capable of unearthing the female subjectivity otherwise censored by patriarchal culture. The all-consuming desire of Lisa for Stefan in *Letter from an Unknown Woman* served as the terrain over which questions of gender politics could be productively discussed: Was Lisa's foolish desire for Stefan merely patriarchal hero-worship, reinforcing men's power over women? Or, conversely, was Lisa's desire uncontainable by the forces of the Hollywood film industry, by male directors, and by the generic constraints of its stories? Was Ophüls' cinema finally able to visualize what Freud was not, the actively sexual woman?

The academic study of Ophüls has nearly completely abated since the 1980s, yet it seems possible to re-group. Paul Thomas Anderson leads us in the direction of Ophüls' undeniable aesthetic importance. Ophüls' intricate mise-en-scène (the rooms in *La Ronde* are loaded with statues, candlesticks, paintings, and much of the material objects of Europe at the turn of the nineteenth into the twentieth centuries) and camera movements (every time Lisa runs after Stefan in *Letter from an Unknown Woman*, Ophüls' camera follows on dollies, tracks and cranes to be right there with her) are undeniably beautiful and influential. However, Kubrick's *Eyes Wide Shut* and Wes Anderson's *The Grand Budapest Hotel* lead us more toward the thematic obsessions of Ophüls' work. They indicate that our fixation with Eros leads inexorably to Thanatos, our inability to keep our productive love and creativity in check against the dark nature of our animalistic souls. We are inexorably drawn like Stefan to the carriages awaiting us to take us to the duel with death that shall end us all.

Ophüls' work is, at the same time, distinctly biographical, historical and political. He lived the tension between America and Europe, and it shows up in profound ways in his films, ways that have been occluded by prior analytical methods. As one example, in *Letter from an Unknown Woman*, the elegant yet very American Joan Fontaine plays Lisa as a smitten teenager, obsessed with the European artist Stefan (played by the highly accented Louis Jourdan). In order to impress him, Lisa studies dance to become more graceful. Lisa's teenage friend out in the courtyard responds completely differently to Stefan's piano playing, screeching with an annoying American accent, "I wish he'd stop that playing." Lisa discards her American identity, enamoured by the culture and civility of Europe, not seeing its dark side of decadence and violence, as Stefan sleeps with every available woman who presents herself to him.

Ophüls' image is filled with pregnant images that allegorize the decaying history of the twentieth century. To further improve herself, Lisa goes to a record library to listen to the works of the great composers whom Stefan plays on his piano. In a stunning image, Lisa puts away a Wagner record to seek out the next higher shelf, labelled Mozart. In allegorical form, Lisa chooses the good German over the anti-Semitic one, all the time not seeing that this choice is of little consequence: her American identity will be forever destroyed by her choice, not of Romantic or classical opera, but of Stefan.

For his part, Stefan gives up his musical career after a disastrous run in America, while Lisa ruins her life by leaving her husband for the cad Stefan late in the film, when she sees him at a performance of

Mozart's *Die Zauberflöte*. Alas, there is no magical music in an Ophüls film! Lisa and her illegitimate son with Stefan, eponymously named, both die of typhus contracted in a quarantined train car. The spectre of Auschwitz looms large over those Ophüls images purportedly set in Vienna in 1900. Like other German émigrés, such as Bertolt Brecht or Douglas Sirk, Ophüls defines a Europe in ruins, protected only by a capitalist America that might save the people, but will seal the fate of the culture that once thrived there.

In *The Reckless Moment* (1949), Ophüls' last American film, the post-war housewife, Lucia Harper (Joan Bennett) defends her teenage daughter from ruin at the hands of shady European blackmailers. In the course of events, Lucia falls in love with Martin Donnelly, a heavily accented Irish hoodlum played by James Mason. Martin too has fallen in love with America, and thus sacrifices himself to keep danger away from his beloved. Recoiling from Ophüls' swirl of Thanatos around Eros, Lucia staggers back to her American suburban home. In the film's final moments, her absent husband calls from Berlin, where he is building bridges. It is a brutal Ophüls irony: the Europe of evil is not quite destroyed, coming to roost in America, but despite that, the Marshall Plan rebuilds the infastructure of Germany, hoping that the next generation will pull its records from the Mozart shelf instead of the Wagner one.

Ophüls, for his part, is building different bridges than the physical ones in 1949 Berlin. His films, by obsessively returning to Vienna in 1900, build a bridge to the past, hoping desperately to unearth the scene of the crime. How did the promise of nineteenth-century Romanticism turn so deadly? With the Andersons—Paul Thomas and Wes—we might be able to retrace Ophüls' tracks and find for ourselves the answers that this great German filmmaker died seeking.

Biography

Born in Saarbrücken, Germany, in 1902 as Maximillian Oppenheimer, the filmmaker known as Max Ophüls was the son of Jewish textile merchants. He decided as a teenager to pursue the theatrical arts. At first merely an unsuccessful actor, Ophüls then directed his first play at age 21, sparking a career that led to the Vienna theatre world, where he embarked on a career-long symbiotic relationship with playwright Arthur Schnitzler. In the early 1930s, Ophüls moved to UFA, the German film studio in Berlin, where he first apprenticed under Anatole Litvak. Later in the 1930s, Ophüls directed films throughout Europe, settling in France in 1938. In an all-too-common German-Jewish exile's tale of that ill-fated decade, and as German military aggression mounted, Ophüls fled first to Switzerland and then to Hollywood. From 1941 to 1947, Ophüls found few defenders of his artistic mastery of mise-en-scène and the German flowing camera for which he is now famous. Finally, in 1947, Robert Siodmak was able to ensure that Ophüls direct a Douglas Fairbanks, Jr. vehicle, *The Exile*, after which Ophüls, in the span of twenty-four months, made three exquisite, though financially unsuccessful American melodramas—*Letter from an Unknown Woman* (1948), *Caught* (1949), and *The Reckless Moment* (1949). Afterward, Ophüls returned to France where he completed a string of international art house masterpieces, including *La Ronde* (1950), an adaptation of Schnitzler's play; *Le Plaisir* (1952), an omnibus film of Guy de Maupassant short story adaptations; and *Lola Montès* (1955), a grandiose colour film shot in widescreen Cinemascope. The film stands as one of the great monuments to art cinema, but was a commercial failure at the box office. Deeply wounded, Ophüls retreated to the theatre, and died of heart failure in Hamburg, Germany in 1957 without having completed another film.

Filmography

Die verkaufte Braut [*The Bartered Bride*] (Germany, 1932)
Liebelei (Germany, 1933)
La Signora di Tutti [*Everybody's Woman*] (Italy, 1934)
Komedie om geld [*The Trouble With Money*] (The Netherlands, 1936)
Yoshiwara (France, 1937)
Werther (France, 1938)
De Mayerling à Sarajevo (France, 1940)
The Exile (1947)
Letter from an Unknown Woman (1948)
Caught (1949)
The Reckless Moment (1949)
La Ronde (France, 1950)
Le Plaisir (France, 1952)
Madame de … [*The Earrings of Madame de …*] (France, 1953)
Lola Montès (France 1955)

Further reading

Bacher, Lutz. *Max Ophüls in the Hollywood Studios*. New Brunswick, NJ: Rutgers UP, 1996.
Metz, Walter. "Who am I in this story?: On the Film Adaptations of Max Ophüls." *Literature/Film Quarterly*. 34.4 (2006): 285–93.

White, Susan M. *The Cinema of Max Ophüls: Magisterial Vision and the Figure of Woman*. New York: Columbia UP, 1995.

Wexman, Virginia Wright (ed.). *Letter from an Unknown Woman*. New Brunswick, NJ: Rutgers UP, 1986.

Willeman, Paul (ed.). *Ophüls*. London: BFI, 1978.

Williams, Alan. *Max Ophüls and the Cinema of Desire: Style and Spectacle in Four Films*. New York: Arno P, 1976.

OTTO PREMINGER

By Patrick Keating

During the original heyday of auteurist criticism, Otto Preminger was one of the most celebrated Hollywood directors. In *Cahiers du Cinéma*, Jacques Rivette praised Preminger's mise-en-scène, and the editors of *Movie* dedicated the second edition of their landmark journal to the director's works.[1] Though Andrew Sarris refrained from including Preminger in his "Pantheon," he counted the director among other notable auteurist favorites such as Nicholas Ray, Vincente Minnelli, and Douglas Sirk in the second tier of great directors.[2] At the time Sarris was defining his canon, Preminger was working at the height of his powers, producing and directing a series of ambitious films featuring ensemble casts and addressing serious social issues, such as *Anatomy of a Murder* (1959), *Exodus* (1960) and *Advise & Consent* (1962). Though Preminger continued directing films throughout the 1960s and 1970s, his critical reputation began to wane after the initial burst of enthusiasm from the auteurists. Some directors' prestige survived the decline of the auteur theory, but for a while it appeared that Preminger's might not.[3]

In a recent essay on the 1949 film noir *Whirlpool*, Christian Keathley elegantly summarizes one of the challenges of writing about Preminger. He writes, "While Ray, Sirk, and Minnelli mounted their critique of American capitalist society indirectly, though carefully designed *mise-en-scène* that communicated visually things that couldn't then be addressed directly, Preminger took the opposite approach," selecting themes such as sex and drugs as the literal subject matter of his controversial films, thereby building a public reputation as a provocateur.[4] Preminger's works were long considered too "obvious" to merit sustained scholarly attention, though happily several thoughtful contemporary scholars have attempted to rehabilitate Preminger's reputation, either by denying the charge of obviousness, or by examining more closely how that effect of obviousness is constructed.

Preminger began his career as an actor and then found success as a theater director, first at Max Reinhardt's Josefstadt Theater in Vienna and then in New York City after emigrating to the United States in 1935.[5] Having directed one film in Austria and two more in Hollywood in the 1930s, Preminger established himself as a major filmmaker with *Laura* (1944) at Twentieth Century-Fox, taking a story that could have served as an upper-class murder mystery and adding layers of depth by hinting at the protagonist's disturbing obsession with Laura, a woman he believes to be dead. Preminger's subsequent output at the studio was eclectic, including several other notable entries in the noir canon, such as *Fallen Angel* (1945) and *Where the Sidewalk Ends* (1950); two period comedy films he directed or co-directed in support of an ailing Ernst Lubitsch; and the two early CinemaScope productions *River of No Return* (1954) and *Carmen Jones* (1954), the latter featuring an all-African American cast with Dorothy Dandridge in the starring role.

While at Twentieth Century-Fox, Preminger often produced his own films, and in the 1950s he established himself as an independent producer. Working outside the studio system allowed Preminger to tackle more controversial subject matter, including topics that were in direct violation of Hollywood's self-censorship norms. Two of Preminger's films from this decade were released without the Production Code seal: *The Moon Is Blue* (1953), a romantic comedy accused of taking its subject matter – the attempted seduction of a "professional virgin" – too lightly; and *The Man with the Golden Arm* (1955), a drama depicting the taboo topic of drug addiction. Both films influenced subsequent changes to the Production Code, and Preminger took advantage of the loosening restrictions to address such difficult topics as rape, in *Anatomy of a Murder*; homosexuality, in *Advise & Consent*; and abortion, in *The Cardinal* (1963). Increasingly, Preminger would present these controversial issues by situating them within institutional contexts. Whereas *The Moon Is Blue* focuses on a small cast of characters, Preminger's later films feature large ensemble casts and extended running lengths, allowing him to dissect the workings of particular institutions, ranging from the U.S. Senate to the Catholic Church. For instance, *Anatomy of a Murder* rejects the conventions of the detective-driven murder mystery in favor of an examination of the courtroom itself. By the end of the film, there are aspects of the central crime that we may not fully understand, but we have learned in great detail how legal norms constrain the ways that the crime may be interpreted and discussed.

In *Movie*'s 1962 issue, Preminger was described as a director with an "objective" style. According to this account, his goal is "to present characters, actions, and issues clearly and without prejudice" and thereby "to show events, not demonstrate his feelings about them."[6] Even in this brief quotation, one can find three distinct but related meanings for the crucial but difficult term "objective." First, the term might refer to the moral stance of the director: the sense that he tries to represent characters "without prejudice." In ensemble films such as *Exodus* and *Advise & Consent*, Preminger presents a large cast of characters who possess conflicting political positions, and yet his directorial strategy does not mark any one position as unambiguously heroic or any other position as unambiguously villainous. Second, Preminger's style might be considered objective in the sense that it is unusually clear and lucid. Though Preminger was a master of camera movement, his compositions are less cluttered than those of more baroque stylists like Max Ophüls. Third, Preminger's style is objective in the sense that he generally eschews subjective techniques. Whereas Hitchcock routinely employs point-of-view shots to encourage spectators to identify with major characters, Preminger favors a more detached style of presentation, often staging two or more characters in medium shot and using the long take to present this ensemble to the audience in a seemingly neutral way. The comparison with the often flamboyant Hitchcock made Preminger's visual style seem remarkably restrained, especially given Preminger's attention-grabbing preference for hot-button social issues.[7] All three senses of the term "objective" can be related: Preminger abstains from moral judgments precisely by offering the viewer a clear but detached view of his characters, without soliciting strong identification with any one character in particular.

Preminger's handling of a riverbank scene in *River of No Return* (1954) won special praise from influential writers Charles Barr and V. F. Perkins for its sensitive use of CinemaScope's extended frame.[8] When Marilyn Monroe's character Kay drops her bag into the river, Preminger does not use elaborate camera movement or complex montage to emphasize its significance. Rather, the bag simply drifts into the background, available for interpretation to any viewer who wishes to contemplate it. In this way, Preminger showed how CinemaScope offered particular advantages for filmmakers who grounded their technique in the nuanced use of mise-en-scène.[9]

Subsequent scholars have considered the implications of these ideas, sometimes by further refining theoretical concepts like detachment and lucidity, and sometimes by questioning the notion of objectivity altogether. For instance, in her thoughtful analysis of *Advise & Consent*, Deborah Thomas re-examines the concept of detachment, describing Preminger's approach as "remarkably unrhetorical in its refusal to persuade."[10] She insists that this characterization does not mean that the camera simply remains planted on one spot, in the manner of a cold and neutral observer. Quite the contrary: Preminger uses the wide screen and the mobile camera to reveal a richly detailed world. Far from expressing coldness, Preminger's detachment indicates a "compassionate interest [that] extends across a broad sweep of characters."[11]

Other scholars who focus on Preminger's alleged objectivity find the director distinctive in his handling of point of view: he is seemingly clear yet ultimately refuses to offer us access to a character's deepest motivations. Situating their analysis within the context of George M. Wilson's discussion of "modes of non-omniscience," John Gibbs and Douglas Pye write:

> Preminger places us epistemologically in relation to the characters in something of the way they are placed to each other – except, of course, that for us they are characters seen through Preminger's direction, both of the actors and of the camera. But what we see of them is what they do. Another way of getting at this is that Preminger's method doesn't imply either a claim to know his characters, especially to know exactly what motivates them to act as they do, or an invitation to us to think that we can know them.[12]

In *Bonjour Tristesse* (1958) and other films, we arrive at the end of the film feeling as though there are key aspects of character psychology that we do not fully understand. While many films may leave a character's mental state ambiguous, what makes these cases important is the paradox – immediately after watching a film that appears to have been shot in an otherwise clear, straightforward, and unpretentious style, we are nevertheless made aware of our own lack of knowledge. This paradox is a key reason why Preminger once again has become a fascinating subject for scholars: his style appears obvious, or objective, or clear, and yet the initial appearance of surface-level clarity gives way to a deeper awareness of opacity.

To better understand this paradox, it might be useful to consider the relationship between two similar but distinct concepts, omniscience and omnipresence. One familiar framework for understanding the classical Hollywood cinema centers on the observation that the camera generally has the power to go anywhere, cutting or moving freely from character to character, or space to space. However, recent work by V. F. Perkins urges us to use the metaphor of omnipresence more cautiously. He writes, "To be in a world is to know the partiality of knowledge and the boundedness of vision – to be aware that there is always a bigger picture. To observe a world humanly is to do so from a viewpoint."[13] To tell a story about a world is to tell a story about a place where, by definition, there is infinitely more to be known than anyone can possibly know. And one reason for this sense of restriction is spatial: the spectator experiences this world from a point of view, which is inevitably limited no matter how much that point of view shifts around from character to character or from space to space.

In spite of these restrictions, a film may still explore the concept of omniscience as a theme, and, correspondingly, it might offer us a fantasy of omnipresence. Historically, many cinematic techniques have been used to offer us such a fantasy: cross-cutting, impossible angles, elaborate camera moves, location shooting. In their different ways, these techniques give us the momentary sense that we can travel anywhere instantly. And yet, following Perkins's line of thinking, this sense of omnipresence is just a fantasy: to see the world from one point of view is to not see it from another. In the cinema as in life, our vision is inevitably limited.

Just as Preminger's narrational strategy seems to promise omniscience only to leave us aware of gaps in our knowledge, his stylistic approach seems to promise omnipresence only to leave us aware of just how limited our perspective in space really is. Preminger might take us to a spectacular exotic location, such as Austria or Israel, offering to immerse us in that world as we enter a widescreen frame, only to stage his scene inside a commonplace room providing a mere glimpse of the outside world through a tiny doorway. A brief example from *Bunny Lake Is Missing* (1965) may serve as an illustration. The film tells the story of an American woman, Ann (Carol Lynley), whose daughter Bunny disappears from a London daycare center. During the investigation, the detective (Laurence Olivier) develops doubts about the daughter's existence – doubts that the spectator is encouraged to share. In the end, the daughter is revealed to be real, her disappearance engineered by Ann's possessive brother. Throughout, we experience the epistemological limitations discussed by Gibbs and Pye, as we struggle to understand the psychology of characters who initially appear easily readable. Preminger's staging reinforces this tension between access and restriction. In one shot, Newhouse (Olivier) listens skeptically to Ann while they examine the school's kitchen. After picking up a bowl of junket, Newhouse proceeds to eat nonchalantly while she explains her concerns. He wanders over to the back door and opens it, to illustrate how Bunny might have escaped, but Ann raises a plausible objection to his theory. Newhouse registers the objection, but continues to insist that there is nothing to worry about, finishing his junket and then moving to leave the room. Preminger films this scene in one of his characteristic long takes. The camera starts out in the front room, and then dollies forward to enter the back room. With this brisk through-the-door movement, Preminger hints at his ability to take us anywhere – and yet, he refuses to push the camera into the back room entirely, instead taking a position behind Ann's left shoulder, where the advantages of sharing her point of view are balanced by several disadvantages: we cannot see her face, and we cannot see very well what is outside the door, a wide open space with cars, police, and pedestrians that we only glimpse for a moment before the detective shuts the door and exits the room entirely. The result is a heightened awareness that the world extends beyond the room we are in, combined with a reminder that we will never be able to explore that world fully. The effect of Preminger's approach is not to give us the sense that the world would be knowable if only we had a more reliable storyteller to guide us. Instead, it is to suggest that the world may not be entirely knowable simply because it is a world, a place of irreducible complexity that we experience only through the boundaries of a frame.

Perhaps Preminger's seemingly objective style is what made him so threatening to the Production Code he challenged so many times. Though the Production Code did forbid certain subjects, its general principles refer to the more abstract concept of sympathy, insisting that sympathy "shall never be thrown to the side of crime, wrongdoing, evil or sin."[14] Preminger's best films contain no obvious heroes or villains, and they refuse to offer the spectator an omniscient position from which right and wrong can be judged clearly. One way of interpreting the famed objectivity of Preminger's style is to see his technique as the systematic production of the ambivalences that classical Hollywood cinema usually avoids.

Biography

Otto Preminger was born in 1905 in Wiznitz, Austria-Hungary (now in the Ukraine), though both the date and the location are uncertain. After a successful career as a theatrical director at Max Reinhardt's Josefstadt Theater in Vienna, Preminger emigrated to the United States in 1935, where he continued to direct plays while establishing himself as a prominent filmmaker, first at Twentieth Century-Fox and then as an independent producer who gained notoriety for challenging the Production Code several times over a career that stretched into the 1970s.

Notes

1 Jacques Rivette, "The Essential," in *Cahiers du Cinéma: The 1950s: Neo-Realism, Hollywood, New Wave,* (ed.) Jim Hillier (Cambridge: Harvard University Press, 1985), pp. 132–35; for the special Preminger issue, see *Movie* 2 (September 1962).

2 Andrew Sarris, *The American Cinema: Directors and Directions, 1929–1962* (New York: Da Capo Press, 1996).

3 John Orr discusses Preminger's shifting critical fortunes in "Otto Preminger and the End of Classical Cinema," *Senses of Cinema* 40 (July 2006), http://sensesofcinema.com/2006/40/otto-preminger.

4 Christian Keathley, "Otto Preminger and the Surface of Cinema," *World Picture* 2 (Autumn 2008), http://www.worldpicturejournal.com/WP_2/Keathley.html.

5 For biographical information, see Chris Fujiwara, *The World and Its Double: The Life and Work of Otto Preminger* (New York: Faber and Faber, 2008).

6 V. F. Perkins, "Why Preminger?" in *The Movie Reader* (ed.) Ian Cameron (New York: Praeger, 1972), p. 43. This volume attributes the essay to Perkins, though in the original 1962 publication the essay was unsigned.

7 For a three-way comparison of Preminger, Hitchcock, and Ophüls, in terms of their use of camera movement, see Robin Wood's celebrated analysis of *Letter from an Unknown Woman* in Wood, "Ewig hin her Liebe Gluck," *Personal Views: Explorations in Film,* rev. ed. (Detroit: Wayne State University Press, 2006), pp. 143–66.

8 See V. F. Perkins, "'How' Is 'What,'" in *Film as Film: Understanding and Judging Movies* (New York: Da Capo Press, 1993), pp. 128–29; and Charles Barr, "CinemaScope: Before and After," in *Film Theory and Criticism,* 3rd edition, ed. Gerald Mast and Marshall Cohen (New York: Oxford University Press, 1985), pp. 147–48.

9 For further analysis of this scene from *River of No Return,* see David Bordwell, "Widescreen Aesthetics and Mise en Scene Criticism," *The Velvet Light Trap* 21 (Summer 1985): pp. 20–23. Bordwell argues that Perkins and Barr underestimate the extent to which Preminger controls our attention through other visual and aural cues.

10 Deborah Thomas, "Cinematic Spaces: Background and Foreground, Onscreen and Offscreen," in *Reading Hollywood: Spaces and Meanings in American Film* (London: Wallflower Press, 2001), p. 71.

11 Thomas, p. 72.

12 John Gibbs and Douglas Pye, "Revisiting Preminger: *Bonjour Tristesse* (1958) and Close Reading," in *Style and Meaning: Studies in the Detailed Analysis of Film,* ed. Gibbs and Pye (Manchester: Manchester University Press, 2005), p. 121. The reference is to George M. Wilson, *Narration in*

Light: Studies in Cinematic Point of View (Baltimore: The Johns Hopkins University Press, 1988).

13 V. F. Perkins, "Where Is the World? The Horizon of Events in Movie Fiction," in *Style and Meaning: Studies in the Detailed Analysis of Film*, ed. Gibbs and Pye (Manchester: Manchester University Press, 2005), p. 20.

14 "The Production Code," in *Movies and Mass Culture* (ed.) John Belton (New Brunswick, NJ: Rutgers University Press, 1996), p. 138.

Filmography

Die grosse Liebe (Austria, 1931)

Under Your Spell (1936)

Danger – Love at Work (1937)

Margin for Error (1943)

In the Meantime, Darling (1944) also producer

Laura (1944) also producer

A Royal Scandal (1945)

Fallen Angel (1945) also producer

Centennial Summer (1946) also producer

Forever Amber (1947)

Daisy Kenyon (1947) also producer

That Lady in Ermine (1948) uncredited; co-directed with Ernst Lubitsch

The Fan (1949) also producer

Whirlpool (1949) also producer

Where the Sidewalk Ends (1950) also producer

The 13th Letter (1951) also producer

Angel Face (1952) also producer

The Moon Is Blue (1953) also producer

Die Jungfrau auf dem Dach (1953) also producer

River of No Return (1954)

Carmen Jones (1954) also producer

The Court-Martial of Billy Mitchell (1955)

The Man with the Golden Arm (1955) also producer

Saint Joan (1957) also producer

Bonjour Tristesse (1958) also producer

Porgy and Bess (1959)

Anatomy of a Murder (1959) also producer

Exodus (1960) also producer

Advise & Consent (1962) also producer

The Cardinal (1963) also producer

In Harm's Way (1965) also producer

Bunny Lake Is Missing (1965) also producer
Hurry Sundown (1967) also producer
Skidoo (1968) also producer
Tell Me That You Love Me, Junie Moon (1970) also producer
Such Good Friends (1971) also producer
Rosebud (1975) also producer
The Human Factor (1979) also producer

Further reading

Fujiwara, Chris. *The World and Its Double: The Life and Work of Otto Preminger*. New York: Faber and Faber, 2008.

Lippe, Richard. "At the Margins of Film Noir: Preminger's *Angel Face*." *Film Noir Reader* (eds) Alain Silver and James Ursini. New York: Limelight, 1996, pp. 161–75.

Simmons, Jerold. "Challenging the Production Code: *The Man with the Golden Arm*." *Journal of Popular Film and Television* 33.1 (Spring 2005): 39–48.

Thompson, Kristin. *Breaking the Glass Armor: Neoformalist Film Analysis*. Princeton: Princeton University Press, 1988.

NICHOLAS RAY

By Lucy Bolton

When reviewing *Bitter Victory* in 1958 for *Cahiers du Cinéma*, Jean-Luc Godard declared as follows:

> There was theatre (Griffith), poetry (Murnau), painting (Rossellini), dance (Eisenstein), music (Renoir). Henceforth there is cinema. And the cinema is Nicholas Ray.
> (Godard, 'Au delà des étoiles', *Cahiers du Cinema* 79, 1958)[1]

Admired for his artistry and respected for his subversions, Ray is considered by many critics and directors to have been one of the greatest directors in Hollywood, but one whose career suffered because of the demands of commercialism and his own personal demons.

Ray's body of work ranges from women's pictures to Westerns, film noir to biblical epic, and from Hollywood studio fodder to personal European projects. Although he is best known for the Hollywood films he directed between 1948 and 1958, Ray's status as a Hollywood director is not straightforward. Ray began directing films at RKO, and worked with stars and genres at the very heart of the studio system, yet he was at the forefront of experiments with CinemaScope, gave the world the first American teenager in the form of James Dean, subverted the gender iconography and sexual politics of the Western, exposed the alienated anti-hero of the American dream, and subsequently left Hollywood for Europe. He worked with Wim Wenders and led an unconventional life, collaborating on various independent projects, all the time battling alcohol and gambling addictions and poor health.

Renowned for an array of intense, alienated and rebellious protagonists, as well as his striking use of colour, shape and space, Ray occupies a particularly liminal place in the history of Hollywood directors: an outsider inside Hollywood. Critic Geoff Andrew describes Ray as 'the first home-grown film-poet of American disillusionment'.[2] David A. Cook writes that, in his films of the fifties, Ray 'provided a definitive statement of the spiritual and emotional ills that beset America during that period'.[3] Although he is frequently aligned with his furious and frustrated characters, it is perhaps more accurate to consider his role as a Hollywood director as one of subversion and rebellion.

Ray came to be beloved by the French *Cahiers du Cinéma* critics as an *auteur par excellence*, but his biographical and directorial beginnings were American. He studied under architect Frank Lloyd Wright, and this is often credited with accounting for the use of buildings and spaces in his films. In Bernard Eisenshitz's (2011) biography of Ray, *An American Journey*, however, the relationship with Lloyd Wright is described in more tempestuous, personal terms, and the characteristics of intensity and frustration are familiar features of relationships and period in Ray's life. David Thomson writes that 'Ray had the looks, talent and friends that might have made a great career. There was always a great film-maker inside him, yet he relentlessly hacked away at his support and supporters.'[4]

These details about Ray's personal life explain why he is considered along with his furious and tempestuous anti-heroes to be an outsider par excellence. As Elsaesser writes,

> it is perhaps this ability to articulate, in terms special to the cinema, a point of view, at once inside (the system) and outside (its limits on personal expression) that makes Ray's cinema so uniquely loved and so vitally important.[5]

For Elsaesser, 'Ray's importance as a film-director is essentially on the level of his *mise-en-scène* and not on the level of ideas.'[6] Ray uses a striking palette of bold colours in his costumes, sets and props, and his use of rooms, buildings, furniture and staircases creates intense and emotive meaning, playing with instability and balance. The scene on the staircase in *Rebel Without a Cause*, where Jim Stark (James Dean) is caught between his father on the ground floor and his mother on the landing above him coveys visually how Jim feels trapped and torn between his parents. This intensity often leads to instances of high style or flamboyance. As Andrew writes, 'Even his most satisfying works feature moments of baroque excess.'[7] The themes of Ray's more personal work are distinctive and powerful: isolation, alienation, adolescence, and the clash between civilisation and natural instincts. These themes are present from the outset of Ray's career, but his body of work demonstrates a struggle to balance artistic expression with commercial demands.

In Ray's first film, *They Live by Night* (1948), fugitive and loner Bowie (Farley Granger) is archetypal of Ray's alienated and desperate anti-heroes to come. For critic David Thomson, it is 'one of the great debuts by an American director'.[8] A wrongly convicted man on the run, trying to battle his way back to respectability through criminal activity, Bowie falls in love with Keechie (Cathy O'Donnell) and the couple live a secret, hopeless life of escapist innocence and illusory safety. When Bowie is shot and killed, leaving Keechie and their unborn child, the film ends on the note that will permeate Ray's most powerful films: the injustice faced by the individual at war with society and pessimism about the possibility of love as a happy ending.

Similar themes are explored in the hugely successful and radical social polemic *Knock on any Door* (1949). 'Pretty Boy' Nick Romano (John Derek) is accused of killing a policeman, and calls upon the lawyer who bears some responsibility for the death of the boy's father. The lawyer, Andrew Morton (played by Humphrey Bogart, whose newly formed company, Santana, produced the film), argues that society is to blame for the way in which Pretty Boy and others like him have turned out. Again, romantic love is not redemptive, and Pretty Boy is guilty of this crime, but the film's challenge is to consider the lot of the individual who grows up like him. The morality of the ending is ambiguous with no easy answers to reassure or comfort the audience.

Around this time Ray also turned out some less personal and more conventional films such as *A Woman's Secret* (1949), *Born to be Bad* (1950) and *Flying Leathernecks* (1951). Working with major Hollywood players such as Joan Fontaine, Robert Ryan and John Wayne, Ray directed these films to satisfy the demands of RKO. *In a Lonely Place*, however, that Ray directed in 1950 (again for Bogart's Santana company) is an unflinching examination of a man consumed with fury and violence and is justly considered a landmark Hollywood film. Screenwriter Dixon ('Dix') Steele, played by Bogart, is cynical about Hollywood and the adaptations of novels on which he works, but he is also a desperately lonely man searching for love. When he is accused of murder, and his neighbour Laurel (Gloria Grahame) provides his alibi, he finds the woman he has been looking for, only to drive her away because of his manic possessiveness and violent temper.

This film not only offers hugely complex characters, it is also like Ray's other significant films in that it transcends narrative concerns. These films are thematic investigations of alienation, isolation, loneliness and frustration, and attempts by characters to reach out to a like-minded individual. Romance in Ray's films lies in this coming together of people who have in some way been searching for each other: but just as violence and criminality leads to Pretty Boy's wife's suicide in *Knock on any Door*, so Dix's temper means that he loses the possibility of sharing his life with Laurel. These lonely men – Bowie, Pretty Boy, Dix, and violent detective Jim Wilson (Robert Ryan) from *On Dangerous Ground* – are a panoply of existential isolation within societies that are unforgiving no matter which side of the law you are on.

The Lusty Men (1952) and *Johnny Guitar* (1954) took Ray out of the city and into the iconography of the Western with rodeo rider Jeff (Robert Mitchum) and saloon-owner Vienna (Joan Crawford), respectively. Both films are concerned above all with issues of love and loyalty as Jeff falls in love with married Louise (Susan Hayward) and essentially sacrifices his life for her marriage, and Vienna calls upon ex-lover and *gunslinger* Johnny Guitar (Sterling Hayden) to help her in her battle with the local posse driven by jealousy fuelled Emma Small (Mercedes McCambridge). The unrealistic backdrops, intense colour, dramatic musical score and passionate performances, particularly those of Crawford and McCambridge, make *Johnny Guitar* a Western like no other. When Vienna plays her piano in a vast white crinoline dress, defying the maniacal Emma and her posse (all dressed head to toe in black) to prove her involvement with the gang of the Dancing Kid, the iconography of the Western in the context of the 1950s is reinscribed with subversive sexual and moral content.

In many ways, *Rebel Without a Cause* (1955) is the culmination of this subversive impulse. The image of Dean in the red windcheater jacket, blue jeans and holding a cigarette is one of the most globally iconic star images, and the furious frustrations of Jim, Judy (Natalie Wood) and Plato (Sal Mineo) are monumental in Hollywood film history as well as American culture. Although expelled from school and under the eye of the police, Jim Stark is in many ways a responsible Ray hero. He resists attempts by the gang to get him involved in fighting as he knows where this kind of trouble can lead. He advises his own father about how to be a better man, and manages to communicate with the disturbed Plato in a reassuring and conciliatory way when police and adults are failing.

Ray consolidates the ways in which the teenagers feel desperate and alienated through visual style. On Jim's first day at his new school, all the students avoid stepping on the school insignia except for Jim who stands directly on top of it. The camera's focus on the students' nimble feet and Jim's stolidly placed brown brogues confirms his outsider status. The chickee run between Jim and Buzz involves many elements that feature in Ray's films, such as the angry posse and conflicting characters, and these conflicts have primal things at stake: life and death in *Johnny Guitar* and *Rebel Without a Cause*. Vienna and Jim Stark want to avoid conflict but they need to stand their ground and fight when persecuted by the gang, alongside their unlikely allies. In this way, these films offer early visions of the family as non-biological, with alliances formed between characters on the margins that need each other, hiding out in places of safety, such as a deserted mansion or beyond a waterfall.

Ed Avery in *Bigger than Life* is a man whose fantasies of domination and self-centred supremacy are unleashed by the cortisone medication that he is prescribed. Thomas Elsaesser writes that in this film 'the guilt-ridden rebel grows into a pseudo-fascist superman'.[9] The way in which Ed speaks his mind bluntly to students, teachers and neighbours is initially amusing, but the film shows the consequences of this mindset for a man who is a husband and father. He places intolerable pressure on his young son, and viciously rejects his loving wife for her inadequacies. The railing against anything that restricts him and the desire for supremacy is a kind of hyper-masculinity, a nightmare vision of a patriarch who sees his way as the only way, results in his despotic declaration that 'God was wrong'. The end of the film sees him taken off medication and reconciled with the wife and son he nearly killed, but facing an uncertain future in terms of health and longevity. Even when there is an image of conventional cinematic closure, like Ed's family around his bed, or Jim's mother smiling in acquiescence at his father in *Rebel Without a Cause*, it cannot be viewed with any reassurance or conviction that all will be well.

Ray worked with Hollywood's major stars in some of their more unconventional roles. He capitalised on ambiguities in the star personas of Robert Mitchum and James Mason, and enabled Humphrey Bogart, James Cagney and Robert Ryan to convey complex masculinities in multifaceted roles. Ray also enabled Ava Gardner to convey the poignancy of an aging beauty, and Natalie Wood the confusion and frustration of a burgeoning one. *In a Lonely Place* may begin as a noir-ish crime movie with a cynical look at Hollywood, but it grows into a film about the difficulties of escaping the grips of a violent man, enabling Gloria Grahame to deliver a performance of emotional depth and sincerity. In *Johnny Guitar*, Crawford's unique role capitalised on the elements of masculinity and femininity in her persona, enabling her to flash her eyes with both fury and with flirtation. Ray tackled the war movie again with the cynical *Bitter Victory* and Richard Burton, the musical *Hot Blood* with Jane Russell as a feisty gypsy, and Anthony Quinn as Inuk the Eskimo in a clash with Peter O'Toole's civilising white man. *Party Girl* in 1958 concluded Ray's American studio period.

The early 1960s saw Hollywood explore epic cinema, with films such as *Spartacus* (Stanley Kubrick, 1960), *El Cid* (Anthony Mann, 1961) and *Cleopatra* (Joseph L. Mankiewicz, 1963). Ray directed two such films, produced by Samuel Bronston. In *King of Kings* (1961) Jesus Christ enters the roster of Ray rebels as Pilate describes how 'he doesn't fit in – he refuses to be like everybody else'. Plagued by health problems and using drugs and alcohol heavily, Ray collapsed on set and was fired from the set of his next epic film about the Boxer rebellion *55 Days at Peking* (1963). This dismissal marked the end of Ray's commercial filmmaking career.

Ray lived and worked outside of the Hollywood system for the next sixteen years until his death. He taught filmmaking at New York University, where he collaborated with students on some experimental projects involving film and video, such as *We Can't Go Home Again* (1973). He also collaborated with German director Wim Wenders in *Lightning Over Water* (1980), a film about his own slow and painful death from cancer.

For Geoff Andrew, Ray's films 'expressed his awareness of inner torment, of solitude and despair, conflict and confusion, and did so through entirely cinematic means'.[10] Ray's protagonists have a fury and a desperation that is borne out of alienation and frustration, often rejection by the cities and communities in which they live. Beyond narrative, however, it is Ray's ability to create visual cinematic intensity adequate to the emotional task that makes his films so powerful, such as when Mildred talks directly to camera in *In a Lonely Place*, overwhelming Dixon Steele and us with her intensity and passion; or when the lighting focused on Dixon's face highlights the mania in his eyes as he directs the scene of the murder re-enactment.

Dialogue also shores up this intensity with memorable and influential lines such as Jim Stark's desperate scream at his parents 'you're tearing me apart', Pretty Boy Romano's motto 'Live fast, die young, have a beautiful corpse'; Johnny Guitar's announcement 'I'm a stranger here myself', or Richard Burton as Captain Leith in *Bitter Victory* wallowing in masochistic bitterness proclaiming that 'I kill the living and save the dead'. As Elsaesser identifies, 'The secret of the Ray heroes is that they are poised between an unlivable individualism and an equally unlivable conformism.'[11] This hopeless irreconcilability means that Ray's Hollywood films do not offer any conventional happy endings, rather they manage something probably unique in Hollywood: bleakly pessimistic but richly satisfying entertainment.

Biography

Ray was born in Wisconsin in 1911, the only boy of the family, with two step-sisters and three sisters. Ray attended the University of Chicago for one term in 1931, before accepting the offer of a scholarship to study with architect Frank Lloyd Wright in 1933. Ray acted and worked in theatre in New York from 1934 and began work as director with RKO in 1944, directing his first feature, *They Live by Night*, in 1948. Ray worked in Hollywood until 1957 when he began to direct films in Europe where he lived until 1969. He then returned to America where he taught film at SUNY Binghamton's Harpur College. He collaborated with students and directors Wim Wenders and Jim Jarmusch on independent projects. He died on 16 June 1979. Ray was married four times, and had four children.

Notes

1 Godard, Jean-Luc, 'Au delà des étoiles' ('Beyond the Stars'), *Cahiers du Cinema* 79, 1958.
2 Andrew, Geoff, *The Films of Nicholas Ray*, London: Charles Letts & Co., 1991, p. 11.
3 David Cook, *A History of Narrative Film*, New York and London: W. W. Norton & Co., 1996, p. 481.

4 Thomson, David, 'The Poet of Nightfall', *The Guardian* Saturday 27 December 2003.
5 Elsaesser, Thomas, 'All the Lonely Places: The Heroes of Nicholas Ray', in *The Persistence of Hollywood*, New York and London: Routledge, 2012, p. 52.
6 Ibid, p. 42.
7 Andrew, p. 3.
8 Thomson.
9 Elsaesser, p. 47.
10 Andrew, p. 1.
11 Elsaesser, p. 46.

Filmography

The Twisted Road (1948) aka *They Live by Night*
Knock on any Door (1949)
A Woman's Secret (1949)
Roseanna McCoy (1949) uncredited
In a Lonely Place (1950)
Born to be Bad (1950)
Flying Leathernecks (1951)
The Racket (1951) uncredited
On Dangerous Ground (1952)
Macao (1952) uncredited
The Lusty Men (1952)
Androcles and the Lion (1952) uncredited
Johnny Guitar (1954)
'The High Green Wall' (1954) TV episode of *General Electric Theatre*
Run for Cover (1955)
Rebel Without a Cause (1955)
Hot Blood (1956)
Bigger than Life (1956)
The James Brothers (1957)
Bitter Victory (1957)
Wind Across the Everglades (1958)
Party Girl (1958)
'High Green Wall' (1959) TV episode of *On Trial*
The Savage Innocents (1960)
King of Kings (1961)
55 Days at Peking (1963)
Wet Dreams segment 'The Janitor' (1974)
We Can't Go Home Again (1973)
Marco (1978) short
Lightning Over Water (1980)

Further reading

Andrew, Geoff. *The Films of Nicholas Ray*. London: Charles Letts & Co., 1991.

Eisenschitz, Bernard. *Nicholas Ray: An American Journey*. Trans. Tom Milne. London: Faber & Faber, 1993.

Ray, Nicholas. *I Was Interrupted, Nicholas Ray on Making Movies*. (ed.) Susan Ray. Berkeley: University of California Press, 1993.

DON SIEGEL

By Pete Falconer

Don Siegel certainly commands a place in the history of Hollywood filmmaking, although there remains some ambiguity as to what that place should be. Perspectives on Siegel have never coalesced into anything resembling conventional wisdom. He has provoked contradictory responses: praised for "demonstrably recurrent thematic concerns"[1] and described as "wrongly deified by auteurists"[2]; credited with a "tight realistic style"[3] and "an elliptical, abstracting dramatic technique"[4]; portrayed as "the auteur who makes action films with meaningful social comment"[5] and accused of trafficking in the "xenophobic tropes that serviced postwar America's current hegemonic constructs".[6] The lack of consensus on the meaning or value of Siegel's work means that it has remained open to various classifications and appropriations. An index of this indeterminate status is that two of Siegel's black-and-white films (*The Big Steal* and *Invasion of the Body Snatchers*) have been colourised. These movies have been judged to be worth marketing to contemporary audiences, but not to be so established in significance or prestige that they cannot be fundamentally altered.

The qualities that have kept a dominant interpretation of Siegel's films from emerging are arguably those that make his films worthy of attention. Siegel's movies emphasise local over global significance, elements that resonate in their immediate context rather than in relation to wider concerns. Moments of obvious visual stylisation, for example, are usually tied to a particular action or motion: the way the camera seems to reel in sympathy with Hogan (Clint Eastwood) when an arrow hits him in *Two Mules for Sister Sara*; the tilting and bouncing of the low-angled camera as Ben Chamberlain (Henry Fonda) is thrown out of the boxcar in *Stranger on the Run*; the close-ups of Coogan (Eastwood again) throwing punches, as if at the audience, in *Coogan's Bluff*. Binding these flourishes to the action or sensation that they accompany serves both to motivate and contain them. These moments pass by quickly, held within a wider style that is more restrained.

Siegel's films often have a processional quality. Events and incidents pass quickly, with few indications of the particular significance of one over another. This may be one reason that Siegel was such an effective director of chases. The climactic car chase in *The Lineup* is one of Siegel's most praised sequences,[7] and many of his other movies are based around extended pursuits or escapes (*The Big Steal* has been called "basically one long chase".[8]) This approach extends to the viewpoint offered on Siegel's characters – they move from one situation to the next, without much time devoted to material that might explain, justify or condemn their behaviour. As Richard Combs puts it, "Siegel expends no footage on expressing an opinion, or in resolving issues which his films raise."[9] This can be seen in *Dirty Harry*. Despite Stuart Kaminsky's claim that Harry Callahan (Clint Eastwood) is "out to avenge the death of his wife"[10], the film makes no overt connection between Harry's bereavement and his behaviour elsewhere. Beyond a general confirmation of Harry's solitude, the death of his wife at some unspecified point in the past is not presented as an insight into his motives or personality. Instead it is offered, almost in passing, as one of many aspects of Harry's life that he cannot explain or account for. When he tells Norma Gonzalez (Lyn Edgington) that his wife was killed in a car accident involving a drunk driver, he remarks that, "There was no reason for it, really." Asked why he remains a homicide detective, Callahan replies, "I don't know – I really don't." Throughout this brief conversation, he wears sunglasses, maintains a neutral expression and speaks in a quiet, even tone of voice (at most, we might detect hints of puzzlement or resignation). The meaning of Harry's life (if it has one) is as obscure to the audience as it is to Harry.

Clint Eastwood seems to have particularly suited the opaque presentation favoured by Siegel. Edward Gallafent notes that in *The Beguiled*, Corporal McBurney (Eastwood), a wounded Union soldier recovering at a girls' school in Confederate territory, is presented as "someone who makes no very profound calculations".[11] His actions respond to the immediate circumstances in which he finds himself, but have no other unifying logic or purpose:

> Wishing to avoid being sent to a Confederate prison once he is well, he uses his charm on the various women who tend him,

but there is no evidence that his motives are more complex than this, or that he contemplates their attitudes to each other.[12]

The character of McBurney largely consists of a series of reactions to the dangers and opportunities that he encounters. It is not that Siegel's films show no interest in their characters, but rather that this interest is not focused on matters of individual psychology. Siegel's best movies demonstrate the level of complexity that can be achieved while still remaining on the surface.

Siegel's examination of surfaces can be seen in his visual style, which often emphasises a quality of flatness. The opening shot of Siegel's early Western *The Duel at Silver Creek* employs a number of the flattening techniques that Siegel would use throughout his career. The shot shows a gang of claim jumpers riding along a dirt track. The riders are backlit, which gives the foreground of the shot a solid, impenetrable quality. The rapid sideways movement of the camera emphasises the impression that the action is taking place on one plane – the background passes too quickly to register any sense of depth. What we do see of the background includes trees, rocks and fences, all of which reduce the visible space behind the riders. The camera stays close enough to the claim jumpers that they are never situated in the kind of expansive space often presented in the opening moments of Westerns. Siegel often stages action in restricted depth. When the inmates in *Riot in Cell Block 11* capture their first guard as a hostage, this is shot along one side of a prison corridor, with most of the action taking place in the tight space between the camera and the stone walls. The scene subsequently opens out into the full depth of the corridor, but the initial flatness is striking, and sustained for a significant proportion of the sequence.

Combs suggests that Siegel favours lighting that "emphasises foreground shadow against bright backgrounds".[13] This is certainly true of a film like *The Shootist* (and the example above from *The Duel at Silver Creek*), but it is only one of several ways in which Siegel uses contrasts of light and dark to divide deeper spaces into a series of shallow planes. Siegel achieves similar effects by contrasting a bright foreground with a dark background – several scenes in *The Beguiled* use this lighting style – and by breaking up spaces into bands of brightness and shadow, as in the shots of Callahan searching the rooftop under the opening credits of *Dirty Harry*.

Siegel often uses sets in a similar way. *Charley Varrick* features a number of spaces that are divided by barriers and thresholds, disrupting the sense of depth. The bank in Tres Cruces is the most striking example of this construction – its old-fashioned interior (which its manager has lovingly restored) is full of panels, partitions and windows. Elsewhere in the movie, bank manager Harold Young (Woodrow Parfrey) and bank president Maynard Boyle (John Vernon) have an extended conversation by the gate to a field where cattle are grazing. The first part of the conversation is shown in long shot, with the gate and the fence cutting across the centre of the frame, flattening the space behind the two men. When the camera moves in closer, the gate continues to block off the background and our view of the surrounding space gets no deeper. It is interesting to note that Andy Warhol's Elvis Presley prints are based on a still from *Flaming Star*, the Western that Siegel made with Presley, and that Siegel was included in the group of Hollywood action directors praised by 1960s art critic Lawrence Alloway.[14] It would be a stretch to draw too close a comparison between Siegel's aesthetic and that of Pop Art, but it is fair to say that both show an interest in the expressive capabilities of flatness.

In the case of Siegel, it is the clear and precise handling of surface details that makes flatness expressive. Although associated with violence, his films also pay close (if characteristically brief) attention to more mundane forms of action. It is easy to overlook how carefully Siegel's movies present the gestures of everyday interaction, the particular ways that relationships are defined and conducted through ordinary behaviour. In *Flaming Star*, for example, the reactions of the multi-racial Burton family to signs that violence might be about to erupt between white settlers and Indians are presented through a series of looks. Neddy Burton (Dolores del Rio), the Kiowa-born mother of the family, looks anxiously at her two sons as she sees them arming themselves. Neddy's fear for her family and sense of her exposure as an Indian woman married to a white man are conveyed through the way her repeated glances at her sons disrupt the rhythm of her speech and movements – she is slow to respond in conversation and keeps pausing while setting the table for dinner. Alongside this, we also see attempts to reassert normality. After Neddy looks over her shoulder at her younger son Pacer (Elvis Presley), her husband Sam 'Pa' Burton (John McIntyre) looks back at him too, giving him a slight nod and making a loose strumming motion with his hand. Pacer takes the hint, stops loading his rifle and picks up his guitar instead. The gestures and reactions of the Burton family are presented clearly, but without heavy emphasis. There is a close-up on Neddy when she looks at her older stepson Clint (Steve Forrest), but it serves more as another interruption to her movements than as an assertion of the dramatic weight of that particular expression. The lightness with which these interactions are presented helps to create the sense that they are only the latest manifestations of the ongoing tensions and established understandings within the family.

One of the most interesting consequences of Siegel's tendency to present events without extensive commentary is the degree to which more troubling implications are allowed to stand. Manny Farber called Siegel's movies "unsettling"[15] and Peter Bogdanovich credited them with "a disquieting ambiguity".[16] The scenes that introduce the main characters in *Private Hell 36* and *Coogan's Bluff* show the characters using violence that seems to exceed the demands of their situation. In *Private Hell 36*, Detective Sergeant Cal Bruner (Steve Cochran) crashes through a drugstore window with a robber (King Donovan) he has caught in the act. The robber appears to be beaten – he barely moves after he hits the pavement – but Bruner punches him three times, seemingly out of spite. Similarly, Coogan slams his rifle butt into the stomach of the fugitive (Rudy Diaz) he was pursuing, after the man has already surrendered. In both cases, a level of conventional justification is established – Bruner and Coogan are main characters, policemen chasing criminals and facing initial danger (both are shot at) – but this explanation is inadequate for the type and level of violence portrayed. There is also the impression in each case that the violence passes without remark, that it will not be reflected upon, or connected to anything that follows – in both films, the scene ends quickly after the last blow is struck. Siegel's movies rarely offer an easy or superior perspective on their more disturbing elements. Scorpio (Andy Robinson) in *Dirty Harry* may be placed in what Gallafent calls "the reassuring category of the psychopath"[17], but no equivalent framework is provided for understanding Harry's violence and estrangement from those around him. In some instances, Siegel's approach can be problematic. His films sometimes leave unpleasant stereotypes and reductive characterisations untroubled – two examples of this tendency would be the portrayal of the 1960s counterculture in *Coogan's Bluff* and that of the gay convicts in *Riot in Cell Block 11*. Often, however, the refusal to overtly situate the unsettling moments in Siegel's movies generates a rich and complex ambiguity.

When obvious explanations and interpretations do seem to be offered in Siegel's movies, this is often a matter of generic convention. *The Beguiled* has been criticised for "obvious and laboured symbolism"[18], but we might equally regard the film's symbolic wildlife, sudden eruptions of internal monologue and *ménage à trois* dream sequence as fitting comfortably within the characteristic tone and atmosphere of the southern gothic subgenre. As Gallafent remarks, "We know immediately where we are, in a world locked into the particular trajectories of collapse that belong to southern melodrama."[19] Equivalent contexts might be suggested for the occasional "speech-making about prison conditions and earnest 'problem picture' approaches"[20] in *Riot in Cell Block 11* or the allegorical dimension to *Invasion of the Body Snatchers*. The latter, as George Turner points out, was made a couple of years after the initial cycle of 1950s alien invasion movies,[21] and thus had a set of newly established conventions to work with, which included gestures to contemporary allegory. Siegel's films acknowledge the value of such conventions, located in their capacity to reduce the necessity of explaining or justifying each individual element. Popular genres provided a level of familiarity that allowed Siegel to stay on the surface without seeming shallow or obtuse.

Andrew Sarris suggests that Siegel "never projected the aura of the 'great' director".[22] He lacked the public persona, the cultural cachet, the thematic and stylistic overtness on which such reputations are often founded. Siegel's characteristic approach, and the modes in which he generally worked, have not served him well against such contingent criteria. Indeed, Siegel's movies highlight the continued inadequacy of many of our critical concepts and vocabularies for recognising the achievement of filmmakers who work within popular forms.

Biography

Don Siegel was born in Chicago in 1912. He studied at Cambridge University and subsequently lived in Paris. After returning to the USA, Siegel found work at Warner Brothers studios, starting in 1934 as a film librarian, moving onto inserts and eventually becoming head of the montage department. He also did Second Unit work in the 1940s for directors including Howard Hawks and Raoul Walsh. Two short films directed by Siegel, *Hitler Lives* and *Star in the Night*, won Academy Awards in 1946. This recognition allowed Siegel to establish himself as a feature director. He directed low-to-mid-budget genre films for a range of companies in the 1940s and 1950s and developed a longer association with Universal in the 1960s. He gained greater critical attention and commercial success towards the end of the 1960s and into the 1970s. Siegel died in 1991.

Notes

1 Colin McArthur, *Underworld U.S.A.* (London: Secker and Warburg, 1972), p. 150.
2 Manny Farber, 'Don Siegel', *Artforum,* December 1969, collected in Robert Polito (ed.), *Farber on Film: the complete film writings of Manny Farber* (New York: Library of America, 2009), p. 675.
3 Alan Lovell, *Don Siegel: American Cinema* (London: BFI, 1975), p. 13.
4 Richard Combs, "Less is More: Don Siegel from the block to the Rock", *Sight and Sound* 49:2, Spring 1980, p. 119.
5 Peter Whitehead, "Coogan's *Bluff*", *Films and Filming,* May 1969, collected in "*Films and Filming* Reviews, 1966–69", *Framework* 52:1, Spring 2011, p. 230.
6 Katrina Mann, "'You're Next!': Postwar Hegemony Besieged in *Invasion of the Body Snatchers*", *Cinema Journal* 44:1, Autumn 2004, p. 65.
7 See McArthur, *Underworld U.S.A.,* p. 153; Combs, 'Less is More', p. 118; Peter Bogdanovich, "B-Movies", in Al LaValley (ed.), *Invasion of the Body Snatchers* (New Brunswick: Rutgers University Press, 1989), p. 174.
8 Al LaValley, "Don Siegel: A Biographical Sketch", in LaValley (ed.), *Invasion of the Body Snatchers,* p. 20.
9 Richard Combs, "Count the Hours: the real Don Siegel", *Monthly Film Bulletin* LI: 601, February 1984, p. 58.
10 Stuart M. Kaminsky, *American Film Genres* (Chicago: Nelson Hall, 1985), p. 184.
11 Edward Gallafent, *Clint Eastwood: Actor and Director* (London: Studio Vista, 1994), p. 77.
12 Ibid., p. 77.
13 Combs, "Less is More", p. 119.
14 Lawrence Alloway, *Violent America: The Movies 1946–1964* (New York: The Museum of Modern Art, 1971), p. 26.
15 Farber, "Don Siegel", p. 675.
16 Bogdanovich, "B-Movies", p. 174.
17 Gallafent, *Clint Eastwood,* p. 38.
18 Robin Wood, "Don Siegel" in Richard Roud (ed.), *Cinema: A Critical Dictionary, Volume 2: Kinugasa to Zanussi* (London: Martin Secker and Warburg, 1980), p. 923.
19 Gallafent, *Clint Eastwood,* p. 73.
20 Combs, "Less is More", p. 121.
21 George Turner, "A Case for Insomnia", *American Cinematographer* 78:3, March 1997, p. 77.
22 Andrew Sarris, "Don Siegel: The Pro", *Film Comment* 27:5, September 1991, p. 38.

Filmography

Star in the Night (1945) short
Hitler Lives (1945) documentary short

The Verdict (1946)
Night Unto Night (1949)
The Big Steal (1949)
The Duel at Silver Creek (1952)
No Time for Flowers (1952)
Every Minute Counts (1953)
China Venture (1953)
Riot in Cell Block 11 (1954)
Private Hell 36 (1954)
The Blue and the Gold (1955)
Invasion of the Body Snatchers (1956)
Crime in the Streets (1956)
Spanish Affair (1957)
Baby Face Nelson (1957)
The Lineup (1958)
Gunrunners (1958)
Edge of Eternity (1959)
Hound-Dog Man (1959)
Flaming Star (1960)
Hell is for Heroes (1962)
The Killers (1964)
The Hanged Man (1964) made-for-television movie
Stranger on the Run (1967) made-for-television movie
Madigan (1968)
Coogan's Bluff (1968)
Two Mules for Sister Sara (1970)
The Beguiled (1971)
Dirty Harry (1971)
Charley Varrick (1973)
The Black Windmill (UK, 1974)
The Shootist (1976)
Telefon (1977)
Escape from Alcatraz (1979)
Rough Cut (1980)
Jinxed! (1982)

Further Reading

Belton, John. *Cinema Stylists.* London: The Scarecrow Press, 1983. 217–27.

Combs, Richard. "8 Degrees of Separation." *Film Comment* 38:4 (July/August 2002): 50–53.

Kaminsky, Stuart M. *Don Siegel: Director*. New York: Curtis Books, 1974.

Kass, Judith. *The Hollywood Professionals, Volume 4: Don Siegel*. London: The Tantivy Press, 1975.

Siegel, Don. *A Siegel Film*. London: Faber and Faber, 1993.

ROBERT SIODMAK

By Tim Snelson

In August 1947, *Life* magazine reported on Hollywood's 'newest top-flight director' Robert Siodmak's long-awaited passage 'over the threshold that, figuratively, separates rags from riches'.[1] At this time, the 47-year-old Siodmak had been in the film business for more than twenty years, directing over thirty films within Germany, France and Hollywood. Siodmak explains his protracted journey towards artistic autonomy and, more importantly, financial security not as a romantic struggle of creative will against commercial imperatives, but one of calculated though sometimes cynical cooperation with studio executives. *Life* moves onto report that in his first Hollywood studio role as jobbing director on Paramount's 'B' status comedy *West Point Widow* (1941), the film's producer commended Siodmak's compliance, stating 'you're about the only imported genius I've met who does what he's told'. The director responded that he didn't care because 'this picture isn't good enough to be a Siodmak picture. It will only be known as a Paramount picture.'[2] True or not, the anecdote exemplifies Siodmak's canny ability not so much to play the system, as work playfully within it.

Furthermore, as Siodmak confidently and correctly asserted, *West Point Widow* was not the contribution to film culture he has been remembered for. With the exception perhaps of contemporary German émigré director Fritz Lang, Siodmak is revered as the quintessential and certainly most prolific director of classic film noirs; these include *Phantom Lady* (1944), *The Suspect* (1945), *The Dark Mirror* (1946), *The Killers* (1946), *Cry of the City* (1948) and *Criss Cross* (1949). Siodmak's films were not understood as film noirs during their production or on release of course. In the 1940s Siodmak was known primarily as the director of horror films, whose penchant for morbid themes and expressionistic style were resultant of his training in German Weimar cinema.[3] This was an entirely inaccurate portrayal of Siodmak's early filmmaking experience and style, which is exemplified far more accurately by his first film *Menshen Am Sonntag / People on*

Sunday (1929) – co-directed with Edgar G. Ulmer and co-written by his brother Curt Siodmak and Billy Wilder – a laconic and lugubrious quasi-documentary of Berlin daily life that was seen as a key influence on Italian Neorealism. Siodmak was more than happy to exploit these fabricated expressionist credentials, however, in order to break into and develop a third career phase in Hollywood, after narrowly escaping Nazi persecution in Germany and then France. As Andrew Sarris explained in his classic auteurist study of Hollywood, *The American Cinema*, 'Siodmak's Hollywood films are more Germanic than his German ones.'[4] However, Sarris's assertion that the director succeeded in spite of rather than because of Hollywood's industrial and aesthetic structures – a 'triumph of form over content'[5] – misrepresents the productive dialectic Siodmak developed within the classical studio system. It was within this third career where he produced his most creatively and commercially successful work and where his status as simultaneously Hollywood insider and outsider was crafted both on and off screen.

During the wartime and immediate post-war era, whilst working under contract for Universal, Siodmak directed a range of horror films, fantasy films, female gothics and crime thrillers that have retrospectively been reclassified under the umbrella terms of film noir. Whilst this regenrification served to elevate some of Siodmak's films, it simultaneously served to characterise him as a 'one trick pony', successful only within one 'genre' of filmmaking perfectly suited to his émigré status. Whilst film criticism usually identifies Siodmak as an exemplary, if unremarkable film noir director – routinely fusing German cinema traditions and style with Hollywood's commercial aesthetic – film critics and scholars rarely discuss the deeper psychological and ideological preoccupations of his films in the way they have at length in relation to Siodmak's closest equivalent Alfred Hitchcock; the directors shared both thematic and stylistic interests and personnel, most significantly producer Joan Harrison. Across his Hollywood films and a range of genres, Siodmak demonstrates a remarkable sense of reflexivity and criticality in his foregrounding of the psychological and ideological implications of cinematic apparatuses. As Lutz Koepnick suggests, 'indexing Weimar cinema performatively, some of Siodmak's most celebrated film noirs directly confront (cinematic) hopes to engineer impressions of essential meaning through apparitical mediations'.[6] Koepnick demonstrates how Siodmak reinscribed German Expressionism's 'doppelganger' character within Hollywood films such as *The Dark Mirror* and *Cobra Woman* (1944) – or 'doubled the doubles of Weimer cinema' – as a means to allow 'their American audiences to see how a liberal modern polity looks from an illiberal viewpoint'.[7] In these films, Siodmak utilises the cinematic technology of split screen to create chaos (deliberately confusing audiences by having the same actress – Olivia de Havilland in the former and Maria Montez in the latter – portray 'good' and 'bad' twin sisters) to critique 'the totalitarian edges of modernism and deny any vision of modern culture as emancipation'.[8]

However, whilst Koepnick interprets this conscious use of doubling and special effects as a way to evoke the canny rather than the uncanny – to espouse principles of political justice, equality, freedom and democracy in the midst and aftermath of Total War – little attention has been paid to Siodmak's engagement with gender politics within his films. Siodmak was the director Universal looked to in attracting an emergent wartime market of female horror and mystery fans;[9] his first film for Universal, *Son of Dracula* (1943), claimed to have feminised the horror genre by casting two female leads in what 'once would have been considered exclusively a male province'.[10] He was then teamed up with Universal's first female producer, Joan Harrison, to direct *Phantom Lady*, billed by Universal as Hollywood's 'first mystery story from a woman's point of view'.[11] Whilst the matching up of Siodmak with female personnel and female-centred projects gives some indication of his proclivity for female characters and concerns, it is his handling of this material which is most telling politically. In *Phantom Lady*, for example, resilient wartime woman Kansas (Ella Raines) is empowered not merely by her placement in the typically male detective role, but in Siodmak's phenomenological use of mise-en-scène, cinematography, editing and music, to interpellate other wartime women. In the film's standout scene Kansas, masquerading as 'good-time girl' Jeannie, visits an underground New York jazz club. This frenetic montage sequence utilises disorientating camera angles and close-ups as it cuts between the musicians performing and Kansas dancing, pouring liquor, kissing drummer Cliff and applying make-up. It culminates in a frenzied drum solo that cuts back and forth between Cliff's increasingly sweaty, manic face and Kansas's feigned ecstatic expression. In 1944, this sequence received considerable praise from respected critics Manny Farber and James Agee and considerable concern from industry regulators, who interpreted the sequence as a metaphor for sex.[12] D'Emilio and Estelle Freedman suggest that World War Two's expansion of women's labour and leisure experiences, particularly in urban centres like New York, brought unprecedented opportunities for women to engage in premarital sex.[13] *Phantom Lady*, rather than condemning or side-stepping this issue, embraces the new sexual liberalism.

If, through Siodmak's phenomenological approach to the material, *Phantom Lady* emphasises and empathises with women's wartime liberations, then *The Spiral Staircase* (1946) directly confronts myths of female spectatorship. At the outset, the film utilises a self-conscious narrative mechanism that immediately hooks the spectators into the female protagonist's perspective, whilst paradoxically alerting them to its overt theatricality. The film commences with a *mise-en-abyme* that shows an early film screening in a village hotel at which the film's mute heroine Helen (Dorothy McGuire), situated amongst an almost entirely female crowd, is excessively emotionally involved in a silent melodrama called *The Kiss*. The camera pans up through the floorboards to reveal the realistic scene of a young girl's murder, before the camera cross-cuts to a drowned girl being pulled from the water in the concluding shot of the melodramatic silent film. This scene, one that does not appear in the source novel, has the effect of linking contemporary (female) spectatorship of *The Spiral Staircase* to that of the protagonist Helen. However, paradoxically it also distinguishes Helen's naïve and stereotypically overly involved spectatorship of *The Kiss* from that of her contemporary counterparts; ones who are cinematically knowing enough to literally take it up a level and brave the horrors on offer in modern movie houses and beyond. The representation of the over-identified female spectator of 1906 encourages the cine-literate female spectator of 1946 to hold this image at arm's length, acknowledging her critical distance from this outdated patriarchal myth.

The Spiral Staircase goes even further, asking its female audience to take a closer look and question the very act of looking at the cinema screen, pre-empting the feminist psychoanalytic approaches to cinema of the 1970s. In her seminal essay on the nature of 'the gaze' in cinema, Laura Mulvey states:

> Woman stands in patriarchal culture as signifier of the male other, bound by a symbolic order in which man can live out his fantasies and obsessions through linguistic command, by imposing them on the silent image of woman still tied to her place as bearer of meaning, not maker of meaning.[14]

Drawing upon Freud and Lacan, Mulvey suggests that the use of the cinematic apparatus in classical Hollywood film reinforces the illusion of a unified male identity (and therefore patriarchal dominance) by positioning women as silent spectacles to be mastered through the look of the male star, and resultantly the spectator (who is automatically addressed as male). However, rather than a hidden mechanism that underlies the ideological functioning of the film, this paradigmatic theorisation of the male gaze is almost a direct plot summation of *The Spiral Staircase* in which the murderer Professor Warren's wielding of the gaze (blatantly represented in the extreme close-ups of his eye) manifests itself in his fantasised image of Helen with her mouth erased. He subsequently offers to give her 'the quiet' in death he believes she secretly wishes for. McGuire revealed in a later interview that the murderer's eye in close-up in the film in fact belonged to director Siodmak.[15] Therefore, pre-empting *Peeping Tom* (Michael Powell, 1960) and the aforementioned feminist psychoanalytic theory, Siodmak consciously actualises the metaphor of the director's sadistic use of the male gaze, with its tyrannical desire to negate the perceived threat of the female body by taking this symbolic control in defining it. Through Helen's murder, Professor Warren hopes to permanently fix her in a unitary and eternal conception of femininity outside the symbolic order of language. Siodmak should be appreciated, therefore, not just as a master of cinematic techniques but also a critic of them.

In recent years there has been some reappraisal of Siodmak, particularly following a Berlin Film Festival Retrospective in 1998.[16] Revisiting his brief 1975 entry on the director in his *Biographical Dictionary of Film*, David Thomson reassesses his conclusion that Siodmak was 'never more than an assignment director' by asserting that he is in fact 'an artist [... who] deserves fuller retrospectives'.[17] He concludes, 'Siodmak had not just a good eye. But a way of seeing life.'[18] As the above discussion of *The Spiral Staircase* suggests, Siodmak was well aware of how the director's good or bad eye could shape the way we understand and navigate the world.

Biography

It is widely reported that Robert Siodmak was born in Memphis, Tennessee, on 8 August 1900, before moving with his parents to Leipzig in Germany at the age of one. However, Joseph Greco suggests that Siodmak fabricated his American birthplace in order to obtain a visa in Paris just prior to the outbreak of World War Two, then continued to utilise this fiction to enhance his wartime Hollywood career by downplaying, or more accurately supplementing, his Germanness.[19] Certainly from the age of one, Siodmak lived in Leipzig, where his parents' Jewish families lived. As a young man he worked in stage directing and banking, moving into the film business in the mid-1920s, firstly titling imported American films and then working as an editor, scenarist and talent scout for the state funded German film company UFA. In 1929 he persuaded his producer cousin Seymour Nebenzal to let him direct his first feature, *Menshen Am Sonntag / People on Sunday*, on which he collaborated with a 'who's who' of German filmmaking talent, which included Edgar Ulmer (co-director), Fred Zinneman (assistant cinematographer), Billy Wilder (screenwriter) and his brother Curt Siodmak (screenwriter). He directed ten further films in Germany between 1930 and 1933 when, following Goebbel's banning of his film *Brennendes Geheimnis / The Burning Secret* (1933), he moved to Paris with his brother Curt. In Paris he undertook the second of his film careers, directing eleven films, including the celebrated Pièges / *Personal Column* (1939), from 1933–39. On the eve of the declaration of war in Europe, Robert and Curt Siodmak fled to America, heading straight to Hollywood where the director signed a two-year contract with Paramount in 1940. However, Siodmak did his most celebrated work after signing a seven year contract with Universal in 1942. He went on to direct a number of commercially and critically celebrated horror films and crime thrillers, including *Phantom Lady* (1944), *The Suspect* (1945), *The Spiral Staircase* (1946), *The Killers* (1946), *Criss Cross* (1949) and *The File on Thelma Jordan* (1950). As the studio system began to disintegrate in the early 1950s, however, Siodmak became frustrated with Hollywood and, after completing filming in England and Spain on the Warner Brother's swashbuckler *The Crimson Pirate* (1952), he decided to remain in Europe. He attempted to reinsert himself into the German film industry in 1955, but, with the significant exception of *Nachts, Wenn Der Teufel Kam / The Devil Came at Night* (1957) he encountered limited commercial and critical success in this fourth stage of his career. He died on 10 March 1973 in Locarno, Switzerland, just seven weeks after the death of his wife Bertha Odenheimer.

Notes

1 Donald Marshman, 'Mister "Seé-Odd-Mack"', *Life* magazine, 25 August 1947, p. 100.
2 Ibid., 107.
3 Mark Jancovich, '"A Former Director of German Horror Films": Horror, European Cinema and the Critical Reception of Robert Siodmak's Hollywood Career', in Patricia Allmer, Emily Brick and David Huxley (eds), *European Nightmares*, New York: Wallflower, 2012, pp. 185–93.

4 Andrew Sarris, *The American Cinema: Directors and Directions, 1929–1968*, New York, Dutton, 1968, p. 138.

5 Ibid., p. 138.

6 Lutz Koepnick, 'Doubling the Double: Robert Siodmak in Hollywood', *New German Critique: An Interdisciplinary Journal of German Studies*, vol. 89, 2003, p. 94.

7 Ibid., p. 88.

8 Ibid., p. 100.

9 Tim Snelson, *Phantom Ladies: Hollywood Horror and the Home Front*, New Brunswick, NJ, Rutgers University Press, 2014.

10 Universal, 'Movie Doors Now Open To Taller Actresses', *Son of Dracula* pressbook, Margaret Herrick Library, California, 1943.

11 Universal, '*Phantom Lady* First Mystery for Lady Fans', in *Phantom Lady* pressbook, BFI Library, London, 1944.

12 Manny Farber, 'Two Phantoms', *New Republic*, March 1944, p. 346; James Agee, '*Phantom Lady* review', *The Nation*, February 26, 1944; Letter from Joseph Breen to Maurice Pivar, September 3, 1943, 're: screenplay dated August 24, 1943', MPAA file, Margaret Herrick Library, California.

13 John D'Emilio and Estelle B. Freedman, 'Redrawing the Boundaries', in *Intimate Matters: A History of Sexuality in America: Second Edition*, Chicago, Chicago University Press, 1997, p. 260.

14 Laura Mulvey, 'Visual Pleasure and Narrative Cinema', *Screen* 16, 1975, p. 7.

15 AFI, 'The Spiral Staircase', AFI Catalogue of Feature Films. Accessed 21 January 2014.

16 Koepnick, p. 104.

17 David Thomson, *Biographical Dictionary of Film*, London, Andre Deutsch, 1995, pp. 699, 700.

18 Ibid, p. 700.

19 Joseph. Greco, *The File on Robert Siodmak, 1941–1951*, Boca Raton, Florida, Universal, 1999, p. 9.

Filmography

Menschen am Sonntag (*People on Sunday*) (1929) codirected with Edgar J. Ulmer

Abschied (*Farewell*) (1930)

Der Mann, der seinen Mörder sucht (*Looking for His Murderer*) (1931)

Voruntersuchung (*Inquest*) (1931) also writer

Stürme der Leidenschaft (*Storms of Passion*) (1932)

Quick I and *II* (1932)

Brennendes Geheimnis (*The Burning Secret*) (1933)

Le Sexe faible (*The Weaker Sex*) (1933)

La Crise est finie (*The Depression Is Over*) (1935)

La Vie parisienne (*The Parisian Life*) (1935)

Mister Flow (1936)
Symphonie D'Amour (1936)
Cargaison Blanche (Woman Racket) (1937)
Mollenard (Hatred) (1938)
Ultimatum (1938)
Pièges (Personal Column) (1939)
West Point Widow (1941)
Fly-By-Night (1942)
The Night Before the Divorce (1942)
My Heart Belongs to Daddy (1942)
Someone to Remember (1943)
Son of Dracula (1943)
Cobra Woman (1944)
Phantom Lady (1944)
Christmas Holiday (1944)
The Suspect (1945)
The Strange Affair of Uncle Harry (1945)
The Spiral Staircase (1946)
The Killers (1946)
The Dark Mirror (1946)
Time Out of Mind (1947)
Cry of the City (1948)
Criss Cross (1949)
The Great Sinner (1949)
The File on Thelma Jordan (1950)
Deported (1950)
The Whistle at Eaton Falls (1951)
The Crimson Pirate (1952)
Card of Fate (1954)
The Rats (1955)
The Devil Came at Night (1957)
Dorothea Angermann (1958)
The Rough and the Smooth (1959)
Adorable Sinner (1960)
My School Chum (1960)
The Nina B. Affair (1961) also writer
Escape from East Berlin (1962)
The Shoot (1964) also writer
The Treasure of the Aztecs (1965)
Pyramid of the Sun God (1965)
Custer of the West (1967)
The Fight for Rome I and II (1968–69)

Further reading

Alpi, Deborah Lazaroff, *Robert Siodmak: A Biography, With Critical Analyses of His Films Noirs and a Filmography of All His Works*. Jefferson, N.C.: McFarland, 1998.

Bernard, Mark. '"A Foreign Man in a Fog": Robert Siodmak, Lon Chaney Jr., and Son of Dracula.' *Journal of Dracula Studies* 14 (2012): 77–99.

Brook, Vincent, *Driven to Darkness: Jewish Émigré Directors and the Rise of Film Noir*, New Brunswick, N.J: Rutgers University Press, 2009.

Snelson, Tim, '"From Grade B Thrillers to Deluxe Chillers": Prestige Horror, Female Audiences and Allegories of Spectatorship in *The Spiral Staircase* (1946)', *The New Review of Film and Television Studies*, vol. 7 (2009): pp. 173–88.

Walker, Michael, 'Robert Siodmak', in Ian Cameron, ed., *The Book of Film Noir*, New York: Continuum, 1993, pp. 110–51.

DOUGLAS SIRK

By Peter William Evans

No Hollywood director of melodrama has attracted as much theoretical and critical attention in recent years as Douglas Sirk. His Universal-International films have sparked lively debates ever since his rehabilitation in the pages of *Cahiers du Cinema* in the 1950s, and *Movie* in the 1960s. In the 1970s, the book of interviews with Jon Halliday and the articles collected for an Edinburgh Film Festival retrospective consolidated the view of Sirk as a major figure whose films appealed simultaneously to mainstream audiences and film theorists. Initially attracting the attention of auteurist critics who identified unifying threads of form and theme, Sirk's melodramas were subsequently considered by Marxists as critiques of American bourgeois ideology, and later by feminists who began questioning notions of authorial control. Feminist criticism has either celebrated Sirk for privileging female protagonists or condemned him for appropriating a female genre. Besides critics and theorists, filmmakers as disparate as François Truffaut, Rainer Werner Fassbinder, Pedro Almodóvar and Todd Haynes have expressed their admiration in print and on screen.

A European left-wing intellectual, he was able to bring to his Hollywood films a double-focused approach that continues to appeal to high and low audiences. The films he made in Germany at

UFA, above all the melodramas *Schlussakkord* (1936), *Zu Neuen Ufern* (1937) and *La Habanera* (1937), are early examples of this tendency. An admirer of American culture before he emigrated from Germany, Sirk quickly found his bearings in Hollywood, directing films handed to him by the studios, initially at MGM, United Artists and Columbia, and subsequently Universal-International, where his films ranged beyond melodrama to other mainstream genres such as the Western (*Taza, Son of Cochise*, 1953), the epic (*Sign of the Pagan*, 1954), and family comedy (*Has Anybody Seen My Gal?* 1951). In Halliday's indispensable book of interviews, Sirk complements references to major European writers—e.g. Euripides, Shakespeare, Calderón, Chekhov—with acknowledgements of Americans such as Thoreau, Emerson, Cather, some of whom are either directly or indirectly alluded to in his films (e.g. Thoreau in *All That Heaven Allows*, Cather in *The Tarnished Angels*). In *Taza, Son of Cochise*, the cinematography of Russell Metty, Sirk's cameraman on several films, rivals some of the evocative landscapes of Ford's great Westerns. The film testifies not only to his expert handling of one of Hollywood's most iconic genres but also to his celebration of America.

Among the many striking features of *Taza, Son of Cochise*, the theme of sibling rivalry, and its showcasing of Rock Hudson in his second Sirk role (*Has Anybody Seen My Gal?* came first), deserve mention. *All I Desire* (1953), *There's Always Tomorrow* (1955), *Written on the Wind* (1956), and *Imitation of Life* (1959) are other films where Sirk touches on siblings. In *Taza, Son of Cochise* the rivalry between brothers is not as finely nuanced as, say, in *Written on the Wind*, where Kyle Hadley (Robert Stack) is locked in a relationship of love/hatred dating back to his father's invitation to Mitch Wayne (Rock Hudson), the son of a less prosperous friend, to live and grow up as a brother to his own children in the luxurious surroundings of a petro-dollar family mansion. In *Taza, Son of Cochise*, the Taza/Naiche relationship draws on one of the Western's traditional motifs, the uneasy co-existence of natives and settlers, to comment indirectly on racial and social issues of relevance to 1950s Americans of all races and backgrounds.

Taza, Son of Cochise gave Rock Hudson an opportunity to excel as a leading man. His persona, ideally suited to the role of Taza, illustrates Sirk's interest in solid characters who clash with divided or 'broken' ones. In this film, Hudson is paired with a minor actor, Bart Roberts, who plays his darker alter ego. But elsewhere the type is played by major stars such as George Sanders in *Summer Storm* (1944), and Robert Stack in *Written on the Wind* and *The Tarnished Angels*

(1957). *Summer Storm*, woven out of Chekhov's only novel, *The Shooting Party*, was made on a budget of under $400,000 at Warner Brothers, with a cast of memorable actors that included, in addition to Sanders, Linda Darnell, Edward Everett Horton, Anna Lee and Sig Ruman. Sanders' role as Judge Petroff, overwhelmed by passion for Linda Darnell's self-seeking peasant girl, is a palimpsest of contradictions. In this film, the divided character, or what Sirk calls the 'in-between character'[1] has no rock-solid complement against whom to measure his ruinous folly.

Whether or not the stable character is coupled with his unstable opposite, his presence in Sirk's films represents a calming influence on others. So, Rock Hudson's priest in *Battle Hymn* (1956), his 'Thoreauvian' gardener in *All That Heaven Allows*, and peace-loving brave in *Taza, Son of Cochise* embody a standard of decency and reliability, often imaged as a benevolent force of nature in a turbulent world. When not played by Hudson, the role is given to others with a similar air of dependability, such as Charles Boyer in *The First Legion* (1950), or John Gavin in *A Time to Love and a Time to Die* (1957) and in *Imitation of Life*. But no one improves on Hudson.

Beyond his professional skills as an actor, Hudson's projection of a cooler, more relaxed, less aggressive persona opens up questions of male identity and sexual orientation. Sirk refers to his unsuitability for playing a 'broken personage' and goes on to define his 'straight goodness of heart and uncomplicated directness'.[2] His involvement in nine Sirk films must be taken into any account of Hollywood representations of 1950s masculinity.

The bombshell revelation of Hudson's homosexuality and his contraction of AIDS had yet to surface. Even so, his masculinity represents an interesting variant on dominant contemporary models. As Richard Dyer notes, he was neither a muscle-bound he-man nor an introverted, moody type.[3] His appeal was primarily to heterosexual female audiences. His virile physique, handsome features and unthreatening, even slightly delicate aura, were enormously attractive as an object of desire for women unimpressed by the aggressive masculinity of the ageing 1950s 'Big Bad Wolves' such as Clark Gable, Errol Flynn, John Wayne and others, or the overgrown adolescence of Marlon Brando, Montgomery Clift or James Dean. Sirk's films may sometimes, as Dyer suggests, surround the Hudson character with heterosexually related difficulties that a gay audience is intended to pick up.[4] For the mainstream female audience his appeal is an embodiment of an uncomplicated dominant form of masculinity. As well as in *Taza, Son of Cochise* and the key melodramas, Hudson appeared in one of Sirk's liveliest family comedies, *Has Anybody Seen My Gal?*

Between 1951 and 1952 Sirk made six family comedies that have attracted surprisingly little attention.[5] This neglect is surprising in view not only of Sirk's interest in stage comedy—Shakespeare, Molière, Wilde and Shaw—some of whose plays he directed in Germany, but also since his own comedies may be regarded as the sunnier versions of his melodramas. Even where the narratives privilege romantic relationship, Sirk's melodramas ground the trials and tribulations of the central couple in the vicissitudes of family life. But, while melodramas such as *Magnificent Obsession, All That Heaven Allows* or *Written on the Wind* stress internal and external pressures that blight the lovers' progress, the comedies prefer harmony and resolution, though even here irony permeates their closure with ambiguity.

Characters such as Samuel Fulton (Charles Coburn) in *Has Anybody Seen My Gal?*, or Vermilion O'Toole (Ann Sheridan) in *Take Me to Town* (1952), are on holiday from their official selves, the former disguised as 'John Smith' to exchange the stuffiness of his life of lonely privilege for the home-grown pleasures of ordinary family life, the latter, forsaking the gaudy ambience of vaudeville for surrogate motherhood, to look after a preacher's (Sterling Hayden) three sons.

The 'Thoreauvian' theme also surfaces in the comedies, and connects with its treatment in the melodramas. The pastoral settings of the comedies function not unlike those in Shakespearean comedy. The atmosphere of literary pastoralism imbues the whole of *Take Me to Town* and *Meet Me at the Fair* (1952). In *Weekend with Father* (1951) the summer camp provides a holiday location for the children and an opportunity for their parents to consolidate their conflicted relationship. The children in these films, as in *The Lady Pays Off, Take Me to Town* and *Meet Me at the Fair* are relatively free of the blocking tendencies of their counterparts in melodramas such as *All I Desire, There's Always Tomorrow, All That Heaven Allows* and *Imitation of Life*. In the comedies, the children are still largely governed by a pre-Oedipal anarchism and creativity. In the melodramas, they have become too socialised, adopting conservative and life-denying attitudes that perpetuate what Sirk regards as the cycle of regression:

> Children are usually put into pictures right at the end to show that a new generation is coming up. In my films I want to show exactly the opposite: I think it is the tragedies which are starting over again, always and always ... [6]

The conflicts between parents and children, more acute and disruptive in the melodramas, are in the comedies characterised by resolution, a sense of the rightness and normality of family life, where parents are benign forces of authority. In *The Lady Pays Off*, for instance, singledom cannot compete with the rewards of motherhood, as Evelyn Warren (Linda Darnell), a seemingly confirmed spinster, is converted to motherhood and, above all, to bonding with her employer's impossibly perfect adolescent daughter Diana (Gigi Perreau), who is determined to reconstruct her broken family by persuading Evelyn to fill the hole left by her dead mother.

If the children in Sirk's melodramas defend the family ideal, they usually do so—as in *All That Heaven Allows*—to endorse conformist notions, in defiance of a parent's reaching out for liberation from traditional attitudes. Yet, even though the comedies embrace resolution and reconciliation, their closures are provisional. Aware of the pressures of conformity, Sirk shows his characters coping under stress, resisting unqualified endorsement of the status quo. Nevertheless, the audience is left to question the effectiveness and durability of these endings. In *No Room for the Groom* (1952), for instance, we wonder whether the patched-up marriage between Alvah (Tony Curtis) and Lee (Piper Laurie) will survive their fundamental incompatibility. How long will it be in *Take Me to Town* before the ex-vaudeville performer Vermilion O'Toole wearies of marriage to the preacher and step-motherhood to his three sons? In *The Lady Pays Off*, we speculate whether Matt's (Stephen McNally) sneaky method of getting Evelyn to pay off her gambling debt at his casino by becoming his daughter's private tutor will eventually undermine her romantic involvement with him. These films ask questions that other child-dominated family comedy films of the 1950s, such as Capra's *A Hole in the Head* (1959), largely ignore.

While the comedies have been mostly neglected in discussions of Sirk's Hollywood career, the melodramas have played a key role in commentary on Hollywood melodrama as a whole, above all in their representation of the family, the relations between the sexes, gender, and the constraints on a European left wing intellectual working for a mainstream studio on largely commissioned material. The majority of the audience responded to the overt meanings of his films, while a minority to more covert ones. The minority-directed hidden text is, however, available precisely through the enhanced melodramatic strategies of music, mise-en-scène, and other formal elements that worked against the grain of the film's overt meanings.

In *All That Heaven Allows*, the projection of a conformist set of beliefs and assumptions through the attitudes of Cary's (Jane Wyman) children and some of her country-club friends is often sabotaged through colour, above all through the shades of blue that spread over the mise-en-scène.

Like the work of any artist, Sirk's films reflect unconscious as well as conscious impulses and desires. The even-handed treatment of male and female characters suggests at the very least an awareness of the constraints of dominant ideology, and provides evidence of a desire to expose, within the limits allowed by Hollywood, the socio-political realities of 1950s America. The 'Woman's Picture' variant of melodrama—the screen equivalent of the women's magazine—of which *Magnificent Obsession, There's Always Tomorrow, All That Heaven Allows, Written on the Wind* and *All I Desire* are prime examples, draw attention to the challenges and allegiances of a society in transition. The 1950s have often been classified as a period of American conservatism overseen by the Republican politics that dominated the country after Eisenhower's election as president in 1953. But the 1950s have also been seen as the seedbeds of 1960s second wave feminism. Sirk's films reflect the equivocal character of the times.

Female protagonists like Barbara Stanwyck's Naomi Murdoch in *All I Desire* (1953) and Jane Wyman's Cary Scott in *All That Heaven Allows* (1954) momentarily defy their fate, even though, ultimately, one is reintegrated into a suffocating status quo, while the other is granted what appears to be a reprieve from family and class prejudice. In *All I Desire* Naomi Murdoch's ill-defined targets of self-fulfilment include, at first, an adulterous affair with a local small-town Lothario, and then a limited career as an actress. These prove to be dead-end routes to liberation, and Naomi settles back as the chastened wife of the man she abandoned for a seemingly more thrilling alternative. The film's closure is superficially conservative. As in the comedies, though, the tone of these films is of melancholic resignation rather than of upbeat reconciliation. We are expected to wonder how permanent Naomi's return to the family will be.

All That Heaven Allows displays a similar pattern of resistance followed by social reintegration although, in a characteristically *deus ex machina* conclusion, Cary is reunited with Ron Kirby (Rock Hudson), the admirer disapproved of by her family and friends on the grounds of class and age, through an accident that forces her to care for him at the end of the film. Here, the female protagonist battles not only against external pressures represented by the country club community to which she belongs, but also her own grown-up children. Ned (William Reynolds) and Kay (Gloria Talbot) in *All That Heaven Allows*, like Vincent (William Reynolds again) and Ellen

(Gigi Perreau) or, more complicatedly, Sarah Jane (Susan Kohner) in *Imitation of Life*, are emotionally damaged by the class and, in the latter case, by the racially-based attitudes of the times.

The pressure in *All That Heaven Allows* to unite Cary and Ron to satisfy mainstream audience preference for the triumph of romantic love is met by an inverse tendency that exposes the tensions of their union. Cary's romance with Ron, slightly complicated anyway by his faintly authoritarian attitude towards her, initially horrifies her children. The children's ideologically-introjected hostility fades as they begin to lead independent lives, but the audience is led to speculate as to whether the doubts implanted in Cary's mind about Ron by Ned and Kay and the country club members will ever be truly dispelled.

Parent/child tensions are even further heightened in Sirk's last Hollywood melodrama, *Imitation of Life*, where two mothers clash with their daughters. Again, Sirk could be accused of undermining the efforts of one of the mothers, Lora Meredith (Lana Turner), to find self-fulfilment by sacrificing the emotional needs of her daughter, Susie (Terry Burnham and Sandra Dee). But in the same film the mother who prioritises her daughter's life is rewarded with her ingratitude.

All but three (*All I Desire*, *There's Always Tomorrow*, *The Tarnished Angels*) of Sirk's Universal-International melodramas were filmed in colour. Drawing on his abiding interest in painting, Sirk relies on colour as a key resource in delineating the films' social and psychological themes: for instance, he uses scarlet to represent the frenzied passion of Marylee in *Written on the Wind*, and dark blue to capture the atrophied emotions of the New England bourgeoisie in *All That Heaven Allows*. The décor and frame composition, especially the mise-en-abyme effects of mirror imagery, in the monochrome as well as in the colour films, are also key devices through which Sirk exposes the one-dimensionality of a decadent society or the veneer of normality obscuring troubled egos. Music, too, often composed by Frank Skinner and supervised by Joseph Gershenson, the 'melos' in the drama, is an integral part of Sirk's melodramatic form, now heightening, now counterpointing the characters' moods.

Whether viewed as the skilful work of a director adapting himself fully to the Hollywood system, or as brilliant double-focused attempts to combine the interests of mainstream and discerning audiences, the best of Sirk's films, especially the melodramas, have earned a justified reputation as among the milestones of Hollywood film history.

Biography

Douglas Sirk was born Hans Detlef Sierck on April 26, 1900, in Hamburg, Germany, to Danish parents. He read law at Munich University and philosophy and history of art at Hamburg University. After a period as a journalist and then as a stage director, he began from 1934 to make films at UFA studios. He left Germany in 1937, following the departure of his Jewish second wife, the actress Hilde Jary. Sirk's first wife, Lydia Brinken, with whom he had a son, was a Nazi sympathiser who denounced Jary. Sirk and Jary eventually ended up in the USA, where at first he made films for independents, MGM and Columbia, before going on to make his name at Universal-International, collaborating with the producers Ross Hunter and Albert Zugsmith, director of cinematography Russell Metty, screen writer George Zuckerman, art director Alexander Golitzen, and composers Joseph Gershenson and Frank Skinner, on some of the most striking melodramas of the 1950s. In 1959 he and his wife left America for Switzerland where he died in January 1987.

Notes

1 Halliday, Jon. 1971. *Sirk on Sirk*. London: Secker and Warburg and BFI, p. 73.
2 Ibid., p. 112.
3 Dyer, Richard. 1993. 'Rock—The Last Guy You'd Have Figured', in Pat Kirkham and Janet Thumim (eds), *You Tarzan; Masculinity, Movies and Men*. London: Lawrence and Wishart, pp. 27–34.
4 Ibid., p. 32.
5 The major exceptions are Stern, Michael. 1977–78. 'Interview with Douglas Sirk', *Bright Lights*, Winter: 29–34; and Babington, Bruce and Peter William Evans. 1989. *Affairs to Remember; the Hollywood Comedy of the Sexes*. Manchester: Manchester University Press.
6 Sirk in Halliday, 1971, p. 107.

Filmography

'T was een April (1935)
April, April (1935)
Das Mädchen vom Moorhof (1935)
Stützen der Gesellschaft (1935)
Schlussakkord (1936)
Das Hofkonzert (1936)
La Chanson du souvenir (1936)
Zu Neuen Ufern (1937)

La Habanera (1937)
Boefje (1939)
Hitler's Madman (1942)
Summer Storm (1944)
A Scandal in Paris (1945)
Lured/Personal Column (1946)
Sleep, My Love (1947)
Slightly French (1948)
Shockproof (1948)
The First Legion (1950)
Mystery Submarine (1950)
Thunder on the Hill (1951)
The Lady Pays Off (1951)
Weekend with Father (1951)
Has Anybody Seen My Gal? (1951)
No Room for the Groom (1952)
Meet Me at the Fair (1952)
Take Me to Town (1952)
All I Desire (1953)
Taza, Son of Cochise (1953)
Magnificent Obsession (1953)
Sign of the Pagan (1954)
Captain Lightfoot (1954)
All That Heaven Allows (1955)
There's Always Tomorrow (1955)
Written on the Wind (1956)
Battle Hymn (1956)
Interlude (1956)
The Tarnished Angels (1957)
A Time to Love and a Time to Die (1957)
Imitation of Life (1959)

Further reading

Elsaesser, Thomas. 'Tales of Sound and Fury: Observations on the Family Melodrama.' *Home Is Where the Heart Is: Studies in Melodrama and the Woman's Film*. Ed. Christne Gledhill. London: British Film Institute, 1987, pp. 43–69.

Evans, Peter William. *Written on the Wind*. London: BFI Palgrave/ MacMillan, 2013.

Fischer, Lucy. *Imitation of Life: Douglas Sirk Director*. New Brunswick, NJ: Rutgers University Press, 1991.

Klinger, Barbara. *Melodrama and Meaning: History, Culture and the Films of Douglas Sirk*. Bloomington: Indiana University Press, 1994.

Halliday, Jon. *Sirk on Sirk*. London: Secker and Warburg and BFI, 1971.

Meyer, Richard. 'Rock Hudson's Body.' *Inside Out: Lesbian Theories and Gay Theories*. Ed. Diana Fuss. New York and London: Routledge, 1991, pp. 259–88.

Mulvey, Laura and Jon Halliday, eds. *Douglas Sirk*. Edinburgh: Edinburgh Film Festival, 1972.

———. 'Notes on Sirk and Melodrama. *Movie* 25 (Winter 1977–78): 53–56.

Screen. Special Issue on Sirk. 1971.

JOSEF VON STERNBERG

By Amanda Ann Klein

After Charlie Chaplin saw a screening of Josef von Sternberg's first feature for United Artists, *The Salvation Hunters* (1925), he enlisted the green director to helm his next picture, *Woman of the Sea* (1926). When von Sternberg's finished film did not match Chaplin's vision, Chaplin withdrew it from circulation and von Sternberg quickly gained a reputation in Hollywood as a "difficult" director.[1] Like many directors working under the Hollywood studio system, von Sternberg chafed at its limitations. Several of his films were never completed, completed by other directors, or withdrawn from release entirely, all due to von Sternberg's inability to bend his creative vision to the demands of commerce. He directed twenty-three (complete) feature films on a range of subjects—from the criminal underworld to the destructiveness of the American Dream to sexual predilections of Russian royalty—but his visual signatures can be found to some degree in all of his films: the emphasis on textures and surface; the use of long, fluid tracking shots; the careful arrangement of light and shadow (chiaroscuro); and the favoring of tableau and spectacle over plot development.

Von Sternberg is probably best known for the six films he directed starring his muse and personal "discovery," Marlene Dietrich. Dietrich's first film role was in the German Ufa production, *The Blue Angel* (1930), where she played the beguiling cabaret singer Lola Lola. *The Blue Angel* exemplifies much of what would come to characterize the von Sternberg/Dietrich sensibility, in particular, we see the beginnings of the director's "masochistic aesthetic," which Gaylyn Studlar offers up as a counter-narrative to Laura Mulvey's foundational claims that dominant cinema's visual pleasure is based on scopophilia, and sadism, psychic mechanisms tied firmly to an active, male subjectivity.[2] Because masochistic desire is defined by the need to maintain a gap between desire and consummation, according to Studlar, the von Sternberg/Dietrich pairings provide an alternative, masochistic model of spectatorship, one which prolongs desire through the absence of the love object, in this case, the cold, two-dimensional screen image of Marlene Dietrich. As von Sternberg himself has said " ... one ... facet of glamour never changes: it promises something it cannot deliver."[3]

Indeed, Professor Rath (Emil Jannings), *The Blue Angel*'s fastidious protagonist, is drawn to Lola Lola because of her cruelty and indifference. Rath is soon disgraced by his infatuation with Lola Lola and consequently fired from his prestigious teaching position, a job upon which he based all of his self worth. To make ends meet, Rath becomes a full-time cuckold, travelling with Lola Lola and selling souvenir postcards of her likeness—the same racy postcards that first lured him to The Blue Angel—to other ogling men. When he can no longer endure his wife's indifference, Rath ends his sham marriage and storms out of the singer's dressing room. But instead of reacting, Lola Lola calmly eats her lunch and gazes at her reflection in the vanity; von Sternberg's patient camera watches and waits until, a few beats later, Rath returns, head hanging. Lola Lola is unsurprised by his sudden return and tonelessly commands, "Give me my stockings." Her husband complies, slowly sliding the fetishized garment over her extended foot. By the end of the film, Rath finds himself prostrate before his jeering former students, forced to crow like the cuckold he is. Rath's masochistic relationship with Lola Lola, this "need to control desire and suspend consummation," is replicated in the spectator's own relationship to the film text.[4] Like von Sternberg's masochistic male protagonists, the viewer privileges Dietrich (as Lola Lola, Amy Jolly, Shangai Lilly, Helen Faraday, Catherine II, or Conchita Perez) as an unfathomable but idealized mother, a fantasy available to all viewers, regardless of gender.

This desire to watch and revel in Dietrich's unknowability explains why so many of the Dietrich-von Sternberg films feature scenes in which Dietrich—a competent but by no means remarkable singer—performs a torch song before a sold-out crowd of eager, enamored spectators. When she sings "Falling in Love Again" to a packed house in *The Blue Angel*, the spotlight illuminating her face, she appears bored and possibly annoyed with the crowd's attentions. And her infamous "Hot Voodoo" number in *Blonde Venus* (1932) is a lesson in ambiguity. As the house band plays, a large gorilla bounds across the stage, scaring the club's posh white patrons with its posturing. The gorilla settles itself in the middle of the stage, grabbing at its hairy paws until a gleaming, bejeweled hand emerges. Soon Dietrich's white-blonde head rises from the gorilla's torso and smirks at her audience. Von Sternberg uses toplighting to highlight her white wig and the angles of her cheekbones, nose, and chin while a mass of faceless, scantily clad dancers with bronzed skin gyrate in unison behind her. This lighting generates Dietrich's glowing, fetishized whiteness by setting her apart from the "natives" who serve as a decorative backdrop. In *Blonde Venus* Dietrich's identity is ambiguous and incoherent: she is white, she is African, and she is animal. Later on in the film Dietrich dons her signature menswear and boldly flirts with the women in her audience, a move duplicated from a performance scene in an earlier film, *Morocco* (1930), co-starring Gary Cooper. In these moments Dietrich embodies hyperbolized sexuality as much as languid androgyny; she is man and woman, heterosexual and homosexual, all at once.

This performance also speaks to von Sternberg's love of the exaggerated—of things "being what they are not," to cite Susan Sontag's canonical "Notes on Camp."[5] The director was less concerned with moving his plots along than with expressing a tableau rife with symbolism, an "outrageous aestheticism." As a teenager von Sternberg worked as an apprentice in a millinery and later, as a stock clerk in a lace warehouse, and that early exposure to fine fabrics and textures was formative for the director; his mise en scène is crowded with fabrics, feathers, furs and lace. These fabrics can be found draped over the skin of Marlene Dietrich but also, frequently, hung in front of the camera, obscuring our view of the main action.[6] "Consequently," Aeneas Mackenzie argued in 1936, "the story does not move his picture; it is his picture which moves the story."[7] Indeed, while most classical Hollywood films aimed for an economy of action, in his Dietrich films von Sternberg painted extravagance and formal play into every frame. For example, for *The Scarlet Empress* (1934), a film von Sternberg describes as a "relentless excursion into style,"[8] the director had Pete Babusch, a Swiss sculptor, create hundreds of statues for the set.[9] These sculptures, primarily images of human figures crying, screaming, or in throes of misery, line the hallways, decorate the royal thrones, and even appear on serving dishes at Catherine II's (Marlene Dietrich) and Peter's (Sam Jaffe) lavish wedding feast. The pieces are such a spectacle in their own right that their presence frequently detracts from other, seemingly more important actions taking place within the frame.

In addition to flamboyant melodramas like *Scarlet Empress* and *The Devil is a Woman* (1935), von Sternberg also made several social realist films. In these pictures, von Sternberg's origins as a poor Jew from Austria come into sharp focus, as they reveal his understanding of poverty and desire and demonstrate empathy for characters who feel themselves on the outside looking in. His first feature, *The Salvation Hunters* (1925), is indicative of this strain of his *oeuvre*. In 1924 English comedian George K. Arthur invited von Sternberg to direct him in an American picture, and von Sternberg suggested a drama he had scripted about vagabonds living in America's urban slums. *The Salvation Hunters'* aesthetic is as reflective of its limited budget as much as it was by von Sternberg's lack of experience. They could not afford track equipment so almost all of the shots are static, a feature that differentiates *The Salvation Hunters* from most of von Sternberg's later works featuring the "unfastened camera" technique indicative of 1920s German *Kammerspielfilm*. Likewise, although von Sternberg is known for his lavish mise en scène, *The Salvation Hunters* features barren settings: blank grimy walls in an urban tenement, the flat grassiness of a country retreat. *The Salvation Hunters'* destitute characters, known only as The Boy (George K. Arthur), The Girl (Virginia Hale) and The Child (Bruce Guerin), are meant to stand as symbols for the "derelicts of the earth," individuals who are unable to earn a living and therefore find themselves faced with difficult moral choices. Despite a pimp's best efforts to convince The Girl to prostitute herself, the film concludes with The Boy pummeling his adversary to unconsciousness. Then The Boy, The Girl, and The Child walk off together, towards the setting sun as an intertitle explains "our faith controls our lives." We are meant to cheer The Girl's preserved chastity and The Boy's bravery, but it is unclear where they will sleep or eat their next meal. Such a conclusion feels disingenuous in a film that labors to show how the poor generally have little control over their poverty.

Von Sternberg addressed this issue of moral choices and class mobility two years later in the iconic gangster film, *Underworld* (1927). At the time of its release *Underworld* represented a fundamental change in the style of silent gangster films, mainly because it was "less fanciful" and "grittier" than its forbearers and because it depicted the criminal environment from the gangster's point of view.[10] *Underworld*'s prominence in the history of the gangster genre can also be linked to its use of certain key icons and conventions which would later become central to the genre: the lavish underworld celebration, the detailed depiction of the crowded, run-down city milieu, the use of newspaper headlines to further key plot points, and the charismatic gangster hero, Bull Weed (George Bancroft).[11] Like the more famous cinematic gangsters who followed in the 1930s—Tony Camonte (Paul Muni), Rico Bandello (Edward G. Robinson), and Tommy Powers (James Cagney)—Bull Weed is uneducated but "street smart," encourages his own media celebrity, and he sees himself destined for greater things—such as when he spots a flashing neon advertisement that reads "The City is Yours" and he believes it to be true. However, unlike the so-called "classic cycle" of the gangster genre, *Underworld* does not focus on the gangster hero's unrelenting greed or his desire to reach the "top" or achieve the American Dream (the desires driving characters like Bandello and Camonte). Rather, Bull Weed executes his rival, Buck Mulligan (Fred Kohler)—a fatal decision resulting in his conviction—to protect the honor of his girlfriend, Feathers (Evelyn Brent). *Underworld's* reliance on the melodramatic codes of sacrifice and redemption align it with many of von Sternberg's later films, including *Shanghai Express* (1932), *Blonde Venus, Crime and Punishment* (1935) and *An American Tragedy* (1931).

An American Tragedy, Josef von Sternberg's adaptation of Theodore Dreiser's social realist novel of the same name, offers up an interesting hybrid of the director's seemingly opposed tendencies towards excess and naturalism. To depict the world of wealth and social prestige coveted by the protagonist, Clyde Griffiths (Phillips Holmes), von Sternberg takes a more subtle approach than he did in films like *The Scarlet Empress.* The film's iconography of wealth is conveyed soberly and objectively, with low contrast lighting and middle distance framings. However, as Clyde's resentment for his working class lover, Roberta "Bert" Allen (Sylvia Sidney) festers, the lighting becomes more high contrast, resembling that of a *film noir.* For example, when Clyde begins pressuring Bert to bring him back to her room, complaining that it is now "too cold" to be walking outside at night on their dates, their faces and bodies are obscured with the shadows from the autumn trees. Later, when Clyde has succeeded in gaining entry to Bert's room, and therefore, her virginity, the room is cloaked in shadow, with only a few shafts of evening light coming in through her fogged windows. These scenes foreshadow the tragedy that will befall the couple once Bert becomes pregnant and threatens Clyde's romance with the pretty socialite, Sondra Finchley (Frances Dee).

Von Sternberg followed *An American Tragedy* with four Dietrich pictures (*Shanghai Express, Blonde Venus, The Scarlet Empress* and *The Devil is a Woman*), bookended with another attempt at adapting a canonical social realist text, Fyodor Dostoyevsky's *Crime and Punishment*. Made for Columbia Pictures, *Crime and Punishment* is the story of Roderick Roskolnikov (Peter Lorre), who murders a greedy pawnbroker out of vengeance and, to a lesser extent, the desperation of poverty. As in *Tragedy*, *Crime and Punishment* uses its characters in tableau, shadows obscuring their faces, to communicate character subjectivity. These scenes most clearly demonstrate the influence of German Expressionism, a film movement that sought to project a character's subjective emotions through carefully placed shadow, fantastical costuming and make up, and mannered acting. *Crime and Punishment*, despite its roots in Dostoyevsky's naturalist novel, relies on visual tableau to convey the character's inner torment. For example, as Sonya (Marian Marsh) reads Bible passages to Rolskolnikov in order to convince him to turn himself in to the police, we don't hear the tortured murderer ruminate at length on his torment, as he does in the novel. Instead we have a close up of his face, breathing heavily and dripping with perspiration and medium shots of a frightened Sonya, reading with a shaky voice in the shadows by her window. These laden images condense Dostoyevsky's 500-page opus into a tight, 84-minute Hollywood story.

The last few years of von Sternberg's Hollywood career were unremarkable. After *The King Steps Out* (1936), von Sternberg's disastrous attempt to recreate the glamour and opulence of a major studio with minor-studio resources, the director left Columbia and denounced the film. This was followed by a bout of illness and several years spent travelling the world. Upon his return von Sternberg was approached by Alexander Korda to direct an adaptation of *I, Claudius* for his London Films studio, a financial disaster that von Sternberg never completed.[12] He followed this up with *Sergeant Madden* (1939), a Wallace Beery crime picture for MGM, *The Shanghai Gesture* (1941), a Code-testing adaptation of a twenties-era play about prostitutes, for United Artists, and *Macao* (1950), a love story starring Robert Mitchum and Jane Russell, a sensual stand-in for Dietrich. Sternberg's final, completed film, *The Saga of Anatahan* (1952), was filmed and set in Japan, and was, according to his autobiography, von Sternberg's favorite.

A year after Josef von Sternberg died, Marcel Oms wrote a loving tribute to his work: "Sternberg's whole work is nothing but an agonized mediation on the difficulty of living. Without this philosophic assumption, his baroque aesthetic would have been merely superficial."[13] It is this dialectic—between realism and fantasy, economy and opulism—that enabled von Sternberg to successfully complete twenty-three feature films while pushing back on every demand made of him by the Hollywood studio system. Though he often complained about Hollywood, famously stating "there is nothing of me in it,"[14] each of von Sternberg's Hollywood films are undeniably his own, reflecting his personal experiences as a poor Jewish immigrant as well as his very adult lusts for cold, indifferent women.

Biography

Born as Jonas Sternberg in Vienna in 1894 to a poor Orthodox Jewish family, Josef von Sternberg changed his name after moving to America in a doubled effort to erase both his ethnic (Jewish) and economic (the addition of "von") past. After working a series of low-skill jobs—dish-washer, farm hand, stock clerk—von Sternberg obtained work servicing and repairing film prints at a New York firm, a job that honed his eye for visual composition and editing. Although von Sternberg held contracts with major studios like MGM and Paramount throughout his career, he often found himself at odds with the studio system and its stars, resulting in numerous abandoned projects. Von Sternberg died in 1969 of a heart attack.

Notes

1 Josef von Sternberg, *Fun in a Chinese Laundry: An Autobiography*. New York: MacMillan Publishing, 1965, pp. 32–33.

2 Laura Mulvey, "Visual Pleasure and Narrative Cinema." *Film Theory and Criticism: Introductory Readings*. 5th ed. Eds. Leo Braudy and Marshall Cohen. New York: Oxford University Press, 1999, pp. 833–44.

3 "The Von Sternberg Principle." *Sternberg*. Ed. Peter Baxter. London: BFI, 1980, p. 53.

4 Gaylyn Studlar, *In the Realm of Pleasure: Von Sternberg, Dietrich, and the Moschistic Aesthetic*. Urbana: University of Illinois Press, 1988, p. 27.

5 Susan Sontag, "Notes on Camp." *Against Interpretation and Other Essays*. New York: Farrar, Straus and Giroux, 1961.

6 Von Sternberg, pp. 16–17.

7 "Leonardo of the Lenses." *Sternberg*. Ed. Peter Baxter. London: BFI, 1980, p. 43.

8 Von Sternberg, p. 265.

9 John Baxter. *The Cinema of Josef Von Sternberg*. London: C. Tinling and Co. Ltd. 1971, p. 10; Von Sternberg, p. 112.

10 John McCarty. *Hollywood Gangland: The Movies' Love Affair with the Mob*. New York: St. Martin's Press, 1993, p. 40.

11 Eugene Rosow. *Born to Lose: The Gangster Film in America*. New York: Oxford University Press, 1978, p. 123.

12 John Baxter, pp. 133–37.

13 "Josef Von Sternberg." *Sternberg*. Ed. Peter Baxter. London: BFI, 1980, p. 63.
14 Qtd. in John Baxter.

Filmography

The Salvation Hunters (1925)
Exquisite Sinner (1925)
Underworld (1927)
The Last Command (1928)
The Drag Net (1928)
The Docks of New York (1929)
The Case of Lena Smith (1929)
Thunderbolt (1929)
The Blue Angel (1930)
Morocco (1930)
Dishonored (1931)
An American Tragedy (1931)
Shanghai Express (1932)
Blonde Venus (1932)
The Scarlet Empress (1934)
The Devil is a Woman (1935)
Crime and Punishment (1935)
The King Steps Out (1936)
Sargent Madden (1939)
The Shanghai Gesture (1941)
Macao (1950)
Jet Pilot (1950)
The Saga of Anatahan (1952)

Further reading

Baxter, Peter (ed.). *Sternberg*. London: BFI, 1980.
Constable, Catherine. *Thinking in Images: Film Theory, Feminist Philosophy and Marlene Dietrich*. London: British Film Institute, 2005.

PRESTON STURGES

By Lindsay Steenberg

The life and films of Preston Sturges are equally bizarre and fascinating. In addition to working as a screenwriter, composer, playwright, and military pilot, he was also an inventor (his creations include a vibrationless diesel engine and long-lasting lipstick) and restaurateur (The Players at 8225 Sunset Boulevard had a Sturges designed system of rotating platforms and its own theatre). None of Sturges' ventures, however, achieved lasting financial success. Sturges' brief but intense triumph in Hollywood was largely due to the series of off-beat comedies he made for Paramount from 1940 to 1944, including *The Lady Eve, The Palm Beach Story, The Miracle of Morgan's Creek* and *Hail the Conquering Hero*. Film critic Andrew Sarris describes Sturges' Paramount films as "one of the most brilliant and bizarre bursts of creation in the history of cinema."[1] By the early 50s, Sturges had lost The Players and Sturges Engineering Company to the IRS, struggled to find work in Hollywood and was living in relative poverty. Sturges himself reported, "It looked as if fate were intent on eradicating every trace of my existence in Hollywood."[2] Sturges was by all accounts as contradictory as his films – extravagant and hard working; loyal and mercurial; self-deprecating and self-congratulatory.

Considerations of Sturges' films generally fuse his exceptional life and career. Yet he is rarely discussed as an auteur in the same way as some of his contemporaries. Like Sarris, the influential French critics at the *Cahiers du Cinema* did not devote the kind of attention to Sturges' films as they did to Howard Hawks or John Ford. Alessandro Pirolini points out:

> Sturges became neither a case study of Classical Hollywood auteur, nor the occasion for more recent postmodern rediscoveries, and he was mainly confined to the territory of the Hollywood personality, whose life (more than his movies) deserves to be told.[3]

Scholarship has emerged that considers the intersection points between his larger than life personality and his films. Pirolini sees Sturges' works as powerful examples of a nascent postmodern sensibility in the cinema and Diane Jacobs argues that he embraces the modernist mantra of 'make it strange!' despite his personal disgust at such labels.[4] Perhaps the most cited source for scholarship on Sturges' life and work is the man himself, whose letters and autobiography feature heavily in many studies of his films. As Jacobs' observes, Sturges was a "deft mythographer"[5] with a strong hand in the manufacture of the Sturges persona as an irascible cinematic and engineering genius.

Although Sturges initially gained Hollywood notoriety as the screenwriter of *The Power and the Glory* (Howard 1933), Sturges was not considered a cinematic force until his 1940 film *The Great McGinty*, when he became the first man to direct his own script. This honour was indicated by a 'written and directed by' credit onscreen, the first of its kind. Typically Sturgean style and preoccupations are most visible in those films he both writes and directs. He uses invisible cinematography, eschews realism, favours single take shots, and often draws on his experience in the theatre. Although rarely displaying the attention-getting stylistic virtuosity of directors such as Orson Welles, Sturges made frequent use of *narratage*, a technique where "the narrator's, or author's, voice spoke the dialogue while the actors only moved their lips."[6] A sequence from *The Lady Eve* demonstrates Sturges' use of this silent cinema inspired technique perfectly: adventuress Jean (Barbara Stanwyck) observes (in her compact mirror) a series of ambitious young women attempt to seduce clueless millionaire snake enthusiast Charles Pike (Henry Fonda). As we watch the women inventing excuses to introduce themselves to Pike, Jean's voiceover comically imagines their dialogue. Sturges' humorous *narratage*, along with his larger than life persona, were used as marketing tools for his films.

During his tenure at Paramount, Sturges built up a solid ensemble of supporting character actors to whom he was intensely loyal and to whose performances he devoted an unusual amount of time and effort.[7] Sturges credits his commitment to actors such as Jimmy Conlin, Harry Rosenthal and Robert Warwick as one of the reasons why Paramount (under the management of Buddy DeSylva) looked to break their working relationship.[8] These actors are the main performers of the vaudeville inspired and slapstick humour in Sturges' films – from the drunken 'Ale and Quail Club' in *The Palm Beach Story* to the well meaning broke marines in *Hail the Conquering Hero*. Sturges' access to a cast of regulars also generated many of the extra-textual references common to his films – e.g., the characters of McGinty and 'the Boss' appear in *The Miracle of Morgan's Creek*, and a publicity poster for that film is visible in the train station in *Hail the Conquering Hero*.

Sturges' films combine physical humour with witty dialogue and social satire, often punctuating comic farce with powerful instances of violence or pathos. One sequence in *Sullivan's Travels*, for instance, features the amnesiac director going to prison for brutally bludgeoning a railroad security guard. Sturges' stories frequently hinge on the collision between the sophisticated and ridiculous upper classes and the equally ridiculous but generous poor. The Sturges story is that of the self-made American man – a trope that expresses his view of the world and his carefully constructed celebrity persona. Yet, this process of self-making is generally due less to perseverance than to luck, coincidence or mistake. In *Hail the Conquering Hero*, Woodrow

Truesmith (Eddie Bracken) is forced into masquerading as a heroic marine returning from the front, and in *Christmas in July* Jimmy MacDonald (Dick Powell) receives a doctored telegram (courtesy of his prankster co-workers) confirming him as the winner of a slogan writing contest. Both cases of mistaken identity are revealed to the community at the films' climaxes and despite the vortex of misunderstandings that surround them, both men prove themselves worthy of admiration. It is not hard work that makes the man in Sturges' films, but innate virtue combined with karmic (and comic) coincidence.

Preston Sturges' films also demonstrate a poignant sensitivity to the absurdities of American society, a sensibility expressed through his female characters' comical mixture of commerce and frank sexuality. As Gerry Jeffers (Claudette Colbert) exclaims to her broke inventor husband (Joel McCrea), "You have no idea what a long legged girl can do without doing anything." Like other irreverent heroines of the screwball comedy, Gerry in *The Palm Beach Story* and Jean in *The Lady Eve* disguise themselves in order to get what they want, often using their sexuality as their most powerful weapon. Lori Landay points out that where pre-war screwball heroines used playful disguises as inside jokes with their male partners, screwball comedies released after the outbreak of war often punished the female masquerader rather than celebrated her ability as a trickster. For Jean "trickery only causes her more misery, and her performance of Lady Eve is unnoticed and unappreciated by the hero".[9] Critics disagree on whether Sturges' jokes come at the expense of characters such as Gerry or Jean. Sturges himself was often dismissive of women, claiming that it was a man's world where women were secondary. For example he maintains,

> Mother had absolutely nothing to do with my development ... I very much fear that this has something to do with the general esteem in which women are held compared with men. I know it is stupid and unfair, but there it is.[10]

Conversely, Diane Jacobs argues that Sturges' female characters owe much of their power to the influence of Sturges' bohemian mother and her close friend Isadora Duncan, both of whom featured prominently in Sturges' early life. Whether or not the Sturges heroine can be reduced to a joke or celebrated as a proto-feminist, she arguably embodies Sturges' views about the ridiculous way American cinema shies away from showing adult sexuality, burying it in stories about money and wartime propaganda.

The quintessential Sturges heroine is Trudy Kockenlocker (Betty Hutton) in *The Miracle of Morgan's Creek*. After a night spent partying with her small town's departing military she returns home married and pregnant but with no memory of the identity of the soldier with whom she spent the night. Her characterization gets to the heart of the gendered tensions in Sturges' body of work. Sturges claims that the moral of the film is to caution "young girls who disregard their parents' advice and who confuse patriotism with promiscuity".[11] Certainly, Trudy has a difficult journey to giving birth to 'miraculous' sextuplets. At the film's close, however, she is happily (if perhaps bigamously) married to the man she loves and the most celebrated mother in America. The sequence in which Trudy returns drunk from her evening with the soldiers hints at the almost subversive nature of her character, since her obvious enjoyment of 'victory lemonade', dancing and sex overshadows her later regret. The film was naturally of great concern to the Breen Office, Hollywood's self-censoring authority. The same is true of many Sturges films, which pushed the limits of what the Production Code deemed acceptable. Trudy is rebellious, charismatic and (through a series of hilarious coincidences) gets everything that she wants. Neither Sturges nor the male characters of his cinematic world can fully contain or understand the precocious women they encounter.

At their core, Sturges' films ask two fundamental questions: what do people do with instant success? What happens when they hit rock bottom? Through these questions the measure of the self-made man (and sometimes woman) is taken. Sturges films are not returns to the essential American working class virtues celebrated in Frank Capra's films. While *Sullivan's Travels* can in many ways be read as a re-working of Capra's wildly successful *It Happened One Night* (1934), its unlikely happy ending is far less stable. Sturges' story of the rich learning lessons by travelling among the poor reveals the immutable inequalities in American society. Sullivan is let out of prison at the film's conclusion not because he is innocent but because he is rich and famous. The pessimism underpinning his comedies earns Sturges the nickname "the anti-Capra".[12]

Like Capra's heroes, however, Sturges' characters show they morally deserve their instant success. In *Christmas in July* Jimmy takes the cheque he thinks he has won and goes on a shopping spree, buying gifts for his girlfriend, mother and neighbourhood. Rather than quitting his job, he shows even greater initiative. In the Sturges universe success is rewarded with more success while failure merits not pathos but laughter. Jimmy's bosses offer him a promotion not because of his abilities but because he has won the slogan contest. Those who have failed also prove their virtue through their generosity. In *Sullivan's Travels* the nameless actress played by Veronica Lake buys Sullivan breakfast, even though she is out of work and fleeing Hollywood. As if to reward the virtues of the comically unsuccessful, Veronica Lake gets her big break and Jimmy actually does win the contest. Sturgean karma both reveals and justifies an unequal system in operation in 1940s America. Success and failure do not arrive as a result of hard work but emerge, almost miraculously, as luck or coincidence. These turns of events make Sturgean karma characteristically contradictory, absurd, harsh and humorous.

At the close of *Sullivan's Travels* newly transfigured director John Lloyd Sullivan comes to the realization that while comedy films cannot provide a cure for America's inequalities, they are the best treatment. As he says, "it isn't much but it's better than nothing in this cockeyed caravan". Sullivan's original crusade involved rejecting his comedic filmmaking career (the film dwells on his successful comedy *Ants in Your Pants of 1939*) in favour of hard-hitting social realist cinema (he wants to adapt a fictional literary tome entitled *O Brother Where Art Thou?*).[13] He ultimately abandons this project after a harrowing prison experience where he witnesses his fellow inmates' sublime joy at watching a Disney cartoon. Sullivan's/Sturges' vision of the world as a cockeyed caravan is a justification of the Hollywood dream factory and a revelation of the world as an absurd place without virtue. *Sullivan's Travels* demonstrates the best and the worst of Preston Sturges as a filmmaker. At their worst, Sturges' films are unfunny jokes at the expense of those marginalized in wartime America. At their best they can both entertain and criticize the system. But unlike Sullivan, Sturges need not choose between *Ants in Your Pants* and *O Brother Where Art Thou?* Through some amusing narrative trickery, his films present both at once.

Biography

Born Edmund Preston Biden in 1898, Sturges spent his early years in France. In Paris his mother opens the Maison Desti, the cosmetics business where a young Sturges learns that he is an enthusiastic inventor and poor businessman. After success as a playwright, Sturges begins in Hollywood as a screenwriter for Universal but finds happiness and financial success at Paramount with the release of *The Great McGinty*. After Paramount, the movie business becomes much less lucrative for Sturges who continues to work on screenplays such as *Roman Holiday* and forms the ill-fated California Pictures with Howard Hughes. Sturges dies in 1959 in the Algonquin Hotel, working on new ventures into the theatre and television and writing his autobiography. The memoir's ironic last lines (written only twenty minutes before his death) are straight out of a Sturges script. They describe his remedy for indigestion: "ingest a little Maalox, lie down, stretch out, and hope to God I don't croak."[14]

Notes

1 Diane Jacobs, *Christmas in July: The Life and Art of Preston Sturges*, Berkeley: University of California Press, 1992, p. 215.
2 Preston Sturges, *Preston Sturges: His Life in His Words*, Sandy Sturges (ed.), New York: Touchstone, 1990, p. 325.
3 Alessandro Pirolini, *The Cinema of Preston Sturges: A Critical Study*, Jefferson: McFarland & Company, Inc., 2010, p. 2.
4 Jacobs, *Christmas in July*, p. xii.
5 Jacobs, *Christmas in July*, p. xiii
6 Sturges, *Preston Sturges*, p. 272.
7 Jacobs, *Christmas in July*, p. 224.
8 Sturges, *Preston Sturges*, pp. 297–98.
9 Lori Landay, *Madcaps, Screwballs and Con Women: The Female Trickster in American Culture*, Philadelphia: University of Pennsylvania Press, 1998, p. 142.
10 Sturges, *Preston Sturges*, p. 260.
11 Sturges, *Preston Sturges*, p. 300.
12 Pirolini, *The Cinema of Preston Sturges*, quoting André Bazin, p. 28.
13 The Coen brothers' film *O Brother Where Art Thou?* (2000) draws on *Sullivan's Travels* (among other sources) to make a postmodern comedy about travelling through depression era America.
14 Sturges, *Preston Sturges*, p. 340.

Filmography

The Great McGinty (1940)
Christmas in July (1940)
The Lady Eve (1941)
Sullivan's Travels (1942)
The Palm Beach Story (1942)
Safeguarding Military Information (1942)
The Miracle of Morgan's Creek (1944)
Hail the Conquering Hero (1944)
The Great Moment (1946)
The Sin of Harold Diddlebock (1947)
Unfaithfully Yours (1948)

The Beautiful Blonde From Bashful Bend (1949)
Mad Wednesday (1950)
Les Carnets du Major Thompson (1955)
The French are a Funny Race (1957)

Further reading

Agee, James. *Agee on Film: Volume 1.* New York: Grosset & Dunlap, 1941.

Farber, Manny and W. S. Poster. "Preston Sturges: Success in the Movies." *Film Culture* 26 (Autumn 1962): 9–16.

Kracauer, Siegfried. "Preston Sturges or Laughter Betrayed." *Films in Review* 1.1 (February 1950): 11–13, 43–47.

Spoto, Donald. *Madcap: The Life of Preston Sturges.* Boston: Little, Brown and Company, 1990.

Ursini, James. *The Fabulous Life and Times of Preston Sturges, An American Dreamer.* New York: Curtis Books, 1973.

FRANK TASHLIN

By Harvey O'Brien

Frank Tashlin began writing and illustrating in his school years. Starting at the Fleischer Brothers animation studio in New York in 1929, he undertook a series of jobs in the animation industry. These positions included two stints at Warner Bros. (where he was a contemporary of Tex Avery and Bob Clampett), one at Disney, and periods at the Van Beuren and Columbia Screen Gems animation studios. He is often credited by these studios as 'Tish Tash', and fulfilled a variety of roles including writing, direction, and 'supervision' (essentially direction). Known as a gag-man in the mould of Tex Avery (whom Tashlin modestly credits as his influence, though some observers equate them), his films were noteworthy for the visual and behavioural refinement of the character of Porky Pig, his deployment of shape (anticipating the graphic style of 1940s and 50s advertising), and the level and precision of camera movement he used. The frequent remark that his cartoons were shot like live action and his live action shot like cartoons is perhaps exaggerated, but not entirely unfounded.

Tashlin's films were noteworthy for featuring knowing and parodic asides and breakages of the cinematic fourth wall in which on-screen characters would acknowledge and even address the audience, frequently about the plot. In *The Case of the Stuttering Pig* (1937) the audience becomes involved in the plot when an irate patron 'in the third row' foils the on-screen villain, who has been taunting him throughout the film. Though arguably characteristic of the Jack Benny-influenced comic ethos of Warner Bros.' legendary 'termite terrace', the sceptical, ironic, and often satirical gaze of Tashlin's animations deepened and darkened as he moved to live action, while his canvas remained broadly unrealistic and irreverent.

In 1944 Tashlin's Porky Pig cartoon *The Swooner Crooner* was nominated for an Academy Award, and in 1946 he published *The Bear That Wasn't*, the first of three storybooks that he wrote and illustrated. These three books were written as Tashlin transitioned into live action, first as a screenwriter and script doctor, then as a director. *The Bear That Wasn't* was followed by *The Possum That Didn't* (1950) and *The World That Isn't* (1951). *The Bear That Wasn't* is a comical but pointedly satirical tale of a bear that awakens from hibernation in a newly built factory. Unable to convince the people that work there that he is not human, he finds himself pressed by management into the frantic and mechanized world of post-war industrial labour. The thematically similar but more melancholy *The Possum That Didn't* recounts the tale of a possum whose smile is seen by humans as a frown because he hangs upside-down. The humans bring the possum to the city and harangue it with the joys of modern consumer culture until the creature's smile turns upside down and its misery is read as happiness by the satisfied humans. *The World That Isn't* is a downright nihilistic story of humanity's race towards nuclear annihilation. Tashlin archivist and documentarian Howard Prouty writes: 'This is not a book that any rational parent would read to their child.'[1]

It is difficult not to see the books and films of Frank Tashlin as a desperate plea for a reality check on the part of humankind. Though his non-naturalistic and borderline surrealist films only rarely deal with characters that are anything more than live action cartoon characters, Tashlin's films savagely confront the fantasies by which human society (more particularly mid-twentieth century American consumer capitalist society) conducts its affairs. While comical, they are also extremely dark when considered as narratives of cultural commentary. His films deal in false worlds—consensual delusions of material success and sexual conquest in which most of the characters are either consciously or unconsciously role-playing. Many of the films are parodic, if not completely deconstructive of their master genres, including *Son of Paleface* (1952), a Western that features a wisecracking Bob Hope getting away with a joke about co-star Roy Rogers' relationship with his horse that still surprises today.² Other films are clearly satirical, most famously *Will Success Spoil Rock Hunter?* (1957), which targets both television and the advertising industry of the mid 1950s. Others still are framed in terms of sexual farce, a recurring idiom that frequently brought mid-career Tashlin into conflict with the Production Code. Women in Tashlin films are grotesquely exaggerated, highly sexualised caricatures based on the manufactured ideals of beauty of the period, most obviously (and literally) embodied by Jayne Mansfield in *The Girl Can't Help It* (1956), whose walk down the street triggers a series of metaphorical ejaculations in delivery men. Tashlin's men are equally troubled; simultaneously disabled and enabled in sexual passive-aggression in the presence of such creatures, they are as often vulgar and infantilized as they are nominally heroic.

There is an overarching sense of black despair in Tashlin's comic vision of what in his interview with Peter Bogdanovich he describes as 'the nonsense of what we call civilization.'³ He is clearly appalled by the self-absorption and (largely sexualized) social rituals of a deluded and broken humanity. He frequently punctures the veneer of functionality and the ethos of success characteristic of post-war American popular culture with the insertion of a sexually innocent but libidinal hero who creates generically predetermined chaos and disorder in the everyday world. (Jerry Lewis is Tashlin's most clearly articulated version of this character, appearing as such in each of the eight films they made together, but the role is also filled by others including Bob Hope and Tony Randall.) Often, there is a frantic energy and a pronounced sense of unreality to these characters and their world that exceeds the Vaudeville-Borscht Belt star vehicle formula that is their typical fare. The actors don't quite stand out or apart from the cinematic aesthetic as they would in a star vehicle: rather they become part of Tashlin's palette, as malleable as a cartoon character in a cartoon universe.

Tashlin's cartoons were often marked with a sense of irreverence for the trappings of marriage and family. In *Porky's Romance* (1937), Porky tries to court Petunia pig, but is knocked unconscious and fantasizes about the loveless, horrific marriage that lies ahead of him given how difficult the courtship has been. Likewise, in *Brother Brat* (1944) Porky tries to manage a gruff, unruly baby while his mother works as a war labourer. If, then, Porky Pig and Daffy Duck were Tashlin's tools for the pillory of romantic ritual and other socio-political mores, so too did he disrupt mannered portrayals of sexuality in his live action films, featuring characters who manage sensual extremes ranging from indulgence to deprivation. Jerry Lewis as a bumbling sexual naïf, for example, enjoys an ersatz orgy in the massage scene in *Artists and*

Models (1955). On the other hand, Tony Randall uncharacteristically resists Jayne Mansfield in *Will Success Spoil Rock Hunter?*, and *The Glass Bottom Boat* (1966) allows Doris Day to update her no longer sustainable 'virgin' character, maintaining an air of sexual mystery as a widow around whom men swarm.

Ethan de Seife's study of Tashlin's cinema argues that traditional readings that stress Tashlin's transition from cartoon maker to filmmaker miss the point. In every medium, de Seife says, Tashlin was first and foremost a director of comedy. This is certainly true, but it is also true that Tashlin viewed the world as such a profoundly overdetermined, absurd, and fabricated place that employing a cartoonist's sensibility was the only way to properly render it. Tashlin's cinematic world is 'cartoony' on many registers: for one, in the mechanical sense of mise-en-scène, particularly his compositions and camera movement, which emphasize strong shapes. Similarly, though the colour range of the pastel-decorated universe of the live action films isn't as vivid as that of the technicolour animations, there is still a pronounced delineation effect in the way the actors are framed against the sets. The pace of his editing employs similar affinities with animation techniques, though these can be deceptive, as it is the action that is frequently frantic rather than the cutting. The 'living Looney Tune' comedians with whom he worked also highlight his roots: personalities including Hope and Lewis, as well as Danny Kaye in *The Man From the Diner's Club* (1963) and Terry Thomas in *Bachelor Flat* (1962). Most importantly, however, Tashlin is a cartoonist in the more profound sense that his films are illustrations – caricatures of reality that draw attention to their own expressivity. Animation scholar Paul Wells argues that animation always calls attention to itself *as* animation, inviting the viewer to both enjoy the illusion and spectacle but also recognize the artisanal and expressive work as work in itself (as drawing, as animation). He notes: 'Animation in essence makes the aesthetic surface of the work more visible, tracking the implications of motion, and offers a perception of spectacle as well as its outcome.'[4] Tashlin's live action films are as direct as cartoons – they are aesthetically expressive and reflexive, inviting the audience to actively 'read' them as illustrations. To make this point, Tashlin filled his cinema with reflexive asides including gag cameos and intertextual in-jokes, direct addresses to the audience, and an overarching sense of absurdist self-parody that refuses empathy and dramatic immersion. Like a Warner Bros. cartoon character letting the audience in on the joke by cracking wise outside the frame of the story, his films draw attention to the constructedness of filmic reality and the representational context within which the film should therefore be seen.

Tashlin's targets are sometimes obvious and seemingly external to cinema, including the comic book industry (*Artists and Models*), the music business (*The Girl Can't Help It*), television and advertising (*Will Success Spoil Rock Hunter?*), Californian college students and professors (*Bachelor Flat*), health care and psychiatry (*The Disorderly Orderly*), big retail (*Who's Minding the Store?*), and espionage/anticommunist hysteria (*The Glass Bottom Boat* and *Caprice*). However, like latter-day mockumentaries that ridicule the subject rather than the object, reading the satire on this level alone is to miss the point. Underlying the quips, gags, and bits of comical business is a refusal of the representational frame itself, almost a dismissal of 'cinema' as it was when Tashlin began to work with it. Jean-Luc Godard saw this, and famously hailed Tashlin's filmography as heralding a truly modern comic cinema. Godard's call to ditch the phrase 'Chaplinseque' in favour of 'Tashlinesque' in 1957 was unquestionably a signal of Godard's own directorial ambitions,[5] and Eisenschitz[6] and de Seife[7] have both analysed the ideological and aesthetic interconnections between the two filmmakers. The two directors' similarities exist not least of all in the Brechtian dimensions of what Ian Cameron identifies as films which 'show a synthetic world in a way that is itself synthetic'.[8] Yet Andrew Sarris would flatly dismiss Tashlin in his taxonomy of directorial authority as 'expressive esoterica' in 1963, an evaluation revised in 1968 with the observation that Tashlin had become 'sympathetically obsolete without ever becoming fashionable'.[9]

Ironically, by the end of his career Tashlin had been eclipsed in French film criticism by his apprentice, Jerry Lewis, who freely acknowledged his indebtedness to Tashlin. Indeed the Tashlin-directed *Cinderfella* (1960) is a clear marker of Lewis' emergence, veering towards a fantastical sentimentality more characteristic of Lewis's oeuvre than Tashlinesque modernism. Curiously, after Lewis' departure, Tashlin's own anarchic imagination nonetheless appeared dulled, and he never quite found another vessel as ideal as Lewis for creating a canvas of cineplastic impossibilities and who could serve as the embodiment of his illustrator's imagination. Though later Tashlin continues to exhibit almost misanthropic scepticism with American society, particularly its constructed desires (sexual, material, and ideological), his aesthetic settled into a calmer and more conventional cinematic register. This even permitted moments of identification and humanity, such as the casual sing-a-long scene in *The Glass Bottom Boat* where Doris Day parodies her own hit *Que Sera Sera*, now in the context of an adult woman entertaining friends and family over a casual drink on the back porch. The scene is shot without compositional complication, and plays with a warmth unseen in Tashlin's earlier work. When compared with the heavily ironic beach scene in *The Girl Can't Help It* where a bathing suit-clad Jayne Mansfield professes her true and heartfelt desire to live a normal family life to an understandably distracted Tom Ewell, the later film seems the work of another director entirely.

Tashlin enjoyed an immediately posthumous upsurge in appreciation with the 1973 Edinburgh Film Festival focus on his work, resulting in Claire Johnson and Paul Willemen's edited volume of essays and criticism. The same result followed Locarno Film Festival programme in 1994, this time inspiring a collection edited by Frank Garcia. Tashlin remains frequently spoken of as an 'underappreciated' director, and yet the body of scholarly work on his films is consistently robust in tackling his many dimensions and arguably subtle legacies (certainly subtler than Godard seemed to imagine in 1957). Ethan de Seife's 2012 monograph remains the only sole-authored analysis of his films, though many and various online journals continue to revisit the director, particularly as the films are reissued on various home viewing formats.[10] Though it is true the phrase 'Tashlinesque' never became the touchstone Godard may have hoped, the cinema of Frank Tashlin is a significant historical link in the evolutionary chain between mechanical and digital cinema. Given how it occupies a unique aesthetic space between live action and animation, the study of Tashlin is both instructive and illustrative.

Biography

Born Francis Fredrick von Taschlein on 19 February 1913 in Weekhawken, New Jersey of French and German parentage, Frank Tashlin worked in animation and live-action cinema, and also authored and illustrated three children's books. Tashlin wrote, directed, and produced feature films through the 1950s and 1960s, most notably a series of comedies starring Jerry Lewis, whose own directorial style is clearly informed by Tashlin. Tashlin earned his first directorial credit for *Hook & Ladder Hokum* (1933) (which he co-directed with George Stallings), and his Warner Bros. short *The Swooner Crooner* (1944) was nominated for an Academy Award. His first live action directorial credit was for the marital comedy *The First Time*, though he had directed approximately one third of *The Lemon Drop Kid* (1951) during re-shoots based on his screenplay. His last directorial credit was for the late-career Bob Hope vehicle *The Private Navy of Sgt. O'Farrell*. Tashlin died in 1972, survived by wife Jean Deines and son Christopher Tashlin.

Notes

1 Howard Prouty, 'Frank Tashlin Bibliography', available http://home. labridge.com:8100/|hprouty.
2 While ogling Jane Russell performing in a saloon, Hope questions a stoic Rogers: 'Don't you like girls?' to which Rogers responds 'I'll stick to horses, Mister.' Hope's reaction goes on for quite some time to underscore that the joke is intentionally risqué.
3 Peter Bogdanovich, 'Frank Tashlin: An Interview and an Appreciation', in Claire Johnston and Paul Willemen (eds) *Frank Tashlin*, Edinburgh, Edinburgh Film Festival 1973 in association with *Screen*, 1973, p. 57.
4 Paul Wells, *Animation: Genre and Authorship*, London, Wallflower Press, 2007, p. 32.
5 In *Cahiers du Cinema*, July 1957, cited in Jonathan Rosenbaum 'Tashlinseque', in Roger Garcia (ed.) *Frank Tashlin*, Locarno, Editions du Festival international du film de Locarno in conjunction with the British Film Institute, 1994, p. 23.
6 Bernard Eisenschitz, 'Pardon my French' in Garcia, op. cit., pp. 103–9.
7 Ethan de Seife, *Tashlinesque: The Hollywood Comedies of Frank Tashlin*, Middletown, Connecticut, Wesleyan University Press, 2012, pp. 190–98.
8 Ian Cameron, 'Frank Tashlin and the New World', in Johnston and Willemen, op. cit., p. 86.
9 Andrew Sarris, *The American Cinema: Directors and Directions 1929–1968*, Cambridge, Da Capo Press, 1996, p. 141.
10 The 2005 Warner Bros. *Looney Tunes Golden Collection Vol. 3* featured a short documentary made for the DVD release entitled *Tish Tash: The Animated World of Frank Tashlin* (producer Constantine Nasr).

Filmography

The First Time (1952)
Son of Paleface (1952)
Marry Me Again (1953)
Susan Slept Here (1954)
Artists and Models (1955)
The Lieutenant Wore Skirts (1956)
Hollywood or Bust (1956)
The Girl Can't Help It (1956)
Will Success Spoil Rock Hunter? (1957)
Rock-a-Bye Baby (1958)
The Geisha Boy (1958)
Say One for Me (1959)
Cinderfella (1960)
Bachelor Flat (1962)
It'$ Only Money (1962)

The Man From the Diner's Club (1963)
Who's Minding the Store? (1963)
The Disorderly Orderly (1964)
The Alphabet Murders (1966)
The Glass Bottom Boat (1966)
Caprice (1967)
The Private Navy of Sgt. O'Farrell (1968)

Further reading

Byron, Stuart. 'Frank Tashlin.' *The National Society of Film Critics on Movie Comedy*. Eds. Stuart Byron and Elisabeth Weis. Harmondsworth: Penguin, 1977, pp. 89–90.
Durgnat, Raymond. 'I Dreamed I Flew through the Air on a Custard Pie: What Could That Mean, Doctor?' *The Crazy Mirror: Hollywood Comedy and the American Image*. New York: Delta, 1969, pp. 231–39.
Garcia, Roger, ed. *Frank Tashlin*. Locarno: Editions du Festival international du film de Locarno in conjunction with the British Film Institute, 1994.
Henderson, Brian. 'Cartoon Narrative in the Films of Frank Tashlin and Preston Sturges.' *Comedy/Cinema/Theory*. Ed. Andrew Horton. Berkeley: University of California Press, 1991, pp. 153–73.
Johnston, Claire and Paul Willemen, eds. *Frank Tashlin*. In association with *Screen*. Edinburgh: Edinburgh Film Festival, 1973.
Leers, Philip. 'Frank Tashlin: The Animated Auteur.' *Bright Lights Film Journal* 69 (August 2010.) http://www.brightlightsfilm.com/69/69tashlinleers.php.
Sikov, Ed, ed. 'Living Looney Tunes: The Art of Frank Tashlin.' *Laughing Hysterically: American Screen Comedy of the 1950s*. New York: Columbia University Press, 1994, pp. 179–242.

JACQUES TOURNEUR

By Yannis Tzioumakis

Jacques Tourneur belongs to a small group of film directors who always have been admired by film critics. Associated primarily with the Hollywood studios' lowly B film units and the Poverty Row firms, filmmakers such as Edgar G. Ulmer, Joseph H. Lewis, Phil Karson, Budd Boetticher, Dorothy Arzner and Tourneur often worked with very limited resources and in a range of genres, especially "disreputable" ones such as the urban crime drama and the horror film. For these reasons, there were few expectations that they could produce anything else but "functional" product that would accompany often infinitely glossier, and in theory more appealing, A pictures in double feature presentations. And yet, these filmmakers used the B film as a platform for creativity, sometimes in response to logistical problems caused by the lack of resources, at others in an effort to find interesting ways to film pedestrian material and more rarely as a conscious attempt to experiment with the properties of the medium. In the process, they made a number of classic films.

In a career that spans four decades, thirty-three feature films, twenty short subjects and work for television,[1] Jacques Tourneur spent most of his time working on B productions, primarily financed and distributed by the Hollywood majors. However, unlike other filmmakers who worked under similar production arrangements and managed to develop their own particular approaches to filmmaking,[2] Tourneur's approach has remained inextricably linked to the practices of RKO unit producer Val Lewton. Having worked together in three successful horror films early in Tourneur's career, and with Lewton often credited as the main creative force behind these films, it has proven difficult for film critics to separate one's work from the other.[3] Exacerbating this confusion, only a handful of films made by Tourneur following the end of his collaboration with Lewton in the early 1940s attracted significant critical attention and/or box office business: the celebrated film noir *Out of the Past* (1947), the Burt Lancaster vehicle *The Flame and the Arrow* (1950) and the British production *Night of the Demon* (1957).

Although Tourneur's first feature for RKO, the breakaway hit *Cat People*, took place in 1942, by that time he had over fifteen years of experience in several aspects of filmmaking, including directing. The son of Maurice Tourneur, an established French filmmaker who had also had a significant career in Hollywood, Jacques Tourneur worked in a number of roles in his father's films, both in France and the United States. This apprenticeship helped him break into filmmaking in France as he directed four features between 1931 and 1934. However, despite this substantial experience, Tourneur only managed to get a job in Hollywood as second-unit director at MGM. Eventually he became one of the company's directors of short subjects, a position he held for six years, while also making three features for the company's B units: *They All Come Out* (1939), an expanded version of one of his short films, and the first two instalments in a film series

on the adventures of detective Nick Carter, a popular literary character of the time in dime novels, *Nick Carter, Master Detective* (1939)
and *Phantom Raiders* (1940).

Tourneur's service at short subject and B units, which in a studio like
MGM were in the business of producing quality product in an efficient
manner, helped the director understand the principles of the producer
unit-system and the ways in which it regulated studio filmmaking
practices while also serving the studio's brand identity or "house style".
Specifically, he became attuned to arrangements designed to draw on
the skills and talent of a close-knit group of contributors under the
close supervision of a creative producer. Arguably, it is the unit
(standing for the studio) that can lay a legitimate claim in the authorship of film, and the experience of Tourneur at RKO where he was
hired to direct films for another B unit testifies to this reality.

His arrival at RKO coincided with a period in the studio's history
when there was an emphasis on building such a house style, "a new
stylised approach to black-and-white filming", employed in both A
and B films, that would eventually find a consistently successful
embodiment in the company's cycle of films noirs in the 1940s. At
the same time, there was an industry wide shift of production management away from executives and into the hands of top talent,
which in RKO's case reached far down the pecking order to its B
units. Placed in a unit with a mandate to direct inexpensive films in
the popular horror genre in the early 1940s, Tourneur found himself
part of a particularly close-knit group that was led by creative producer Val Lewton, who had worked previously with Tourneur when
they were both at MGM. Furthermore, the unit was supported by a
host of RKO below-the-line production personnel, many of whom
would work with Tourneur in all eight films he directed for the
studio in the 1940s, and not just in the three films he made with
Lewton. Any questions about authorship, then, should not be seen
solely in conjunction with the role Lewton played in the production
process of the unit's films but more importantly, in association with
the very specific function B unit filmmaking had to perform at the
dawn of a new era for RKO and the rest of the industry.

With the budgets for the unit set to a lowly $150,000 per film, it
was clear that RKO could not aspire to make the often premium
quality brand of horror that market leader Universal specialised in and
which involved elaborate settings, monsters, mad scientists and special
effects. In this respect, the widely celebrated visual style of the films
the unit made with Tourneur as director was a necessity born out of
the allocation of limited resources to the unit by the studio, but

which also dovetailed RKO's endorsement of a stylised black and white cinematography as a hallmark of its emerging house style.

Cat People proved a breakaway success, especially for a B production.[4] Focusing on the story of a woman who seemingly transforms into a panther when she gets angry or sexually aroused, the film presented a horror story that was different from the ones associated with Universal. *Cat People* makes effective use of lighting and shadows, using the play between darkness and light to create striking aesthetic effects and imbues the narrative with a tense atmosphere, which suggests that horrific events could take place at any time, in any place and in any shape. Furthermore, the film utilises editing creatively, juxtaposing images and shots to create anxiety for the viewer. Intimating that something horrific is about to happen, the suggested danger often turns out to be false alarm, as in a masterful 90 second long sequence in which Irena, the film's protagonist, is stalking Alice, a young woman who works with Irena's husband and with whom he has developed a friendship. Alice thinks she is about to be attacked, while the roar of a panther starts becoming audible before the roar of an engine from a bus that suddenly bursts into the frame drowns it, suggesting that the stalking and panther attack might have been in Alice's (and the spectator's) imagination, despite earlier shots having shown Irena following Alice. Such a visual style gave the film's narration a degree of playfulness, and highlighted a more general ambiguity, which is seemingly resolved only at the end when the protagonist permanently transforms into a wild cat. This transformation is shown in shadows, however, which leaves a final question mark as to the exact nature of the narrative events.

The playful narration, the dark, tense atmosphere and the allusions to erotic passion as motivation for horrific events are replicated in the unit's second film, *I Walked with a Zombie* (1943). However, the ensuing ambiguity is much more pronounced, with even the main narrative strand, the efforts of a nurse to understand the reasons behind the "zombification" of a woman she was hired to care for, characterised by indeterminacy.[5] Even the lyrics of a calypso song performed by a character/narrator who functions similarly to a chorus in a Greek tragedy do not provide much more clarity than the actual narrative events when he sings "the wife fall down and the evil came and it burnt her mind in the fever flame". This suggests that the film's narrative strategies are resistant to the principles of unity and clarity that permeated filmmaking in the studio era.

Similarly, *The Leopard Man* (1943), with a story about an escaped leopard and its potential attacks on a number of women in a New

Mexico town, provided ample opportunity for menacing shadows, scenes in dark places and moments of horror expectation that do not always materialise. Made by the same key personnel that also worked on *Zombie* (though with a different director of photography), the film additionally eschewed a classical narrative structure, opting instead for a much looser collection of long sequences, each of which features different leading characters. In this respect, the narration presents challenges as the spectator is asked to connect events whose relation to one another is made clear only when, at the end of each sequence, one of the leading characters is seemingly attacked by the leopard.

The success of these films, which reviewers of the time often credited not only to Lewton and Tourneur but also to many of the RKO crew that worked below them,[6] convinced the studio to assign Tourneur to A pictures. However, despite the "upgrade", Tourneur found himself yet again working under the supervision of creative producers who also doubled up in the production process as screenwriters: Casey Robinson, writer-producer of *Days of Glory* (1944) and Warren Duff, writer-producer of *Experiment Perilous* (1944), respectively. Like the arrangements in the Lewton unit, both *Days of Glory*, a World War II film about Russian resistance to the German invasion of the Soviet Union, and *Experiment Perilous*, a gothic thriller, were served by a number of RKO's contracted personnel, many of whom had worked with Tourneur in the Lewton unit, as well as renowned cinematographer Toni Gaudio who shot both films. In this respect, the main difference from his work on the previous three RKO films was that as an A list director, Tourneur had more resources and higher budgets at his disposal.

Experiment Perilous and *Days of Glory* utilise visual styles that do not have many points of contact with the Lewton films, except perhaps for a few instances of experimentation with narration that could link them to the director's previous films. *Experiment Perilous* continues what seems to be a fascination with narrational agency, especially as various characters assume the role of narrator at different points in the film, questioning the meaning of fixed images and facts.[7] *Days of Glory*, on the other hand, utilises an extra-diegetic narrator who does not only introduce the story world and the characters who occupy it but also offers information about the actors portraying these characters, breaking key rules of classical filmmaking. These loose connections to Tourneur's earlier work, however, remained unnoticed by reviewers of the time who focused more on these films' links to other similarly themed pictures around the time of their release. Tourneur's A list pictures were instead placed within a canon determined by a production trend (the gothic thriller of the 1940s for *Experiment Perilous*; the pro-Soviet Union film made during and immediately after the end of World War II for *Days of Glory*), rather than authorship.

Tourneur's seeming inability to differentiate a personal style from a more general, producer/unit/studio approach to filmmaking continued in *Out of the Past*, where he was reunited with the producer of *Experiment Perilous*, Warren Duff.[8] Surprisingly, however, film criticism has almost unanimously credited Tourneur as the main agent responsible for the critical and commercial success of *Out of the Past*. Often cited as one of the best films noirs of the 1940s,[9] the film contains numerous hallmarks of the cycle: stylistically (the dark *mise en scène* with an extensive use of shadows, the use of voice over), narratively (a complex story about a former private detective who betrayed a big crime boss for a woman of dubious morality and later tries to lead a new life until the past catches up with him), and thematically (post-war male anxieties produced by strong, confident women). Given RKO's panache for stylishly shot black and white crime films, the expertise of its employees in making this type of film (many of whom had been instrumental in developing techniques that were both utilised in the film and more generally fed into the studio's house style) and Tourneur's propensity for complex and narrationally challenging material (for which the film noir lends itself perfectly), *Out of the Past* seems to represent the peak of an era in the studio's history when all the right elements fell into place. In this respect, the film likely serves as an example of the "genius of the system", rather than existing as a uniquely "Tourneur film".

Following the critical and commercial success of *Out of the Past*, Tourneur was assigned to writer-producer Bert Granet for *Berlin Express* (1948), arguably the most stylistically distinct film he directed while at RKO but one that still fit the studio style in the 1940s. Like in *Days of Glory*, the opening credits provide extra-textual information, this time revealing that the scenes in Frankfurt and Berlin were filmed in these locations after special permission was granted to the filmmakers. With Germany occupied after the end of World War II, it was a considerable achievement for a Hollywood film crew to get permission to shoot in the country, especially as this was also expected to reinforce the film's realism and potentially make it more "mature" and comparable to the European post-War productions.[10] Also like many earlier Tourneur-directed films, it made use of voice over narration, though in this case its use is excessive, with a particular sequence accompanied by a five minute-long voice over narration that attracts attention to the technique.

Such an unusual dependence on the voice over device suggests that *Berlin Express* was a film that did experiment with style. Indeed, a recent review of the film in the *Village Voice* called it "a strange rarity that inserts a noir thriller into post-war Germany, augmented with documentary travelogues of rubble-strewn cities",[11] which besides style also draws attention to the film's issues with genre. The elements of noir thriller were perhaps not surprising given both the director's pedigree in the specific genre but also the opportunities provided by a number of night scenes amidst the rubble of destroyed German cities and in the claustrophobic environment of the train's compartments where a large part of the action takes place.

Tourneur's final film for RKO, *Easy Living*, which tells a story about a professional footballer who discovers he has a heart condition and therefore has to make a decision between honouring his commitment to the team (that could prove fatal) and retiring (that would mean a much less "easy living"), failed to attract any critical attention and remains one of the least known of Tourneur's films. Despite an interesting effort to present a realistic portrayal of professional football as a business and the dark side of upward social mobility post World War II, and an elaborately edited high society party sequence that is brought together by an African American singer's live performance, if the film is now remembered for anything it is mostly for being one of the first features to focus on professional sports, with members of NFL team Los Angeles Rams portraying the players of the fictional Chiefs team. Following this feature, RKO decided not to renew Tourneur's contract, amidst other cost-cutting exercises that took effect in the studio after its takeover by Howard Hughes in 1948.

Following a brief return to unit filmmaking at MGM for the film *Stars in My Crown* (1950), the rest of Tourneur's career in the 1950s was dominated by a series of films for key independent producers, including Harold Hecht and Burt Lancaster (*The Flame and the Arrow*), Benedict Bogeaus (*Appointment in Honduras*, 1953), Leonard Goldstein (*Stranger on Horseback*, 1955), the Mirisch brothers (*Wichita*, 1955) and Edward Small (*Timbuktu*, 1959), while also directing for key exploitation independent company American International Pictures. He also worked on some British productions including his best known film from that time, *Night of the Demon*, while also undertaking some unit production under the supervision of leading 20th Century-Fox writer-producers George Jessel and Philip Dunne (*Way of A Gaucho*, 1952 and *Anne of the Indies*, 1951, respectively).

The minimal critical engagement with most of the above films suggests that they have been placed outside whatever auteurist canon has existed for Tourneur's work. This is despite the fact that many of these films contain stylistic, narrative or thematic elements that could potentially link them to the RKO ones, for instance, narrational ambiguities in *Appointment in Honduras* and *Anne of the Indies*.[12] One potential explanation for this shift in critical attention is the industrial and institutional context within which Tourneur operated. Because the means of production shifted into one off deals or short-lived arrangements, Tourneur was unable to continue working with the same collaborators and building on a body of work that, until his exit from RKO, was perceived as "coherent" and occasionally significant. This would explain why the majority of his post-RKO work is deemed "authorless", consisting of little seen and now forgotten films that tend to be excluded from almost all critical and scholarly engagement with his work. On the other hand, the industrial and institutional arrangements that exemplified unit production at MGM and especially at RKO seem to have allowed Tourneur not only to establish a coherent body of work, but on certain occasions to also hit an artistic peak that for many critics tends to stand in for his whole body of work, perhaps unjustifiably so. In this respect, the most appropriate label to describe Tourneur might not be "Hollywood filmmaker", but instead, "Hollywood director".

Biography

Jacques Tourneur was a French filmmaker who made most of his films in Hollywood. Born in 1900, he entered the filmmaking business at a young age, working with his father, Maurice Tourneur. After making a small number of films in France, Tourneur emigrated to Hollywood where he worked first for MGM and then for RKO. It was during his years at the latter studio when he found significant success, first with a string of low budget horror films produced by Val Lewton, and later with the noir film *Out of the Past*. This success, however, was not replicated in the rest of his career when he worked primarily for independent producers and for a number of television shows. He died in 1977.

Notes

1 These figures have been taken from Chris Fujiwara (1998) *The Cinema of Nightfall: Jacques Tourneur*, Baltimore: Johns Hopkins University Press, pp. 301–12. This is the only book in the English language examining all of Tourneur's output.

2 See Yannis Tzioumakis (2008) "Edgar G. Ulmer: The Low-end Independent Filmmaker par excellence" in Rhodes, Gary (ed.) *Edgar G Ulmer: Detour on Poverty Row*, Lanham: Lexington Books, pp. 3–23.

3 Paul Willeman (1975) "Notes towards the Construction of Readings of Tourneur" in Paul Willeman and Claire Johnston (eds) *Jacques Tourneur*, Edinburgh: Edinburgh Film Festival, p. 16.

4 *Cinema Texas: Program Notes*: Vol. 7, No 39, 7 November 1974, p. 4.

5 Pierre, Sylvie (1975) "The Beauty of the Sea" in Paul Willeman and Claire Johnston (eds) *Jacques Tourneur*, Edinburgh: Edinburgh Film Festival, p 45.

6 See, for instance, Anonymous (1942) *"Cat People"* in *Variety*, 13 November 1942; and Anonymous (1943) *"I Walked With a Zombie"* in *Variety*, 16 March 1943.

7 Willeman, 1975, p 26.

8 In between *Days of Glory* and *Out of the Past*, Tourneur also made *Canyon Passage* (1946) for another creative producer, Walter Wanger, when RKO loaned him out to Universal where Wanger was heading a successful unit in the 1940s.

9 See, for instance, Gary Morris (2000) "High Gallows: Jacques Tourneur's *Out of the Past*" in *Bright Lights Film Journal*, Issue 29, online, at www.brightlightsfilm,com/29/outofthepast.php.

10 Wright, Virginia "Berlin Express" in *Los Angeles Daily News*, 28 March 1947.

11 Halter, Ed (2002) "Wait Until Dark" in *Village Voice*, 28 August 2002 http://www.villagevoice.com/2002-08-27/film/wait-until-dark/

12 Noames, Jean Louis (1975) "Three Tourneurs" in Paul Willeman and Claire Johnston (eds) *Jacques Tourneur*, Edinburgh: Edinburgh Film Festival, p. 15.

Filmography

Tout ça ne vaut pas l'amour (France, 1931)

Pour être aimé (France, 1931)

Toto (France, 1933)

Les Filles de la concierge (France, 1934)

They All Come Out (1939)

Nick Carter, Master Detective (1939)

Phantom Raiders (1940)

Doctors Don't Tell (1941)

Cat People (1942)

I Walked with a Zombie (1943)

The Leopard Man (1943)

Days of Glory (1944)

Experiment Perilous (1944)

Canyon Passage (1946)

Out of the Past (1947)
Berlin Express (1948)
Easy Living (1949)
Stars in My Crown (1950)
The Flame and the Arrow (1950)
Circle of Danger (1951)
Anne of the Indies (1951)
Way of a Gaucho (1952)
Appointment in Honduras (1953)
Stranger on Horseback (1955)
Wichita (1955)
Great Day in the Morning (1956)
Nightfall (1957)
Night of the Demon (UK, 1957)
The Fearmakers (1958)
Timbuktu (1959)
The Giant of Marathon (Italy, 1959)
The Comedy of Terrors (1963)
War-Gods of the Deep (UK, 1965)

Further reading

Fujiwara, Chris. *The Cinema of Nightfall: Jacques Tourneur*. Baltimore:
    Johns Hopkins University Press, 1998.
Newman, Kim. *Cat People*. London: BFI Classics, 1999.
Willeman, Paul and Claire Johnston, eds. *Jacques Tourneur*. Edinburgh:
    Edinburgh Film Festival, 1975.

RAOUL WALSH

By Giuliana Muscio

Often defined as a Hollywood professional, most efficient in story-telling and directing actors, Raoul Walsh was actually an innovative and energetic filmmaker. Notable for swift action films, Walsh's filmography coincides with the history of the studio system, from silent cinema to the crisis of the sixties, and includes more than 150 titles.[1] He created and/or innovated several genres, from Western, gangster and war films, to comedies, dramas, women films, boxing movies, costume epics and even musicals. Appreciated by critics and audiences alike for his narrative efficiency and for the ability to construct memorable characters with a few perfect strokes and a spare or witty dialogue, he became a favorite of the "Nouvelle Vague" and of several filmmakers of recent generations such as Steven Spielberg and Martin Scorsese.

A tall man with square shoulders, Raoul Walsh always wore cowboy boots in order to recall the experiences of his youth. As would a hero in his films, he led an adventurous life. Born in a middle class family in New York, he quit college to sail to Cuba with his uncle, and then traveled and worked in Mexico, Texas and Montana, where he learned to break horses, to do rope tricks and labor as a cowboy. In fact his debut on stage was in the theatrical adaptation of *The Clansman*, the popular civil war drama, where he was hired to ride a horse. Back in New York, still the main site for filmmaking in the US, he became an amateur actor and worked as a stuntman for Pathé Westerns and action shorts, shot in Fort Lee, New Jersey.[2] He started directing one- or two-reelers, which he often also performed in as an actor. In the early 1910s he also met D. W. Griffith and worked with him as an assistant (especially for action scenes) and "casted" horses and cowboys. In 1913 Griffith assigned him to co-direct (with Christy Cabanne) *The Life of General Villa*, a film of seven-reels with re-enactments and real footage of Villa himself. Walsh filmed moments of the civil war in Mexico, even the shocking scene of peasants breaking the teeth of corpses to extract the gold fillings, and interacted with Pancho Villa himself, whom he ended up portraying on the screen.[3] Griffith hired Walsh as an assistant for the battle scenes in *The Birth of a Nation*, based on *The Clansman*, and cast him as John Wilkes Booth, Lincoln's assassin. Walsh acted in, and directed a dozen two-reelers, mostly Westerns interpreted by his brother George Walsh, in addition to writing and, at times, producing films.

At age twenty-eight Walsh left Griffith and returned to New York, lured by a generous offer from William Fox. He stayed with the company for almost twenty years, often in conflict with his difficult boss. In 1915 he directed his first feature, *Regeneration*, considered the first American gangster film. The film was shot on location in the Lower East Side, and Walsh cast interesting figures he found on the waterfronts and docks of New York. He soon demonstrated that in addition to being efficient at making quick action films, he could also make spectacular pictures. (Walsh's *Carmen*, staring Fox's Theda Bara, was in fact more successful at the box office than Cecil B. DeMille's *Carmen* with Geraldine Farrar.) He directed Douglas Fairbanks in the swashbuckling fairytale *The Thief of Bagdad*, nowadays often cited as one of the magic titles of silent cinema, and was at the helm of cult women's films such as *Sadie Thompson* (which he scripted too), one of Gloria Swanson's best performances.[4]

Walsh's most accomplished title of the silent period is *What Price Glory*, a war film full of vitality which also displays an instinctual disgust towards war. Spiced by bawdy antics (which at times can be read on the lips of the characters) *What Price Glory* is an action film where action is elided. Instead, war is invoked as a series of close ups of bolts on a convoy of tanks, as the livid reflection on a row of bayonets, and as cruel traveling shots of the trenches. As in many of Walsh's films, male rivalry/comradeship creates robust comedy, which takes place mostly in taverns. "Men are cannon fodder; there are no hidden, idealized goals," comments Peter von Bagh in the catalog presentation of the Bologna retrospective.[5] The contrast between the vitality of sexual attraction and the opaqueness of war makes a moral but not preachy statement: Walsh expresses ethics through physicality. (Starring together in *What Price Glory*, *The Cock-Eyed World* and *Women of All Nations*, the macho couple McLaglen-Lowe completed a trilogy defined by male comradeship and sexual appetite.)

Like other film pioneers, Walsh learned the basics of filmmaking from Griffith, but he differed from his master in several ways: he co-wrote or wrote his scripts and was more inclined to improvisation, in general rejecting the "iron script." From Griffith he learned a sense of dramatic *crescendo*, but was much more elliptical in showing action; he made effective use of close ups but not only for psychological emphasis. He also became quite sophisticated in the organization of space on screen—an early version of deep focus composition—and in the use of natural landscape. He did share with Griffith a sensitive alternation of action and intimate scenes. Walsh also had an exceptional gift for making his films on time, and was often used as a "film doctor," completing the shooting of uncompleted films, even though he was not always credited for them.

Contrary to Griffith, Walsh had a very successful and creative career even after the introduction of sound. He directed the spectacular wide-screen production of *The Big Trail* (1930), where he launched Marion Morrison and, changing his name to John Wayne, cast him in his first Western. Walsh was known for his patience and for advising actors in a way that often produced their best performances, and he theorized the need for "spontaneity."[6] Having started his career as an actor himself, he refused any intellectualistic approach and aimed straight at character and narrative needs. Probably he would have continued working in both capacities, had it not been for the accident during the filming of *In Old Arizona* (1929), which caused him to lose his right eye. He was supposed to play Cisco Kid, the protagonist of the film, but was replaced by Warner Baxter, who, under Walsh's direction, won an Academy Award for his role. Walsh was able to extract the best work from Errol Flynn as an ambitious Custer in *They Died With Their Boots On*, in the boxing classic *Gentleman Jim*, and in the realistic war film *Objective Burma*; from Humphrey Bogart as a loner and a loser in *High Sierra*; and from James Cagney as a psychotic gangster of *White Heat*.

Walsh is known mostly for his virile, swiftly paced action and adventure films in typical masculine genres—war, Western and gangster. He directed the first sound Western to be shot outdoors, *In Old Arizona*, as well as the epic odyssey of the conquest of the West, *The Big Trail*, and the recently rediscovered *Wild Girl*. In his films, adventure and war imply in the protagonist strong feelings moving toward extreme consequences—from self-destruction to a possible regeneration. War is not explosions and hectic battle scenes, but tension, even immobility, and individual choices, which can transform a gangster into a patriot. In addition to his great silent drama *What Price Glory,* his war films include *Battle Cry* (memorable for the intense moment in which the marines insert their bayonets to go and take revenge for Van Heflin's death), and the sober *The Naked and the Dead* from Norman Mailer's novel.

Surveying Walsh's filmography, most modern critics favor Walsh's *noirish*/energetic work at Warner Bros., visible in films such as *The Roaring Twenties*, with gangsters James Cagney and Humphrey Bogart; *They Drive by Night*, with truckers George Raft and Bogart; *Manpower*, with Raft and Edward G. Robinson competing for the love of Marlene Dietrich; and later, *White Heat*. Most of all, however, they applaud *High Sierra*, with Bogart as a fugitive assisted by Ida Lupino. While several actors (Cagney, Muni, Raft and Robinson) refused to play Roy Earle (loosely based on John Dillinger's real life), *High Sierra* made Bogart a star. Written by John Huston and W. R. Burnett, this *noirish* cult criminal drama ends with the hero facing death with a stoic fatalistic attitude, typical of Walsh and prophetic of the noir development of crime drama, though untypically he is immersed here in nature.

"Walsh gave the most natural, spontaneous, relaxed rendition of any genre," writes von Bagh. "The essence seems to be born of a state of undisciplined happiness in breaking the conventions of each of them."[7] This versatility is confirmed by such diverse works as the early adaptation of Ibsen's *Pillars of Society* (1916); *Sadie Thompson*, with Gloria Swanson as a prostitute finding love in the humid tropics; the spicy *Me and My Gal* with its witty dialogue between

Spencer Tracy and Joan Bennett and its experimental sound; *The Red Dance* with Dolores Del Rio as a rebellious dancer in czarist and revolutionary Russia; and *Yellow Passport* with Elissa Landi as a Jewish girl traveling in imperial Russia with the type of passport usually assigned to prostitutes. Walsh's diverse canon also includes dramas, comedies and women films, which are as dynamic as his action pictures. Walsh is able to represent sexual attraction or social idealism in a fresh, dry though intense manner. His tough and earthy heroes are often loners, but without bitterness or sadness, though they are skeptical about inner search. "Walsh was equally tough about society and human nature: whether a boxing ring, a business enterprise, the primitive accumulation of money in a Western boom town or a war," comments von Bagh.[8] Behind it all looms the erotic energy and the vitality that energizes everything: stars, genre, the sense of story, as well as his concrete sense of nature, often defined as a beautiful space trembling with grotesque death." [9]

Walsh represents Hollywood professionalism in his multifaceted abilities, developed when the division of labor on the set was still weak. He has nineteen credits as a writer, mostly in the silent part of his career but not exclusively, and he wrote scripts until the 1970s. He also has twenty-nine credits as a producer, significantly working in these capacities on his own films both at the beginning and at the end of his employment in Hollywood, where he aimed to have fuller control of his work. A skillful and dynamic director, Raoul Walsh nurtured a natural enjoyment for his profession and always avoided high aesthetic proclamations. In a way the Walshian hero recalls the personality of his creator—a cowboy whose adventures in real life lent authenticity and energy to his films. He worked within the system and its rules, but in a way he also created the system and the rules, achieving creative liberty within its frontiers.

Biography

Walsh was born in New York on March 11, 1887, and died in Simi Valley, California, on December 31, 1980. His father was Thomas Walsh, an Irish immigrant, owner of a profitable garment business, while his mother, Elizabeth, was of Irish/Spanish descent; both were Catholics. In silent cinema he directed such diverse and successful films as *The Thief of Bagdad*, *Sadie Thompson* and *What Price Glory*. Under contract at Warners he directed some of his most famous gangster and action films, such as *They Drive by Night and High Sierra*, crowning the gangster series with *White Heat* in 1949. He kept making movies until 1964, when he retired to his ranch.

Notes

1 The published filmographies differ greatly in numbers of titles: IMDB lists 139 credits overall; in his presentation of the retrospective at the Harvard Archive devoted to Walsh, Tom Conley states that the filmography is constituted by 176 titles; finally, in her recent biography of the director Marilyn Ann Moss proposes about 200 titles. If we take into account both the early phase of the industry history in which he worked and his uncredited participation at salvaging diverse films, this vagueness is not surprising.
2 See Richard Koszarski, *Fort Lee: The Film Town*, Rome: John Libbey – CIC Publishing, 2004.
3 Villa signed a contract with Mutual to finance the revolution and even agreed to re-enact battle scenes. *And Starring Pancho Villa as Himself* (Bruce Beresford, 2003) described the making of this film with Antonio Banderas playing Villa.
4 He also acts in the film, playing a marine in love with the desperate prostitute.
5 Peter von Bagh, *La grande avventura di Roul Walsh*, Bologna: Cinema Ritrovato, 2012.
6 Interview, *The New York Times*, April 27, 1924.
7 Von Bagh, p. 177.
8 Ibid.
9 Ibid.

Filmography

The Pseudo Prodigal (1913)
A Mother's Love (1913)
Paul Revere's Ride (1913)
The Double Knot (1913) also producer and scriptwriter
The Mystery of the Hindu Image (1913) also producer and scriptwriter
The Life of General Villa (1914) re-released as *The Outlaw's Revenge* (1915)
The Double Knot (1914)
The Mystery of the Hindu Image (1914)
The Fatal Black Bean (1914)
Regeneration (1915) also co-scenarist and scriptwriter
Carmen (1915) also producer, scenarist, and scriptwriter
The Death Dice, His Return (1915) also producer
The Greaser (1915) also producer and scriptwriter
The Artist's Wife (1915)

The Fencing Master (1915) also producer and scriptwriter
A Man for All That (1915) also producer and scriptwriter
The Comeback (1915)
The Smuggler (1915)
11.30 P.M. (1915) also producer and scriptwriter
The Burned Hand (1915) also producer and scriptwriter
The Celestial Code (1915) scriptwriter
A Bad Man and Others (1915) also producer and scriptwriter
Home from the Sea (1915)
The Lone Cowboy (1915) also co-scriptwriter
Peer Gynt (1915)
Blue Blood and Red (1916) also producer and scriptwriter
The Serpent (1916) also producer and scriptwriter
Pillars of Society (1916)
The Honor System (1917)
The Lone Cowboy (1917)
The Silent Lie (1917)
The Innocent Sinner (1917) also scriptwriter
Betrayed (1917) also scriptwriter
The Conqueror (1917) also scriptwriter
This Is the Life (1917)
The Pride of New York (1917) also scriptwriter
The Woman and the Law (1918) also scriptwriter
The Prussian Cur (1918) also scriptwriter
On the Jump (1918) also scriptwriter
Every Mother's Son (1918) also scriptwriter
I'll Say So (1918)
Should a Husband Forgive (1919) also scriptwriter
Evangeline (1919) also scriptwriter
The Strongest (1920) also scriptwriter
The Deep Purple (1920)
From Now On (1920)
Headin' Home (1920)
The Oath (1921) also producer and scriptwriter
Serenade (1921) also producer
Kindred of the Dust (1922) also producer and scriptwriter
Lost and Found on a South Sea Island (1923) aka *Passions of the Sea*
The Thief of Bagdad (1924)
East of Suez (1925) also producer
The Spaniard (1925) also co-producer
The Wanderer (1926) also co-producer
The Lucky Lady (1926) also co-producer

The Lady of the Harem (1926)
What Price Glory (1926)
The Monkey Talks (1927) also producer
The Loves of Carmen (1927) also scriptwriter
Sadie Thompson (1928) also co-scriptwriter
The Red Dance (1928)
Me Gangster (1928) also co-scriptwriter
In Old Arizona (1929) also co-director
The Cock-eyed World (1929) also co-scriptwriter
Hot for Paris (1929) also co-scriptwriter
The Big Trail (1930)
The Man Who Came Back (1931)
Women of All Nations (1931)
The Spy (1931)
The Yellow Passport (1931)
Wild Girl (1932)
Me and My Gal (1932)
Sailor's Luck (1933)
The Bowery (1933)
Going Hollywood (1933)
Under Pressure (1935)
Baby Face Harrington (1935)
Every Night at Eight (1935)
Klondike Annie (1936)
Big Brown Eyes (1936) also co-scriptwriter
Spendthrift (1936)
O.H.M.S. (1937) aka *You're in the Army Now*
Jump for Glory (1937)
When Thief Meets Thief (1937)
Artists and Models (1937)
Hitting a New High (1937)
College Swing (1938)
St. Louis Blues (1939)
The Roaring Twenties (1939)
Dark Command (1940) also producer
They Drive by Night (1940)
High Sierra (1941)
The Strawberry Blonde (1941)
Manpower (1941)
They Died With Their Boots On (1941)
Desperate Journey (1942)
Gentleman Jim (1942)

Background to Danger (1943)
Northern Pursuit (1943)
Uncertain Glory (1944)
Objective Burma (1944)
Salty O'Rourke (1944)
The Horn Blows at Midnight (1944)
The Man I Love (1946)
Pursued (1947)
Cheyenne (1947)
Silver River (1948)
Fighter Squadron (1948)
One Sunday Afternoon (1948)
Colorado Territory (1949)
White Heat (1949)
Along the Great Divide (1951)
Captain Horatio Hornblower (1951)
Distant Drums (1951)
Glory Alley (1951)
The World in His Arms (1952)
The Lawless Breed (1952)
Blackbeard the Pirate (1952)
Sea Devils (1953)
A Lion in the Streets (1953)
Gun Fury (1953)
Saskatchewan (1954)
Battle Cry (1955)
The Tall Men (1955)
The Revolt of Mamie Stover (1956)
The King and Four Queens (1956)
Band of Angels (1957)
The Naked and the Dead (1958)
The Sheriff of Fractured Jaw (1958)
A Private's Affair (1959)
Esther and the King (1960) also producer and scriptwriter
Marines, Let's Go (1961) also producer and scriptwriter
A Distant Trumpet (1964)

Further reading

Bachman, Paolo. *Raoul Walsh*. Turin: Quaderni del Movie Club, 1969.
Bogdanovich, Peter. *Who the Devil Made It*. New York: Knopf, 1997.

Canham, Kingsley. *The Hollywood Professionals, Volume 1: Michael Curtiz, Raoul Walsh, Henry Hathaway*. London: Tantivy Press, 1973.

Hardy, Phil, ed. *Raoul Walsh*. Edinburgh: Edinburgh International Film Festival, 1974.

Marmin, Michel. *Raoul Walsh*. Paris: Seghers, 1970.

Moss, Marilyn Ann. *Raoul Walsh: The True Adventures of Hollywood's Legendary Director*. Lexington: University Press of Kentucky, 2011.

Smith, John M. *The Films of Raoul Walsh: A Critical Approach*. Kindle Edition, 2013.

Von Bagh, Peter. *La grande avventura di Raoul Walsh*. Bologna: Cinema Ritrovato, 2012.

Walsh, Raoul. *Each Man in His Time*. New York: Farrar, Straus, and Giroux, 1974.

Wilson, Michael Henry. *Raoul Walsh ou la saga du continent perdu*. Paris: Cinématéque Française, 2001.

ORSON WELLES

By Celestino Deleyto

At the end of *Touch of Evil* (1958), Tanya (Marlene Dietrich), the prostitute on the Mexican side of the border, says of her old friend, Hank Quinlan (Welles), who has just died: "He was some kind of a man." Given the close identification between the characters Orson Welles played and his public image, it is hard to resist thinking of the filmmaker himself when we hear these words. One of the few directors already considered an auteur before auteurism was invented by the *Cahiers du cinema* critics in the 1950s, Welles had co-written, produced, directed and starred in *Citizen Kane* (1941), his first Hollywood film, before turning twenty-six. By then he had already become a prominent theater director in New York, first as part of the Federal Theatre, a project subsidized by the Roosevelt administration, and then with the Mercury Theatre, the repertory company he and John Houseman put together in 1937. He had also risen to popular fame as a consequence of his radio adaptation of H. G. Wells' *The War of the Worlds*, broadcast on October 30, 1938, which caused a panic when many people, who had not listened to the introduction, took the program for the report of a real alien invasion of the Earth. Partly as a consequence of this success, RKO offered Welles an unprecedented deal to direct two films over which he was to have complete artistic control. After various failed attempts, including an adaptation of Joseph Conrad's *Heart of Darkness*, the first of these was *Citizen Kane*.

Kane is universally considered one of the most important films in the history of cinema. Co-written with Herman J. Mankiewicz, it tells the story of media tycoon Charles Foster Kane, from his childhood in a cabin in Colorado to his death in his extravagant mansion "Xanadu" in Florida. The film is structured around a series of flashbacks, following a journalist's investigation of the meaning of "Rosebud," the last word uttered by Kane before dying. With Gregg Toland as director of photography and Bernard Herrmann as composer, Welles took advantage of some recent technical innovations to offer a unique and remarkably coherent visual style, based on the use of deep focus photography, forced perspectives, including painterly foreshadowing and frequent low angles, fast cutting, long takes, overlapping dialogue and various types of special effects.

Assuming that the figure of Kane was based on him, real-life media tycoon William Randolph Hearst mobilized his newspapers and radio stations around the country in an attempt to boycott the film and stop its release. In part due to this campaign, *Kane* did not do particularly well at the box office, and although it was nominated at the following year's Academy Awards in nine categories, it only won one, for best original screenplay. However, the critical reception was overwhelmingly positive and the film has since continued to grow in momentum and prestige. French critic André Bazin contributed decisively to the film's centrality in cinema history with his 1967 article "The Evolution of the Language of Cinema." In it he argued that Welles in *Citizen Kane*, along with William Wyler in his movies of that period, brought about a revolution of sorts in the history of cinema by substituting depth of field for editing as the basic stylistic way to tell a story. This option was for Bazin less manipulative and more democratic than that implicit in continuity editing, bringing the relationship of the spectator with the screen closer to real experience. Bazin's argument is more complex than can be developed here, but it is surely ironic that Welles is presented as a champion of depth of field and therefore an "enemy" of editing, given that the filmmaker was a master of editing and that many of his later films relied more obviously on his bold and inventive use of the cutting room than they did on deep focus.

Welles's next film, the second of his deal with RKO, was *The Magnificent Ambersons* (1942), the story of the decadence of a nineteenth-century upper-class family caught in the throes of progress and social change. In this adaptation of a novel by Booth Tarkington, the filmmaker continued his exploration of the American Dream and recent U.S. history, developing his trademark mixture of romanticism and iconoclasm and his characteristic cinematic style. A scene introducing the spectator to a party at the Amberson mansion that combines the long take with sophisticated camera movement, deep focus and overlapping sound illustrates the extent to which Welles's films were different from those of the majority of his Hollywood contemporaries, who tended to favor visual and aural schemas that were less complicated. *The Magnificent Ambersons*, however, would never see the light as Welles conceived it. Before finishing, Welles left for Brazil to shoot the documentary *It's All True* for the U.S. government, which he would never complete. While he was away, RKO, following negative audience responses at a preview in Los Angeles, thoroughly recut *Ambersons*, had some new scenes reshot, even changed part of Bernard Herrmann's score, and released the film in a sadly truncated form (reduced from 132 to 88 minutes). As James Naremore has convincingly argued, such alternations changed some of the film's meaning, particularly in its final part.[1] Signs of Welles's brilliance are still apparent everywhere in the film, even though the knowing spectator cannot help wondering what could have been had the director not travelled to Brazil before completion.

The case of *Ambersons* became the norm rather than the exception in Welles's career. Many of his subsequent completed movies were released following tampering by the producers, while projects that were never made or not finished easily outnumber those films that were finally released. The myth built around the director, to a large extent fueled by Welles himself, suggests that he was a misunderstood maverick artist destroyed by a cruel industry. While this was indeed the case on many occasions, the incompleteness of his projects was as much a consequence of Welles's own attitude to his films, which he always saw as works in progress, as the responsibility of his producers and financial backers. His long cherished project of a film adaptation of *Don Quixote* is a case in point. After working on various versions in the course of several decades, the film was never released. The director himself ironically referred to it as *When Will You Finish Don Quixote?* Several years after his death, a dismal version was released in Spain put together by his one-time collaborator Jesús Franco from various existing materials (1992).

It is also a commonplace of Wellesian criticism to observe that after the peak of *Citizen Kane* his career went into a slow but unstoppable decline, and his European films became second-rate substitutes of what he would have been capable of had he continued to receive the financial support he got for *Kane*. In fact, however, his *oeuvre* was enriched by his constant travelling, by his unorthodox production methods and even by the numerous unfinished projects, which, as Jonathan Rosenbaum suggests, are as much part of his output as the thirteen films he completed.[2] The modernity of *Citizen Kane* and the movies that followed challenges the concept of classical Hollywood cinema and, more pointedly than other recognized auteurs, questions current periodizations of U.S. film history. But, perhaps more importantly, placing his European films and unfinished projects on an equal footing with his American ones allows us to see Welles as a truly transnational director, both preoccupied with very specifically U.S. tropes and the product of a cosmopolitan sensibility, more at home in various European countries than in his native U.S.

After *Citizen Kane* and *The Magnificent Ambersons*, Welles completed three films in the U.S. in the 1940s: the spy movie *The Stranger* (1946), the *noir* thriller *The Lady from Shanghai* (1946) and his first Shakespearean adaptation, *Macbeth* (1948). Ten years later he would return to Hollywood to make *Touch of Evil* (1958). As well as remaining quintessentially Wellesian texts, both *The Lady from Shanghai* and *Touch of Evil* became landmarks of *film noir*. Both movies met with changes by the studios after Welles finished with them, particularly in the case of *The Lady from Shanghai*. The director produced a rough cut of 155 minutes but, after a thorough reedit on the part of the studio, including, as with *Ambersons*, new footage filmed by somebody else, the release and only extant version was reduced to 86 minutes. Still, Welles's presence can be felt everywhere in this story of an Irish sailor (played by the director) and his involvement with *femme fatale* Elsa Bannister (Rita Hayworth), not least in the climactic San Francisco fun house scene. The changes made by Universal to Welles's edit of *Touch of Evil* were comparatively minor, although three versions exist today. The film is as justly remembered for the filmmaker's imprint as director as for his performance as Hank Quinlan, a crooked and decadent policeman operating on the border with Mexico.

Touch of Evil is often considered the last of the classical *films noirs* but it is equally important as a border film. Shot in the Los Angeles district of Venice, the fictional town of Los Robles admirably conveys the complexity of border life much before borders took on the symbolic significance they have within contemporary consciousness. The famous long take that opens the film, apart from showcasing the director's technical virtuosity, derives much of its significance from its fascinating portrayal of the borderlands and its engagement with the transnational experience.

Given the proliferation of perspectives from which Welles's *oeuvre* has been approached, it is surprising that the transnational dimension is generally absent. In her excellent monograph on *Citizen Kane*, Laura Mulvey (1992) is an exception when she situates the tension between Europe and America as the key to understanding Kane's character and the signifying structure of the text. In most of his other films, the transnational dimension is much more obvious. One of Welles's best-remembered creations, his brief appearance as attractive but depraved villain Harry Lime in Carol Reed's *The Third Man* (1949), illustrates the border consciousness that permeates his career: Lime is the product of a historical context in which borders were being redrawn and the fragility of national boundaries opened up novel spaces of identity and power. In this sense, *The Third Man* is a forerunner of *Mr. Arkadin* (1955), another notoriously "incomplete" text and Welles' most openly transnational film. Shot with an international group of actors across various cities and countries of Europe in the course of many months, this tale of power and the search for identity constructs a unique cosmopolitan sensibility in which the uncertain and fluid national identity of characters and places points towards a new understanding of citizenship. The film is often linked with *Kane* through the enigmatic central figure of Arkadin and its investigative structure. Disparaging appraisals of this movie have failed to do justice to its forward-looking cultural agenda.

Like all Welles films, *Mr. Arkadin* is centrally concerned with the ambivalence of power, its tyrannies and oppressions as well as its endless fascination. The transnational canvas for the articulation of this preoccupation becomes a nationally unmarked one in the film adaptation of Franz Kafka's *The Trial* (1962), in which Welles again uses an international cast (and geographically unmarked but visually impressive locations) to highlight the universality of his hero Joseph K's (Anthony Perkins) ambiguous relation to power and victimization. In keeping with this theme, it is probably the centrality of power in William Shakespeare's *oeuvre* that attracted Welles to the universe of the English playwright. Welles made three filmic adaptations of Shakespeare's plays: *Macbeth*, a very humble cinematic version of a theatrical production Welles had staged at the Utah Shakespeare Festival in 1947; *Othello* (1952), his first film outside Hollywood and, like *Mr. Arkadin* later, shot over a long period of time in various European and North-African locations; and *Chimes at Midnight* (1966), based on the two parts of *Henry IV*, with some minor additions from *Richard II*, *The Merry Wives of Windsor* and *Henry V*, which derived from Welles's earlier stage productions of these plays. *Chimes at Midnight* was the first film since *Citizen Kane* in which Welles had final cut and is still today considered one of the best in the long history of cinematic adaptations of Shakespeare's works. Like the original plays, the movie places Falstaff (Welles) at the center of the power realignments in European politics that brought about the end of the Middle Ages and the advent of the modern nation-states. Justly famous for its central battle scene, a prodigy of rhythmic editing and expressionistic denunciation of the horrors of war, the film also displays the border consciousness of earlier efforts. One of its most characteristic set-ups, repeated several times, shows the Eastcheap tavern, the space dominated by Falstaff, in the foreground with the king's castle looming in the background, the area in between constructed as a borderland and meeting point of two historical periods and two attitudes to life, embodied by Falstaff and Prince Hal (Keith Baxter). The film was shot and produced in Spain and continued Welles's fascination with this country, which, like the plays of Shakespeare and the world they create, he saw as caught in the turmoil of momentous changes, between the innocence of a utopian past and the inevitability of modernity. In this sense Spain stood for the whole of Europe and its relation to the new world, and therefore, through the lens of Shakespeare, Welles revisited in *Chimes at Midnight* some of the central themes of his first two films.

Welles's mastery at the editing table can be attributed to his love of magic and trickery and his awareness of the manipulative nature of the creation of alternative realities through storytelling. His TV film *The Immortal Story* (1968) reflects some of these preoccupations, but they are much more prominent in his mock documentary *F for Fake* (1973), another cosmopolitan film about forgery and storytelling, one which starts with Welles assuring the spectator that he will tell nothing but the truth and ends with the embodied narrator admitting that for the last twenty minutes he has been lying. This exploration of the elusiveness and arbitrariness of what we call reality and truth points at the gaping hollowness at the center of identity, another recurring concern of the filmmaker, which energizes the mirror sequence of *The Lady from Shanghai*, reverberates through the massive Gare d'Orsay locations of *The Trial*, permeates Lucy (Anne Baxter) and Eugene's (Joseph Cotten) famous long-take conversation in *Ambersons* and resonates in the smoke coming out of the Xanadu chimney at the end of *Kane* as a metaphor of the ultimate meaning of Rosebud. This emptiness of existence, also present at the climactic moment of *Macbeth* ("life's but a walking shadow [...], a tale of sound and fury, signifying nothing"), reappears in the final shot of *Chimes at Midnight*, with Falstaff's corpse slowly traversing the borderland between tavern and palace as history marches inexorably forward, in the words of the offscreen narrator. Or, as Tanya concludes in the final line of *Touch of Evil*: "What does it matter what you say about people?"

Biography

A director, writer and actor, Orson Welles was born in 1915 in Kenosha, Wisconsin, and died in 1985 in Hollywood, California. His major films include *Citizen Kane* (1941), *The Magnificent Ambersons* (1942), *The Lady from Shanghai* (1946), *Mr. Arkadin* (1955), *Touch of Evil* (1958), *The Trial* (1962) and *Chimes at Midnight* (1966), in most of which he played one of the leading parts. His performance in Carol Reed's *The Third Man* (1949) is also well remembered. He was given an Honorary Academy Award in 1981 as well as many other life achievement awards, and won, with Herman J. Mankiewicz, the Oscar for Best Original Screenplay for *Citizen Kane*.

Notes

1 James Naremore, *The Magic World of Orson Welles* (revised edition), Dallas: Southern Methodist University Press, 1989 (1978), pp. 106–10.
2 Jonathan Rosenbaum, *Discovering Orson Welles*, Berkeley, Los Angeles and London: University of California Press, 2007, pp. 8–14.

Filmography

Citizen Kane (1941)
The Magnificent Ambersons (1942)
The Stranger (1946)
The Lady from Shanghai (1946)
Macbeth (1948)
Othello (1952)
Mr. Arkadin (1955) aka *Confidential Report*
Touch of Evil (1958)
The Trial (1962) aka *Le procès*
Chimes at Midnight (1966) aka *Campanadas a medianoche*
The Immortal Story (1968) aka *L'histoire immortelle*
F for Fake (1972) aka *Vérités et mensonges*
Filming Othello (1978)
Don Quijote de Orson Welles (1992)

Further reading

Bazin, André. *Orson Welles.* Paris: Editions Chavane, 1950.

Carringer, Robert. *The Making of Citizen Kane.* London: John Murray, 1985.

Higham, Charles. *The Films of Orson Welles.* Berkeley, Los Angeles and London: University of California Press, 1970.

Kael, Pauline. *The Citizen Kane Book.* Boston: Little, Brown, 1971.

McBride, Joseph. *Orson Welles.* London: Secker and Warburg/BFI, 1972.

Mulvey, Laura. *Citizen Kane.* BFI Film Classics. London: BFI, 1992.

WILLIAM A. WELLMAN

By Sudarshan Ramani

William A. Wellman's life has much in common with that of his film's heroes. On his father's side, he belongs to the New England elite, the Wellman name extending up to the arrival of Thomas Wellman, a Puritan who arrived at Massachusetts Bay Colony in 1640. His mother, however, was an Irish immigrant, Cecilia McCarthy, who was noted for her work in juvenile reform but who famously complained about her failure to keep her rambunctious son in check. On the outbreak of World War I, he signed up well before America's engagement in the conflict. He served as an ambulance driver for the Narton-Hartjes Ambulance Corps and later the French Foreign Legion as a fighter pilot and then as the first American to join the Lafayette Flying Corps (not to be confused with the more famous *Lafayette Escadrille*, the title and subject of his final film, made in 1958).

His career as an aviator and his zestful boasting of the same earned him the lifelong nickname of "Wild Bill" Wellman and the attention of Douglas Fairbanks who cast him in *The Knickerbocker Buckaroo* (1919). Wellman however, chafed under the discipline of performing and became more interested in the process of filmmaking. His first major work was *Wings* (1927), the first recipient of the Oscar for Best Picture at the inaugural Academy Awards. It is an ironic aspect of Wellman's life that the films that came closest to his life experience as an aviator, *Wings* and later *Lafayette Escadrille* (1958) seem less visually and formally inspired than his gangster films and Westerns. Indeed seen in light of his pre-code period, *Beggars of Life* (1928), starring Louise Brooks (before she went to Weimar Germany) seems more important.

Wellman was a man of paradoxes. He was a macho director who claimed to hate working with actresses, yet he directed some genuine proto-feminist films like *Night Nurse, Midnight Mary*, and *Westward the Women*. An aviator who hated infantrymen and passed on working on *The Story of G. I. Joe* (1945) when it was first offered to him, he then embraced the film and considered it his greatest work. He was conservative and right wing in politics, indeed a militant anti-communist who shared John Wayne's views, but he also made some of the harshest critiques of family values, authentic New Deal propaganda and the definitive anti-lynching film.

Indeed, during the period known as the Pre-Code era, Wellman made some of the defining films of the 30s, works that endure as great documents of the early years of the Great Depression. Wellman made seventeen features in the period of 1931–33, with seven released in 1933 alone. Wellman finds his mark early with *Other Men's Women*, which led critic Bertrand Tavernier to remark on the film's "confounding vitality," its integration of "real exteriors, and the bits of daily life," which creates a naturalistic atmosphere, "a style close to Renoir."[1]

Wellman's films from this era are filled with powerful images, particularly death scenes. Bodies fall haplessly, easily, like a victim of machine gun fire in *The Public Enemy*. When Tom Powers (James Cagney) enacts his final revenge against his enemies at the climax, all we see is Powers' body staggering out and falling in the gutter. His corpse is later presented to his family home as a grotesque tribal ornament, a scene that apparently shocked some thin skinned producers at a preview screening.[2] More sudden and less logical is the shocking death of Loretta Young in *Heroes for Sale*, who, while searching for her husband in the middle of a riot is indifferently felled by a simple club to her head by a police truncheon. Years later, Wellman would cite the war journalist Ernie Pyle's maxim, "a man only falls dead once." Violence in Wellman's films has a reality and candor rare for American cinema—for him, death is merely a sudden finality.

Wellman's films of the early Depression prefigure the "Living Newspaper" of the Roosevelt backed WPA Theatre Project of the mid-30s. In *The Conquerors*, a highly topical Depression-era saga, the economic anxieties are filtered through the prism of "financial crises through the ages." Much of the film's force comes from its sense of the epic-as-newsreel, an attempt to put on screen American capitalism itself. Its hero, Roger Standish (Richard Dix) is presented as a sympathetic, upstanding businessman but the rise of his company is based on violence and death. In the film's early section, Standish and his wife arrive at a town assailed by bandits and thieves. He inspires the crowd to take charge and fight them, instigating the same lynch mob mentality that Wellman would denounce ten years later with *The Ox-Bow Incident*. Standish even leads the early charge, but a convenient injury prevents him from being part of the mob that summarily hangs the bandits. He profits clearly in the aftermath, establishing the first banking institution in the town. The rest of the film charts how the corporate dynamic of the business is at one with the family's daily life and how Standish's bank remains "Too Big to Fail" up until the crash of 1929.

Heroes for Sale is another Depression epic, the reverse image of Wellman's paean to big capital. Inspired by the 1932 Veterans March to Washington D.C., his focus shifts to the topical issue of out-of-work WW1 veterans. The same event inspired Busby Berkeley's "Remember My Forgotten Man" number from *Gold Diggers of 1933* (on the set of which, Wellman met Dorothy Coonan, who played the female lead in *Wild Boys of the Road* and whom he would later marry). Like Tom Joad after him, Thomas Holmes (Richard Barthelmess) endures the trauma of America during the Depression, a landscape that is urban, violent and dark, full of breadlines, broken families and senseless deaths. Much of the film's action is shot at night, like a gangster film albeit with the real public enemies – the unemployed, the workers on strike and suspected "reds." The sense of persecution descending into paranoia and vain hopes prefigures post-war film noir in many ways.

Wellman's heroes are rarely actors and choosers of their own destiny and circumstances. The exception is *Wild Boys of the Road*, which features sons and daughters of unemployed parents, teens who illegally cross state lines by stowing away on trains, risking and losing life, limb and personal dignity – as in the case of a girl who is raped by a brakeman on a train. This film, rare for casting actual age-appropriate teenagers, presents the migration of young people to the cities in search of work as a strategy to fund their parents back home. Yet, they flee only to form a commune of slums where they are threatened by thug-like truncheon wielding cops. *Wild Boys of the Road* marks the end of Wellman's golden age. The enforcement of the Hays Code instituted a period of censorship that lasted twenty-five years, crippling his instinctive fervor to offer a glimpse of American society from below

Wellman did direct such enduring classics as the first version of *A Star is Born* (1937), for which he won his only Oscar for Best Story, and *Nothing Sacred* (1937), a screwball comedy with Carole Lombard.

Yet, neither film has the same spirit that animates his best work, being more journeyman and anonymous than personal. Wellman did find inspiration and freedom in a series of Westerns, where he returns to his pre-code style, namely by employing a *mise-en-scène* attuned to hostile circumstances where his characters confront the absurdity of life. *The Ox-Bow Incident*, Wellman's most celebrated work, is a return to the spirit of the 30s yet also a correction; refusing compulsory optimism, heroic figures fail to rescue the downtrodden.

The film also benefits greatly from a cast composed of several John Ford stock players, including in addition to Henry Fonda, Jane Darwell (Ma Joad from *The Grapes of Wrath*), Francis Ford (offering a less comical variation of his usual role in his brother's films), and screenwriter Lamar Trotti and DP Arthur C. Miller. Much of the film's portrayal of community reads like a dark parody of John Ford's films, which typically feature enlightened lawmen quelling mob violence and channeling resentment to peaceful resolutions. Wellman's film, on the other hand, offers well-meaning but powerless dissidents who fail to prevent the lynching of three innocent men by a mob comprising falsely comic dim-wits who mime boastfully about their atrocity after the event. The film takes a broad view by foregrounding deeper motivations behind lynching, namely that the Western town of Bridger Wells suffers from a stagnant economy, with its townsfolk bored and corrupted by unemployment.

Wellman's *Yellow Sky* deals with similar themes, featuring a Western town that, like Bridger Wells, has seen its economy collapse, and is visited by a gang of outlaws. Led by James Dawson (Gregory Peck) they tread over a barren landscape, deteriorating from the heat, thirst and starvation. The mise-en-scène of *Yellow Sky* is surprising throughout, precise in outlining the tensions of Dawson's posse. The fact the crooks are former Civil War soldiers places the film in the tradition of post-war Westerns such as *Pursued* (1947), *Fort Apache* (1948), *Winchester '73* (1950), films that all retrofitted post-WW2 trauma in the Wild West.

Wellman's Westerns deal with the West not as a mythological backdrop but as a landscape that determines the economy and circumstances of communities. *The Ox-Bow Incident* was, for example, shot on sound stages to amplify the confinement and claustrophobia of a dying town. *Yellow Sky* makes use of actual locations, including Death Valley, California, to create a primordial world of heat, sand and charred rock. Drastically cut by the studios, *Across the Wide Missouri*, tells the story of the fur trapping industry and makes use of the Rocky Mountains, shooting at high altitudes. Finally, like Anthony

Mann's *The Far Country* (1954), Andre DeToth's *Day of the Outlaw* (1959) and Robert Altman's *McCabe & Mrs. Miller* (1971), *Track of the Cat* is a "White Western" relocating the frontier on snowy plains. White Westerns tend to be bleak and desolate, the environment denying any of the mythic grandeur of the more common "Red Westerns" set in desert landscapes.

Track of the Cat breaks new formal ground while its content in many ways brings many threads in Wellman's earlier films to a close. Featuring a family home located in a barren valley, the film features brothers who ask for a share in the family produce. The nature in this film is beautiful and primordial while civilization, as typified by the nuclear family is savage and vicious. Far from the image of idealized motherhood, Ma Bridges (Beulah Bondi) ruthlessly exploits the ritual of grief and the burial of her dead son to emotionally castrate her youngest son, Harold (Tab Hunter), the most vulnerable of the three brothers and the one who harbors dreams of escape. The Bridges family embodies the Protestant Ethic gone to seed; every member of the family is defined by their capacity to earn and in the absence of a strong patriarch, is ruled by a dictatorial mother whose hand is always near the Bible. *Track of the Cat* serves as the capstone of a career devoted to showing the absurdity, violence and madness hidden below the surface of American life.

Wellman retired early at a time when Howard Hawks, John Ford and Alfred Hitchcock remained active into the mid-60s and late-70s, and as such he missed out on the period of reevaluation that enshrined their reputations. Wellman's revival occurred later, when he found champions like Manny Farber, Bertrand Tavernier and director Martin Scorsese who cited the influence of *The Public Enemy* on *Mean Streets* (1973). Though Wellman's films lacked the heroic or tragic figures redolent in that of his more storied contemporaries,[3] his heroes were essentially normal people with a "common sense" approach to adventure. To be an outcast or an outlaw in Wellman's films is to face real consequences, as discovered by the titular characters of *Wild Boys of the Road* and *Heroes for Sale*. Wellman's films are driven by a fascination with process, the basics of trying to survive. When it comes in Wellman's films, success tends to be qualified and frequently rings hollow; his "happy endings" offer poor compensation for the torment his characters undergo. To unrelenting universal indifference, Wellman proposes constant persistence. Persistence sometimes devolves into self-destructive obsession, as in *Track of the Cat*, but it also inspires, as when in *The Story of G. I. Joe* the soldiers of C. Company, 18th

Infantry fight against constant exhaustion, maintaining their bodies to last until the day the war ends.

Biography

William Augustus Wellman was born on February 29, 1896. A meeting with Douglas Fairbanks led to his entry into the motion picture business as an actor. His interest drifted to behind the scenes production work, and he served under director Bernie Dunning as an assistant director, with his first credited work coming in 1923. In 1927, he directed *Wings* which won Best Picture at the inaugural Academy Awards ceremony. His career as a director continued in full swing for over three decades including classics such as *The Public Enemy* (1931), *A Star is Born* (1937), *The Ox-Bow Incident* (1943) and *The Story of G. I. Joe* (1945). He retired in 1958 with *Lafayette Escadrille*, his final film. He died on December 9, 1975.

Notes

1 Bertrand Tavernier, "Wild Bill Wellman, Back in the Saddle." *L. A. Weekly*, April 2009. http://www.laweekly.com/2009-04-30/film-tv/wild-bill-back-in-the-saddle/
2 "WILD BILL": WILLIAM A. WELLMAN. Interview by Scott Eyman. Originally published in *Focus on Film #29* http://filmlinccom.siteprotect.net/fcm/online/wellmanextra.htm
3 Eyman, Scott and Allen Eyles. "'Wild Bill' William A. Wellman," *Focus on Film* (London), no. 29. 1978.

Filmography

The Man Who Won (1923)
2nd Hand Love (1923)
Big Dan (1923)
Cupid's Fireman (1923)
The Vagabond Trail (1924)
Not a Drum Was Heard (1924)
The Circus Cowboy (1924)
When Husbands Flirt (1925)
The Boob (1926)
The Cat's Pajamas (1926)
You Never Know Women (1926)
Wings (1927)
The Legion of the Condemned (1928)

Ladies of the Mob (1928)
Beggars of Life (1928)
Chinatown Nights (1929)
The Man I Love (1929)
Woman Trap (1929)
Dangerous Paradise (1930)
Young Eagles (1930)
Maybe It's Love (1930)
Other Men's Women (1931)
The Public Enemy (1931)
Night Nurse (1931)
Star Witness (1931)
Safe in Hell (1931)
The Hatchet Man (1932)
So Big (1932)
Love Is a Racket (1932)
The Purchase Price (1932)
The Conquerors (1932)
Frisco Jenny (1932)
Central Airport (1933)
Lily Turner (1933)
Midnight Mary (1933)
Heroes for Sale (1933)
Wild Boys of the Road (1933)
College Coach (1933)
Looking for Trouble (1934)
Stingaree (1934)
The President Vanishes (1934)
The Call of the Wild (1935)
The Robin Hood of Eldorado (1936) also co-screenwriter
Small Town Girl (1936)
A Star Is Born (1937)
Nothing Sacred (1937)
Men with Wings (1938) also producer
Beau Geste (1939) also producer
The Light That Failed (1939) also producer
Reaching for the Sun (1941) also producer
Roxie Hart (1942)
The Great Man's Lady (1942) also producer
Thunder Birds (1942)
The Ox-Bow Incident (1943)
Lady of Burlesque (1943)

Buffalo Bill (1944)
This Man's Navy (1945)
The Story of G. I. Joe (1945)
Gallant Journey (1946) also producer and co-screenwriter
Magic Town (1947)
The Iron Curtain (1948)
Yellow Sky (1948)
Battleground (1949)
The Next Voice You Hear (1950)
The Happy Years (1950)
Across the Wide Missouri (1951)
Westward the Women (1951)
It's a Big Country: An American Anthology (1952) co-director
My Man and I (1952)
Island in the Sky (1953)
The High and the Mighty (1954)
Track of the Cat (1954)
Blood Alley (1955)
Good-bye My Lady (1956)
Darby's Rangers (1958)
Lafayette Escadrille (1958) also producer and co-screenwriter

Further reading

Tavernier, Bertrand. "From the Archives: William Wellman by Bertrand Tavernier." *Film Comment* (February 2012.)

Thompson, Frank T. *William A. Wellman (Filmmakers Series)*. Metuchen, NJ: Scarecrow Press, 1983–84.

Wellman, William A. *A Short Time for Insanity: An Autobiography*. New York: Hawthorn Books, 1974.

JAMES WHALE

By Michael Williams

James Whale was born in Dudley, England, in 1889, and had been a stage actor and director in London, as well as a talented artist, before working successfully in a wide range of Hollywood genres. However, Whale is primarily remembered for his association with Universal horror, and for his cultivation of an image of refined, occasionally reserved, but often macabre and devilishly witty, Britishness.

Whale came to fame through his direction of R. C. Sherriff's harrowing Great War play, *Journey's End*, which became an international success on the stage following its London debut. Both men had experienced the trenches in World War I, and Whale's set design displayed his keen sense for atmosphere, which framed the drama claustrophobically beneath heavy overhead beams. Transferring to Broadway, the play would bring him to the attention of Hollywood, where Whale's theatrical credentials were sought to direct dialogue, most notably for Howard Hughes' *Hell's Angels* (1930). Having thus served his apprenticeship in talking pictures, Whale's first film as director, the Gainsborough / Welsh-Pearson adaptation of *Journey's End* (1930), filmed at Tiffany-Stahl's Sunset Boulevard studios, remains one of the finest war films, a status that would be more widely recognised today had Lewis Milestone's *All Quiet on the Western Front* (1930) not been released two months later.[1] As with the theatrical production, audiences were left speechless by what they saw, with the complex sound effects Whale devised for the theatre transformed into the film's brooding soundscape of booms, rumbles and whistles—all heard before the action begins. Britain's *Picturegoer* magazine hailed the film as 'intensely realistic and poignant', the publication's headline announcing that *Journey's End* presents 'War as it Was'. The review's final words, portentous of a future line in Whale's most famous film, concluded that the film defied analysis: 'it is alive'.[2] American critics agreed, with *Photoplay* hailing it as 'a magnificent milestone in motion picture history'.[3]

Universal lured Whale away from Tiffany for a five-year contract, and it was under Carl Laemmle Jr.'s supervision at the studio that Whale flourished. Following another successful drama set during the war, *Waterloo Bridge* (1931), Whale's *Frankenstein* (1931) crystallised his modern reputation. Whale had watched a number of German 'expressionist' films in preparation for the project (and had himself directed a rare British venture in the Grand Guignol theatre in which a corpse is brought to life with electricity), including *The Cabinet of Dr Caligari* (1919), and told his lead actor, Colin Clive, that the film would contain 'a great deal of us' and that 'I think it will fit you as well as Stanhope'.[4] Clive had received acclaim for his extraordinary performance on both stage and screen as the alcoholic, neurotic, officer Stanhope in *Journey's End*, and the press felt him to have 'merged his name indissolubly' with the role.[5] Whale clearly felt there was some shared cultural or psychological DNA between Clive and the characters he interpreted for him. Indeed, the strength of sympathy is such that their screen collaborations seem to find Clive acting as Whale's muse, channelling obliquely the men's experience in the war, along perhaps with their sexuality (Whale was gay, and Clive may have been, albeit highly repressed), and their identity as outsiders. Soon *Frankenstein* itself would supplant any other associations in the careers of both Clive and Whale. It is more than a biographical contrivance to read the horror film as bearing the traces of the war, which from the outset is illuminated by dim light recalling the dugout of *Journey's End*, with expressionistic, chiaroscuro flourishes in lighting, staging and performance. Indeed, the film is electrified by Clive's jittery, impassioned determination to bring a dead man to life, crying ecstatically 'It's alive!' as his creation's arm – the product of Boris Karloff's legendary performance – erects itself before him.[6] Indeed, war-damaged men seem to haunt Whale's films, directly and more implicitly, returning as often as Frankenstein's creation would prove to do.

The self-description of ex-soldier Roger Penderel (Melvyn Douglas) in *The Old Dark House* (1932) – 'War generation, slightly soiled. A study in the bittersweet, the man with the twisted smile' – could describe any number of Whale's characters, and might eloquently represent the persona of the director himself. Many of his characters strive to escape the present, to become someone else, or return to who they were before some frightful life-changing event occurred. 'There must be a way back!' exclaims the Invisible Man of Whale's 1933 film, frustrated by the chemicals that have produced his tormented and optically challenged situation. The motley assortment of passengers in *Sinners in Paradise* (1938) who find themselves plane-wrecked on a Pacific island, all seem torn between a desire to return home, and a desperate need to forget the troubled pasts from which they have seemingly escaped. 'We don't care much where we're going', one character remarks, 'so long as it isn't back', while another quips that the island group resembles 'a rest camp for nervous patients'.

Frankenstein proved a great commercial success for Universal, at a time when they needed one, although some critics sneered. 'Of its type, it is very good', Britain's Lionel Collier damned with grudging praise, suggesting that while the film's 'goose-flesh' sequences were well-designed, a tendency to 'over-emphasis and over-elaboration simply lead to an artificiality which renders them nugatory', but revealingly compares the film to *Der Golem* (Boese and Wegener, 1920), an expressionistic German horror.[7] The *Monthly Film Bulletin*, meanwhile, dismissed the film upon its 1938 reissue (in an evidently poor print) as a 'superficial' feature with 'no deeper purpose' than 'thrills' and 'sensation'.[8] Similar responses met the release of *The Bride of Frankenstein*. The *Monthly Film Bulletin* was deferential to the 'extraordinarily good' technical and acting prowess on show, but overall felt it to be a poor sequel. 'The Monster is less terrifying', it opined, 'partly because the dawning in him of human qualities arouses sympathy for him'.[9] One might argue that this precisely misses the point, that it is in Whale and Karloff's portrayal of the creature's vulnerable humanity and poignant longing for companionship that the film triumphs. Such comments are surprising to read now given that the film is prized for its skilled direction and hailed as a genre classic. They also must have rankled with Whale at the time, and might partly account for his retrospective desire to distance himself from his four horror features, and attempt to align himself with projects deemed by critics to be more culturally elevated.

Evidently, many contemporary critics were unsure how to read Whale's use of theatricality, which produced moments that might seem mannered or predictable. We might now appreciate this as Whale's foregrounding of 'the "phoniness" of performing', as Paul Jensen puts it.[10] Whale's films are shot through with a type of trench humour, never more so than in *The Old Dark House* and *The Bride of Frankenstein* (1935), which also imbued them with a tone – part of their 'campness' – that enabled them to function on a number of levels. The latter film, for example, features performance styles ranging from Valerie Hobson's RADA-trained poise as Elizabeth, which contrasts with Clive's nervous intensity, which turns near-woodenness into a virtue, to fellow Briton Una O'Connor's outrageous comic turn as hysterical villager Minnie. Each figure teases the fine line that lies between sending up these archetypes and exemplifying them, but somehow the blend of performances, as vivid and contrasting as the cinematography and exuberant set design, just works. These films were highly unconventional, suiting the director whose successful debut had transgressed nearly every tradition of commercial filmmaking.

Since *Journey's End*, Whale introduced a number of British artists to Hollywood, adding to the already-strong European influence upon the system, not least Sherriff and Clive. In *The Old Dark House*, Charles Laughton made his US debut as a broadly comic but rather sympathetic northern industrialist, as did Canadian Raymond Massey, who had been working in British stage and screen. Also brought to America was the extraordinary Ernest Thesiger, whose acid intonation and distinctively waspish appearance is a strong part of the film's enduring appeal, as is his delicious performance as Dr. Pretorius in *The Bride of Frankenstein*. Thesiger was flamboyantly camp in both theatricality and the enunciation of his homosexuality, adding a caustic quality to his entreaty in *The Old Dark House* to 'have a potato', or in holding up a bunch of flowers, explaining that his sister intends to arrange them, before disdainfully casting them into the fire. Thesiger and Whale became good friends, and the director vicariously delighted in his star's on and off-screen performances while being more muted in his gay identity himself. The needlepoint-loving Thesiger's declaration of himself on set as "'the stichin' bitch'" probably says it all.[11]

The queerness of *The Old Dark House* is capped by the cross-gender casting of Elspeth Dudgeon as the 102-year-old Roderick Femm. The film was a brilliant exercise in functioning at one level as an entirely satisfactory horror film, while also offering a smorgasbord of innuendo and sub-textual readings. Gloria Stuart's Margaret, for example, is subjected to the macabrely intense attention of Rebecca Femm (Eva Moore), who fingers her 'fine' gown while speaking of 'fleshy love' before pointing to her chest, remarking that it was 'finer stuff still, but it will rot too, in time'. Later, after her rain-swept visit to the barn with another man, Laughton's Penderell remarks to his chorus girl girlfriend Gladys Perkins (Lillian Bond) 'you got your feet wet?', to which she quips with provocative innuendo 'Yes, Bill, and that wasn't all either.' The film includes fine performances from a starry cast, including Karloff as the sinister Morgan, introduced in disconcerting close-up, and Stuart as the flame-like figure benighted with her fellow travellers at the titular house on a stormy night. The talent for sound design Whale had nurtured from the outset of his career is nowhere stronger than in this film, where the eerie whistling wind heard throughout the film exemplifies the aural distinctiveness of the Universal horror. As with many films now viewed as classics, the 1932 production received mixed reviews before becoming unavailable for a time. While in 1933 Britain's *Picturegoer* magazine praised the film's camerawork and exploration of psychology and the 'quite brilliant' direction, a trade review on the film's reissue in 1945 stated that it was merely 'an unpleasant thriller which might well have been left in the vaults from which it was resurrected'.[12] Thankfully, the film – and its reputation – have been restored. *The Old Dark House* and *The Bride of Frankenstein* have both risen in critical status, and are now accepted as testament to any auteurist argument for Whale's status within the Hollywood system of the era.

The Kiss Before the Mirror (1933) demonstrated once more that Whale was a master of adaptation, drawing on the camera skills of Karl Freund (the first of three collaborations) to fully transform a stage play into something specifically cinematic. Whale nevertheless declared himself dissatisfied with this earlier treatment, and later remade the film as *Wives Under Suspicion* (1938), a rapidly produced drama that was dismissed by the press as 'a crude and artificial melodrama with stilted dialogue and direction'.[13] Nonetheless, the opening sequence in which a complex tracking shot reveals the machinery of the electric chair is remarkable, as is the abacus of skulls with which the central attorney counts off the city's suspected murderers, a brilliantly macabre presentation of the technologies of death perpetrated by modern society. The psychological impact, and sometimes 'hubristic' ambition, of science are likewise at the heart of one of Whale's most celebrated films, *The Invisible Man*. With a screenplay by Sherriff, the film was given the prestigious endorsement by the novel's author, H. G. Wells, for being a faithful version 'filmed flawlessly'.[14] It offered a characteristic blend of thrills, uncanny effects, male emotional angst and broad humour and comic grotesques, the latter exemplified, once more, by Una O'Connor as the Innkeeper's wife. While *Frankenstein* and *The Old Dark House* offered Karloff a chance to act while largely unheard, this time Claude Rains was cast for his mellifluous voice, with his face glimpsed only in the final moments of the film. Following the film's critical and commercial success, Whale developed another science-fiction script with Sherriff entitled *A Trip to Mars*. The project suffered a series of delays, and once Universal began production of the first *Flash Gordon* serial (1936), Whale's project was shelved.[15] The irony remains that the *Flash Gordon* serials can be seen re-using props, sets and music from *The Bride of Frankenstein*.

It is often forgotten that the film that gained Whale some of his most glowing notices was his 1936 version of Kern and Hammerstein's *Show Boat*. One review's reference to the film representing 'a revolution in sound recording' rightly points out the way a certain intimate quality is achieved in the musical's vocals, and most particularly those of Paul Robeson.[16] The actor's performance of 'Ol' Man River', reprising his stage role, is the standout sequence of the film. The camera tracks around Robeson in a sequence interspersed with expressionistic inserts of slaves toiling in the fields, before framing the black performer's face in a lingering extreme close up. Unusual for Hollywood in that era, the bold close-up (and trademark Whale touch) allowed Robeson's charisma to overcome the stereotypes inherent in the material and is another instance, as David Lugowski has pointed out, of Whale using 'theatrical illustration, a hyperbolic and stylised pointing-out' to explore the pressures on racial or cultural outsiders.[17] This critical and commercial high watermark proved a turning point in the director's career, but not towards the positive end that might have been expected.

Largely due to changes at Universal, Whale subsequently lost the kind of creative control he had enjoyed under Laemmle, and was increasingly vulnerable to the action of the censors and unsympathetic producers alike. *The Road Back* (1937), where Whale worked with another R. C. Sherriff script, suffered greatest in this respect. Making what should have been a prestigious adaptation of Remarque's follow-up novel to *All Quiet on the Western Front*, Whale found himself under great pressure to reduce costs and speed up production. Then, as the political situation in Europe grew more troubled and Hollywood grew anxious about its foreign markets, the film was mercilessly cut to address concerns expressed by the German govern-ment about scenes perceived to be anti-German. Although Germany did not pursue the matter, and despite positive previews, the studio still imposed thirty-three separate cuts and removed the ending, which warned of a future war. Whale refused to direct the new scenes.[18] Thus, while some visually striking scenes remain, including some virtuoso camerawork, contemporary reviews pointed to the 'confused' direction of the story, and it performed poorly at the box office.[19] Whale's original version is believed lost.

Not helping his reputation in this context, biographies also indicate that Whale's persona, and sometimes uncompromising personality, was rather alienating to some actors, particularly if they were not part of the very English tea-drinking rituals that he cultivated at the studio. There were later successes, as in his 1939 swashbuckler *The Man in the Iron Mask*, but also films that were widely derided such as the jungle melodrama *Green Hell*, released the same year. Mark Gatiss, in his biography of Whale, reproduces the accepted wisdom that this film was 'probably one of the worst pictures ever to come out of Holly-wood'.[20] However, written by Frances Marion and photographed once more by Karl Freund, the film has much to offer, including some remarkable flood scenes staged on a huge set recreating an ancient temple, and the obligatory thunderstorm that recalls Whale's earlier work. There is certainly some risible dialogue and clichés in abun-dance, but its critical reception indicates that it was far from a complete disaster; even the usually-reserved *Monthly Film Bulletin* exclaimed that Whale, and the 'wholehearted' cast including Douglas Fairbanks Jr., Joan Bennett, and George Saunders, overcame the 'somewhat ordinary plot' to produce a film that is 'exciting and thrilling'.[21]

After making the anti-Nazi drama *They Dare Not Love* (1941) for Columbia, along with a propaganda film, occasional stage work, and then *Hello Out There* (1949), which was planned to be part of a 1949 compendium film, but was not actually included, Whale retired from the screen. His later life, where he returned to painting and sketching, before finally being discovered dead at the bottom of his famous Los Angeles swimming pool, is imaginatively evoked by Bill Condon's 1999 film *Gods and Monsters*. It has become a truism to connect Whale's horror films, particularly *Frankenstein*, to his experiences in the trenches of the First World War, and indeed one of the underlying themes of his work is the painful longing – an expressionistic *nostalgie de la boue* – for the 'road back' to his working-class origins in Britain, and to the war itself. *Photoplay's* 1930 review of *Journey's End* distilled many of the qualities that made that film so special. Articulating many observations that hitherto remained unsaid about the war, his characters and, dare one say, Whale himself, the review pronounced with varying degrees of irony: 'Raw nerves, tender memories of home, fear, grasping at every straw to forget thoughts of death beyond.'[22] Yet while his horror features function as a Rosetta stone for Whale's key influences and personal talent they, like his sexuality, are but one part of his identity and achievements, many of which too rarely emerge from the archive; like Karloff's creature, reaching for the light they so richly deserve.

Biography

James Whale was born into a large working class family in the industrial town of Dudley, UK, on 22 July 1889. Whale's experience in the First World War was arguably key in shaping the themes of his work, and unexpectedly provided the young officer with a creative theatrical outlet while he was held captive as a prisoner of war. Returning to Britain, Whale developed his talents as an actor, set designer and director, first for the stage and then film, a move that would take him to Hollywood in 1930. Living in California for the rest of his life, Whale worked imaginatively across a range of genres making visually striking films, often infused with dark humour. Whale became disillusioned by their varying critical success and the restrictions of studio and commercial pressures, and his film career had weakened by the late 1930s. Following a series of strokes, the director was found dead in his swimming pool on 29 May 1957; his suicide note was later released by his long-time partner, David Lewis.

Notes

1 Mark Gatiss, *James Whale: A Biography*. London and New York: Cassell, 1995, p. 46.
2 Lionel Collier, 'War as it Was', *Picturegoer*, June 1930, pp. 20–21.
3 *Photoplay*, June 1930, p. 56.
4 Gatiss, pp. 18, 72, 74. Quoting letter from James Whale to Colin Clive, quoted in 'Frankenstein Finished', *New York Times*, 11 October 1931.
5 Collier, op. cit.
6 See also Christiane Gerblinger, 'James Whale's Frankensteins: Re-animating the Great War', *CineAction!*, n. 82/83, 2010, pp. 2–9.
7 Lionel Collier, *The Picturegoer*, May 1932, p. 18.
8 *Monthly Film Bulletin*, vol. 5 1938, pp. 183–84 (reissue).
9 *Monthly Film Bulletin*, July 1935, p. 83.
10 Paul Jensen, 'James Whale', *Film Comment*, Spring 1971, pp. 52–57.
11 James Curtis, *James Whale: A New World of Gods and Monsters*. Minneapolis: University of Minnesota Press, 2003. p. 240.
12 Lionel Collier, *The Picturegoer*, 28 January 1933, p. 19; *Kinematograph Weekly*, January 1945 (reissue), p. 5.
13 *Monthly Film Bulletin*, August 1938, p. 206.
14 Curtis, p. 221.
15 Curtis, p. 235.
16 'A Big Musical in the Making', *Picturegoer*, 2 January 1927, p. 29.
17 David Lugowski, 'James Whale', 'Senses of Cinema': http://sensesofcinema.com/2005/great-directors/whale/ (accessed 20 December 2013).
18 Gatiss, pp.132–33.
19 *Monthly Film Bulletin*, August 1937, p. 175.
20 Gatiss, p. 144.
21 *Monthly Film Bulletin*, August 1940, p. 91.
22 *Photoplay*, June 1930, p. 56.

Filmography

The Love Doctor (1930) also dialogue director
Hell's Angels (1930) uncredited; also dialogue director
Journey's End (1930)
Waterloo Bridge (1931)
Frankenstein (1931)
The Impatient Maiden (1932)
The Old Dark House (1932)
By Candlelight (1933)
The Invisible Man (1933)
The Kiss Before the Mirror (1933)
One more River (1934)
The Bride of Frankenstein (1935)
Remember Last Night? (1935)

Show Boat (1936)
The Great Garrick (1937)
The Road Back (1937)
Port of Seven Seas (1938)
Sinners in Paradise (1938)
Wives Under Suspicion (1938)
Green Hell (1939)
The Man in the Iron Mask (1939)
They Dare Not Love (1941)
Personnel Placement in the Army (1942)
Hello out There (1949)

Further reading

Curtis, James. *James Whale: A New World of Gods and Monsters.* Minneapolis: University of Minnesota Press, 2003.
Jensen, Paul. 'James Whale.' *Film Comment* (Spring 1971): 52–57.

BILLY WILDER

By Neil Sinyard

At one point during a seminar at the American Film Institute on 13 December 1978, Billy Wilder told his interviewer that 'it is not necessary for a director to know how to write. However, it helps if he knows how to read'.[1] In his early days as Hollywood screenwriter, Wilder had clashed furiously with director Mitchell Leisen and actor Charles Boyer over their deletion of a scene he had written for *Hold Back the Dawn* (1941). His enraged retaliation had taken two forms: rewriting the ending of the film with his co-writer Charles Brackett so that Boyer was left with virtually nothing to say; and (following the examples of his contemporaries Preston Sturges and John Huston) deciding to branch into direction in order to protect his own scripts. They proved to be eminently worth protecting.

After his arrival in Hollywood, Wilder initially made a precarious living selling stories and ideas whilst learning to master the language. His big break came when he was teamed with Charles Brackett as a writer for Paramount. They rapidly gained prestige through their work for directors such as Ernst Lubitsch (*Bluebeard's Eighth Wife, Ninotchka*), Mitchell Leisen (*Midnight, Arise My Love*) and Howard Hawks (*Ball of Fire*). These early associations were a significant influence on Wilder's work. Like Hawks, he was to show a predilection for extravagant impersonations, assertive heroines, pungent social comedy and lack of visual pretension. In common with Lubitsch, to whom he was devoted, he was to treat risqué subjects with a sardonic humour. Yet Wilder also had his own distinctive personality and these early screenplays were fascinating harbingers of things to come. Disguise and role playing in *Midnight* (1939), the attraction of innocent male and experienced female in *Ball of Fire* (1942), the romantic aura of Paris in *Ninotchka* (1939) and the idealization of America in *Hold Back the Dawn* were all themes that would find their way, with ingenious embellishments, into Wilder's own films as a director.

Wilder's directing debut in Hollywood, *The Major and the Minor* (1942) was a sparkling comedy about the dawning romance between an Army major (Ray Milland) and someone he initially believes to be a 12-year-old girl (actually Ginger Rogers in disguise). The masquerade by a two-faced woman intriguingly anticipates one of Wilder's beautiful late works, *Fedora* (1978), and the tricky comedy material is handled with nonchalant ease. Not the safest of projects with which to launch a directing career, *The Major and the Minor* established what would be a crucial facet of Wilder's filmic personality: namely, his willingness to take risks. Several aspects of his films can be seen as acts of defiance against Hollywood convention. His range – comedy, film noir, prisoner-of-war film, courtroom drama, Gothic melodrama, romance, social problem picture – reflected a refusal to submit to genre specialization. His use of familiar actors in unfamiliar roles (Fred MacMurray, Ray Milland, Humphrey Bogart, Gary Cooper) gave them a chance to flex hitherto untried dramatic muscles whilst simultaneously examining their screen image: note, for example, how wittily Wilder played with Bogart's persona as the existential loner in *Sabrina* (1954). Thus Hollywood formulae were revised rather than reproduced and were also sometimes led into unexpected and controversial areas.

Wilder quickly made a reputation for himself as Hollywood's resident cynic. Films such as *Double Indemnity* (1944), *The Lost Weekend* (1945), *Sunset Boulevard* (1950) and *Ace in the Hole* (1951) shone a harsh spotlight on unsavoury aspects of American life, but did so with such style and panache that audiences and critics were, for the most part, beguiled more than dismayed. 'We didn't need dialogue, we had faces,' claims the former star of silent movies, Norma Desmond (an imperious performance from Gloria Swanson) in a famous line from Wilder's glittering critique of modern Hollywood, *Sunset Boulevard*; paradoxically, though, the line demonstrates that Wilder was writing some of the sharpest dialogue in movies. In the mid-50s he began a happy and enduring collaboration with screenwriter I. A. L. Diamond and a rewarding partnership with the actor Jack Lemmon, which paid off almost immediately with two of his greatest artistic and commercial successes. *Some like it Hot* (1959) daringly put Lemmon and Tony Curtis in women's clothes as Jazz Age musicians on the run after inadvertently witnessing the St Valentine's Day Massacre. The resulting mayhem was a triumph, thanks to the sheer pace and outrageous logic of the film's comic invention, the delightful drag performances, the spectacle of Marilyn Monroe at her most sensually alluring and poignantly vulnerable, and an unforgettable last line. In a poll conducted by the American Film Institute in 2000, the film was voted best screen comedy of all time. Wilder's next film, *The Apartment* (1960) was a study of urban loneliness and corporate concupiscence that walked on a tightrope poised between comedy and tragedy, sustaining its balance through pitch-perfect performances from Lemmon, Shirley MacLaine and Fred MacMurray and the exquisite precision of its narrative structure and wide-screen composition. Trenchant but also tender, the film won Oscars for Wilder as producer, director and writer, and was to prove the highpoint of his career.

When reviewing *Kiss Me, Stupid* (1964), the critic of the London *Times*, John Russell Taylor began his column with the ringing declaration: 'In a world all too obsessively infected with the cult of ghastly good taste, thank heaven for Mr Billy Wilder.'[2] By contrast, an aghast American press thought that this time Wilder had finally gone too far. A bittersweet comedy that satirized attitudes to marriage, sex, success and celebrity in small-town America, *Kiss Me, Stupid* was widely attacked for its alleged lewdness and immorality. The film earned a 'Condemned' rating from the Catholic Legion of Decency and was a critical and commercial disaster from which Wilder's career never fully recovered. Even before this, influential critic Pauline Kael had queried his exalted reputation, attacking *One, Two, Three* (1961) for what she called his 'brazen contempt of people'.[3] In the classification of Hollywood directors in his book, *The American Cinema*, auteurist critic Andrew Sarris placed Wilder ignominiously in his 'Less Than Meets the Eye' category (alongside, it must be said, other great directors such as William Wyler, John Huston, Elia Kazan and David Lean) describing Wilder as 'too cynical even to believe his own cynicism'.[4] Most distressing of all for Wilder at this stage of his career was the failure of one of his most cherished projects, *The Private Life of Sherlock Holmes* (1970), which, at the insistence of United Artists, had its original running time of three hours cut by about a third, arguably the cinema's saddest act of artistic vandalism since the fate of Orson Welles's *The Magnificent Ambersons* (1942).

After the critical setbacks of the 1960s, Wilder's reputation gradually revived. In the film journal, *Cinema*, Robert Mundy offered a useful corrective to the 'bad taste cynic' characterization of Wilder's films, and suggested a more objective structural approach, which identified recurrent motifs such as Wilder's use of the dance and disguise for comic and character purposes.[5] Moved by *The Private Life of Sherlock Holmes* and *Avanti!* (1972), which he described as 'mellow masterpieces', Andrew Sarris revised his harsh evaluation of Wilder and confessed that he had 'grossly underrated' his films.[6] More recent criticism has tended to focus particularly on Wilder's vital contribution to film noir with movies such as *Double Indemnity* and *Sunset Boulevard*; on his skilful and individualistic mode of operation within the Hollywood studio system during its heyday; on how he worked with his writer collaborators; and on a reappraisal of the significance of his early film career in Berlin and Paris. A lavish book-length tribute from writer-director Cameron Crowe, *Conversations with Wilder* (1999) seemed designed to do for Wilder what François Truffaut's interview book had done for Alfred Hitchcock, but, unlike Hitchcock, Wilder, although characteristically waspish and witty in conversation, was not inclined to disclose his cinematic secrets to a young pretender. For him, film style was at its best when invisible and was a means to an end and not the end itself.

Wilder once said: 'I always think of my style as a curious cross between Lubitsch and von Stroheim.'[7] As well as drawing attention to the mixture of sophisticated comedy and macabre drama that was a hallmark of his work, the comment is a reminder of Wilder's European background and of its importance to an understanding of his films. Perhaps he can criticize American urban life and bourgeois values in such films as *The Apartment* and *Kiss Me, Stupid* because he and his co-writer I. A. L. Diamond were Europeans who could observe nuances of American behaviour with an outsider's perception and detachment, and who brought a different set of cultural assumptions to Hollywood stereotypes. American critics might have been appalled by Wilder's presentation of a sympathetic prostitute (Kim Novak) in *Kiss Me, Stupid* who seems more morally sensitive than anyone else in the film. However, for Wilder, the whore is not a sexual siren trying to subvert so-called respectable society but just another human being coping as best she can with life's adversities.

Of course, a number of Hollywood directors (Lang, Preminger, Sirk etc.) of Wilder's generation had European backgrounds not dissimilar to his, but in no other Hollywood director's work does Europe appear so often and so potently. Half of his Hollywood feature films are actually set in Europe. When not adapting European sources (e.g. *Love in the Afternoon, One, Two, Three*) or transposing European material into American settings (e.g. *Some like it Hot, Kiss Me Stupid, Buddy Buddy*), he often sets his films in an expressive European location, a landscape felt as a moral as well as a physical presence. Under Audrey Hepburn's loving guidance, for example, Humphrey Bogart's movement from America to Paris in *Sabrina* symbolizes nothing less than a spiritual liberation. The confrontation between American and European values is Wilder's most insistent preoccupation: indeed, his Big Theme. His fascination with Innocence and Experience derives particularly from that cultural contrast. His interest in America's international role in *A Foreign Affair* (1948) and *One, Two, Three* reflects his concern over America's coming to terms with her national and international identity, but implicitly it is also a self-interrogation of his own identity as a European American.

From the vantage point of an immigrant who has settled contentedly and successfully in the land of opportunity, Wilder presented his boldly ambivalent vision of America. His admiration for its pioneering past and its vigour and vivacity in films such as *The Spirit of St Louis* (1957) and *Some like it Hot* is set against his horror at urban alienation and rat-race materialism in films such as *Double Indemnity*, *The Apartment* and *The Fortune Cookie* (1966). In *The Emperor Waltz* (1948), *A Foreign Affair* and *One, Two, Three*, he explores the situation of the American abroad, where the hero either attempts to transform, exporting his own ambition and drive, or is himself transformed by Europe's differing tempo and morality. A sublime late film like *Avanti!* is particularly significant in this regard. In Ischia to reclaim his father's corpse, a brash conservative American executive (brilliantly played by Jack Lemmon) finds himself having to adjust to the island's leisurely charm and transcendent beauty. Ostensibly a light romantic comedy (albeit lasting nearly two-and-a half hours), *Avanti!* is an epic personal survey of America/Europe interaction in which both hero and director, in a moving personal pilgrimage, achieve an enriching reconciliation between their identities as Americans and Europeans. The film also hints at something that Wilder critics have only belatedly begun to perceive: that one of Hollywood's most coruscating cynics might also have been one of its subtlest romantics.

Biography

Born on 22 June 1906 of Jewish parents in Sucha, Austria (now a part of Poland), Wilder had begun work as a journalist in Berlin. His entry into the film world came through his involvement as writer in the 1929 film, *People on Sunday* (which also launched the film careers of directors Robert Siodmak, Edgar G. Ulmer and Fred Zinnemann). He wrote a number of screenplays for German films of the early sound era, and directed his first film, *Mauvaise Graine* in Paris in 1933 before leaving for America after Hitler came to power. After a long career in Hollywood, Wilder was to receive numerous awards in recognition of his achievements, including the Irving G. Thalberg Memorial Award from the Motion Picture Academy in Hollywood (1988) and Lifetime Achievement Awards from the Directors Guild of America (1985), the American Film Institute (1986) and the European Film Awards (1992). He died of pneumonia at his home in Beverly Hills, California on 27 March 2002.

Notes

1 Stevens Jr, G. *The Great Moviemakers of Hollywood's Golden Age*, New York: Alfred Knopf, 2006, p. 317.
2 Madsen, A. *Billy Wilder*, London: Secker & Warburg, 1968, p. 133.
3 Kael, P. *I Lost it at the Movies*, New York: Little, Brown & Co, 1968, p. 138.
4 Sarris, A. *The American Cinema: Directors and Directions 1929–1968*, New York: Dutton, 1968, p. 166.
5 Mundy, R. 'Wilder Reappraised', *Cinema*, October, 1969, pp. 14–19.
6 Sarris, A. 'Billy Wilder: Closet Romanticist', *Film Comment*, July–August, 1976, p. 7.
7 Higham, C. and Greenberg, J. *The Celluloid Muse: Hollywood Directors Speak*, London: Angus & Robertson, 1969, p. 247.

Filmography

Mauvaise Graine (France, 1933) also co-director and co-screenplay
The Major and the Minor (1942) also co-screenplay
Five Graves to Cairo (1943) also co-screenplay
Double Indemnity (1944) also co-screenplay
The Lost Weekend (1945) also co-screenplay
The Emperor Waltz (1948) also co-screenplay
A Foreign Affair (1948) also co-screenplay
Sunset Boulevard (1950) also co-screenplay
Ace in the Hole (1951) also producer and co-screenplay

Stalag 17 (1953) also producer and co-screenplay
Sabrina (1954) also producer and co-screenplay
The Seven Year Itch (1955) also co-producer and co-screenplay
The Spirit of St Louis (1957) also co-producer and co-screenplay
Love in the Afternoon (1957) also producer and co-screenplay
Witness for the Prosecution (1958) also co-screenplay
Some like it Hot (1959) also producer and co-screenplay
The Apartment (1960) also producer and co-screenplay
One, Two, Three (1961) also producer and co-screenplay
Irma la Douce (1963) also producer and co-screenplay
Kiss Me, Stupid (1964) also producer and co-screenplay
The Fortune Cookie (1966) also producer and co-screenplay
The Private Life of Sherlock Holmes (1970) also producer and co-screenplay
Avanti! (1972) also producer and co-screenplay
The Front Page (1974) also co-screenplay
Fedora (Germany/France, 1978) also producer and co-screenplay
Buddy Buddy (1981) also producer and co-screenplay

Further reading

Armstrong, R. *Billy Wilder: American Realist*. Jefferson, NC: McFarland & Co. 2000.
Chandler, C. *Nobody's Perfect: Billy Wilder, A Personal Biography*. New York: Simon & Shuster, 2002.
Crowe, C. *Conversations with Wilder*. New York: Alfred Knopf, 1999.
Farber, S. 'The Films of Billy Wilder.' *Film Comment* (Winter 1971–72): 8–22.
Germunden, G. *A Foreign Affair: Billy Wilder's American Films*. Oxford: Bergham Books, 2008.
McBride, J. and Wilmington, M. 'The Private Life of Billy Wilder.' *Film Quarterly* 23.4 (1979): 2–9.
Poague, L. *The Hollywood Professionals Volume 7: Wilder and McCarey*. London: Tantivy Press, 1988.
Seidman, S. *The Film Career of Billy Wilder*. Boston: G. K. Hall & Co, 1977.
Sikov, E. *Sunset Boulevard: The Life and Times of Billy Wilder*. New York: Hyperion, 1998.
Sinyard, N. and Turner, A. *Journey Down Sunset Boulevard: The Films of Billy Wilder*. Ryde: BCW Publishing, 1979.
Zolotov, M. *Billy Wilder in Hollywood*. New York: Limelight, 1977.

WILLIAM WYLER

By Sarah Kozloff

William Wyler, who by any measure should be counted as one of the most illustrious Hollywood directors, has been relatively ignored by film academics because he presents a conundrum for auteur theorists. He does not, like many directors, repeatedly circle around the same genres or the same thematic antinomies. His more than forty feature films range from Westerns, romantic comedies, period adaptations, to Biblical epics.

Similarly, although Wyler *does* have a characteristic style—marked by the use of the depths of the set, long takes with subtle camera movement, deep focus (he worked with famed cinematographer Gregg Toland seven times), "invisible" editing, emphasis on performance, and the evocative use of music—his mise-en-scène is not instantly recognizable. His style is restrained, rather than showy; perfectionist, rather than casual; an amalgam of studio gloss and realistic touches. His style often leads to quiet nuance.

Take for instance, a shot midway through *The Heiress*. Catherine Sloper (Olivia de Havilland) has matured since the fortune hunter Morris (Montgomery Clift) jilted her and her cruel father died. We now see a self-assured, reasonably contented woman, bidding farewell to some visitors as they settle in their carriage. As Catherine returns through the archway back towards her mansion, however, she pauses for a moment. Wyler frames the movement in depth in a long shot; he does *not* cut to a flashback of Morris kissing her in that very spot; he does not overlap an aural flashback of Morris promising to marry her; he doesn't even show us Catherine's face. He just captures her momentary pause in the shadow of the darker archway, while Aaron Copland's love theme repeats. Viewers feel as if we have independently read her mind and seen into her still-broken heart. The French critic André Bazin would claim that Wyler's style allows the viewer more freedom and gave his films more ambiguity. I believe that Wyler's guidance is just subtler.

Wyler fervently believed in the primacy of the script. Although he never gave himself credit for screenwriting, he collaborated extremely closely with each writer during a script's development; all of the screenplays went through numerous drafts. The last-hired screenwriter would often be present on the set, and during shooting Wyler and this screenwriter would rewrite the script every night. Numerous line changes in the "revised final" screenplays are written in Wyler's large flowing cursive. (Although raised speaking German and French, his English was flawless.)

Actually, Wyler approached every aspect of the filmmaking process with equal intensity. At the AFI Life Achievement Award ceremony in his honor, George Stevens Jr. spoke of Wyler's "infinite capacity for taking pains," and noted that he placed poem on pedestal, not the poet. Greer Garson similarly vouchsafed that Wyler "cared sincerely and sensitively about every moment on film."[1]

Such perfection is expensive, and Wyler became notorious for shooting multiple takes and going over budget. The veteran Warner Bros. producer Hal Wallis went through the roof, fuming in a memo:

> Possibly Wyler likes to see these big numbers on the slate, and maybe we could arrange to have them start with the number '6' on each take, then it wouldn't take him so long to get up to nine or ten.[2]

Once Wyler gained a certain amount of power in the industry, he almost never worked on a film unless he was committed to its political content and themes. He gravitated towards humanistic dramas dealing with social issues by Pulitzer Prize winning playwrights or classic or award-winning novelists. A cohesive thread runs through many of his disparate works: an interest in the ethical choices an individual makes in the face of his or her moment in history. In particular, Wyler was drawn towards material condemning social inequities and prejudice: his films treat anti-Semitism, economic class, greed, and homophobia. His later movies question bellicose masculinity and the legitimacy of violence.

William Wyler was born in 1902 in the city of Mulhouse, which is located in the border area between France and Germany called Alsace-Lorraine. When his mother's cousin, the generous Carl Laemmle, head of Universal Studios, came to visit in 1920, his mother asked Laemmle to take Wyler to the US. Wyler's directing career spans from 1925 to 1970. He worked on silent two reelers, as a contract director in the classic studio era, as his own producer, and as a hired hand.

In the first phase of his career, Wyler worked for Universal, learning his craft through directing numerous low budget Westerns, shorts and silent features, and then larger budget sound films. *Hell's Heroes*, an accomplished Western, and *Counsellor-at-Law*, an adaptation of a play about class snobbery and anti-Semitism, figure as his most famous works for Universal. In his second chapter, from 1935 to

1946—although during these years he was periodically loaned out to other studios and the U.S. military—Wyler worked primarily for Samuel Goldwyn, a willful independent producer, who sometimes changed Wyler's endings. Together, Wyler and Goldwyn would produce a string of films that have become synonymous with the classic polish of the studio years, including: *These Three, Dodsworth, Dead End, Wuthering Heights, The Westerner, The Little Foxes* and *The Best Years of Our Lives*. In the third part of his career during the late forties and fifties, while Wyler was deeply involved in trying to fight the blacklist, McCarthyism, and censorship, Paramount placed Wyler under contract to produce and direct five films: *The Heiress, Detective Story, Carrie, Roman Holiday*, and *The Desperate Hours*. Finally, from 1956 until he ended his career in 1970, Wyler worked for a variety of studios and roamed through various genres. *Friendly Persuasion*, a period film about Quakers, appeared through Allied Artists; *The Big Country*, a Western, was independently produced by Wyler and Gregory Peck and distributed through United Artists. Wyler then spent two years in Rome working on M-G-M's mammoth remake of *Ben Hur*. His next film, *The Children's Hour*, adapted Lillian Hellman's play about school teachers who are shunned because of a rumor they are lesbians. *Funny Girl*, his second to last film, and the first time he attempted a musical, was his only big-budget project in the sixties. *The Liberation of L. B. Jones*, his last film, is a searing indictment of corrupt policemen and lawyers and racial prejudice in the South.

Dead End (1937) demonstrates Wyler's reformist zeal. The film presents a long day on a block of the riverfront of NY, where a new luxury apartment building abuts a slum. We follow multiple characters and their interactions, and especially focus on the clashes between the inhabitants of the tenements and their new, well-off neighbors. What sets *Dead End* apart from other films about poverty is the texture created by throwaway dialogue and carefully staged bits of business. In an offhand early moment, a woman coos over a toddler in a pram ... so she can steal away his cracker for herself. The tenement slums are littered with garbage and infested with roaches; ragged children swim in the filthy water of the East River; women are forced to choose prostitution over starvation; trained professionals can't find work. The police are inattentive, self-absorbed, and heartless at best; at worst they are beating up workers out on a legal strike. Reform schools educate kids in advanced criminology and spread tuberculosis. As one of the characters (Joel McCrae) says about the young hoodlums: "Enemies of society, it says in the papers. Why not? What have they got to be so friendly about?"

The family is not a reliable haven: a drunken father beats his wife and children; a despairing mother (Marjorie Main) disowns her long lost son who has become a gangster, her total exhaustion and despair embodied by the breathy weakness of her voice and her glassy eyes: "Just stay away and leave us alone and die. But leave us alone." And yet the very harshness of her treatment betrays a depth of feeling; when her son is gunned down Mrs. Martin (Marjorie Main) screams her anguish into the night. Under Wyler's direction Baby Face Martin (Humphrey Bogart) is both a yellow dog and a lonely man for whom we can't help but feel some sympathy. Martin's passion turns to anguished disgust when he realizes that his former girlfriend Francie (Claire Trevor) has become a whore. "Why didn't you starve?" he accuses her. "Why didn't you?" she slings back, in a stinging condemnation of the sexual double standard.

The Best Years of Our Lives (1946), Wyler's most famous and most lauded film, winning seven Academy Awards including best director and best picture, also focuses on class and social inequities. It tells the story of three returning servicemen, one upper class, one middle, and one working-class, who face the traumas of re-adjusting after their war experiences. Al (Frederic March) has become an alcoholic; he is literally sickened by the hypocrisy of the bank he works for. Homer, who is physically injured (played by Harold Russell, a non-professional actor who lost his hands in the service), must cope with the stifling pity and close quarters of his middle-class milieu. Fred (Dana Andrews), who comes from a poor background, suffers from post-traumatic stress syndrome and can't find a decent job. Each shot, set, costume, line of dialogue, and musical theme works to create a portrait of America, sliding towards hyper-consumerism and the red scare immediately after World War II.

All three of *Best Year*'s servicemen are finally fully integrated into American society through love. Thirteen of Wyler's sound films give first billing to women actors and present stories primarily focalized through female characters. Bette Davis, who worked with Wyler on *Jezebel, The Letter*, and *The Little Foxes*, has stated that he was the best director she'd worked for in her career. M-G-M borrowed Wyler to make Greer Garson a star in *Mrs. Miniver*. Unlike Ford or Hawks, Wyler did not choose scripts about male camaraderie or the pleasures of an elite male group. Much more so than some directors who have been labeled "women's directors," Wyler's interest in and respect for his female characters animates his films.

Wyler presents a galaxy of fictional women who seem fully human. His ingénues, played by Bette Davis, Teresa Wright, Olivia de Havilland, Audrey Hepburn, Jean Simmons, or Barbra Streisand, have an odd habit of growing spines of steel. The marriages between mature adults in *Dodsworth*, *The Letter*, *Best Years*, *Friendly Persuasion*, and *The Desperate Hours* show marriage in a realistic light: sometimes stifling and best dissolved, often demonstrating the deep—but not trouble-free—connection of a lifetime together.

During World War II, Wyler was certainly no pacifist. His documentary, *The Memphis Belle*, still retains its power to put the viewer in the position of American pilots of a B-17 and makes one hunger to drop bombs on Germany or at least donate blood to the Red Cross. But his post-war films collectively demonstrate an interest in redefining true masculinity away from violence, in showing the strength it takes to be a man of reason when all around you are bellicose. Gary Cooper in *Friendly Persuasion*, Frederic March in *The Desperate Hours*, Gregory Peck in *The Big Country*, and even Charlton Heston in *Ben Hur* demonstrate strength by refraining from killing and revenge. From the opposite angle, Kirk Douglas in *Detective Story* comes to grief because he cannot temper his rage and violence.

Personally, Wyler was known for his warmth and impish humor and he had a wry wit. Billy Wilder recounts, "So sometimes, you know, when I started directing and people don't quite listened [to the difference in the names] 'Wyler' or 'Wilder,' much to my delight they confused the two of us, and he would put the arm around me and say, 'Come on now – Monet, Manet, who cares?'"[3] However, unlike his friend Billy Wilder, while Wyler's films could be light-hearted, they were never cynical or sarcastic. In general, Wyler's comedies are not as memorable as his dramas. Writing about *Roman Holiday* and its bittersweet romanticism, Stanley Kauffmann notes: "To glow with this film, to chuckle with it, to cry—as I certainly do every time I see the last scene—is to enjoy a special triumph. We have slipped one over on modernity."[4]

Wyler was always trying "to slip one over on modernity." Rather than being ironic or full of in-jokes, his films are humanistic and morally serious. His masterpieces present quietly devastating portraits of social ills and people under pressure. They enlarge viewers' hearts.

Biography

William Wyler was born in Mulhouse, then part of Germany in 1902, the son of a successful small business owner and his educated German-Jewish wife. He immigrated to the US in 1920, and began working for Universal in New York. Moving to Hollywood, he worked various odd jobs on the set before being given a chance to direct in 1925. His first marriage to the actress Margaret Sullavan quickly dissolved, but his second marriage to Margaret Tallichet lasted the rest of his life. He died in 1981, survived by five children.

Notes

1 *American Film Institute Presents a Salute to William Wyler* (Broadcast in 1976). Copy available at the Paley Center for Media, NYC.
2 Quoted in *Inside Warner Bros.* ed. Rudy Behlmer, New York: Simon and Schuster, 1985: 42–43.
3 Quoted in Aviva Slesin, director. *Directed by William Wyler.* Tatge Productions, 1986. New York: Kino Video, 2002.
4 Stanley Kauffmann, "Take Two: *Roman Holiday,"American Film*, 3:6 (April 1978): 79.

Filmography

Lazy Lightning (1926)
The Stolen Ranch (1926)
Blazing Days (1927)
Shooting Straight (1927)
The Border Cavalier (1927)
Desert Dust (1927)
Thunder Riders (1928)
Anybody Here Seen Kelly? (1928)
The Shakedown (1929)
The Love Trap (1929)
Hell's Heroes (1930)
The Storm (1930)
A House Divided (1931)
Tom Brown of Culver (1932)
Her First Mate (1933)
Counsellor-at-Law (1933)
The Good Fairy (1935)
The Gay Deception (1935)
These Three (1936)
Dodsworth (1936)
Dead End (1937)
Jezebel (1938)
Wuthering Heights (1939)
The Westerner (1940)

The Letter (1940)
The Little Foxes (1941)
Mrs. Miniver (1942)
The Memphis Belle (1944)
The Best Years of Our Lives (1946)
The Heiress (1949)
Detective Story (1951)
Carrie (1952)
Roman Holiday (1953)
The Desperate Hours (1955)
Friendly Persuasion (1956)
The Big Country (1958)
Ben Hur (1959)
The Children's Hour (1961)
The Collector (1965)
How to Steal a Million (1966)
Funny Girl (1968)
The Liberation of L. B. Jones (1970)

Further reading

Herman, Jan. *A Talent For Trouble: The Life Of Hollywood's Most Acclaimed Director, William Wyler*. New York: Da Capo Press, 1995.

Kozloff, Sarah. *BFI Classics The Best Years Of Our Lives*. New York: Palgrave Macmillan, 2011.

Kozloff, Sarah. "Wyler's Wars," *Film History: An International Journal* 20:4 (2008): 456–73.

Miller, Gabriel. *William Wyler: The Life And Films Of Hollywood's Most Celebrated Director*. Lexington: University Press of Kentucky, 2013.

NEW HOLLYWOOD

ROBERT ALTMAN

By Marc O'Day

> I've always said that making a film is like making a sand castle at the beach. You invite your friends and get them down there and you say – you build this beautiful structure, several of you, and then you sit down and watch the tide come in, and the ocean just takes it away. And that sandcastle remains in your mind.
>
> (Robert Altman accepting his Oscar for Lifetime Achievement, March 2006)[1]

Altman often compared his films to sandcastles, making a film to playing on the beach. In another version of this anecdote, he adds: 'But that, for me, is the real joy of it all, that it's just fun, and nothing else.'[2] He viewed filmmaking as an exploratory collaborative effort, always in the here and now, an end in itself. On set he treated the screenplay as only a starting point, he liked his actors and creative personnel to surprise him, to go with the flow and create an event – the film – which would be unique in conveying the fleeting nature of life as we experience it. 'Good disintegration', he once remarked as his actors strayed further and further away from the script.[3] And, reflecting on his role as director, he tosses auteur theory into the ether: 'The author that I'm looking for is the event itself.'[4] The better the (working?) party on set, the more we can make it really real, I'm just the facilitator, he seems to be saying.

If all this sounds casual, throwaway or just plain puzzling, well, it is. But it *was* Altman's way of seeing and doing his work and we don't need to be (too) taken in by it. Robert Altman was a restless and energetic man *driven* to make films, a cinematic iconoclast, an adventurer and a gambler (literally: he loved gambling and it's the subject of one of his most passionate films, *California Split*). He was arguably the most important independent film director to come out of America in the last fifty years, a resilient survivor who had an ongoing love-hate relationship with Hollywood, a wheeler-dealer with a gift for financing project after project and a leader wedded to control who resented interference from anyone who he saw as trying to constrain his creative work. Above all he was a modernist auteur with a vision which, in the late 1960s and 1970s especially, saw him in the forefront of the New Hollywood, alongside such contemporaries as Arthur Penn, Stanley Kubrick, Francis Ford Coppola and Martin Scorsese. These figures thrived in a period when the traditional studio system was fragmenting and television was still the *new* popular entertainment. They drew at least as much of their aesthetic and ideological sustenance from European Art cinema as they did from classical Hollywood.[5]

The term 'Altmanesque' today denotes the provisional and open-ended flavour of the multi-protagonist films for which Altman is renowned, with their emphasis on rich visual tapestries, the often dark nuances and mysteries of human behaviour, on accident, coincidence, chance and luck (or the lack of it) and on the radical relegation into the background of traditional storytelling and plotting in favour of numerous interrelating vignettes, which often seem to remain fragmented or incomplete. These elements are evident in films such as Altman's breakthrough anti-war satire *M*A*S*H*, which captured the zeitgeist of late sixties countercultural anti-Establishment and anti-Vietnam sentiment; the menacing country-and-western epic *Nashville*; the hugely ambitious comedy drama *A Wedding*, which features no fewer than forty-eight 'characters'; the diffuse, rambling, and querulous LA-based *Short Cuts*; the entrancing and at times sublime ballet film *The Company*; and his last film, about the death of a radio show, the gentle *A Prairie Home Companion*. Equally important to his current reputation as an 'Indie' pioneer are his quirky genre-revisionist films such as the Western *McCabe & Mrs Miller*, his neo-noir remake of *The Long Goodbye*; the crime spree drama *Thieves Like Us* (also a remake, of Nicholas Ray's *They Live By Night*); the weird, gothic psychodramas *That Cold Day in the Park*, *Images* and *3 Women*, which together make up what we can call the loosely-linked 5 Women Trilogy; and his English country house murder mystery parody, *Gosford Park*.

Altman knew genres and formulas inside out, having learned his filmmaking the hard way. He had been in the business for over twenty years before *M*A*S*H*'s runaway success in 1970, by which time he was in his mid forties: first as a novice screenwriter, then as an industrial filmmaker for the Calvin Company (with subjects ranging from how to play sports to war veteran celebrations), and subsequently as a director and writer for popular television series, doing dramas, mysteries, Westerns, crime shows, war adventures and comedies for the American TV networks. Notably he contributed to *Alfred Hitchcock*

Presents, Whirlybirds ('a Western with helicopters'[6]), *Maverick*, the much celebrated *Bonanza, Bus Stop* (loosely based on the 1956 Marilyn Monroe film) and *Combat!*. It looked as if the move into Hollywood features that he craved was not going to happen until *M*A*S*H*, his sixth film, which had been passed on by a number of higher profile directors, serendipitously launched him as a name in the industry. While his 1970s pictures mostly didn't make much profit and their critical reception was often mixed, a small group of devoted aficionados repeatedly endorsed his work and he gradually built a reputation as an idiosyncratic maverick with an offbeat style and a disturbing vision of contemporary American society. The live action musical comic strip adaptation *Popeye*, however, made for Paramount and Walt Disney on his biggest ever budget (somewhere between $20 and $30 million) unjustly sank him with the studios, even though it did well at the box office. Thereafter he spent the 1980s making small theatrical adaptations – some of which, such as the searing woman-centred melodrama *Come Back to the Five and Dime, Jimmy Dean, Jimmy Dean*, still showed him in remarkable form – and television miniseries, including the excellent political 'mockumentary' *Tanner '88*, as well as branching out into theatre and opera. In the early 1990s, the Hollywood satire *The Player* (its protagonist, Griffin Miller [Tim Robbins] is one of the blockbuster-obsessed studio executives Altman detested) saw his return to feature film success. From then until the end of his career Altman was the grand old man of American independent cinema.

Nashville, possibly his masterpiece, is a prime example of the Altman multi-protagonist film. A self-consciously State of the Nation American epic – the Stars and Stripes flag fills the screen more than once during its closing sequence – it's a country and Western musical film (often a kind of concert film) encased in a political paranoia film. It intercuts scenes and performances in the fractured lives of Nashville's music community – old trooper Haven Hamilton (Henry Gibson), vulnerable Barbara Jean (modelled on the real-life Loretta Lynn, Ronee Blakley), the black in town Tommy Brown (Timothy Brown), the cold Connie White (Karen Black), the argumentative trio Bill, Tom and Mary (Allan Nicholls, Keith Carradine and Cristina Raines) and Nashville wannabes Sueleen Gay (Gwen Welles) and Albuquerque (Barbara Harris), among others, fictional and real – against the back-cloth of Replacement Party Presidential candidate Hal Philip Walker's political campaign, orchestrated by the malign smoothie John Triplette (Altman stalwart Michael Murphy), to reach the White House. The film does feature an outsider, the British BBC interviewer Opal (Geraldine Chaplin), who seems at the outset as though she may be able to help the spectator gain insight into the community and its operation. Yet she is quickly swallowed up in this shallow if compelling world, fawning over the actor Elliott Gould (featured in *M*A*S*H*, *The Long Goodbye* and *California Split*, here playing himself), sleeping with the cad Tom Frank and recording surreal meanderings as she wanders alone through a gigantic car tip.

Nashville grew out of field research by screenwriter Joan Tewkesbury – Altman himself knew nothing about the music until he came to make the film – and at one level is an almost verité exploration of the Nashville entertainment world.[7] The actors wrote and performed their own songs, much to the hostility of the 'real' Nashville music community and (ironically?) Carradine won a Best Song Oscar for his composition 'I'm Easy'. The songs are also important to the film's unfolding action, much as they would be in a traditional integrated musical, highlighting emotions and counterpointing gender and ethnic issues.[8] The political dimension, however, was Altman's idea, as was the assassination of Barbara Jean by mother-fixated Kenny Fraiser (David Hayward) at the closing party rally, an event that he stumbled upon to somehow bring the narrative to a (temporary) close. In fact the structuring device of the campaign is vital to both the film's form and ideology. The party van circulates throughout, with Walker's amplified voice delivering vague populist messages that are at once vacuous and threatening; this is a world that evokes Big Brother and *1984*. Entertainment and politics are both to be distrusted, accidents, violence and even death itself are just a moment away; the fantastically mounted freeway pile up near the film's opening, which echoes Godard's *Weekend*, was apparently experienced by Tewkesbury herself during her trip. Barbara Jean – exploited, distracted, and almost Ophelia-like in her funereal white dress – is the sacrificial victim for the carnival rites of Nashville and by extension, contemporary American culture as a whole. The film's bleakness and pessimism – ideologically it isn't perhaps one of Altman's most 'open' films – place it securely within a cycle of 1970s films reflecting disillusion with both American consumer and media culture and the political process itself in the wake of Vietnam and the Watergate scandal.[9]

Setting Altman's multi-protagonist films in a context that encompasses *Grand Hotel*, Renoir, Hawks and disaster films, Maria Del Mar Aczona succinctly outlines the techniques that Altman and his crew deploy, in *Nashville* and elsewhere, to construct his unusual and disorientating film worlds.[10] These include, of course, the large casts and characters who we sometimes struggle to recognise, let alone identify with; intercutting of many locations, scenes and sequences (often in uncertain time schemes), which are themselves frequently interrupted by set pieces such as the songs in *Nashville*; widescreen (often Panavision) combined with use of a telephoto lens, enabling densely populated and crowded frames where foreground and background are on almost the same plane; and an equally crowded soundtrack, including overlapping dialogue, complex sound effects, sound bridges and an imaginative use of music. The combined effect of these techniques is to create a densely textured and ambiguous world where it often feels as if too much is going on and where we as spectators must work to decide what is central and what is peripheral in visual, sonic and narrative terms. In short, we must struggle to make sense of what it's all 'about'. And what it's about, of course, can change over time and with repeated viewings, as David Thomson suggests: 'Altman is [...] a man whose films alter or shift at different viewings like shot silk.'[11] Altman himself seems to have revelled in placing us in ambiguous viewing positions. He spoke in 1971 of enjoying taking the narrative and story out of his films: 'The audience will sit and see the film and understand the movie's intention without being able to articulate it.'[12] Later, in the 2000s, David Thompson notes that 'Altman has often said that the greatest films are the ones you leave not being able to explain but knowing that you have experienced something very special.'[13] We can't be sure that he was alluding to his own work but it seems highly likely and it's certainly the case that a number of his films work on us in exactly this way.

Altman never ran out of energy as he went on exploring what he called, relating Raymond Carver's stories (the basis of *Short Cuts*) to his own films, the 'idiosyncrasies of human behaviour [...] that exist amid the randomness of life's experiences', right up to the end of his life. He saw Carver's work as 'one story [and] the mosaic of [...] *Short Cuts* [is] one look. But the film could go on forever, because it's like life.'[14] Working in a period of increasing social and cultural fragmentation, paradoxically in a shrinking global environment overseen by multinational conglomerates (including the entertainment industry), his vision perhaps reflects the alienation and disempowerment of many people in American consumer society. But he himself just carried on doing his thing. As his contemporary and fellow traveller Martin Scorsese summed up: 'He made independent pictures in Hollywood, with Hollywood money, ultimately. And he had an individual point of view and a personal statement with every picture. Every one. [...] He's an inspiration. I don't think there's any career like that in the history of Hollywood.'[15]

Biography

Altman was born in Kansas City, Missouri, in 1925. Educated at Catholic schools and at Wentworth Military Academy, Lexington, he flew bombers for the United States Army Air Force during the Second World War. Joan Tewkesbury said of Altman's filmmaking that 'he was insightful enough to get exactly what he needed. I think that came from his days of flying airplanes in the war. He knew what to target. He knew how to get along in situations where he had to survive.' After the war, his education was in the School of Life and Film. As Mitchell Zuckoff writes: 'the entire process of filmmaking *was* his adult life, a stage for his passions, his rages, his triumphs, his humor, his visions, his failures, his gifts.'[16] He died in 2006, aged 81, in Los Angeles, California. His wife Kathryn recalls how after his death her daughter Konni repeated 'Bob's favourite exit line: "See you in the next reel."'[17]

Notes

1 Mitchell Zuckoff, *Robert Altman: The Oral Biography*, New York, Alfred A. Knopf, 2009, p. 500.
2 David Thompson (ed.), *Altman on Altman*, London, Faber and Faber, 2006, p. xviii.
3 Ibid., p. xv.
4 Zuckoff, op. cit., p. 503.
5 On these directors and their milieu, see Robert Kolker, *A Cinema of Loneliness*, 4th edn, Oxford, Oxford University Press, 2011 (first pub. 1980).
6 Thompson, op. cit., p. 262.
7 For an entertaining journalistic account of the film's production, see Jan Stuart, *The Nashville Chronicles: The Making of Robert Altman's Masterpiece*, New York, Simon & Schuster, 2000.
8 See Richard Ness, '"Doing Some Replacin'": Gender, Genre and the Subversion of Dominant Ideology in the Music Scores', in Rick Armstrong (ed.), *Robert Altman: Critical Essays*, Jefferson, North Carolina and London, McFarland & Company, 2011, pp. 46–50.
9 Excellent studies that explore 1970s Hollywood in context are Robin Wood, *Hollywood from Vietnam to Reagan and Beyond*, rev. and expanded edn., New York, Columbia University Press, 2003 and Michael Ryan and Douglas Kellner, *Camera Politica: The Politics and Ideology of Contemporary American Film*, Bloomington and Indianapolis, Indiana University Press, 1990.
10 Maria Del Mar Azcona, 'A Cinema of Plenty: Robert Altman and the Multi-Protagonist Film', in in Armstrong, op. cit., pp. 139–55.
11 David Thomson, *The New Biographical Dictionary of Film*, London, Little, Brown, 2002.

12 Aljean Harmetz, 'The 15th Man Who Was Asked to Direct M*A*S*H (and Did) Makes a Peculiar Western,' in David Sterrit (ed.), *Robert Altman, Interviews*, Jackson, University Press of Mississsippi, 2000, p. 8.

13 Thompson, op. cit., p. xx.

14 The quotations on Carver and Altman are from Raymond Carver, *Short Cuts*, New York, Vintage Books, 1993, p. 7.

15 Zuckoff, op. cit, pp. 506–7.

16 Ibid., pp. 285, xii, 505.

17 Thompson, op. cit., pp. 219–75; Zuckoff, Ibid., p. 527.

Filmography

The Delinquents (1957) also producer and screenwriter

The James Dean Story (1957) co-director and producer

Nightmare in Chicago (1964) also producer

Countdown (1968)

That Cold Day in the Park (1969)

*M*A*S*H* (1970)

Brewster McCloud (1970)

McCabe & Mrs Miller (1971) also co-screenwriter

Images (1972) (screenwriter)

The Long Goodbye (1973)

Thieves Like Us (1974) also co-screenwriter

California Split (1974) also producer

Nashville (1975) also producer

Buffalo Bill and the Indians, or Sitting Bull's History Lesson (1976) also producer and co-screenwriter

3 Women (1977) also producer and screenwriter

A Wedding (1978) also producer and co-screenwriter

Quintet (1979) also producer and co-screenwriter

A Perfect Couple (1979) also producer and co-screenwriter

HealtH (1980) also producer and co-screenwriter

Popeye (1980)

Come Back to the Five and Dime, Jimmy Dean, Jimmy Dean (1982)

Streamers (1983) also producer

Secret Honor (1984) also producer

O.C. and Stiggs (1984) also co-producer

Fool for Love (1985)

Beyond Therapy (1987) also co-screenwriter

Aria (1987) director and screenwriter of 'Les Boreades' segment

Vincent and Theo (1990)

The Player (1992)

Short Cuts (1993) also co-screenwriter

Prêt-à-Porter (aka *Ready to Wear*) (1994) also producer and co-screenwriter
Kansas City (1996) also producer and co-screenwriter
The Gingerbread Man (1998)
Cookie's Fortune (1999) also producer
Dr. T and the Women (2000)
Gosford Park (2001) also producer
The Company (2003) also producer
A Prairie Home Companion (2006) also producer

Further reading

Kagan, Norman. *American Skeptic: Robert Altman's Genre-Commentary Films*. Ann Arbor, MI: Pierian Press, 1982.
Karp, Alan. *The Films of Robert Altman*. Metuchen, NJ: Scarecrow, 1981.
Kass, Judith M. *Robert Altman: American Innovator*. New York: Popular Library, 1978.
Keyssar, Helen. *Robert Altman's America*. New York and Oxford: Oxford University Press, 1991.
McGilligan, Patrick. *Robert Altman: Jumping Off the Cliff*. New York: St. Martin's Press, 1989.
O'Brien, Daniel. *Robert Altman: Hollywood Survivor*. London: B. T. Batsford, 1995.
Plecki, Gerard. *Robert Altman*. Boston: Twayne Publishers, 1985.
Self, Robert T. *Robert Altman's Subliminal Reality*. Minneapolis: University of Minnesota Press, 2002.
—. *Robert Altman's McCabe & Mrs Miller: Reframing the American West*. Lawrence: University Press of Kansas, 2007.

JOHN CASSAVETES

By Marc O'Day

> Cassavetes' people must make, or fail to make, peace with each other. There is no "larger story." There are only common people facing each other in rooms as common as any. [...] Two people, able or unable to look into each other's eyes – that was his ultimate test for all codes, manners, morals, politics, psychologies, and beliefs. To give that test its due, he reshaped the vocabulary of film.[1]

If the true criterion of auteur film theory is authentic personal expression – salient vision, style and themes – then John Cassavetes is the litmus test. Cassavetes was the great pioneer of United States Independent cinema: his work was his life and his life was (in) his work. His films are seminal actor cinema as auteur cinema, akin to theatre, dance, jazz and performance art: an actor by trade himself, he made actor-centred naturalist movies in which 'small emotions' and the looks between ordinary, everyday people formed the basis of colossal (giant, great) – even epic – conflictual dramas.[2] Today Cassavetes still stands as an emblem of the artist as independent creator and entrepreneur: like a playwright with his own troupe, he financed, wrote, directed and sometimes appeared in his films, which were often truly 'home movies' featuring family and friends and shot on location in the places where his family and relations lived. Nevertheless, he also exemplifies the artist as collaborator: loneliness is the killer in his universe, he saw self as always related to other, identity itself as dramatic and relational and he worked relentlessly on his sets to create spontaneous and fluid interactions between his actors, such that no one knew what would happen next. In the process of making each film real life person would become actor would become character would become 'person' on film – life transformed into art and back again, to the extent that in interviews he would interchangeably use his actors' and characters' names – as though they were the same person – a real life human entity that elided the boundaries between fact and fiction. At the centre of his achievement, also, was his lifelong partnership with the actress Gena Rowlands, his wife, his muse, the star of many of his best films and one of the greatest non-Hollywood American film stars.[3]

Cassavetes grew up the son of a self-made Greek immigrant; the family moved frequently and oscillated between poverty and wealth. He would celebrate the scenes of his New York childhood in the lyrical location shots of *Gloria* (contemporary with and comparable to Woody Allen's *Manhattan*). His favourite director was the paean of domestic comedy Frank Capra and his favourite film star was James Cagney, with whom he identified for his shortness and pugnacious character. Not wanting to follow his father into business, he trained under Charles Jehlinger at the American Academy of Dramatic Arts, well known as the alternative to the Method acting that was dominant in the States at the time (ironically Cassavetes would be viewed as a Method actor in some of his early roles). He acted in stock theatre and television during the 1950s, learning about popular genres and formulaic production by appearing in TV soaps, comedies, melodramas and tragedies. He also began to land big screen roles, in films such as *The Night Holds Terror* (1955), *Crime in the Streets* (1956) and *Edge of the City* (1957). His nervy, macho performance as army deserter Axel North in the latter inspired typically mixed feelings in the young Michael Ventura, who would later become his friend and make the documentary *I'm Almost Not Crazy* about him: '[he was] edgy, contradictory, tense with violence and a desperate grace. You wanted to like him, but there was something about him that you didn't trust. You wanted to dislike him, but there was something about him which you couldn't help liking.'[4] Such ambivalence towards Cassavetes the actor would also be felt towards Cassavetes the man by those who knew him and worked with him throughout his life. Ray Carney, for instance, his greatest critical supporter and another friend, notes in the introduction to *Cassavetes on Cassavetes* that 'he could be stunningly generous and thoughtful; but he could also be exasperating, foolish, willful and manipulative.'[5]

Cassavetes often said that 'I really am more an actor than a director',[6] so perhaps it's not surprising that the origin of his first film *Shadows* lay in a theatre workshop improvisation. Featuring scenes from the bohemian lives of three young New Yorkers, its documentary and verité feel allied it to the French New Wave, and especially Godard's *A Bout de Souffle* (1960) and offered an alternative take on the youth-as-social-problem cycle in vogue at the time. Now seen as the single most influential film in launching the American underground and indie scene, its eventual release in America (by British Lion) facilitated Cassavetes' first foray into Hollywood, with the musical drama *Too Late Blues* and the social issue picture *A Child is Waiting* (starring Burt Lancaster and Judy Garland, in one of her final roles), from which he was fired after fighting with producer Stanley Kramer over the film's final cut. It would end his Hollywood career for seventeen years; but it launched him once and for all as a committed independent filmmaker. From the late 1960s to the mid 1980s – and arguably peaking in the mid 1970s – he went on a run of seven extraordinary films, all but two of which starred Gena Rowlands. *Faces* is a nightmare vision of middle-class marital breakdown, with Rowlands as the most sympathetic character, the prostitute Jeannie Rapp. At one point the screenplay was titled *The Dinosaurs*, fitting for a film in which people often behave like hysterical animals caught up in a sex war they barely understand and which calls to mind the argument of Thorstein Veblen's *Theory of the Leisure Class*: that underlying a materially affluent society lies a barely concealed primitive barbarism. The follow-up *Husbands* was, if it were possible, even bleaker, a homosocial drama in which three married men – played by Cassavetes stalwarts Ben Gazzara and Peter Falk and Cassavetes himself – go on a prolonged alcoholic bender in London and New York. (Michael Ventura notes how much of Cassavetes' oeuvre is suffused with alcohol and drunken people.[7])

Thereafter only *The Killing of a Chinese Bookie*, a tour de force mixing existentialism, film noir and the gangster film, with Gazzara as a put-upon stripclub owner driven to murder through a debt to the Mob, would not star Rowlands. She appears with long-time associate and friend Seymour Cassel in the marvellously eccentric screwball comedy *Minnie and Moskowitz*; with Falk in another harrowing marital breakdown drama *A Woman Under the Influence*; with Gazzara and Cassavetes in the backstage/onstage metafictional *Opening Night* (the film in which it is most tempting to try to 'read off' the real-life Cassavetes-Rowlands relationship, and one which frighteningly veers off into possession horror territory); the studio-financed chase film *Gloria*, which Cassavetes wrote for Rowlands as a vehicle for her to act with a child, the hilariously macho Latino boy Phil (John Adames), whom she has to protect from the Mob after they have murdered his family; and the valedictory *Love Streams*, a final mid-life crisis drama in which she stars as the emotionally effusive Sarah Lawson, with Cassavetes as her emotionally stifled writer brother Robert Harmon. This is indeed an epic film (at 141 minutes), with shades of Dostoevsky, Eugene O'Neill and Tennessee Williams, and also of fantasy, farce and surrealism, too, which Tom Charity memorably describes as: 'a beautiful, obstreperous, funny, crackpot, bewildering, bleak and unutterably moving film.'[8]

A Woman Under the Influence was written by Cassavetes specifically for Gena Rowlands as a star performance vehicle; she was nominated for the best actress Academy Award for her role as the generous yet unstable Italian immigrant housewife and mother Mabel Longhetti, playing opposite Falk as her construction worker husband Nick. It was originally intended to be a play but when she saw how gruelling the part was Rowlands said she would not be physically capable of playing it repeatedly. The filmmaking process and the film itself are exemplary Cassavetes. On set the director pursued his habitual strategies for drawing out the small emotions and nuances from his actors: dictating the script to his assistant as the production developed, with the actors delivering the lines he created but in general without direction as to their characters' emotions and behaviour; shooting the script in chronological order to give the actors maximum opportunity to inhabit their characters as people; playing out the parts himself in rehearsals (see, for instance, the pictures in Carney's *The Films of John Cassavetes*, in which Cassavetes looks almost demonically possessed in his intensity);[9] frequently taking over the camera himself; and not always letting the actors know whether the camera was rolling or not. He pushed his actors to the limit and at one point, during the climactic scene where Mabel defends herself against Nick and his equally hostile mother-in-law (played by Cassavetes' own real-life mother Katherine) by outlining the five points that make their relationship worthwhile as he is about to get her committed to a mental hospital, Cassavetes' interruption of his wife in full flow led to a huge showdown between them.[10] All the elements of Cassavetes' style are present to enhance the film's performance dimension: mobile camerawork following the actors; close ups; frequent long takes and long scenes or sequences; group scenes interspersed with two handers; ordinary speech punctuated with silences, as well as non-verbal and gestural eccentricities. It is supremely naturalistic and at the same time it is really expressionistic; indeed, the *Cahiers du Cinema* writers Sylvie Pierre and Jean Narboni (actually reviewing *Husbands*) adroitly characterised Cassavetes' style as 'natural expressionism'. Representationally, thematically and ideologically, the film also inhabits Cassavetes' primary domain: the difficulty people – usually heterosexual partners – have in knowing, trusting, relating to or loving one another. And, as is so often the case in Cassavetes' work, it is the man who is the narrow-minded oppressor and who runs away from commitment or emotional truth, while the woman is open, adventurous – and persecuted.

Cassavetes' influence has been huge. At a structural level, he paved the way for independent filmmaking as a cottage industry, at its most pure still – at least in terms of the actual filmmaking process – undertaken outside Hollywood commerce and business (although increasingly this is no longer the case; capitalism always seems to manage to co-opt the forces and energies which oppose it). At a formal level, he was not only one of the pioneers of any so-called independent film aesthetic but also profoundly affected the look and feel of subsequent popular film and television drama: for instance, as Michael Ventura argues, the work of Stanley Kubrick, Martin Scorsese, Robert Altman, Woody Allen and even Steven Spielberg would not have been what it was without his prior example; and the look and feel of contemporary quality popular television series such as *Lost* owe much to his mobile and fluid camerawork.[11] At a philosophical level, the example of Cassavetes poses some of the 'deep' questions about the relationship between art (here, cinema) and life. Cassavetes wasn't being jokey or evasive when he said: 'My life? It's not very exciting. The excitement is in the work. I live through my films.

They are my life.'[12] As Carney explains, Cassavetes means first and foremost the activity of making the films, with his family and friends, as an exploratory and sometimes liberatory collaborative experience.[13] This was what gave him the greatest satisfaction and where the life-art boundary was at its most enigmatic – and perhaps even sometimes mysteriously dissolved. The films themselves were, for Cassavetes, merely the traces or residues of that primary activity. And – immensely arrogant as it may seem – as a result of this view, Cassavetes seems not to have been that interested in the audience for his work. Certainly the last thing he was concerned with was entertainment – yet he managed to produce some of the most searing and aesthetically fresh dramas in world cinema. If, representationally and ideologically, the restless, conflictual energy of heterosexual relationships is his core theme – even where peace is made, it is only ever going to be a temporary truce – it is nevertheless the messiness, open-endedness and unfinished-ness of the films that makes them so instructive – still intriguing and absorbing – and like life itself.

Biography

Cassavetes was born in New York in 1929. While his cult reputation derives from his position as the Father of American Independent Cinema, his relationship with Hollywood was nevertheless ongoing and vital. The money he poured into his 'home movies' often came from his acting in Hollywood; four of his twelve completed films were made for the studios – and each bears at least some of the hallmarks of his vision and style (especially *Gloria*); and his work did not go unnoticed by the Hollywood cognoscenti: he was nominated for Academy Awards in no fewer than three separate categories – for best supporting actor (*The Dirty Dozen*), screenplay (*Faces*) and director (*A Woman Under the Influence*). His relationship with Hollywood *was* certainly adversarial but it also supported his independent artistic practice *and* helped to shape his filmic philosophy. He died young, aged 59, of cirrhosis of the liver, in 1989.

Notes

1 Michael Ventura, *Cassavetes Directs: John Cassavetes and the Making of Love Streams*, Harpenden, Kamera Books, 2007, pp. 9–10.
2 Cited in Tom Charity, *John Cassavetes: Lifeworks*, London, Omnibus Press, 2001, p. 103.
3 Writing of the Cassavetes troupe, David Thomson suggests that 'Gena Rowlands was not just the greatest talent in the group, but the one that

might have gone other ways.' *The New Biographical Dictionary of Film*, London, Little Brown, p. 762.

4 Ventura, op. cit., p. 18. In the 1980s, Ventura feels similarly ambivalent towards the look in Cassavetes' eyes, pp. 24–25.

5 Ray Carney (ed.), *Cassavetes on Cassavetes*, London, Faber and Faber, 2001, p. xv.

6 Ibid., p. 335.

7 Ventura, op. cit., p. 81.

8 Charity, op. cit., p. 184.

9 Ray Carney, *The Films of John Cassavetes: Pragmatism, Modernism and the Movies*, Cambridge, Cambridge University Press, 1994, pp. 178–79.

10 Charity, op. cit. p. 128.

11 Ventura, op. cit., pp. 11–12.

12 Charity, op. cit., p. x.

13 Carney, op. cit., pp. 273, 276.

Filmography

The following lists Cassavetes' films as director. For his numerous acting credits, see, for instance, Appendix III of Charity's *Lifeworks*.

Shadows (1959) also screenwriter, cameo
Too Late Blues (1962) also co-screenwriter
A Child is Waiting (1963)
Faces (1968) also screenwriter
Husbands (1970) also screenwriter, actor
Minnie and Moskowitz (1971) also screenwriter, actor
A Woman Under the Influence (1974)
The Killing of a Chinese Bookie (1976) also screenwriter
Opening Night (1978) also screenwriter, actor
Gloria (1980) also screenwriter
Love Streams (1984) also co-screenwriter, actor
Big Trouble (1986)

Further reading

Carney, Ray. *American Dreaming: The Films of John Cassavetes and the American Experience*. Berkeley and Los Angeles: University of California Press, 1985.

Fine, Marshall. *Accidental Genius: How John Cassavetes Invented the American Independent Film*. New York: Hyperion, 2005.

Kouvaros, George. *Where Does It Happen?: John Cassavetes and Cinema at the Breaking Point*. Minneapolis and London: University of Minnesota Press, 2004.

ROGER CORMAN

By Jan Johnson-Smith

Writing in the 1980s, critic Tony Rayns characterised filmmaker Roger Corman thus: 'The contradictions are manifold, and unique in Hollywood ... Perhaps they should not be surprising from a man who seemed unable to reconcile his taste for "exploitation values" with his fundamental seriousness of purpose.'[1] The inconsistencies and contradictions of Corman's extensive career – between seriousness and exploitation as Rayns puts it – illuminate the importance of a man who perhaps best exemplifies the meaning of 'maverick operator' in the history of American cinema. As writer, he was reputedly appalled by the gap between script and screen; as director, he made manifest a journey from ingénue to cult revisionist; as an actor, he has been cast by Oscar-winning alumni of his studio/school; as a producer, he gave outlets to victims of HUAC black-listing and to overseas directors such as Truffaut, Kurosawa, Fellini and Bergman, and as a man committed to equality, he took on a project tackling racism in America – *The Intruder* (1961) – which no major studio was prepared to touch. An honorary Academy Award winner, acclaimed King of the B-movies, and the youngest director to receive a retrospective from the Cinémathèque Française, Corman is enjoying a twenty-first century resurgence as producer/executive with the SyFy channel's in-house blood fests such as *Dinoshark* (2010) and *Piranhaconda* (2012). Corman's extensive career and multiple roles in different aspects of filmmaking mark him as both an agent of change and a figure who is persistently obscured by his reputation.

Discussing 1950s American horror Mark Jancovich summarises the three ways in which Corman is generally written about: a fan-based adulatory approach – which is certainly genuine but not always reliable; the anecdotal examination of ' ... several generations of new talent within Hollywood ... ' who have been found, nurtured and encouraged by Corman; and thirdly an academic approach, which ' ... falls into two main subsections: those studies produced out of auteur-structuralism and those studies produced out of genre criticism.'[2] Taken in isolation, each of these approaches elides major aspects of Corman's work. Cutting across these categories are two crucial facets of Corman's practice: a willingness to challenge societal norms, and an intense commitment to making 'pictures' (as he frequently termed his productions). Despite the challenging and/or risky content of his films, the very term 'pictures' connects Corman to an audience and a cinephilic fan-base in a manner quite different from the model of the 'auteur' or filmmaker-as-artist.

Whether working on the fringes of Hollywood or as an outright independent, throughout his career Corman has undoubtedly been an innovative force. Condemning the 1950s science fiction output of Hollywood as unimaginative and in need of 'cerebral wings,'[3] Corman's team (often including camera operator Floyd Crosby and designer Daniel Haller) set to work on reinvigorating the genre. Admittedly some of the resulting films are not genre landmarks, yet the conceptual innovation or 'novum' crucial to science fiction seldom fails to intrigue, whether the device is x-ray vision, replicants or apocalypses.[4] Corman revitalised the dying black and white B-movie format, creating cult cinema for audiences receptive to haphazard, innovative Westerns, gangster, drug and horror flicks. He also argued a case for equality and opportunity in production, opening the door to women at a time when the film industry mostly ignored them.[5] Gale Anne Hurd, one of the most successful producers in Hollywood, responsible for science fiction films such as the Terminator series and *Armageddon* (1998), began her career at Corman's New World Pictures. Speaking of Hollywood's institutional sexism she observes 'I didn't realize it at the time because I worked with Roger Corman … Anywhere else, it was a huge liability.'[6]

The Last Woman on Earth (1960) is typical of both Corman's legendarily thrifty filmmaking practices and the socially challenging themes of his work. Made in Puerto Rico while filming *Creature from the Haunted Sea*, local Puerto Ricans are used as supporting actors with Antony Carbone, Betsy Jones-Moreland and Robert Towne starring in both films (when *The Last Woman* script was not ready in time, Corman cast Towne – screenwriter for both – to save time and money). The plot centres on indicted businessman Harold Gern and wife Evelyn, holidaying with Harold's lawyer, Martin. The three are scuba diving when an unidentified apocalypse apparently wipes out all life on earth. As tensions build between the three survivors, the men fight over Evelyn, who with Martin rebels against Harold's 'rules'. More than the love interest in a doomed triangle, Evelyn's role articulates a pointed critique of her social positioning as woman and wife. Harold becomes increasingly frustrated by her blossoming romance with Martin and their joint lack of order.

Harold repeatedly demands structure and continuity, 'a system' – clearly hypocritical since he has himself broken those rules, whilst Evelyn calmly explains: 'Your system never really worked for me, Harold. With or without the world your system's the same: it gives me everything but you.' Evelyn will later make another considered attack: 'You really don't see, do you? Harold, in the last world you didn't give me a chance to find out where *I* belonged, you're not doing it in this world either.' In response, Harold forces her onto the bed, asserting his sense of sexual entitlement ('you're my wife'), at which point the film cuts to the image of a dead woman on the beach underscoring the imagery of violence. Consistently, visually and verbally, the film and Evelyn shame Harold – his victories forced through a muted yet still ugly demonstration of sexual power and marital rites. Repeatedly Corman's films articulate, sometimes despite the overt narrative, a quiet, dignified and potent tone of critical defiance from women in the face of conservatism and sexism.

On completion of the Puerto Rican films Corman threw himself into productions of Edgar Allen Poe's gothic tales, a celebrated sequence of films spanning cinematic horror and the American literary canon. A fascination with the human condition and the American psyche comes into its own via the Poe adaptations, prominently foregrounding the uncanny qualities of Poe's characters, intruders into a hidden world. Disdaining social conservatism, Corman's Poe cycle – made with slightly higher budgets – sustains the inventive use of exploitation cinema with which he would become synonymous. Indeed there is nothing conservative about these adaptations. Devoid of castles and ancient European history to bolster fear, Corman turns American space into a wild and operatic landscape, using an elemental mise-en-scène to articulate terrors in the night. At the centre is Vincent Price, living a Freudian nightmare of neuroses constructed through fluid camerawork and a garish, artificially intense colour palette. The films represent a remarkable cycle, displaying the director's personal journey from B-movie ringmaster to self-awareness

> ... through an expositional shock phase (*The Pit and The Pendulum*, 1961), a phase of self-parody (*Tales of Terror*, 1962; *The Raven*, 1963) and on to both outright pretension (*The Masque of the Red Death*, 1964) and persuasive seriousness (*The Tomb of Ligeia*, 1964).[7]

This neat horror cycle has been written about at great length; commanding probably the most interest from audiences and critics, these films and their reception underline the way in which exploitation and other broadly 'independent' modes of filmmaking came to fascinate both critics and scholars.

Yet the real exploitation and terror for Corman emerges in everyday realities rather than Poe, Price and *Grand Guignol*. The bigotry of a small southern town is Corman's most gripping horror: *The Intruder* serves as shocking testimony to American social attitudes to racial integration, articulated with monstrous charisma through the character of Adam Cramer (William Shatner). Dividing critics, it was pulled from Cannes but won accolades at Venice and Los Angeles. A rare box-office failure for Corman, his experience with *The Intruder* reputedly ensured that subsequent films would veil any social critique within genre contexts. Released before *To Kill a Mocking Bird* (1963), in which the conceit of Harper Lee's child narrator Scout facilitates an examination of small town racism, Corman's film is based on a novel by Charles Beaumont. But whereas *To Kill a Mocking Bird* is genteel and considered, with Scout's father Atticus Finch (Gregory Peck) examining racial prejudice via court room rhetoric, Corman's work is raw and bloody, highlighting its concerns through an ugly rhetoric of incitement and a grim realism.

The Intruder concerns the induction of ten black students to the previously all-white Caxton High School. Racist activist Cramer arrives in town to explain the evils of integration ('you might say I'm a "social worker"'), quickly forging allegiances with willing locals. But as Caxton falls in line, Cramer also sets about seducing women, including the local news editor's teenage daughter Ella McDaniel and salesman Sam Griffin's wife, Vi. His words to a disdainful, numbed Mrs Griffin sum up his entire role: 'You despise me but you're attracted to me, isn't that right? Isn't it?' Problematically, Cramer's repulsive character is fully fleshed out whilst the black characters remain ciphers – the innocent student, the resigned father, the priest who begs for peace. The black population of Caxton thus has no voice – a position the film does not address. Instead Corman leaves it to Griffin, Vi and local newsman Tom McDaniel to verbalise critique. As the flaming cross in Caxton's main street is superimposed over Cramer's fanatical face, Vi remarks with heavy irony on his 'religious' nature. Her husband has already recognised the troublemaker as a sharp operator, confronting him at gunpoint about his opportunistic adultery, quickly demolishing the façade of power and influence Cramer has painstakingly erected: the racist bully crumbles as he recognises that his control is mere illusion. When his 'mob' turns, ready to lynch a black student over alleged rape, confessions arise: there was no violation, only entrapment. Cramer is moved through the film from centre-frame close-up to a distant sideline, liberal editor McDaniel noting ruefully: 'One thing Adam Cramer's done for us; he's made us face ourselves.'

Filmed on location in the tinderbox towns of Charleston and East Prairie, Missouri, the film incorporates storylines of inter-racial rape, miscegenation, lynching and the KKK – encapsulating the burning resentment of the Confederate states. Corman and his crew filmed without admitting the anti-racist narrative to their local amateur cast, and were barred by the local Sheriff when their real intention was exposed. William Shatner delivered Cramer's main incendiary speech late at night with few present, the feverish crowd scenes having been shot earlier when the actor shouted banalities to an audience roaring carefully directed approval. The final sequence filmed, the horrendous Nazi-like arrival of the KKK, its cars thundering along the road like tanks, was set against a backdrop of real streets with genuine danger of gang violence, black and white, threatening the crew.[8]

New York Times' reviewer Bosley Crowther expressed mixed feelings for the film, saying that the ' … highly explosive material is handled crudely and a bit too clumsily for either conviction or comfort in *The Intruder*, an angry little film turned out by Roger and Gene Corman'. But whilst vacillating between praise and condemnation, he concludes that

> … it does break fertile ground in the area of integration that has not yet been opened on the screen. And it does so with obvious good intentions and a great deal of raw, arresting power in many of its individual details and in the aspects of several characters.[9]

Fifty years on and in context the determination of Corman and the bravery of the film – despite its flaws – are far more widely appreciable.

Corman's versatile work has always contained social commentary, but his films are primarily about exhilaration and innovation; he dared to do things other directors eschewed, even when Hollywood was in a period of flux and experimentation. Corman's films are not always 'crafted', and despite his envy of contemporary CGI effects, ironically the spate of films from SyFy with which he has been involved demonstrate the same flaws in coherence and continuity as *Attack of the Crab Monsters* (1956). Yet Corman's legacy – as director, producer and independent pioneer in a fast-changing industry – remains extraordinary. If enthusiasm outweighs expertise, if perfection is sacrificed at the behest of entertainment, if this requires indulgent, lenient and forgiving audiences, then we are rewarded with an experience never pretentious or tedious. Echoing David Thomson, who remarks that in Hollywood 'there is room for a hundred such figures amid so much dullness',[10] we can note that while no Roger Corman film has ever been made for awards, academics or academies his work has come to stand for a celebration of cinema.

Biography

Roger William Corman was born on 5 April 1926, Detroit, Michigan. He attended Stanford, graduating in industrial engineering, a career he did not pursue. Corman began working in Hollywood as a scriptwriter at Fox, moving on to production and direction during the 1950s. After extensive work with AIP, Corman founded New World Pictures in 1970 operating successfully in the youth and exploitation markets. In addition to the celebration of films he directed such as the Poe cycle, Corman has received recognition for his extensive career as a producer and for his championing of generations of filmmakers. Retrospectives of his work have been held in Europe and the United States. He was awarded an honorary Academy Award in 2009.

Notes

1 Tony Rayns, 'Roger Corman' in Richard Roud (ed.), *Cinema A Critical Dictionary The Major Film-makers* Vol. 1., London, Secker and Warburg, 1980, p. 233.

2 Mark Jancovich, *Rational Fears: American Horror in the 1950s*, Manchester, Manchester University Press, 1996, pp. 268–69.

3 Roger Corman, 'Science Fiction in Danger' in *The Hollywood Reporter* 18 November, 1957.

4 The novum is the central concept in science fiction and requires a renegotiation of expected norms. See Darko Suvin, *Metamorphoses of Science Fiction*, London, Yale, 1979.

5 Wheeler Winston Dixon, 'In Defense of Roger Corman', *The Velvet Light Trap*, 16 (Fall 1976) pp. 11–14, and David Chute: 'The New World of Roger Corman', *Film Comment*, 18, No 2, 1982, pp. 27–32. Also Wheeler Dixon, 'An Interview with Roger Corman'. *Post Script*, Vol. 8, No. 1, (Fall 1988) pp. 2–15.

6 Available at: http://www.stumpedmagazine.com/interviews/gale-anne-hurd/ Accessed 01/10/13. Gary Morris explores this in 'Feminism and exploitation. Roger Corman's New World Pictures.' *Bright Lights*, No 10 (July 1993), pp. 18–23.

7 Rayns, 1980, p. 233.

8 Roger Corman in interview with William Shatner. DVD *The Intruder* STAX Pictures.

9 Available at http://movies.nytimes.com/movie/review?res=9E06E0D9153 CE637A25756C1A9639C946391D6CF

10 David Thomson, *The New Biographical Dictionary of Film*. New York: Knopf, 1994, p. 149.

Filmography

Five Guns West (1955)
Apache Woman (1955)

The Day the World Ended (1955)
Gunslinger (1955)
Swamp Women (1955)
The Oklahoma Woman (1955)
It Conquered the World (1956)
Not of This Earth (1956)
The Undead (1956)
The She Gods of Shark Reef (1956)
Naked Paradise (1956)
Attack of the Crab Monsters (1956)
Rock all Night (1956)
Teenage Doll (1957)
Carnival Rock (1957)
Sorority Girl (1957)
The Viking Women and the Sea Serpent (1957)
War of the Satellites (1957)
Machine Gun Kelly (1958)
Teenage Caveman (1958)
I, Mobster (1958)
A Bucket of Blood (1959)
The Wasp Woman (1959)
Ski Troop Attack (1960)
The House of Usher (1960)
The Little Shop of Horrors (1960)
The Last Woman on Earth (1960)
Creature from the Haunted Sea (1960)
Atlas (1960)
The Pit and the Pendulum (1961)
The Intruder (1961)
The Premature Burial (1961)
Tales of Terror (1961)
The Tower of London (1962)
The Young Racers (1962)
The Raven (1962)
The Terror (1962)
The Man With the X-Ray Eyes (1963)
The Haunted Palace (1963)
The Secret Invasion (1963)
The Masque of the Red Death (1964)
The Tomb of Ligeia (1964)
The Wild Angels (1966)
The St. Valentine's Day Massacre (1967)

The Trip (1967)
De Sade (1969) co-directed with Cy Endfield
Bloody Mama (1970)
Gas-s-s-s! – *or* – *It Became Necessary to Destroy the World in Order to Save It* (1970)
The Red Baron (1971) aka *Von Richtofen and Brown*
Deathsport (1978) uncredited
Battle Beyond the Stars (1980) uncredited
Frankenstein Unbound (1990)

Further reading

Corman, R. with Jim Jerome. *How I Made a Hundred Movies in Hollywood and Never Lost a Dime*. New York: Da Capo Press, 1998.

Frank, A. G. *The Films of Roger Corman*. London: Batsford, 1998.

Gray, B. *Roger Corman: Blood-Sucking Vampires, Flesh-Eating Cockroaches, and Driller Killers*. 3rd edition. Santa Monica, California: AZ Ferris Publications, 2013.

Koetting, C. *Mind Warp! The Fantastic True Story of Roger Corman's New World Pictures*. Sussex: Hemlock Books Ltd, 2009.

Morris, G. *The Films of Roger Corman: 'Shooting My Way out of Trouble'*. Boston: Twayne Publishers Inc., 1986.

Naha, E. *The Films of Roger Corman: Brilliance on a Budget*. New York: Arco Press, 1982.

Nashawaty, C. *Crab Monsters, Teenage Cavemen, and Candy Stripe Nurses Roger Corman: King of the B Movie*. New York: Abrams, 2013.

Nasr, C., ed. *Roger Corman: Interviews*. Jackson: University Press of Mississippi, 2011.

Silver, A. and James Ursini. *Roger Corman: Metaphysics on a Shoestring*. Los Angeles: Silman-James Press, 2006.

Whitehead, M. *Roger Corman*. Harpenden: Kamera Pocket Essentials, 2003.

Willeman, Paul, David Pirie, David Will and Lynda Myles, eds. *Roger Corman*. Edinburgh: Edinburgh Film Festival, 1970.

WILLIAM FRIEDKIN

By David Greven

Though an Oscar-winning director who made two of the 1970s biggest box-office hits, *The French Connection* (1971) and, especially,

The Exorcist (1973), William Friedkin is the perpetual outsider, a stranger within the strange land of the New Hollywood. While Friedkin has consistently made films from the 1970s to the present, he has rarely done so within the security of industry support and box-office success. An abiding sense of estrangement characterizes his work as well as his persona.

Friedkin began his filmmaking career with the remarkable documentary *The People vs. Paul Crump* (1962). The documentary genre provided a crucial foundation for his signature style, which applies documentary technique to mainstream narrative film. Long shots that herald their seeming objectivity; hand-held, often shaky cameras; gritty, unvarnished, even ugly locales; the determination to show poverty and social decay unsentimentally; the use of non-actors: all contribute to the realist aesthetic that would appear to be Friedkin's overriding concern. Friedkin's "realism" is conveyed through these characteristic formal devices and his penchant for long, lingering sequences in which quotidian, routine, time-consuming tasks are performed in close approximations of real time, though often with startling results. The seemingly endless sequence in *The French Connection* for instance, features the hero, Jimmy "Popeye" Doyle (Gene Hackman) and his detective partner Buddy "Cloudy" Russo (Roy Scheider), looking for evidence of stashed-away heroin in a towed car, exhausting the garage mechanics with unceasing demands that every last bit of the car be disassembled and searched. After what feels like hours of tedious unscrewing, removal, and reassemblage, a weight discrepancy is discovered between the owner's manual figure of 4,675 lbs and the reassembled car's weight of 4,795 lbs. Tracing this disparity to the bags of heroin hidden in the car's side doors, Doyle's obsessive, embarrassing persistence pays off.

Reflecting on his childhood, Friedkin notes that, as a boy, his walk to school took him past the home of William Heirens, the infamous Drake Hotel serial killer who dismembered young women's bodies.[1] The influence of such imagery is present in Friedkin's frequent images of amputation and related bodily trauma, such as the limbs floating in the Hudson River in *Cruising* (1980), the young Yemeni girl missing a leg (but not a machine gun) in *Rules of Engagement* (2000). The body provides no barrier against assault in his work; indeed, it incites it. Unflinchingly graphic depiction of assaults to the body and of the mortification of the body itself are also present in *The Exorcist*, which features shots of the possessed girl Regan's horrifically brutalized and suppurating flesh, as well as scenes where she undergoes medical procedures in search of evidence of a lesion in her temporal lobe.

If anything, these scenes of forensic medical realism were chiefly responsible for producing the legendary mass-displays of nausea and retching in theaters. The immense, thunderously loud, rotating machines make modern medical science and technology appear medieval, barbaric, the true, monstrous threat, a stunning extension of the film's blend and confusion of archaism and modernity, ancient evil and Catholic ritual, on the one hand, contemporary medicine and psychiatry, on the other.

Despite Friedkin's graphic realism, it is also true that he has made some of the most stylized and expressionistic films of the postclassical Hollywood canon. His style is distinguished by his use of ellipsis, scenes and shots that cut off disjunctively with no clear conclusion and with jagged abruptness, lending the seemingly ordinary a level of ominous foreboding; fast cutting that jostles the film image along with the spectator, creating a never-ending, perilous sense of anything-goes; subliminal imagery; and, perhaps most crucially, meticulous attention to and distortions of the sound design all add to the expressionistic stylization. It is the blend of unflinching verisimilitude and irreal, poetic, uncanny effects that make his films so unsettling and unusual. Friedkin has cited the paintings of Francis Bacon as an influence, a linkage that can be traced to their choice of dark subject matter as well as the vitality of such death-infused art, images that are "sad" and "frightening" yet also "exhilarating."[2]

Friedkin's influences can be traced to his early upbringing in a middle-class Jewish neighborhood in Chicago during the 1930 and 1940s; not one to sentimentalize, he remarks, "it was a fucking slum."[3] Television's emerging cultural centrality in the United States in the 1950s and 60s and the fierce independence of Chicago also strongly influenced the young Friedkin. After working in the mailroom of the WGN TV station, Friedkin got a job in 1959 at WTTW, a local station in a system that would eventually become PBS. Friedkin found himself incorporated into the social circle of Lois Solomon, who edited and published a progressive journal and held literary salons in her home that included prominent cultural figures such as Studs Terkel, a documentarian. The budding young director soon surreptitiously began working on what would become his breakthrough work, the documentary *The People vs. Paul Crump*, which investigated the trials of an African American man convicted of murder and sentenced to the electric chair. Friedkin's film took the position that Crump was innocent and that his confession of murder had been coerced by the Chicago police officers who beat it out of him. In one of the first instances of Friedkin's professional brutality, a quality that is indistinguishable from his inspired touches as a director, he verbally abused Crump on camera, forcing him to break down. Friedkin has even admitted to hitting Crump, offscreen, to get the particular emotional effect he wanted on camera.[4] Such anecdotes attest to the stylized, manipulated elements within Friedkin's vaunted "realism." As Segaloff observes, "His strength as a filmmaker is not just to make fiction look real but to make reality dramatic."[5] The film did manage to save Crump from the electric chair, but not to commute his sentence of life imprisonment.

One of Friedkin's first directing assignments was the last episode of *The Alfred Hitchcock Hour* (1965). (He never got over being reprimanded by Hitchcock for not wearing a tie.) Several distinct films would come Friedkin's way in the 1960s, including *The Night They Raided Minsky's* (1968), a comedic film about the invention of the striptease, starring Jason Robards; an adaptation of Harold Pinter's play *The Birthday Party* (1968); and, especially, his adaptation of Mart Crowley's notable Off-Broadway play *The Boys in the Band* (1970), which ran for over 1,000 performances. As his 1960s output and his more recent films as well as the operas he has directed in the 2000s attest, Friedkin is adept at transforming stage drama into lively, kinetic cinema. Crowley's play concerns the travails of a group of gay men, some closeted, all troubled one way or another, who get together for the birthday of a member of the group, Michael, played unrelentingly by Kenneth Nelson. While initially comedic in its then-provocative frank exploration of gay life, the film turns decidedly more aggressive and melancholy in tone, as the tormented Michael forces each member of the group to divulge their most wrenching secrets publicly, himself falling apart at the end of the narrative. *Boys* anticipates *Cruising* in its exploration of gay stereotypes that are presented as such, indulged in even, but then turned inside out. While the film was not a box-office success, it got Friedkin noticed as a significant new director successful at "opening up" a stage play and handling difficult material.

With astonishing speed, Friedkin catapulted onto the A-list with his next movie, the galvanizing blockbuster *The French Connection*, a crime thriller based on a real-life case of New York City cops in the Narcotics Bureau investigating a heroin-smuggling ring that originated in France. The film features the most famous car chase in movie history, in which Gene Hackman's Popeye Doyle chases down a paid assassin who has commandeered an elevated train, and as so many of Friedkin's films do, intensively explores male relationships. The slobby, beefy, racist, yet doggedly earnest Doyle of Gene

Hackman is counterbalanced against Alain Charnier (Fernando Rey), as a debonair and slyly knowing gentlemanly figure who is a criminal mastermind. In one of the best sequences in the film, the bull-in-a-china-shop Doyle attempts to follow Charnier unnoticed as he boards a subway train, a ruse involving numerous feints and distractions. Ultimately, his goodbye wave reveals that Charnier has been on to Doyle the entire time. Friedkin's use of fast cutting, handheld camera, long shots, quotidian detail, "gritty," squalid displays of real-life poverty, including the lengthy scenes in which Doyle brutalizes suspects who are not really suspected of anything and most of whom are African American (in one infamous exchange, Doyle questions a black man mystifyingly: "Have you ever picked your toes in Poughkeepsie?"), and enigmatic, elliptical editing and pacing all give this film an unmistakably cohesive aesthetic and emotional tone. The interaction between Doyle and his police partner Cloudy is an index of buddy movie conventions, with Cloudy the voice of reason and responsibility trying to keep erratic Doyle in line, yet always aware that it is Doyle's very erraticism that signals his genius and his unrelenting determination to solve the crime and catch Frog One. In a characteristically Friedkinian touch, Doyle never catches, indeed can never catch, Charnier.

The Exorcist, Friedkin's greatest film and arguably the most important work in the horror genre other than *Psycho* (Hitchcock, 1960), begins with a prologue in Iraq in which the aged Father Merrin (Max Von Sydow) discovers an ancient talisman of the demon Pazuzu. The prologue ends with a stunning shot that counterbalances Merrin, on the right side of the screen, against a looming statue of Pazuzu, on the left, as two snarling dogs fight vociferously and a blinding sun makes Merrin squint. This is an indelible, archetypal image of good and evil; it is also a catalogue of Friedkin's effects: the visual, aural (the sound of the dogs' snarls from offscreen space, the brooding minimalist music), and thematic elements of the sequence, work together to create an image at once cohesive and maddening.

Friedkin also elicits masterful performances from the entire cast of *The Exorcist*, especially Ellen Burstyn as Chris MacNeil, an actress making a movie in D.C. whose daughter Regan (Linda Blair) becomes possessed, and Jason Miller as Father Damien Karras, a priest and a psychiatrist who is losing his faith even as he counsels fellow priests losing their own. So much of the film occurs in "the cold purple room where the devil has set up camp," in the words of one of Friedkin's best critics, Kent Jones.[6] Friedkin brilliantly isolates the bulk of the film's action in Regan's bedroom, a menacing death zone, conveyed by the extraordinary effect of the warm breath of the characters condensing in the arctic room. Despite its considerable display of pyrotechnics, much of the film is quiet, pensive, and gravely sad. "Can you help an old altar boy, Father?" an aged, booze-besotted bum on the subway platform asks Father Karras. As the train whizzes past, a kaleidoscopic image of the ruined man's face in close-up uncannily fills the screen. The world of the Friedkin film falls prey to such disorienting effects. When Karras' mother is hospitalized and placed in the charity ward, Friedkin's realism is at its most devastatingly and troublingly acute: he uses real mental patients in their harrowing isolation and suffering to suggest the atmosphere of poverty and underfunded facilities, with one lone African American woman, who leads Father Karras in, being forced to be both admitting nurse and security guard. The depth of Karras's guilt over his inability to help his mother, especially once she dies, saturates the film and intensifies his eventual commitment to helping Regan. The film also contains one of the best dream sequences in the cinema, as Karras—running in the New York City streets silently in a sweatshirt—sees his mother, oblivious to his silent screams, descending into the Stygian depths of the subway system, the urban space as underworld. *Cruising* will take this idea to the breaking point.

Sorcerer (1977) has been steadily gaining followers over the years, and many critics have come to regard it as Friedkin's best work. The film teems with indelible images, particularly of weathered, lurching trucks crawling their way across tattered, rotting bridges in the South American jungle, and of Roy Scheider's climactic drive through an utterly barren desert landscape that evokes a lunar surface, all counterbalanced against the non-sequitur of Tangerine Dream's score. *Cruising*, however, is, along with *The Exorcist*, Friedkin's most definitive film. The story, based on Gerald Walker's novel (which itself was a riff on a real-life series of blackmailing and killings of gay men in the 1960s) concerns a New York City detective, played by Al Pacino, enlisted to investigate the gay leather underworld of Manhattan while posing as one of its denizens. A killer is targeting gay men in the leather scene, and by the end of the film Friedkin has left it maddeningly unclear who the real killer is, one suggestion being that it might be Pacino's character himself.

While gay activism that vociferously targeted the film as homophobic came from a genuine place of rage and justifiable concern about the demonization of homosexuals, this film is remarkable as a deconstruction of homophobic attitudes. The leather underworld emerges as an arena for the display of a series of masculine styles and for a consideration of sexual desire unfettered by social and even moral constraint. All of this is to say that what makes *Cruising*—an irreducibly troubling film—distinctive is that it, in effect, invents queer theory. *Cruising*, like queer theory, treats gender as a social construction, views sexuality and gender both as a performance, and treats the very idea of subjectivity as deeply suspect.

Friedkin's subsequent output has been highly varied. While no great work informs his post-70s period, *To Live and Die in L.A.* (1985) has many admirers, some of whom view it as his best work. Post-70s, the director continues to push himself, even if the material is questionable (the 2000 *Rules of Engagement*, which has some interesting elements but is, ultimately, a racist depiction of the Arab world precisely because it fails to shed any real light on Middle East conflicts and settles for shock effects) or highly conventional (*Blue Chips*, 1994). While little-seen, one of the most interesting and Friedkin-like of his subsequent films is *Deal of the Century* (1983), with the unlikely casting of Chevy Chase as an arms dealer. This film blends the surreal, the political, the humorous, and the downright obscure in off-putting, incoherent, but fascinating ways; it's Friedkin's *Dr. Strangelove* (Kubrick, 1964). *Jade* (1995), written by Joe Eszterhas, contains one of Friedkin's best car chases and offers a deconstructive corrective to Paul Verhoeven's lurid *Basic Instinct* (1992), also written by Eszterhas. Friedkin is more interested in dissecting the various male obsessions with the female sexual virago than in elevating her to the status of invincible archetype. In addition to his successful mounting of opera works in the 2000s, Friedkin's collaboration with Tracy Letts in *Bug* (2006) and *Killer Joe* (2011), both well-received, provide ample evidence of creative juices flowing. Friedkin's post-70s career matches that of many in the New Hollywood, though not, quite, their level of concession to commercial taste. Friedkin remains the Stranger of the New Hollywood, a visionary with no clear agenda but a demonstrable range of signature effects and preoccupations.

Biography

Friedkin was born in Chicago on August 29, 1935, the son of Louis and Raechael ("Rae") Friedkin, Jewish émigrés from Kiev, Russia. Friedkin began his film career in documentaries, and was celebrated for films such as *The French Connection* and *The Exorcist*. The end of Friedkin's status as an A-list Hollywood director came with the financial disaster of *Sorcerer*, a remake of H. G. Clouzot's *The Wages of Fear* (1953). *Cruising*, which was set in the gay leather underworld of contemporary Manhattan, also courted incendiary controversy from the gay community while alienating mainstream audiences.

Notes

1 Nat Segaloff. *Hurricane Billy: The Stormy Life and Films of William Friedkin.* New York: Morrow, 1990, p. 24.
2 Thomas D. Clagett. *William Friedkin: Films of Aberration, Obsession and Reality.* Expanded and updated 2nd. Los Angeles: Silman-James Press, 2003, p. 20.
3 Segaloff, pp. 22–23.
4 Ibid., p. 34.
5 Ibid., p. 39.
6 Kent Jones. *Physical Evidence: Selected Film Criticism.* Middletown, Conn.: Wesleyan University Press, 2007, p. 181.

Filmography

The People vs. Paul Crump (1962) TV documentary
The Bold Men (1965) TV documentary
"Off Season" (1965) TV episode of *The Alfred Hitchcock Hour*
Pro Football: Mayhem on a Sunday Afternoon (1965) TV documentary
Time-Life Specials: The March of Time (1965) TV documentary
The Thin Blue Line (1966) TV documentary
Good Times (1967)
The Birthday Party (1968)
The Night They Raided Minsky's (1968)
The Boys in the Band (1970)
The French Connection (1971)
The Exorcist (1973)
Fritz Lang Interviewed by William Friedkin (1974) documentary
Sorcerer (1977)
The Brink's Job (1978)
Cruising (1980)
Deal of the Century (1983)
"Little Boy Lost" (1985) TV episode of *The Twilight Zone*
"Wish Bank" (1985) TV episode of *The Twilight Zone*
"Nightcrawlers" (1985) TV episode of *The Twilight Zone*
To Live and Die in L.A. (1985)
Putting It Together: The Making of the Broadway Album (1985) short
C.A.T. Squad (1986) TV movie
Rampage (1987)
C.A.T. Squad: Python Wolf (1988) TV movie

The Guardian (1990)
"On a Deadman's Chest" (1992) TV episode of *Tales from the Crypt*
"Jailbreakers" (1994) TV episode of *Rebel Highway*
Blue Chips (1994)
Jade (1995)
12 Angry Men (1997) TV movie
Rules of Engagement (2000)
The Hunted (2003)
Bug (2006)
The Painter's Voice (Video documentary short) (2007)
"Cockroaches" (2007) TV episode of *CSI: Crime Scene Investigation*
"Mascara" (2009) TV episode of *CSI: Crime Scene Investigation*
Killer Joe (2011)

Further reading

Berliner, Todd. *Hollywood Incoherent: Narration in Seventies Cinema*. 1st ed. Austin: University of Texas Press, 2010.

Friedkin, William. *The Friedkin Connection: A Memoir*. 1st ed. New York: Harper, 2013.

Greven, David. *Psycho-Sexual: Male Desire in Hitchcock, De Palma, Scorsese, and Friedkin*. 1st ed. Austin: University of Texas, 2013.

STANLEY KUBRICK

By Maria Pramaggiore

With a majestic visual lexicon marked by the discipline of rigorous tracking shots and the disorientation associated with the wide-angle lens, Stanley Kubrick's thirteen feature films explore compelling questions that haunted humanity in the latter half of the twentieth century, when the progress and perfectibility of humankind were increasingly called into question by the events of World War II, the Holocaust, and the advent of nuclear warfare. Critics and fans alike characterize Kubrick's eclectic body of work, which ranges from *film noir* and black comedy to science fiction and costume drama, as intellectual, ironic, distanced, and even, at times, cynical. After he earned widespread popular and critical acclaim with the nuclear nightmare comedy, *Dr. Strangelove, or How I Learned to Stop Worrying and Love the Bomb* (1964), fans eagerly awaited new Kubrick films, only to find themselves leaving the theater shocked and puzzled. Prominent critics initially panned such films as *2001: A Space Odyssey* (1968), *A Clockwork Orange* (1971), and *Barry Lyndon* (1975), only to reclaim them as classics and even masterpieces a decade or more later. To American audiences from the early 1960s onward, Kubrick's importance was never in doubt, even while the accessibility and amiability of his films always remained under suspicion.

Kubrick's fifty-year long filmmaking career is remarkable not only because of the simultaneously iconic and iconoclastic status of nearly all of his films, but also because of his ability to maintain a degree of independence from the Hollywood film industry. The popular notion that Kubrick was a fully autonomous auteur, *sui generis*, has been somewhat overstated, however. Paradoxically, the aspects of his career that are often cited as evidence of his singularity – both in terms of his creative audacity and his working methods – render him, in point of fact, an exemplary figure of post-studio era filmmaking, not an anomaly. In the decades that followed the Paramount consent decree of 1948, as major studios began to dismantle themselves, film directors became free agents rather than paid staff members, participating in production deals in a variety of industry contexts. The studios increasingly began to rely on distribution and ancillary marketing, rather than in-house production units, for profitability. Finally, commercial filmmaking became an insistently global enterprise. In all of these areas, Kubrick was a critical figure, if not a pioneer: he secured his name brand both aesthetically and commercially by establishing his own production companies and negotiating financing and distribution deals with major studios. Robert Sklar observes that Kubrick's reputation as a maverick has obscured the ways in which his career represented not a retreat from the industry but, instead, a prototype for post-studio film production. "He and his films," Sklar writes, "have played a much more central role than has heretofore been recognized in the transformation of industry practices in the era since the breakup of studio monopolies".[1]

Kubrick's example was central to postwar American film culture in another industrial context: that of the publicity industry's construction of his star persona, an ineluctable process of hagiography and defilement that Kubrick mostly chose to avoid rather than to participate in, particularly after the preponderance of negative responses to *2001* in the American press. Despite (or perhaps because of) his distance from the star-making apparatus, a Kubrick mystique and mythology emerged, comprising speculation that his withdrawal from Hollywood and his life in the UK were indicative of a profound anti-sociality and rumors regarding his misanthropic perfectionism as a director. The latter charge gained credence after the release of his daughter Vivian's BBC documentary, *The Making of The Shining* (1980), which depicted an impatient Kubrick admonishing the actress Shelly Duvall. The discourse of Kubrick as a hermit savant played a critical role within American film culture in the late 1970s and 1980s, as the younger "film generation" directors who had emerged during the Hollywood Renaissance, including George Lucas, Steven Spielberg, Francis Ford Coppola, and eventually, even Martin Scorsese, moved into big-budget blockbusters. Kubrick's status as the crackpot American auteur ratified the presumed dichotomy between art cinema and commerce in an era in which financial success rather than creative risk taking, once again became the *sine qua non* of Hollywood success.

If Kubrick's films "met with indifference and incomprehension, and, only later, with hindsight, revealed their place in a given generic history"[2] they served as counterpoint to the blockbuster and ensured the continuing possibility of cinema as art. Known for his painstaking research, preparation, and time-consuming production methods, including shooting numerous takes and deferring editing until principal photography was completed, Kubrick was cast as the pathological patriarch, his only rival being Robert Altman, whose mercurial but ultimately dependent relationship with the Hollywood industry also became stuff of legend. Regardless of whether the stories of Kubrick's eccentricities were true—and many clearly were not—the hype preserved the dream of Kubrick as the last bastion of American art cinema, despite the fact that his career had always been based on medium-sized productions that were moderately profitable. *Dr. Strangelove* was made for less than $2 million and grossed just under $10 million. Even *2001*—an admittedly ambitious undertaking that went over-budget and ultimately cost upwards of $10 million—took in $68 million at the box office, its 6:1 ratio comparing favorably to other popular films released in 1968, including *Funny Girl* (4:1) and *Planet of the Apes* (5:1).

The star discourse that came to envelop Kubrick and his legacy, a mantle he wore uneasily, speaks to the critical importance of the celebrity director model that emerged during the breakup of the studio system. Thomas Elsaesser rightly acknowledges the tremendous "effort required in the latter half of the 20th century to control one's image, if one wished to remain (in and for the film industry) that totemic individualist *par excellence*."[3] It is arguable whether or not Kubrick wished to become or remain a "totemic individualist"; he certainly strove to maintain control over the creative, fiscal, and marketing aspects of his product—that is, to control not his image, but his images—at a time of industry decentralization that, ironically, minimized the autonomy of the new class of star directors engendered by the breakup of the studios.

Kubrick is frequently compared to Orson Welles, another postwar American whiz kid whose career proceeded in fits and starts and only flourished, when it did so at all, outside of Hollywood. Despite Stanley Kubrick's expatriate status and much-lauded independence, however, the analogy is flawed, at least in terms of the two directors' relationships with major studios. Unlike Welles, Kubrick managed to work successfully with studios throughout his career, including United Artists (*The Killing, Paths of Glory*), Universal (*Spartacus*), MGM (*Lolita* and *2001*), Columbia (*Dr. Strangelove*) and Warner Brothers (*A Clockwork Orange, Barry Lyndon, The Shining, Full Metal Jacket* and *Eyes Wide Shut*). Granted, the studios that Kubrick worked with in the 1960s through the 1990s were vastly different institutions than the RKO and Universal that Welles encountered in the 1940s and 1950s. And Kubrick was able to secure his autonomy by establishing a reputation for business acumen by delivering profitable projects on time and within budget. Early in his career, when Kubrick moved from making short documentaries for RKO and the March of Time into feature filmmaking, he formed Harris-Kubrick Productions with James Harris, and together they produced or co-produced *The Killing, Paths of Glory*, and *Lolita*. *The Killing* established several career patterns for Kubrick: adapting the work of an established writer and obtaining financing and distribution from a major studio but overseeing production in-house. *The Killing* caught the eye of Dore Schary, head of production at MGM, but not long after Kubrick moved to Southern California from his native New York, the studio unceremoniously dumped Schary, and by extension Kubrick. Whereas some aspiring directors moved into the new medium of television (Altman, Roger Corman, Coppola), Kubrick stayed true to the film medium, co-producing *Paths of Glory* with Kirk Douglas's independent Bryna Films and serving as director for hire on *Spartacus* at Douglas's insistence after Anthony Mann had been fired from the project. The *Spartacus* stint refreshed Kubrick's memory about the importance of creative autonomy. Kubrick was not merely a man of ideas and a savvy businessman, he was also a painstaking craftsman and, after MGM sent him to the UK to shoot *Lolita* (anticipating a 40 percent savings) he found the arrangements there to his liking. He formed several independent production companies, including Hawk Films and subsidiaries Peregrine Productions and Harrier Films, which served him well for the next thirty years. Kubrick spent the remainder of his life in Hertfordshire,

UK, not because of any antipathy toward the United States, but because his children were in school and his trusted colleagues and friends were located there. From that "outpost," a half hour from London, Kubrick sustained and maintained a solid working relationship with Warner Brothers, the studio that ultimately financed and distributed his last five films. The several decades-long relationship between Kubrick and Terry Simmel, Head of Production, was predicated on the fact the Kubrick not only knew what he was doing behind the camera but also controlled expenditure and had good ideas about marketing his films. Mike Kaplan, who worked on publicity for Kubrick in the 1970s, wrote in *The Guardian* in 2007 that "instituting new distribution methods fascinated Stanley as much as film-making, which he also called 'an exercise in problem solving.'"[4] The two men designed marketing strategies that continue to be used today, such as creating advertising copy that is difficult to distinguish from editorial content.

While Kubrick was highly respected for his analytical approach to production and marketing, certainly the filmmaking process itself was where his vast knowledge of aesthetics, interest in history and culture, and his passion for film technology were most in evidence. In many ways, Kubrick's *oeuvre* represents the expanded possibilities of film as a photochemical medium in the postwar era, due to his extensive knowledge of black and white and color photography and his understanding of the mechanics of lenses, cameras, and projectors. He began his career as a still photographer, hired by *Look* magazine at the age of 17 and specializing in gritty portraits of New York and Chicago street life, covering everything from commuters to showgirls, from steelworkers to lingerie models, from wrestler Gorgeous George to boxer Rocky Graziano. Not surprisingly, the moody sensibility of *film noir* predominates as an influence in Kubrick's early films: his pictorial study of boxer Walter Cartier, published in *Look* in 1949, formed the basis of his first motion picture, a sixteen-minute long documentary entitled *The Day of the Fight*. His second film, *Flying Padre*, explores the life of a New Mexico priest who ministers to his far-flung flock through the modern miracle of air travel. That deep-seated understanding of photographic representation—not merely the technical elements but the emotions that might be addressed through the medium—remained salient throughout his filmmaking career. Kubrick was constantly pushing the envelope of technological innovation, pioneering the use of front projection (*2001*), adapting state of the art scientific lenses for cinematic purposes (*Barry Lyndon*), and becoming an early adopter of the Steadicam (*The Shining*). It was precisely through his confident embrace of the technological aspects of filmmaking that Kubrick was able to exert his formidable grasp over the power of images to convey abstract ideas and complex emotions.

A famous anecdote from the production history of *The Killing* (1956) suggests Kubrick's intimate familiarity with the technology he used to arrange the visual worlds of his films. Cinematographer Lucien Ballard explained to Kubrick, who, because of union rules, could not serve as both director and cinematographer on the film, that there would be no visible difference in perspective between a scene filmed with the 25mm lens Kubrick had requested and the 50mm lens that Ballard substituted for it. Kubrick's response was to ask Ballard to replace the lens and shoot the sequence as requested or to leave the set.

In the visual design of his films, Kubrick's heightened formalism is tempered by gestural camerawork—more linear and restrained than that of Welles and Tolland—which, together with the wide angle lens, creates a sense of spaciousness (which does not necessarily translate into a feeling of freedom or openness). Tracking the heroic Colonel Dax through the French trenches in *Paths of Glory*, orchestrating a motif of evolution and revolution in *2001* (where Strauss waltzes and Beethoven symphonies choreograph the regular movement of the heavens), or conveying the horrific void at the center of the Overlook Hotel in *The Shining* by means of Steadicam shots of Danny driving his Big Wheel straight into the emptiness, Kubrick's studied cinematography grows out of and, in turn, has influenced cinematic modernism and postmodernism. The deep focus and clarity afforded by the wide-angle lens, as well as its subtly rendered surreal distortions have become a signature feature of Kubrick's films. As James Naremore perceptively notes: "much like Franz Kafka, [Kubrick's] most bizarre effects emerge from the very clarity with which his imagery is rendered."[5]

The director's technical explorations did not come at the expense of story. An inveterate reader, Kubrick greatly admired literary artistry, remarking in a 1971 interview with Penelope Houston that "a great narrative is a kind of miracle."[6] He was committed to narrative filmmaking, adapting screenplays from the work of authors such as Vladimir Nabokov, Anthony Burgess, Stephen King, Arthur Schnitzler, and William Makepeace Thackeray. He confided in Diane Johnson, who co-wrote the screenplay for *The Shining*, that he looked for novels that were not masterpieces so that he could improve upon them, the one exception being *Lolita*.[7] It's interesting to note that the authors whose work he adapted specialized in creating indelible characters such as Humbert Humbert, Alexander the Large, and Redmond Barry, whereas Kubrick was often denounced for a visual style whose scale, to some, dehumanized characters and for a coldness that betrayed an attitude of indifference. Countering this view is director Martin Scorsese, who said in a 2001 interview: "somehow I keep coming back to *Barry Lyndon*. I think that's because it's such a profoundly emotional experience"[8] and film scholar James Naremore, who writes that "the emotions [Kubrick] elicits are primal and mixed."[9]

Like the European master Max Ophuls, Kubrick produced grandiose films whose themes transcend national, generic, and industrial contexts. Unlike Ophuls, Kubrick deflates any pretensions toward melodrama with a near-surgical form of satire reflecting a well-developed mistrust of the powerful and pompous. In films from *Spartacus* to *Paths of Glory*, *Barry Lyndon* and *Full Metal Jacket*, he championed the common man and indicted the careerism and megalomania embedded within military and class hierarchies. In *Lolita*, *Dr. Strangelove*, *A Clockwork Orange*, *The Shining* and *Eyes Wide Shut*, he underscores the connections between and among gender, power, and madness, not only within the intimate context of the nuclear family but also upon the global stage of the nuclear arms race. In *2001*, he simultaneously celebrates and calls into question the sanity of scientific thinking, inaugurating in a thorough-going manner the cinema's discourse of the post-human by creating an artificially intelligent computer, the HAL 9000, whose foibles prove more interesting to the audience than the human astronauts. Advertised as the "ultimate trip" in order to consolidate the college-age audience that soon became Kubrick's fiercest fans, *2001*, better than any of his films, exemplifies the director's profound understanding of American genres and his sophisticated philosophical perspective on the promises and pitfalls of modernity.

Stanley Kubrick's producer and brother-in-law, Jan Harlan, has stated that Kubrick "wanted to make films that mattered,"[10] and it is abundantly clear that, by whatever standard one uses—awards, critical interest, name recognition, film references, box office performance—he succeeded. He won the Directors Guild of American Lifetime Achievement Award; was named a BAFTA Academy Fellow; and won one Academy Award and earned thirteen nominations for writing, direction, or special visual effects. *Dr. Strangelove* was Columbia's highest grossing release of 1964; *A Clockwork Orange* was one of Warner's biggest hits of the 1970s. His influence on other filmmakers is well documented by directors such as Martin Scorsese, who describes Kubrick's films as a "well" or a "source" for learning how to make pictures[11] and Steven Spielberg, who directed *AI*, which was produced by Kubrick and released after his death. Moreover, Kubrick's sphere of influence is not limited to film culture: his ideas and sensibility, as embodied in his film, have become a defining feature of twentieth-century culture, not simply its art or entertainment. Standard accounts of American film history and, indeed, international film history are dominated in large part though discussions of war, nationalism, industrial organization, and technological change, taking their place alongside the rise and the fall of the Hollywood Studio System, the advent of home viewership and (eventually) portable screen viewing, as seminal film historical events of the twentieth century. In all of these areas, Stanley Kubrick emerges from the background to take his place alongside the more easily legible figures of postwar American cinema as an innovator, an intellectual, and an entertainer.

Biography

Born in Brooklyn, New York, Stanley Kubrick (1928–99) began his film career as a documentary photographer, publishing his work in *Look* magazine at the age of 17. He began making short documentary films at the age of 23 and made his first (and, in one sense, last) Hollywood feature film, *Spartacus*, in 1960. He went on to become a director of world renown, best known for iconic films dealing with the central historical, political, and philosophical concerns of the twentieth century, including *Paths of Glory* (1957), *Dr. Strangelove or: How I Learned to Stop Worrying and Love the Bomb* (1964), *2001: A Space Odyssey* (1968) and *Full Metal Jacket* (1987).

Notes

1 Robert Sklar, "Stanley Kubrick and the American Film Industry." *Current Research in Film: Audiences, Economics and the Law*, vol. 4 (1988): 115.
2 Thomas Elsaesser, "Evolutionary Imagineer: Stanley Kubrick's Authorship," in *Stanley Kubrick*. Frankfurt am Main: Deutsches Filmmuseum, 2007, p. 140.
3 Ibid., p. 137.
4 Mike Kaplan, "Kubrick: A Marketing Odyssey." *The Guardian*, November 1, 2007.
5 James Naremore, *On Kubrick*, London: BFI, 2007, p. 40.
6 Penelope Houston, "Kubrick Country." *Saturday Review*, December 25, 1971. Reprinted in *Stanley Kubrick Interviews*, ed. Gene D. Phillips. Jackson: University Press of Mississippi, 2001, p. 115.
7 Michel Ciment. *Kubrick: the Definitive Edition*, London, Faber and Faber, 2003, p. 293.
8 Charlie Rose. "An hour about the life and work of filmmaker Stanley Kubrick." June 15, 2001. www.charlierose.com/view/interview/3069.

9 Naremore, op. cit., p. 40.
10 Charlie Rose, op. cit.
11 Charlie Rose, op. cit.

Filmography

Day of the Fight (1951)
Flying Padre (1952)
Fear and Desire (1953)
The Seafarers (1953)
Killer's Kiss (1955)
The Killing (1956)
Paths of Glory (1957)
Spartacus (1960)
Lolita (1962)
Dr. Strangelove or: How I Learned to Stop Worrying and Love the Bomb (1964)
2001: A Space Odyssey (1968)
A Clockwork Orange (1971)
Barry Lyndon (1975)
The Shining (1980)
Full Metal Jacket (1987)
Eyes Wide Shut (1999)

Further reading

Baxter, John. *Stanley Kubrick: A Biography*. New York: Carroll and Graf, 1997.

Chion, Michel. *Kubrick's Cinema Odyssey*. Trans. Claudia Gorbman. London: BFI, 2001.

———. *Kubrick: the Definitive Edition*. London: Faber and Faber, 2003.

Cocks, Geoffrey, James Diedrick and Glenn Perusek, eds. *Depth of Field: Stanley Kubrick, Film, and the Uses of History*. Minneapolis: The University of Minnesota Press, 2006.

Duncan, Paul. *Stanley Kubrick: Visual Poet, 1928–1999*. Cologne, Germany: Taschen, 2003.

Elsaesser, Thomas. "Evolutionary Imagineer: Stanley Kubrick's Authorship." *Stanley Kubrick*. Frankfurt am Main: Deutsches Film-museum, 2007, pp. 136–47.

Howard, James. *The Stanley Kubrick Companion*. London: Batsford, 1999.

Kolker, Robert. *Stanley Kubrick's 2001: A Space Odyssey: New Essays*. Oxford, UK: Oxford University Press, 2006.

Krohn, Bill. *Stanley Kubrick*. Paris: Cahiers du cinéma Sari, 2010.

Lobrutto, Vincent. *Stanley Kubrick: A Biography*. Boston: Da Capo Press, 1999.

Naremore, James. *On Kubrick*. London: BFI, 2007.

Rose, Charlie. "An hour about the life and work of filmmaker Stanley Kubrick." 15 June 2001. www.charlierose.com/view/interview/3069

SIDNEY LUMET

By Joanna E. Rapf

Sidney Lumet was not what one would call "a Hollywood director." He was a New York director, although he did make a few movies abroad. But New York was his home: he found his inspiration there, and he knew that world, especially the underbelly of dirty cops and desperate criminals. Lumet largely shunned Hollywood and in turn, was shunned by Hollywood in spite of numerous Academy Award nominations. In 2005 he finally achieved a much-deserved "Lifetime Achievement" Oscar. At the ceremony, after almost fifty years behind the camera, Lumet had too many people to thank. He had worked with just about every famous actor and actress in Hollywood and been influenced by all the great directors – he mentioned Buster Keaton, Carl Dreyer, and Martin Scorsese, among others. And so, ever the individualist, he concluded that he simply had to thank "the movies," and he was adamant about calling them "movies" and not what he considered the pretentious term "films."

Lumet also denied the label of "auteur." He refused the possessive credit – "a film by" – believing it demeaned the collaborative nature of moviemaking. He knew the importance of script, and of working together with his screenwriters such as Walter Bernstein, Frank Pierson, Jay Presson Allen, David Mamet, and E. L. Doctorow, to mention just a few. When he received the Evelyn F. Burkey Award from the Writers Guild of America, he was honored as "one whose contribution has brought honor and dignity to writers everywhere." Although he always stressed collaboration, on the set he was "the boss," and since *Murder on the Orient Express* in 1974, he had right of final cut. His knowledge of every aspect of production is evident in his anecdotal, influential, and detailed handbook, *Making Movies*. The chapter on the camera in particular is regarded by cinematographers as one of the clearest descriptions of a complex art. As for cutting, editor Ralph

Rosenblum said of him that he was "the only filmmaker I've ever worked with who could tell me cut-for-cut what he wanted in a scene," and because of this, and careful preproduction, he was usually able to come in under budget.[1] Lumet had a background in acting, and he was exceptionally sensitive to the needs and nuances of his performers. Known as an "actor's director," he worked with an unequaled roster, including Henry Fonda, Sophia Loren, Marlon Brando, Paul Newman, Katharine Hepburn, Sean Connery, the Redgraves, Richard Burton, Michael Jackson, Helen Mirren, and the list goes on.

In spite of insisting that each film is unique and that style should be invisible and tailored to the story, Lumet was fairly consistent in returning to certain themes and even stylistic techniques, such as his fondness for long takes and his refusal to cater to the MTV generation with a lot of rapid cutting. He favored naturalism or realism and he did not like what he called the "decorator's look."[2] The cinematographer on his last projects, Ron Fortunato, jokingly once said, "Sidney flips if he sees a look that's too artsy."[3] When HD [high definition] technology came along, he embraced it, saying it gave him what his eye saw, a "real" look, and after 2000 he worked exclusively in HD with a multiple camera format.

Thematically, his movies cover a vast range of topics and he was not afraid to experiment; the musical *The Wiz* (1978) is an example of this openness. He also took work just for the sake of working, to pay the bills, and the oddly uncharacteristic *Lovin' Molly* (1974), based on a Larry McMurtry novel set in Texas, is probably an instance of this. He was fond of using novels and plays as source material, and he considered his word-for-word adaptation of Eugene O'Neill's *Long Day's Journey Into Night* (1962) one of his best achievements. The film tells its story visually in a way that could never be done on stage, utilizing the stunning black and white cinematography of Boris Kaufman and what Lumet called a "lens plot," which involves the lens and position of the camera helping to tell the story. In the case of this film, for example, he used a longer and longer lens on Katharine Hepburn, who played Mary Tyrone, as she gradually slipped into madness. Personally, *The Seagull* (1968) always evoked powerful emotions in him. In 1990 he told Michel Ciment that "Chekhov teaches you the sense of the ridiculous in some of our aspirations, of our illusions," a feeling he came back to with more profound understanding as an older man.[4] After rereading *The Seagull* one weekend in 2003, he commented,

> all of the aspirations are noble, and it's wonderful to fall in love, and it's wonderful to ride horses across the lake, and it's

wonderful to see older people in love, and it's wonderful to pursue this one and pursue that one, and finally, it is so futile.[5]

Did Lumet's view of human struggles grow darker towards the end of his life? Certainly, the tragic vision of his last movie, *Before the Devil Knows You're Dead* (2007) might suggest this.

Lumet's *New York Times* obituary headlined him as a director of "conscience," and from his first movie, *Twelve Angry Men* (1957) to his last, he explored deeply flawed characters wrestling with moral choices. Sometimes he seemed to specialize in angry men, like Al Pacino's character, Sonny, in *Dog Day Afternoon* (1975) stirring up a crowd with his evocation of "Attica, Attica!" or like Peter Finch's Howard Beale yelling, "I'm mad as hell and I'm not going to take it anymore," an outcry in *Network* (1976) that has since become part of American vernacular. That film's exploration of the amorality stemming from ambition and greed in the television industry spoke also to Lumet's investigations of justice.

Not all his movies, of course, are about victims of society's inequities and human failings. *Garbo Talks* (1984) for example, is a touching story of a son trying to fulfill his dying mother's last wish, yet even in that narrative the mother, Estelle, played by Anne Bancroft, is a diehard activist with a social conscience, doing what she can to educate and empower women, minorities, hospital workers, and police officers. *Garbo Talks* also embraces another of Lumet's favorite subjects: family and the relationship between parents and children. Perhaps the most touching moment in *Twelve Angry Men* is when Juror # 3 (Lee J. Cobb), tears up the photograph of his son as he painfully realizes that his bigotry toward the defendant stems from the relationship he has had with his own child. Lumet's last film, *Before the Devil Knows You Are Dead*, also features an anguished father who has to confront, this time in a most extreme way, a situation with his son. The theme of parents and children even appears in Lumet's formative television years when he worked with Reginald Rose (author of *Twelve Angry Men*) on "+" which aired on *The Alcoa Hour* in February 1956. A reworking of the story of Emmett Till, the fourteen year-old who had recently been lynched for allegedly whistling at a white girl, the teleplay ends when the boy's life is saved by a man who, like Juror #3, comes to recognize his own racial prejudice and also that his own son was guilty of brutally beating the boy.

Race, such a prominent issue in postwar American society, is an ongoing concern in most of Lumet's work. His one foray into documentary was *King: A Filmed Record ... Montgomery to Memphis* (1968).

He similarly centered his 2001–2 television production *100 Centre Street* around racial conflict, a series that testified to his fascination with the law, with the workings of justice, and with the minds of criminals. Judge Joe Rifkin (Alan Alda), a "bleeding heart Jew" who discovers an unconscious racism behind his overt liberalism, and his colleague, Judge Attallah Sims (Tanya Richardson), who is black, wrestle with the racial and ethnic biases that permeate the workings of the judiciary. Thematically, this focus on justice and the law regularly appears in Lumet's movies, from *Twelve Angry Men* in 1957, to *Prince of the City* (1981), *The Verdict* (1982), *Q & A* (1990), *Night Falls in Manhattan* (1997), and *Find Me Guilty* (2006). He once said,

> I've never been aware of it as wanting to do movies about the criminal justice system, and then I look back and there are seven, eight, nine of them involved with it ... I guess when you're a Depression baby, someone with a typical Lower East Side poor Jewish upbringing, you automatically get involved in social issues. And as soon as you're involved in social issues, you're involved in the justice system.[6]

In *The Hill* (1965), an agonizing portrait of the warped justice system in a British army prison camp in North Africa during World War II, Ossie Davis gives a memorable performance as Jacko King who cracks under the degrading punishments of white officers. *The Hill* was the first collaboration between Lumet and actor Sean Connery who rose above his James Bond roles to go on to star in *The Anderson Tapes* (1971), a film that presciently saw the increasing presence of surveillance in modern life; *The Offence* (1973), in which he plays a police officer who, in a rage, commits murder as he confronts unconscious perverse desires; *Murder on the Orient Express*, an all-star Agatha Christie caper that Lumet made for fun; and *Family Business* (1989) where Connery is an Irish-American patriarch whose family bungles a crime.

Connery's roles highlight the range of Lumet's work and his recurring focus on ideological critiques of aspects of postwar society. With screenwriter Paddy Chayefsky, Lumet explored the dangerous potential of television in *Network*; in *Power* (1986) he clearly foresaw how the media can manipulate human reality in politics, while in both *The Verdict* (1982) and *Critical Care* (1997) he turned his attention to corruption in the medical establishment.

In hindsight, Lumet also recognized that a number of his movies dealt with "the cost that others pay for one's passion."[7] He knew this personally, from his own passion for making movies, but it is poign-antly expressed in *Daniel* (1983), based on a book by E. L. Doctorow that loosely tells the story of how the children of Ethel and Julius Rosenberg, who died in the electric chair for "conspiring to sell atomic secrets," were twisted and hurt by their parents' convictions. Lumet followed *Daniel* with *Running on Empty* (1988) and *Family Business*, films that similarly deal with children who pay for the pas-sions and commitments of the parents. Thematically, the human cost involved in following passions and commitment may be at the core of all his movies.

Not all are masterpieces; Lumet made forty-four films and admits that some were just "gigs."[8] But an impressive number can be regarded as "classics." In an interview with Don Shewey in 1982 he recognized that the theme in his work of "men who summon the courage to challenge the system" reflected his own image as a New York filmmaker in an industry dominated by Hollywood.[9] The best of his movies are about personal struggles towards self-knowledge, struggles that always come with a "human cost." Among his "human" movies he has listed *Long Day's Journey Into Night* [for him this was the first], *The Hill*, *The Seagull*, *Dog Day Afternoon*, *Prince of the City*, and *Daniel*. A human movie, according to Lumet, doesn't sentimentalize, is honest, and "earns its own emotion."[10] He privileged acting, emphasized characters with back stories, and avoided spectacle, with the possible exception of *The Wiz*. Although he liked to tell his stories visually, he loved dialogue, as long as it was not used to give what he called "rubber-ducky" explanations. It was important to him to make movies that mat-tered. Even if he believed – and he did – that art ultimately does not have the power to change anything, his art, reflective of his con-science and craftsmanship, had something to say about human life in a system that is too often rigged against a smooth sail.

Biography

Born on June 25, 1924 in Philadelphia, Pennsylvania, Sidney Lumet was the son of Yiddish actor Baruch Lumet. He made his acting debut with his father at the age of five, and continued a career as a child actor, spending six years in the Yiddish theater. Lumet per-formed in fourteen Broadway plays, including as one of the Dead End Kids in *Dead End* in 1935. He briefly attended Columbia Uni-versity, then enlisted in the Army Signal Corps in 1941. After the War, he founded an off-Broadway acting group and began work in the new medium of television, learning his craft by directing a steady stream of close to two hundred and fifty live-action teleplays. He credits his early TV experience with teaching him about the importance of thorough preparation, how to shoot quickly and efficiently, how to edit in the camera, and about the emotional meaning of lenses. His first feature was *Twelve Angry Men* in 1957, and until his death in 2011, "Speedy Gonzales" as he was affectionately known, made almost a movie a year, forty-four in all. Although often nominated for an Academy Award, he did not receive the trophy until 2005 when he was given an Oscar for "Lifetime Achievement."

Notes

1 Rosenblum, Ralph and Robert Karen, *A Film Editor's Story: When the Shooting Stops ... the Cutting Begins.* New York: Penguin Books, 1980, p. 152.
2 Lumet, Sidney, *Making Movies.* New York: Vintage Press, 1998, p. 51.
3 Rudolph, Eric, "A Favorable Verdict for 24p." *American Cinematographer.* 84.4 (April 2001), p. 64.
4 Michel Climent, "A Conversation with Sidney Lumet," in Joanna Rapf (ed.) *Sidney Lumet: Interviews*, Jackson: University Press of Mississippi, 2005, p. 90.
5 Joanna Rapf, "An Interview with Sidney Lumet," in Joanna Rapf (ed.) *Sidney Lumet: Interviews*, Jackson: University Press of Mississippi, 2005, p. 193.
6 Margolick, David, "Again, Sidney Lumet Ponders Justice." *The New York Times*, Section 2, December 31, 1989, p. 9.
7 Rapf, p. 181.
8 Margolick, p. 9.
9 Rapf, pp. 117–18.
10 Ibid., p. 193.

Filmography

Crime Photographer (1951–52) TV series; 2 episodes
Danger (1950–55) TV series; 9 episodes
"Don Quixote" (1952) TV episode of *CBS Television Workshop*
You Are There (1953–57) TV series; 11 episodes
The Best of Broadway (1954–55) TV series; 3 episodes
The United States Steel Hour (1955) TV series; 2 episodes
"*In Nebraska*" (1955) TV episode of *Frontier*
The Elgin Hour (1955) TV series; 2 episodes
Goodyear Playhouse (1956) TV series; 2 episodes
The Alcoa Hour (1956) TV series; 5 episodes

Twelve Angry Men (1957)
Hans Brinker and the Silver Skates (1957) made-for-television movie
"School for Wives" (1957) TV episode of *Omnibus*
"The Changing Ways of Love" (1957) TV episode of *The Seven Lively Arts*
"*The Deaf Heart*" (1957) TV episode of *Studio One in Hollywood*
Mr. Broadway (1957) made-for-television movie
"Mr. Broadway" (1957) TV episode of *Producers' Showcase*
Stage Struck (1958)
The DuPont Show of the Month (1957–58) TV series; 2 episodes
Kraft Theatre (1958) TV series; 7 episodes
All the King's Men (1958) made-for-television movie
That Kind of Woman (1959)
The Fugitive Kind (1959)
Play of the Week (1960) TV series; 4 episodes
Rashomon (1960) made-for-television movie
The Iceman Cometh (1960) made-for-television movie
John Brown's Raid (1960) made-for-television movie
Sunday Showcase (1960) TV series; 2 episodes
Playhouse 90 (1960) TV series; 2 episodes
A View From The Bridge (1961)
Long Day's Journey Into Night (1962)
Fail Safe (1964)
The Pawnbroker (1965)
The Hill (1965)
The Group (1966)
The Deadly Affair (1967)
Bye Bye Braverman (1968)
The Seagull (1968)
The Appointment (1969)
King: A Filmed Record ... Montgomery to Memphis (1969)
The Last of the Mobile Hot-Shots (1970)
The Anderson Tapes (1971)
Child's Play (1972)
The Offence (1973)
Serpico (1974)
Lovin' Molly (1974)
Murder on the Orient Express (1974)
Dog Day Afternoon (1975)
Network (1976)
Equus (1977)
The Wiz (1978)

Just Tell Me What You Want (1980)
Prince of the City (1981)
Deathtrap (1982)
The Verdict (1982)
Daniel (1983)
Garbo Talks (1984)
Power (1986)
The Morning After (1986)
Running on Empty (1988)
Family Business (1989)
Q & A (1990)
A Stranger Among Us (1992)
Guilty as Sin (1993)
Night Falls on Manhattan (1997)
Critical Care (1997)
Gloria (1999)
100 Centre Street (2001–2) TV series; 9 episodes
Strip Search (2004) made-for-television movie
Rachel, quand du seigneur (2004) short
Find Me Guilty (2006)
Before the Devil Knows You're Dead (2007)

Further reading

Blake, Richard A. *Street Smart: The New York of Lumet, Allen, Scorcese, and Lee.* Lexington: The University Press of Kentucky, 2005.

Cunningham, Frank. *Sidney Lumet: Film and Literary Vision.* 2nd ed. Lexington: The University Press of Kentucky, 2001.

Georgakas, Dan and Leonard Quart. "Still 'Making Movies': An Interview with Sidney Lumet." *Cineaste.* 31.2 (Spring 2006): 6–13.

ALAN J. PAKULA

By Steven Doles

Alan J. Pakula directed a series of remarkable thrillers during the 1970s, as well as a number of other critical and popular successes in the 1980s and 1990s, but he is seldom thought of as one of the major auteurs of the New Hollywood era. It is not difficult to see why this would be the case, as the director's output is frequently disparate in style and genre and uneven in quality. As strong as many of his films are, Pakula often followed his major triumphs with unsuccessful projects. Perhaps more harmful to the filmmaker's reputation, his final films were a series of competently made but forgettable thrillers, which inevitably invite comparisons to his best work of the 1970s. The director worked in a number of other genres besides the thriller, but with the exception of the historical Holocaust drama *Sophie's Choice* (1982), this material has received relatively little attention. This essay will not dispel the association of Pakula with the thriller genre, for *Klute* (1971), *The Parallax View* (1974), and *All the President's Men* (1976) truly provoke critical thought and provide compelling entertainment. Their concerns and aesthetics are also, however, present in Pakula's other works. Featuring complex and enigmatic female leads who are observed by male protagonists in an attempt to comprehend them, Pakula's films often revolve around narrative patterns of investigation and flashback, calling attention to the different ways that the present relates to and contains its own past. They are organized around the opposition between physical traces such as photographs and recordings, and more evanescent and irrational remainders such as memory, fantasy, and dreams. Architecture and space are often important, as are the ways characters inhabit and move through them.

The films Pakula made from the late 1960s through the late 1970s respond to shifts in Hollywood production practices, censorship, and representational techniques, which formed the basis for the appearance of New Hollywood. Following from his work as the producer for several of Robert Mulligan's early films, including *To Kill a Mockingbird* (1962), Pakula produced many of his own films, developing long-lasting working relationships with actors such as Jane Fonda, cinematographers such as Gordon Willis and Sven Nykvist, and with composer Michael Small. This post-studio system approach to assembling the cast and crew of the films, however, makes it difficult to establish Pakula as a sole authoring presence; for instance, activist actors such as Fonda, whose IPC Productions hired Pakula for *Rollover* (1981), and Robert Redford, who instigated the production of *All the President's Men*, were largely understood to be the source of their respective film's political content.[1] The frankness about prostitution and sexuality in *Klute*, or the violence of *The Parallax View* register new freedoms from rigid production codes, due to the replacement of the PCA's strict censorship standards with the MPAA's more open age-based restrictions. Pakula's films also demonstrate the emphasis on fragmented, elliptical, and subjective narratives characteristic of New Hollywood filmmaking. This focus on narrative complexity remained part of the director's work even into the '80s and '90s, and is linked to his overriding concerns with psychology and power.

Pakula's career tracks the emergence of feminism as a popular movement, responding to its demand for greater agency for women in complex, sometimes anxious ways. Pakula's first film as director was 1969's *The Sterile Cuckoo*, starring Liza Minnelli as college freshman Pookie Adams. Pookie initiates a relationship with the taciturn Jerry (Wendell Burton), a freshman attending the college down the road from her own all-women school. Outside of a brief scene with Pookie's distant father at the start of the film and a handful of scenes with Jerry's roommate, the film has essentially no other characters besides Pookie and Jerry. It creates a strong impression of the pair's isolation through repeated use of long shots, which capture the couple alone together in fields, on beaches, and in interiors such as an empty chapel and a gymnasium. Although Minnelli does all the heavy acting, the film essentially recounts Jerry's experience of Pookie's neurotic personality. *The Sterile Cuckoo* resembles other narratives about disaffected youth from the late 1960s, such as Mike Nichols's *The Graduate* (1967), but the film ultimately offers less a critique of the outside world than an investigation of Pookie's psychology. Later films take on a more directly satirical (or at least pessimistic) dimension in depicting the social world, but uncovering the truth of the central woman's subjectivity remains a preoccupation for Pakula.

The Sterile Cuckoo's interest in setting a romance between a naïve man and a complicated, troubled woman in spaces of loneliness and solitude carries over into both *Klute* (1971) and *Love and Pain and the Whole Damn Thing* (1973). Although *Klute* can be read profitably as a member of the cycle of outsider-romance films to which *The Sterile Cuckoo* also belongs, its most important role in film history is as a key text in the emergence of neo-noir, and it thus participates in the New Hollywood trend of revising genres associated with Classical Hollywood. The film works to establish parallels between prostitute Bree and the figure of the femme fatale, as well as between private investigator Klute and the hard-boiled detective, while maintaining an ironic tension with these earlier character types and their up-to-date counterparts. Particularly significant is the prominence given to Fonda's voice as Bree; Bree's speaking voice recurs throughout in scenes of psychiatric confession and through media such as the telephone and tape recordings, all linked to the film's themes of power and control. For these reasons, *Klute* was a major text for feminist film studies, and debate centered on the question of how much the titular private investigator (Donald Sutherland) determines and controls the audience's perception of Bree. Critics pondered whether viewers get Bree in herself, as a completely individuated and self-possessed woman, or as men see and experience her.[2]

Such questions are equally relevant in many of Pakula's later films, especially *Sophie's Choice, Presumed Innocent* (1990), and *Consenting Adults* (1992). Each of these films focuses on women who obsess their male protagonists, and who have violence enacted upon them over the course of the narrative. According to Maggie Humm, "Pakula's misogyny is a constant and consistent pressure in all his films even in those he made later in the 1990s."[3] Yet there are moments in these films that open up the possibility of articulating a critique of misogyny, in part because they often foreground the limited perspectives of their male protagonists, and also because of the extradiegetic category of stardom, which can work to give greater agency to actresses like Fonda or Meryl Streep outside the film text even as the narrative works to contain their characters.

Pakula directed two films about divorce and remarriage, the low-key comedy *Starting Over* (1979), and *See You in the Morning* (1989), which has comic moments but treats the divorce narrative with more pathos than the earlier film. These films reconfigure some of Pakula's typical patterns of gender representation in that they allow for a greater interest in the unique psychology of their male protagonists, as well as demonstrate a less condemnatory attitude toward female characters. Peter Lev likens *Starting Over* to Robert Benton's *Kramer vs. Kramer* (1979), considering them both "male 'backlash' film[s] about the difficulties caused by feminism," yet notes that *Starting Over*'s depiction of the negotiations involved in achieving the new relationship by the end of the film "is not inconsistent with feminism."[4] The film recalls the isolation and loneliness of the characters of Pakula's earlier treatments of romance through its richly dark interiors photographed by Sven Nykvist, and through the setting of much of the film during snowy Boston winters. However, unlike *The Sterile Cuckoo, Klute*, or *Love and Pain and the Whole Damn Thing*, the film does not drive toward an uncovering of the desired woman's secret, but instead focuses on the couple's mutual problem as to how to create a space for their relationship while the past continually impinges upon the present. The partially autobiographical *See You in the Morning* resembles a cross between the divorce and remarriage subject matter of *Starting Over* and the narrative strategies of *Sophie's Choice*, employing a complex system of flashbacks and temporal disjunctions to examine the characters' experiences and feelings. Here the protagonist Larry (Jeff Bridges) is a psychologist, and he is both subject and object of the film's concern with memory and identity, as the film's narrative in part is driven by the question of whether or not he is "a shit," as one character refers to him early on.

Besides its central role in articulating Pakula's gender politics, *Klute* is also the first of three major conspiracy thrillers the director made during the 1970s, along with *The Parallax View* (1974) and *All the President's Men* (1976). What is perhaps most remarkable about these films is their increasingly complex vision of the operation and abuse of power. In *Klute*, the villain's abuse of power is understood primarily in individual terms of psychosexual deviancy. Peter Cable (Charles Cioffi) secretly records his sessions with prostitutes in order to revenge himself upon those he sees as humiliating him and robbing him of self-control. The film develops a visual analogy for Cable's isolated power by repeatedly associating him with heights and barriers: he gazes down on Bree through her sky-light, he stalks her from behind a fence, he closes off his office to outsiders with an automated sliding door painted with an image of the moon landing, he ascends above the city in a helicopter, and finally he crashes suicidally to his death through a high window.

Cable's is an individual psychopathology, but the assassins of *The Parallax View* are not fully individuated psychologically, and are instead depicted as embodying a general type. When reporter Joe Frady (Warren Beatty) poses as an applicant to the sinister company Parallax Corporation, he receives a psychological test to determine whether he fits the personality type of a hired assassin. Through increasingly ironic juxtapositions of text and still photographs, the visual test suggests a shared personal history for the killers of Parallax; traditional values of God, family, and home are denied to these men both by traumas at the national level (the Great Depression, lynchings, riots, Nixon) and the level of the family (editing between photographs creates an Oedipal triangle between an eroticized mother figure and a castrating father). As compensation for these traumas, the sequence offers a new image of the self as a being of penetrative violence and sexuality, an association it achieves by cutting between images of the comic book superhero Thor, bullets fired from a gun, and the prone bodies of nude women. The film as a whole expresses the confusion and fallout over the political assassinations of the 1960s, yet this sequence stands out as a particularly vivid encapsulation of the experience of historical traumas that marked the 1970s. At the end of the film, Frady is killed for his attempt at exposing Parallax, and in his death becomes a scapegoat, further obscuring the truth of the conspiracy he attempted to uncover. In interviews about the film, Pakula discussed the ending as representing a loss of faith in the ideal of the American hero provided by earlier Hollywood representations, saying, "We can't believe in him anymore."[5]

In contrast, *All the President's Men* offers faith in the trace, in the way that every act leaves its mark. The Nixon administration cannot achieve its criminal ends without generating an enormous paper trail, nor without relying on the work of any number of bureaucrats spread throughout Washington D.C. and the wider nation. The city thus becomes a surface on which the conspiracy has inscribed its power, yet such an inscription also serves as a track to be followed by Woodward and Bernstein (Robert Redford and Dustin Hoffman). Heights here tend to be aligned with the protagonists, rather than with the villains. The well-known scene in the Library of Congress reading room begins with an overhead shot of thousands of bundled records stacked on a table. In the next shot, Woodward and Bernstein have evidently been rifling through the records for some time, as the papers lie in different piles on the table, with rubber bands scattered amongst them. The camera continuously rises upward across two dissolves until it is looking down at the reporters from the ceiling high above. From this height the walkways in the reading room become lines heading off in every direction, suggestive of the connections that the pair, dead center here in the heart of the city, will make through their efforts.

According to biographer Brown, Pakula thought of *All the President's Men* as a conscious effort at depicting the "resurrection of the hero" he had killed off with *The Parallax View*.[6] This project continues in Pakula's other two films with Fonda, *Comes a Horseman* (1978) and *Rollover* (1981). The former is a late-era Western with conspiracy elements, set in the 1940s as oil-drilling displaces cattle ranching as a more profitable, more destructive use of the land. Ella Connors (Jane Fonda) is a rancher who resists the attempt of a more powerful land owner, J. W. Ewing (Jason Robards), to run her off the land. *Rollover* (1981) is another conspiracy thriller, depicting a scheme by wealthy (and stereotyped) Arab investors to secretly remove their money from American banks, aided by an evil banker (Hume Cronyn), with Fonda and her good banker lover (Kris Kristofferson) uncovering the plan. Across *All the President's Men, Comes a Horseman,* and *Rollover,* a common pattern of narrative resolution emerges: in each film the protagonists confront a catastrophe at the conclusion, demonstrating their moral fortitude by carrying on anyway. In each film the catastrophe grows in size, from the personal and professional embarrassment of Woodward and Bernstein at the end of *All the President's Men,* to the burning of the family farm in *Comes a Horseman*, and finally to the collapse of the global economy in *Rollover*.

Pakula, like other New Hollywood directors, faced difficulties in funding and distribution in the 1980s. After a decade of uneven and generically disparate projects, the director's output in the 1990s again became coherent and largely consistent in quality. *Presumed Innocent* was followed by *Consenting Adults*, *The Pelican Brief* (1993), and *The Devil's Own* (1997), all of which demonstrate that Pakula was working comfortably within different subgenres of the thriller at a time in which the genre was again highly visible. *The Pelican Brief* even calls attention to the film's connections to the director's earlier work in its final scene, as a TV announcer compares Julia Roberts's character Darby Shaw to the Watergate scandal's Deep Throat, for whom *All the President's Men* created the definitive visual representation. Yet the comparison is not necessarily to *The Pelican Brief*'s credit, as the thrillers of this decade are less surprising and audacious than those of the 1970s. However, reading them in light of the director's earlier work often reveals intriguing connections to Pakula's long-standing obsessions. *Presumed Innocent*, for instance, offers perhaps the bleakest image of the process of investigation and its relation to power in the filmmaker's entire body of work. Rusty Sabich (Harrison Ford) is a prosecutor tasked with leading an investigation into the murder of his colleague, Carolyn Polhemus (Greta Scacchi), with whom he had been having an affair, but is soon himself charged with her murder. Sabich is innocent, and the legal case works to exonerate him of the murder, but only because of a series of errors, corruption, and deliberate subterfuge on the part of all parties involved in the investigation and trial. Worse still, by the end of the film Sabich himself becomes complicit in undermining the operation of justice by suppressing evidence. Unlike *The Parallax View*, in which a massive conspiracy completely overrides the ability of individual heroes to establish the truth, and unlike *All the President's Men*, with its optimistic suggestion that journalism can function as a check on power, *Presumed Innocent* pessimistically challenges the legitimacy of the justice system as a truth-finding institution through a focus on small-scale, everyday forms of corruption.

Biography

Alan Jay Pakula was born on April 7, 1928. Early in his career he produced a number of films directed by Robert Mulligan, including *To Kill a Mockingbird* (1962). Pakula began directing his own films in 1969, ultimately directing sixteen films in total. He died on November 19, 1998, following a road accident.

Notes

1 See Jared Brown's biography of the director (*Alan J Pakula: His Films and His Life*, New York: Back Stage Books, 2005) for highly detailed accounts of the production contexts of Pakula's films.
2 For two major statements of different positions on *Klute*, see Diane Giddis, "The Divided Woman: Bree Daniel in *Klute*" in Bill Nichols (ed.) *Movies and Methods: Volume I*, Berkeley: University of California Press, 1976, pp. 194–201, and Christine Gledhill, "*Klute 2*: Feminism and *Klute*," in E. Ann Kaplan (ed.) *Women in Film Noir*, London: BFI, 1998, pp. 99–114.
3 Maggie Humm, "Sight and Sound: Pornography, The Gaze, *Klute* and *Variety*," in *Feminism and Film*, Bloomington: Indiana University Press, 1997, p. 50.
4 Peter Lev, *American Films of the 70s: Conflicting Visions*, Austin: University of Texas Press, 2000, pp. 152–53.
5 Quoted in Brown, p. 135.
6 Brown, pp. 197–98.

Filmography

The Sterile Cuckoo (1969)
Klute (1971)
Love and Pain and the Whole Damn Thing (1973)
The Parallax View (1974)
All the President's Men (1976)
Comes a Horseman (1978)
Starting Over (1979)
Rollover (1981)
Sophie's Choice (1982)
Dream Lover (1986)
Orphans (1987)
See You in the Morning (1989)
Presumed Innocent (1990)
Consenting Adults (1992)
The Pelican Brief (1993)
The Devil's Own (1997)

Further reading

Brown, Jared. *Alan J. Pakula: His Films and His Life*. New York: Back Stage Books, 2005.
Kerpius, Pamela L. "'Zero Percent Chance of Rain': The Watergate History and *All the President's Men*." *Violating Time: History, Memory,*

and Nostalgia in Cinema. (ed.) Christina Lee. New York: Continuum, 40–56.

Narine, Neil. "Film Sound and American Cultural Memory: Resounding Trauma in *Sophie's Choice.*" *Memory Studies* 3.1 (2010): 33–54.

Palmer, James W. and Michael M. Riley. "America's Conspiracy Syndrome: From Capra to Pakula." *Studies in the Humanities* 8.2 (March 1981): 21–27.

SAM PECKINPAH

By Zoran Samardzija

Not many directors have inspired sketches on *Monty Python's Flying Circus* but by the time "Sam Peckinpah's Salad Days" aired in 1972 – presented as footage from his supposed adaptation of the musical in which upper-class picnickers are dismembered as blood spurts everywhere – the image of Peckipah as purveyor of excessive violence was well established even in London. His film *Straw Dogs* (1971) was so controversial that it received an X certificate by the British Board of Film Censors and was later banned from home video release. Contrary to this popular image, however, Peckinpah's films are not obsessed with violence. Rather, the overarching theme of his films is a tragic sense of outmodedness. This is especially true of his Westerns which, alongside the works of John Ford and Anthony Mann, represent the creative high point of the genre in post-WWII American cinema. While Westerns are most frequently set in the years surrounding the American Civil War, Peckinpah's four major Westerns—*Ride the High Country* (1962), *The Wild Bunch* (1969), *The Ballad of Cable Hogue* (1970), and *Pat Garret and Billy the Kid* (1973) take place in the late nineteenth and early twentieth centuries. This allows him to dramatize protagonists who have the misfortune of living past their time and who must struggle to maintain a personal code of behavior that is no longer relevant. For Peckinpah, the idealized frontier depicted in the classical Western has been destroyed by capitalist progress and greed and his characters often meet violent fates as a result.

Released the same year as John Ford's superb *The Man Who Shot Liberty Valance*, Peckinpah's second feature, *Ride the High Country* advances the "death of the West" theme hinted at in his debut, *The Deadly Companions* (1961). Like *Liberty Valance*, Peckinpah's film also functions as a meta-commentary on the Western genre and its foundational myths, though it differs considerably in affect. As the famously cynical dialogue from Ford's film makes clear ("when the legend becomes fact, print the legend") the myth of the frontier is already founded upon lies and distortions of facts. Peckinpah, however, is much more ambivalent. He embraces the idea of the frontier while at the same time mourns its passing. *Ride the High Country* efficiently visualizes this idea of outmodedness in its first fifteen minutes, which presents practically all the ideas Peckinpah will develop throughout his career. His casting of the aging Joel McCrea and Randolph Scott, who audiences would have recognized as icons of B-Westerns from the 1940s and 1950s, gives the film a strong sense of mortality instead of the heroics more commonly associated with the Western. For example, Peckinpah immediately upends the iconography of the heroic cowboy riding into a new town by highlighting the aging and awkwardness of McCrea. His character, Steve Judd, can't hear well and thinks the crowds of people are greeting him by waving. In reality, they are trying to get him off the street before a horse and camel race begins—a race which we subsequently learn is rigged. Steve is told he is "in the way" and, in a scene that foreshadows the death of Cable Hogue in the *The Ballad of Cable Hogue*, he is referred to as an "old-timer" by the police-officer who moves him out of the way of an oncoming automobile.

Steve has arrived in town so he can work for a bank, protecting its gold shipment, which is hardly a heroic job for a former marshal. As the banker who hires him explains, "The days of the forty-niners are past and the days of the steady businessmen have arrived." This dialogue summarizes Peckinpah's vision of the Western. The frontier has been colonized by business interests, and there is no more freedom for self-discovery. In other words, the age of the cowboy has given way to the age of the corporation and Peckinpah's protagonists face the choice of either dying or selling out to big business. This stark choice is dramatized in all his Westerns. In *The Wild Bunch*, Robert Ryan's character, Deke Thorton, is released from prison and hired by the railroad to find his former gang and its leader Pike Bishop, only to declare to his incompetent posse that, "We're after men, and I wish to God I was with them." Similarly, the entire plot of *Pat Garret and Billy the Kid* hinges on the fact that Pat Garret works for corrupt land speculators to capture his former friend.

This theme of friends who respond differently to their outmodedness, often on opposite sides of the law, is introduced in *Ride the High Country* through the relationship between Steve Judd and Randolph Scott's character, Gil Westrum, who was his former deputy. Gil has adapted to the death of the frontier by becoming a performer and a carny. He is introduced as operating a shooting booth at a sideshow while dressed like Buffalo Bill. He and his partner agree to accompany Steve on his bank job with the ultimate plan of robbing all the gold with or without Steve's help. Steve, though, can't be corrupted and even tries arresting Gil once he discovers his deception. Before the conflict between Steve and Gil can resolve, however, Steve is mortally wounded in a gunfight. Before dying Steve tells Gil he must "go it alone" and that he knew Gil still had a code of ethics intact even if Gil himself had forgotten it. The film ends with Steve dying in the extreme foreground of the last shot. His historical moment has past.

Peckinpah's next film was the financially and artistically unsuccessful *Major Dundee* (1965). It was the first of many Peckinpah projects to experience production difficulties and to be edited against his wishes by producers. With the exception of the excellent television movie, *Noon Wine* (1966), it would be four years before Peckinpah would direct again. While his *Major Dundee* film remains flawed even in its restored longer cut, it does introduce the hyper-masculinity and violence that flourishes in his subsequent Westerns. In *The Wild Bunch*, for example, there is no trace of the innocent morality Steve Judd expresses in *Ride in the High Country*. The "last cowboys" in *The Wild Bunch* are thieves whose masculine code of ethics is preferable only to the utter crassness exhibited by the railroad company, its deputies, or the Mexican warlord Mapache whom they encounter. As Pike Bishop declares, "When you side with a man, you stay with him! And if you can't do that, you're like some animal, you're finished!"

Peckinpah expresses cynicism about "moral progress"—particularly the kind supposed brought by corporations—through violent imagery and chaotic disruptions of the classical continuity of Hollywood film style. On their way to the botched robbery at the railroad office, Pike's gang passes a group of children who are grinning as they torture small scorpions by placing them in swarms of ants. Later the children set both the scorpions and ants on fire. The children's sadism foreshadows the first violent gunfight, which erupts once the men realize they are cornered by the railroad and its hired posse. Visually, the nearly eight-minute gunfight marks the birth of the recognizable Peckinpah style, which was subsequently parodied in the infamous *Monty Python* sketch. To emphasize the violence, he employs rapid cuts, varying frame-speeds, aggressive zooms, and oblique camera angles. While such stylistic gestures have been integrated into the mainstream conventions of action films, Peckinpah's visual chaos was disconcerting when it arrived on screens in 1969, amplifying the graphic violence shown in Arthur Penn's *Bonnie and Clyde* (1967) to much greater extremes.

The connection between technological advancement and increased violence is reinforced in the middle of the film when the bunch escapes to Mexico while pursued by Deke Thorton and his makeshift posse. In a satirical gesture, Peckinpah introduces the warlord, Mapache, riding in an automobile. Pike explains to his gang, who are amazed by the sight, that he has seen one before and they even have ones with "motors and wings" that will be used in the war. His comment places the setting of *The Wild Bunch* against the backdrop of World War I, which is very belated for a Western. The First World War marks a historical turning point for the efficiency of mass slaughter through technology like the machine-gun, which figures heavily in the remainder of the film's plot. Forced to work for Mapache, the bunch robs an army train carrying weapons including a machine gun. Angel, the only Mexican working with Pike, convinces the others to keep a crate of rifles for his village. Mapache learns of the double-cross and captures and tortures Angel. Reluctant at first, the group goes on a suicide mission to rescue Angel, echoing Pike's earlier comment that "When you side with a man, you stay with him!" A manic gun-fight erupts with the bunch gaining control of the machine-gun on the turret. This eight-minute sequence, arguably the most formally sophisticated of Peckinpah's career, remains one of the bloodiest in cinema history with imdb.com estimating the death count at 112. The sequence also returns full circle to the skepticism about moral progress expressed by the earlier scene with the children: it is a menacing child with a rifle, shown in medium close-up, who shoots Pike. The film ends with Deke Thorton surveying the wreckage of the battle and joining forces with a posse of Mexican rebels, presumably to drift through the Mexican Revolution along with them.

Peckinpah's subsequent Westerns, *The Ballad of Cable Hogue* and *Pat Garret and Billy the Kid*, also engage with themes of outmodedness and the death of the frontier but in surprisingly different tones. *Cable Hogue* contains broad comedy, musical numbers, self-conscious theatricality, and even cartoonish sped-up action. It may seem nothing like a Peckinpah film but, as David Weddle writes in his biography, Peckinpah "frequently referred to it as his favorite film, and it's easy to see why, for it exposes the tender inner core of this turbulent, often misunderstood artist."[1] *Cable Hogue* is certainly a more "tender" iteration of the death of the frontier theme, told from the perspective of a likeable protagonist. Left to die in the desert by former partners, Cable Hogue discovers water in between two towns. He stakes a claim for a small plot of land that contains the water and turns it into a successful business, an oasis for stage-coaches. It does not take long, though, for Hogue to become outmoded. Three years after working at the Oasis and plotting his revenge against his former partners, one day Hogue sees an automobile, Peckinpah's recurring symbol of progress, driving through the desert with no need to stop on its journey between towns. Realizing his time has passed, he plans to abandon his oasis to meet up with his girlfriend Hildy. Before he can do so, Hildy arrives on another automobile, which later runs over Hogue after its brakes fail. Hogue soon dies and the metaphor could not be blunter: he is killed by progress.

Pat Garret and Billy the Kid is Peckinpah's final Western. Much has been written about its troubled production history and its three different edits. In terms of its dramatization of the death of the frontier, however, it is Peckinpah's most melancholy film. Aided by Bob Dylan's depressed score, its tone is persistently mournful and its eruptions of violence even lack the visual exhilaration exhibited in *The Wild Bunch*. The "days of the steady businessmen" have become the age of corrupt oligarchs like the Santa-Fe Ring, land speculators amassing capital. Pat Garret agrees to capture Billy the Kid for them, justifying his sell-out by claiming he has arrived at an age where he needs stability. The central conflict in the film, between acquiescing to capital or maintaining one's individuality and freedom, is expressed in a crucial bit of a dialogue:

> Billy the Kid: Sheriff Pat Garrett. Sold out to the Santa Fe ring. How does it feel?
> Pat Garrett: It feels like times have changed.
> Billy the Kid: Times, maybe. Not me.

Billy is quite literally *the last cowboy*, the last individual resisting corporate fraudulence. When Garret catches and kills Billy at the end of the film, he existentially splinters, as suggested by the iconic image of shooting his own reflection in the mirror. More so than that, his sell-out and murder of Billy is an error of mythological proportions. It marks the historical moment when the colonization of the frontier by capitalism becomes irreversible. In the film's quick postscript set several decades later, Garret himself is killed by henchmen of the Santa-Fe Ring, undercutting the so-called stability he thought he was getting by working for the group in the first place.

Peckinpah's next film, *Bring Me the Head of Alfredo Garcia* (1974) is his greatest feature outside of the Western genre and his last masterpiece before his alcoholism and drug-addiction made him increasingly unstable and unable to find projects. His war-film, *Cross of Iron* (1977) has some merits, but his last four features are mostly formally awkward and thematically underdeveloped. With the exception of the underrated rodeo film *Junior Bonner* (1972), *Alfredo Garcia* is his one film set in the modern era that successfully engages with his theme of outmodedness. His two other modern-era films, in contrast, reveal the limitations of Peckinpah's romantic vision. Separated from the frontier, his misogyny and cruelty come to the forefront in *Straw Dogs* and the popular, *The Getaway* (1972), both of which lack the subtly and melancholy of earlier works. The latter never amounts to more than a technically proficient exercise in genre filmmaking that celebrates violence. *Straw Dogs*, on the other hand, regresses into nihilism. For example, the rape scene in the controversial film is made all the more horrific by the implication that Susan George's character, Amy, "enjoys" her rape by a former lover before trying to resist a second violation by one of his friends. Moreover, Dustin Hoffman's transformation from arrogant intellectual to brutal sadist willing to protect his home at all costs plays more like an expression of the futility of civilization itself than a meaningful statement against violence.

Despite its morbid premise, *Alfredo Garcia* is more emotionally sophisticated than the aforementioned films and is a genuine cry against nihilism and violence. At first Benny (Warren Oates) agrees to bring the head of Alfredo Garcia for a substantial reward to the patriarchal "El Jefe," whose daughter Garcia impregnated. Benny justifies his crass mission as the only way he and his fiancée, Elita, can get a fresh start in life. When Elita objects to his plan to desecrate the grave of Alfredo Garcia and decapitate his corpse, Benny violently declares to her that "there is nothing sacred about a hole in the ground or a man that's in it." However, he quickly learns otherwise when Elita is killed by men also seeking the head of Alfredo Garcia. After retrieving it from them, Benny develops a bizarre relationship with Garcia's head, which he keeps in a cloth sack with ice. He is determined to understand why it has sparked so much violence and mayhem. When he brings the head to El Jefe, Benny is angered that El Jefe no longer seems to care and instead hypocritically embraces his grandchild. The violence and murder have been entirely purposeless. Benny kills "El Jefe" and his guards – repeatedly shouting "no" as if trying to reject the corrupt value system of the world around him – before being gunned down by numerous men with rifles and automatic weapons. The film's final image is an extreme close-up of the barrel of gun, which serves as a perfect summation of the world-view depicted in Peckinpah's best films: men who try to maintain a code of ethics and reject the world around them are violently destroyed.

Therein lies Peckinpah's importance to American cinema. His formal achievements may have been integrated into the aesthetics of current action cinema, but this cinema nevertheless lacks the moral seriousness of Peckinpah's melancholy and fatalistic vision. He began his career at a moment of great uncertainty in Hollywood, the decade between the exhaustion of the classic era of 1930–60 and the emergence of New Hollywood in 1967 after the success of films like *The Graduate* (1967) and *Bonnie and Clyde* temporarily led to more experimental aesthetics. Peckinpah helped turn the classic genre of the Western away from the transcendent heroics of the frontier toward a deep reflection of the values we lose when we despairingly accept there are no alternatives to progress and "the days of the steady businessmen" in American life.

Biography

Samuel Peckinpah was born in 1925 in California. After an early career in theater and television, he began directing Westerns. His breakthrough film was *The Wild Bunch* in 1969, which led to a brief but intense career in Hollywood. His increasing alcoholism, drug abuse, and antagonisms with studios, made it difficult for him to make films after 1975. He died of heart failure in 1984.

Notes

1 David Weddle. *"If They Move … Kill 'Em!:" The Life and Times of Sam Peckinpah*. New York: Grove Press, 1994, p. 388.

Filmography

The Deadly Companions (1961)
Ride the High Country (1962)
Major Dundee (1965)
Noon Wine (1966) made-for-television movie
The Wild Bunch (1969)
The Ballad of Cable Hogue (1970)
Straw Dogs (1971)
Junior Bonner (1972)

The Getaway (1972)
Pat Garret and Billy the Kid (1973)
Bring Me the Head of Alfredo Garcia (1974)
The Killer Elite (1975)
Cross of Iron (UK/West Germany, 1977)
Convoy (1978)
The Osterman Weekend (1983)

Further reading

Bliss, Michael, ed. *Peckinpah Today: New Essays on the Films of Sam Peckinpah.* Jackson: University Press of Mississippi, 2012.
Dukore, Bernard F. *Sam Peckinpah's Feature Films.* Urbana-Champaign: University of Illinois Press, 1999.
Engle, Leonard, ed. *Sam Peckinpah's West: New Perspectives.* Salt Lake City: University of Utah Press, 2003.
Hayes, Kevin J., ed. *Sam Peckinpah Interviews.* Jackson: University Press of Mississippi, 2008. Conversations with Filmmakers Ser.
Prince, Stephen. *Sam Peckinpah and the Rise of Ultraviolent Movies.* Austin: University of Texas Press, 1998.
——, ed. *Sam Peckinpah's The Wild Bunch.* Cambridge: Cambridge University Press, 1998. Cambridge Film Handbooks.
Seydor, Paul, *Peckinpah: The Western Films A Reconsideration.* Urbana-Champaign: University of Illinois Press, 1999.
Simmons, Garner. *Peckinpah: A Portrait in Montage.* 3rd ed. New York: Limelight Editions, 2004.
Simons, John L. and Robert Merrill. *Peckinpah's Tragic Westerns: A Critical Study.* Jefferson, North Carolina: McFarland, 2011.

ARTHUR PENN

By Oliver Gruner

Nearly fifty years after it first appeared on cinema screens, *Bonnie and Clyde* (1967), Arthur Penn's elegy to the infamous outlaw couple, maintains an iconic place in American film history. Popular accounts of the late 1960s and early 1970s 'Hollywood Renaissance' often suggest that this film helped usher in a new era of cutting-edge auteur cinema. On the back of *Bonnie and Clyde*'s success, so the story goes, studio executives desperate to tap the youth market handed over unprecedented creative control to directors such as Mike Nichols, Francis Ford

Coppola, Martin Scorsese and Robert Altman. Experimenting with innovative formal techniques and explicit thematic content, these directors have since come to symbolise Hollywood's last golden age – a final flash of inspiration before *Jaws* (1975) and *Star Wars* (1977) set the industry on a conservative path once more.[1] Within this celebratory narrative (which, as several film historians have observed, greatly oversimplifies post-World War II American film production[2]), Penn is both prophet and proponent of a countercultural sensibility sweeping the movies in the late 1960s.

To view Arthur Penn as simply a director of the Hollywood Renaissance is nevertheless to elide the continuities present across his back catalogue, and its relationship to broader filmmaking trends. Long before any notion of a 'Renaissance' had emerged, the critic Robin Wood observed that 'there is nothing in *Bonnie and Clyde*, stylistically, technically, thematically, which was not already implicit' in Penn's first feature, 1958's *The Left Handed Gun*.[3] Changing norms regarding censorship and the impact of sixties' political and social movements might have brought certain concerns further to the surface, but the director's films speak more to the tensions and contradictions pervading cinema in the post-war years than any radical break circa 1967. What then makes a 'Penn' film? Penn's collaborations with screenwriters Robert Benton and David Newman (*Bonnie and Clyde*) and William Gibson (*The Miracle Worker*), actor/producer Warren Beatty (*Bonnie and Clyde, Mickey One*) and editor Dede Allen (six films, from *Bonnie and Clyde* to *The Missouri Breaks*) have been discussed in some detail.[4] Nevertheless, as Wood notes, 'Penn's films reveal a strikingly consistent personality.'[5] Combining social comment and a reflection on the pervasiveness of national myths, they intersected and engaged with a period of transformation in Hollywood, and in post-World War II America more generally.

Penn's directorial debut *The Left Handed Gun* introduces a man by the name of William Bonney, known in popular legend as Billy the Kid (played here by Paul Newman), staggering through the New Mexico prairies. This was not the first time that Penn and Newman collaborated on a project. As did a number of New Hollywood directors (William Friedkin, for instance), Penn began his career in television. Penn directed Newman in the 1956 television drama *The Battler*, which told the story of a boxer's physical and mental decline. *The Left Handed Gun* similarly followed the rise and demise of a hero. Incorporating generic elements associated with the melodrama and the juvenile delinquency film, it endeavours both to offer a psychological explanation for Billy's violent awakening, and, as Robert Kolker notes, to scrutinise 'the myth of the hero itself'.[6]

Allusions to Freud litter *The Left Handed Gun*, a film in which Billy's actions are influenced by failed relationships with paternal surrogates. Billy's short-lived tutelage under Mr. Tunstall (Colin Keith-Johnston) begins the film's exploration of father-son conflicts. Tunstall espouses the virtues of unarmed diplomacy and reads Billy excerpts from the Bible. Sweeping long shots of the prairies provide visual accompaniment, heightening the sense that this is a moment of possibility in Billy's life. Billy is conceived here as an unwilling outlaw; had he just enjoyed the right paternal guidance, the film implies, he would never have turned out the way he did. If family relationships give *The Left Handed Gun* a powerful narrative thrust, so too does the emphasis on Wild West mythology. Tunstall's death at the hands of four townsfolk sets Billy on a vengeful path. A particularly striking moment of formal inventiveness occurs as he plots to kill his old mentor's murderers. Standing by the window of his hotel room, Billy etches out his plans on the pane. This action instigates a dissolve so slow that the protagonist can be seen for several seconds both in the hotel room and down in the street below where he is about to execute two of the culprits. Billy temporarily becomes witness to, and agent in, these slayings, as if he is having an out-of-body experience. Figuratively speaking, he is, for now 'William Bonney' – that is, the youth still visible in the hotel room – can do little more than look on as his alter ego, Billy the Kid, is born in a hail of bullets on Main Street. Throughout, Billy is nourished by his own mythic status. Whether posing for a photograph, or being informed of his notoriety in the East, Billy's moments of lionisation inevitably precede acts of violence. Billy murders a man just after his picture is taken; he shoots his way out of jail after reading newspaper reports of his exploits. He is finally betrayed when Moultrie (Hurd Hatfield) announces that Billy is 'not like the books'. The 'death' of the legend leads to the literal death of the man.

Billy is clearly a precursor to the protagonists of *Bonnie and Clyde*. Like Billy, Clyde Barrow (Warren Beatty) is energised by hearing tales of his own renown. Impotent for much of the film, Clyde has his virility restored after hearing Bonnie (Faye Dunaway) read her poem about 'Bonnie and Clyde'. 'You made me somebody they're gonna remember,' gushes Clyde, before the relationship is consummated. If the sun is at last shining on the outlaws' sexual relationship, such an achievement has come at the expense of their criminal career, for, as the film's remainder attests, death is now imminent. Their accomplice's father, Ivan Moss (Dub Taylor), is unimpressed by Bonnie and Clyde's infamy ('shoot, they ain't nothing but a couple of kids'), and sees to it that the police are informed of the outlaws' whereabouts.

Ivan's sneering treatment of Bonnie and Clyde mirrors that of another Penn protagonist, David Braxton (John McLiam) in 1976's *The Missouri Breaks*. This, the last of Penn's three revisionist Westerns, presents Braxton as a heartless cynic, interested only in financial gain. Near the beginning of the film, he presides over a mock trial in which a man is charged with a catalogue of outlaw offences that are so predictable as to be cliché. Braxton asks if the defendant has any last words. 'We would prefer that it be something colourful, life on the frontier being what it is,' he adds. The defendant obligingly reels off a list of killing, robbing, whoring and gambling escapades and demands that he be forever remembered as 'The Lonesome Kid'. Those present greet this declaration with much hilarity. There is little space for mythology in this film; it is, rather, about the corruption lurking behind the Wild West's romantic exterior.

Penn's films celebrate mythic figures in whom he can invest a countercultural sensibility. In *Little Big Man* (1970), audiences are encouraged to feel well disposed toward Wild Bill Hickok and lament his death, while laughing at the deconstruction of General George Custer's 'heroic' image. Hickok has a rebel status favourable to 1970s counterculture values; Custer is on the side of the establishment – a stand-in for US generals sending young men to their deaths in Vietnam. But such myths must at last be revealed for what they are, imaginative constructions, and eventually killed off. In the 1975 neo-noir *Night Moves* private detective Harry Moseby (Gene Hackman) is mockingly compared to his hard-boiled cinematic precursors. 'Come on, take a swing at me, Harry, the way Sam Spade would,' says the man with whom Moseby's wife is having an affair. As the film unravels it becomes clear that Moseby is no Sam Spade. At the film's end he helplessly gazes through the glass bottom of a boat as the man he thought was his friend, but who turns out to have been a criminal, drowns beneath him. Moseby's 'impotence' becomes here a metaphor for the impotence of the mythic American hero.

Directing thirteen features over thirty-one years (*The Left Handed Gun* to 1989's *Penn and Teller Get Killed*), Penn was not prolific. Four years elapsed between his first film and 1962's *The Miracle Worker*. Between 1958 and 1962, however, Penn did successfully direct stage shows such as *Two for the Seesaw*, *Toys in the Attic*, and *The Miracle Worker*. A dramatic rendition of the relationship between Helen Keller, a deaf and blind girl, and her teacher, Annie Sullivan, the film adaptation of *The Miracle Worker* was Penn's first critical and commercial success in Hollywood (*The Left Handed Gun* had received unfavourable reviews in the US, but was much admired by French critic-directors François Truffaut and Jean-Luc Godard). If *The Left Handed Gun* took a scalpel to Wild West mythology, *The Miracle Worker* does something similar to the image of a 'civilised South'. At a time when national attention was being drawn to prejudice and inequality in the Deep South (and civil rights activism in this part of the country), *The Miracle Worker* provides an apt appraisal of the contradictions that lay at the heart of a well-to-do southern family. Here this condemnation is not related to racism.[7] *The Miracle Worker* is, however, an attempt to disrupt the image of serene family life. While courtesy is preached at the Keller family dinner table, Helen (Patty Duke) is treated little better than an animal. She is allowed to eat with her hands and run around in rags, as if civilising her would be a futile endeavour. Only Sullivan (Anne Bancroft), the Irish woman from Boston, treats Helen with the respect she deserves. Considered ill-mannered by Captain Keller (Victor Jory), Sullivan nevertheless proves the most sympathetic to Helen's plight. She rescues the young girl from complete dehumanisation, teaching her the ability to communicate and to think for herself.

If calm comes at last for the Keller family, the southern town portrayed in *The Chase* (1966), is not so fortunate. *The Chase* was released one year after another commercial failure for Penn: *Mickey One*. The latter's Kafkaesque plot about a hunted man unsure what he has done wrong, combined with obscure visual motifs and unconventional form, make *Mickey One* the most difficult of Penn films to understand and, indeed, enjoy. Many critics saw it as a failed attempt at imitating the French New Wave. *The Chase*, on the other hand, was a star-studded studio production. Bubber Reeves (Robert Redford) escapes from prison and finds himself wanted for a murder he did not commit. While Bubber hides in the shadows, the town of Tarle awaits his expected arrival by descending into chaos. Combining elements familiar to oil-town melodramas of the 1950s like *Written on the Wind* and *Giant* – strained relationships between wealthy fathers and sons, tensions between urban and agrarian lifestyles – as well as themes that would become increasingly familiar in late 1960s and 1970s cinema such as the sexual revolution and vigilantism, *The Chase* incorporates a range of social, psychological and countercultural concerns.

Watching the brutal beating of Sheriff Calder (Marlon Brando) at the hands of three townsfolk, it is clear that *Bonnie and Clyde* was not the first instance of Penn 'overturn[ing] decades of polite bloodless movie violence in American cinema'.[8] By this stage in *The Chase*, the town is moving toward self-destruction. Paranoia and gossiping pervade the town, as does casual racism – Lester (Joel Fluellen) is nearly killed, for instance, for daring to visit a white woman's house after dark. The film likewise narrates the split between a repressed older generation and a sexually liberated trio of youngsters, Bubber, his wife Anna Reeves (Jane Fonda) and her lover Jake Rogers (James Fox), and shows greed permeating the town's business affairs. With Calder battered to a pulp, the last semblances of law and order seem to have evaporated. The apocalyptic concluding section of the film sees Bubber safely apprehended by Calder. Yet, in a reference to the assassination of Lee Harvey Oswald (just as, in his next film Penn would quote the Kennedy assassination during Clyde's death throes), Bubber is shot in the stomach outside the police station. The intolerance existing in this town cannot, it seems, be contained by anything as old fashioned as the law. Bubber and Jake end the film dead, and Anna winds up a desolate shell of a woman. The final scene of her leaving the Rogers mansion acts as her symbolic rejection of everything the town represents. Like Moseby at the end of *Night Moves*, or the complicated zoom/pan that provides a sense of stasis at the end of *Alice's Restaurant*, a feeling of helplessness concludes *The Chase*. Perhaps this sensibility serves as an apt metaphor for a filmmaker whose films always trod a contradictory path between emotional excitement and pessimism. Film, in the hands of Arthur Penn, was a window through which to experience and empathise with social and political transformation (from the 1950s onward), but one which ends up offering a view of America, as *The Left Handed Gun* put it (quoting the Bible), 'through a glass darkly'.

Biography

Arthur Penn was born in 1922. After a successful 1950s career in television – where he directed for prestige drama series such as *Philco Playhouse* and *Playhouse 90* – he made his first feature film, *The Left Handed Gun,* in 1958. Penn died in 2010.

Notes

1 See, for example, Peter Biskind, *Easy Riders, Raging Bulls: How the Sex 'n' Drugs 'n' Rock 'n' Roll Generation Saved Hollywood*, London: Bloomsbury, 1998.

2 Steve Neale, '"The Last Good Time We Ever Had?" Revising the Hollywood Renaissance', in Linda Ruth Williams and Michael Hammond (eds) *Contemporary American Cinema*, Maidenhead, Open University Press, 2006, pp. 90–108; Peter Krämer, *The New Hollywood: From Bonnie and Clyde to Star Wars*, London: Wallflower, 2005.

3 Robin Wood, *Arthur Penn*, London: Studio Vista, 1967, p. 72.

4 Mark Harris, *Scenes from a Revolution: The Birth of the New Hollywood*, Edinburgh: Canongate, 2009; Nat Segalhoff, *Arthur Penn: American Director*, Kentucky: The University Press of Kentucky, 2011, pp. 84–98.

5 Wood, op. cit., p. 40.

6 Robert Kolker, *A Cinema of Loneliness: Penn, Stone, Kubrick, Scorsese, Spielberg, Altman*, third edition, Oxford: Oxford University Press, 2000, p. 20.

7 Indeed, if Penn can be said to have tackled a number of political issues throughout his career, there is little sustained treatment of racial conflicts in his films. There is a very brief scene in *Bonnie and Clyde* in which a black man shoots some holes into his master's house, which has just been repossessed by the bank. *Little Big Man's* portrayal of atrocities against Native Americans could be seen as a metaphor for US activities in Vietnam. But the only film where any detailed attention is paid to racism is his 1966 feature *The Chase*.

8 Stephen Prince, 'The Haemorrhaging of American Cinema: *Bonnie and Clyde's* Legacy of Cinematic Violence', in Lester D. Friedman (ed.) *Arthur Penn's Bonnie and Clyde*, Cambridge: Cambridge University Press, 2000, p. 139.

Filmography

The Left Handed Gun (1958)
The Miracle Worker (1962)
Mickey One (1965)
The Chase (1966)
Bonnie and Clyde (1967)
Alice's Restaurant (1969)
Little Big Man (1970)
Visions of Eight (1973) co-director
Night Moves (1975)
The Missouri Breaks (1976)
Four Friends (1981)
Target (1985)
Dead of Winter (1987)
Penn and Teller Get Killed (1989)

Further reading

Cawelti, John. *Focus on Bonnie and Clyde*. London: Prentice Hall, 1973.

King, Geoff. *New Hollywood Cinema: An Introduction*. London: I.B. Tauris, 2002.

ROMAN POLANSKI

By Thomas Schur

The peculiar contours of Roman Polanski's career bear witness to the vagaries of life as much as his films themselves do. Since his first feature in 1962, Polanski has worked in Poland, England, Italy, France, Spain, Germany, and the Czech Republic. The first film he made in Hollywood, *Rosemary's Baby* (1968), capitalized on his reputation as a director of horror films, but his subsequent career—including his other Hollywood film, *Chinatown* (1974)—has shown a wide range of generic and stylistic proclivities. His earliest European films incorporate influences of Hollywood, and his films after his Hollywood stint can be said to reflect an emergent post-Hollywood aesthetic in world cinema. His sensibility from the start has been decidedly eclectic, combining an attitude of old European existentialist detachment with a pop attunement to the most sensational aspects of cinema.

Polanski was left an orphan at the end of the Second World War—his mother died at Auschwitz; his father survived at a different camp, though was absent for years. A precocious child, Polanski taught himself to read, cultivated his interests in cinema and theater, and was eventually enrolled at Krakow's School for Fine Arts. He later attended the prestigious Lodz Film School, though never formally graduated, having failed only to write the required thesis. By that time, however, he had seen behind the Iron Curtain—having traveled to Paris, with a stopover at the Cannes Film Festival—and had made an award-winning short film, *Two Men and a Wardrobe* (1958), a darkly allegorical fable of exile and anomie.

In the 1960s, Polanski is married and then divorced three years later. He visits the United States for the first time to attend the 1964 Academy Awards where his first feature, *Knife in the Water* (1962), is nominated for Best Foreign Film. He lives hand to mouth in London, but manages to make *Repulsion* (1965), *Cul-de-Sac* (1966) and *The Fearless Vampire Killers* (1967) there—the last financed by a Hollywood producer, Martin

Ransohoff. He returns to the U.S. to direct *Rosemary's Baby*; he also returns to Cannes as a juror, but the festival is cancelled amid the political events of May 1968. That year he marries Sharon Tate, who is then tragically and notoriously murdered by followers of Charles Manson a year later.

In the 1970s, Polanski pursues an even more cosmopolitan array of projects, directing *Macbeth* (1971) in Great Britain, *What?* (1972) in Italy, *Chinatown* in the U.S., and *The Tenant* (1976) in France—a striking series of films made in a wide array of film industries. In 1977, while in Los Angeles, he is charged with the rape of a 13-year-old girl. After pleading guilty to unlawful sexual intercourse, he is incarcerated for 42 days for a pre-sentencing psychiatric evaluation. Upon his release, fearing malfeasance by the judge assigned to his case, Polanski, a French citizen by birth, flees to France, where he has lived since. In Europe, he has continued to make films, including *The Pianist* (2002)—about a Jewish musician's struggle to survive the Nazi occupation of Poland during World War II—for which he won the Academy Award for Best Director. A fugitive from justice whose return to the U.S. would likely have resulted in arrest, Polanski was absent from the award ceremony.

As this brief account attests, there is an improbable quality to Polanski's career. The twists and turns are worthy of a Gothic novel repurposed through the figure of a modern-day Candide. A biographical portrait of the director by Lawrence Wechsler is called "The Brat's Tale,"[1] and Polanski himself writes in his memoir that Hollywood is "like a spoiled brat that screams for possession of a toy and then tosses it out of the baby buggy."[2] Whether or not these echoes bespeak some elective affinity, Polanski's work has certainly evinced an interesting relation to Hollywood sensibilities throughout his career.

The fact that Polanski made *Rosemary's Baby* and *Chinatown* in Hollywood—both for Paramount, each a major commercial and critical success—is the obvious justification for including the Polish-French director in this volume. But there are other reasons, too. As of this writing, Polanski's most recent U.S. release is *Carnage* (2011). Despite having been produced in Europe with a European crew and financing, it is an English-language film, made with the benefit of the latest technology, featuring prominent Hollywood stars (Jodie Foster, John C. Reilly, Kate Winslet, and Christoph Waltz). The same things can be said of virtually all of Polanski's films since *Chinatown*. Still, *Carnage*'s cramped and claustrophobic setting—the action takes place inside a single apartment, ostensibly in Brooklyn—is a distinct contrivance that recalls a major trope of Polanski's work since *Knife in the*

Water, a film set within the confines of a small yacht. In fact, the influence of Hollywood can be felt even in that first feature made in Poland, in both its technique—sharp editing, sleek camerawork, and incisive sound design more attuned to classical Hollywood conventions than most European films and even many films made in Hollywood at the time—and its mode, a psychological thriller with erotic overtones, à la Hitchcock.

Polanski's working relationship with Hollywood was nevertheless complicated, given that his love of "glamour" was matched only by his loathing of accounting and bureaucracy. Robert Evans, a producer who helped to usher in the post-classical Hollywood era with its cabal of "young Turk" auteurs, provided Polanski with his entrée to Hollywood by inviting him to direct *Rosemary's Baby*. Whereas *Psycho* had already made the family the locus of American horror, it took *Rosemary's Baby* to thematize that concern around pregnancy. Polanski's treatment turns a jaundiced eye on American culture, satirizing the childbirth industry as tartly as the counterculture Satan craze. The movie's distinctive tone derives largely from the clash between its sympathy with the innocent mother who becomes pregnant with the devil's progeny, and its simultaneous revelry in the most sensational aspects of the material, indulged with a vivid, exacting elegance.

However, by the time it was clear that their partnership was successful, the relationship between Evans and Polanski turned sour. Polanski had been attached to another high-profile project at Paramount, a drama about an American skier who competes in the Olympics, but when he proposed shooting primarily in Europe as indicated by the script, the studio balked at the notion. The film, *Downhill Racer* (1969), was directed instead by Michael Ritchie, starring Robert Redford; and Colorado was made to double for the Alps. It was not until five years later that Polanski returned to Hollywood to make another film, and then it was with some reluctance. In his memoir, Polanski recalls: "My months in Rome had convinced me that Europe was my true home—I loved the sheer antiquity and asymmetry that made it so different from modern, four-square America."[3] But he was in need of money, and *Chinatown*—a film that both mythologizes 1930s Los Angeles and exposes the brutality that underlies "civilized progress"—was in many ways a perfect project.

Whereas several of Polanski's prior films had shadings of Chandler or Hammett, *Chinatown* was an opportunity for the director to immerse himself in the atmosphere of noir, the most simultaneously enchanted and disillusioned of American styles. Polanski's approach to noir is less deconstructive than that of European contemporaries such as Godard, Fassbinder, and Wenders, however; in his memoir he recounts that he wanted *Chinatown* to seem as much as possible like a classical Hollywood film, "only in Panavision and color." The audience response was overwhelmingly positive, suggesting that Polanski and screenwriter Robert Towne had struck an effective balance of nostalgia and malaise; yet by the time box office receipts had been counted, Polanski and Evans were on bad terms once again.

The aspect of Polanski's work that joins to a commercial sensibility like Hollywood's most seamlessly is his romanticization of youth, and of youthful femininity in particular. Other aspects of his profile, though, might appear to place him at odds with Hollywood. Many have recognized a strain of surrealism that runs through Polanski's work, including the director himself, who has cited Bruno Schulz and Kafka as influences. Polanski's commitments are less redolent of André Breton, however, and more suggestive of a proto-surrealist like Arthur Rimbaud. The following artistic credo from Rimbaud could just as well have come from Polanski:

> What I liked were absurd paintings, pictures over doorways, stage sets, carnival backdrops, bright-coloured prints, old-fashioned literature, church Latin, erotic books full of misspellings, the kind of novels our grandmothers read, fairy tales, little children's books, old operas, silly old songs, the native rhythm of country rimes.[4]

With its hectic aura of an old curiosity shop, this fanciful compendium recalls many scenes and details in Polanski's films, by turns charming, anachronistic, haunting: the street musicians that creep along like crabs in his earliest shorts and features; the hole in the wall behind the heavy wooden armoire, stuffed with a wad of cotton concealing a tooth in *The Tenant*, or the murky panel covered in hieroglyphics in the same film; the rare books in *The Ninth Gate* (1999) with their tarot-like illustrations, and the rambling castle ruins that figure at the end; the perfectly manicured snowscapes, like icing on cake, in *The Fearless Vampire Killers*, and the large, whimsical red bow tied around the neck of Alfred (a character played by Polanski himself); the lilting lullaby sung by Mia Farrow at the beginning and end of *Rosemary's Baby*; and so on. One might also discern a connection between Polanski's enchanted worlds, populated by wistful ephemera, and Joseph Cornell's quasi-surrealist shadow boxes, which use familiar objects such as buttons and seashells to conjure their mysteries.

One reason Polanski was able to make such rich films in Hollywood— and that Hollywood was able to incorporate Polanski's surrealist gestures into its own aesthetic so fully—is because Hollywood cinema itself has always been more stylistically varied, less committed to naturalism, than many influential accounts have alleged. It is well known that the surrealists in their heyday, in the 1920s, were fascinated by Hollywood cinema precisely because they saw it as an expression of esoteric knowledge of a sort. The contemporary film theorist associated most with the argument that Hollywood cinema is essentially surrealist is Robert Ray, who has written admiringly of *Chinatown*.

What most clearly separates Polanski's cinema from that of Hollywood, meanwhile, is a certain pessimism toward human nature and society that informs much of the director's work. While Polanski would appear to have a gift for accommodating change, his resilience depends in its essence on a profound sense of the absurd. His films are unremittingly without faith in reason and rationality, though not necessarily despairing for all that; indeed they are comic much of the time. Hollywood, for its part, rarely surrenders the guiding conviction that (since Voltaire has already been invoked) all is for the best in this best of all possible worlds. Optimism is the limit beyond which change might be impossible for Hollywood. A case in point: when Polanski and Towne worked together on the script for *Chinatown*, it was by all accounts a happy collaboration, and so it seems telling that their only major dispute was over the film's finale. Towne, a Hollywood insider, had wanted a redemptive ending; Polanski insisted on a tragic one. The conclusion in which the fated Evelyn Mulwray (Faye Dunaway) is shot as she attempts to keep her daughter from the hands of the father who raped her, is perhaps the *most* tragic ending, in fact, of any Hollywood film.

Yet, putting aside the question of whether the wrong person dies at the finish, a striking feature of the film's closing scene is its recourse to a common Polanski trope, frequently treated with darkly comic overtones. In sluggardly postures, a wayward group of people surround the body of the victim. It is hard to say what accounts for the power of this recurrent staging. It has something to do with the temporal lag in the midst of urgency, the wanly impromptu nature of the assemblage, casual strangers turned unexpectedly into official witnesses, and how Polanski's wide-angle lens deforms the many staring faces. Polanski must be aware of the intensely eerie effect because he has created a version of this same tableau at key moments in other films—*Repulsion*, *Rosemary's Baby*, and *The Tenant*.

Curiously enough, an odd echo of this sort of tableau occurred in the broadcast of the Academy Awards ceremony when Polanski won his Oscar for directing *The Pianist*. The other nominees that year were two directors from the U.S. (Rob Marshall and Martin Scorsese), one from Great Britain (Stephen Daldry), and one from Spain (Pedro Almodovar)—an example of how Hollywood strategically endorses the idea of a unified film culture centered on a "global cinema." After the names of the nominees were read, the television screen filled with squares, one for each of the directors who were all seated in the theatre; all except for Polanski, of course. His square was occupied by a still image of him on a set calling into a bullhorn, an image as ironic as it is clichéd. That Polanski might win was hinted by the selection of presenter—Harrison Ford, who starred in *Frantic* for Polanski, after the director had decamped to Europe and when he was considered persona non grata in Hollywood. Prior to the ceremony, Polanski's nomination had been surrounded by controversy, a feverish round of vitriol such that when Ford opened the envelope, the silence was filled with tension. When Polanski was announced the winner, the theater burst into wild applause. Cut to shots of the audience: some stand awkwardly; all turn their heads in various directions, like gawkers at the scene of an accident. Not knowing where to look, they wind up gaping at each other, confused, as if already struggling to remember why they had felt so anxious only seconds ago. Rife with strange and unassimilable energies, and not a little bit of dark humor, this moment of Polanski's greatest recent professional triumph is uncanny for its resemblance to a scene from a Roman Polanski film.

Biography

Polanski was born on August 13, 1933, in Paris, to a Polish father and a Russian mother. The family returned to Poland in 1935. Four years later, when Germany invaded Poland, they were interned in the Krakow ghetto with the rest of the city's Jews. According to his memoir, one of his first memories of watching movies is peering through barbed wire from inside the ghetto and seeing German pro-paganda films projected on a building opposite. Polanski fortuitously escaped before the final liquidation of the ghetto by the Nazis in 1943. He currently lives in Paris with his wife, the actress Emma-nuelle Seigner, and their two children.

Notes

1 Wescher, Lawrence "The Brat's Tale." In *Vermeer in Bosnia: Cultural Comedies and Political Tragedies*. New York: Pantheon, 2004, pp. 83–150.
2 Roman Polanksi, *Roman*, New York: Morrow, 1984, p. 262.

375

3 Polanksi, p. 346.
4 Arthur Rimbaud, *Complete Works*, trans. Paul Schmidt. New York: Harper, 1967, p. 204.

Filmography

Bicycle (Poland, 1955) short
Toothy Grin (Poland, 1957) short
Break Up the Dance (Poland, 1957) short
Murder (Poland, 1957) short
Two Men and a Wardrobe (Poland, 1958) short
The Lamp (Poland, 1959) short
When Angels Fall (Poland, 1959) short
The Fat and the Lean (France, 1961) short
Mammals (Poland, 1962) short
Knife in the Water (Poland, 1962)
River of Diamonds (France/Italy/Japan/Netherlands, 1964) segment in
    The World's Most Beautiful Swindlers
Repulsion (UK, 1965)
Cul-de-Sac (UK, 1966)
The Fearless Vampire Killers (US/UK, 1967)
Rosemary's Baby (1968)
Macbeth (US/UK 1971)
What? (Italy/France/West Germany, 1972)
Chinatown (1974)
The Tenant (France, 1976)
Tess (France/UK, 1979)
Pirates (France/Tunisia, 1986)
Frantic (1988)
Bitter Moon (France/US/UK, 1992)
Death and the Maiden (France/US/UK, 1994)
The Ninth Gate (France/US/Spain, 1999)
The Pianist (France/Poland/Germany/UK, 2002)
Oliver Twist (France/Czech Republic/UK/Italy, 2005)
Cinéma Erotique (France, 2007) segment in *To Each His Own Camera*
The Ghost Writer (France/Germany/UK, 2009)
Carnage (France/Germany/Poland, 2011)
Venus in Furs (France/Poland, 2013)

Further reading

Cronin, Paul, ed. *Roman Polanski: Interviews.* Jackson: UP of Mississippi, 2005.
Morrison, James. *Roman Polanski.* Urbana: U of Illinois P, 2007.

Orr, John, and Elżbieta Ostrowska, eds. *The Cinema of Roman Polanski: Dark Spaces of the World*. London: Wallflower, 2006.
Polanski, Roman. *Roman*. New York: Morrow, 1984.

STEPHANIE ROTHMAN

By Alicia Kozma

Cinema history comprises bold personalities. Notoriously controlling studio executives, ethereal stars, uncompromising auteurs, self-promoting producers—these are the names that litter our historical cinematic consciousness. There is, however, a secret history, found in footnotes, parenthetical references, side comments, and anecdotes that inevitably raises more questions than answers, and which points to a vast reserve of undisclosed ephemera. Stephanie Rothman, and her oeuvre of films brimming with revolutionary sexual, racial, and gender politics, is hidden in these asides.

Rothman, who directed seven feature films concerned with the changing social and political atmosphere of the 1960s and 1970s over the course of her eleven-year career, was also a screenwriter and an independent studio executive. As such she is a unique figure in film history: a female director whose work was profitable, widely screened, and infused with a progressive socio-political consciousness. Her films are populated by women who were of color, sexual, desirous, political, smart, and most importantly, treated equitably. Yet Rothman, who stopped making films in 1974, faded from film history as quickly as she appeared in it.

Rothman belongs to the robust canon of creative professionals who have been marginalized both historically and culturally because their work has garnered the label of "exploitation film." A vast and often misunderstood category, exploitation films have a parallel history to Hollywood, emerging as a shadow industry to the classical studio system. While classical exploitation films produced from 1919 to 1959 were primarily concerned with highlighting spectacles of vice, sex, and sin, beginning in the 1950s exploitation films moved toward quasi-mainstream standing, when they began to replace the B-films no longer produced by the studios. These films, which I term second wave exploitation, were concerned with integrating controversial subjects, taboo materials, and trendy countercultural topics. In an effort to attract the burgeoning youth and drive-in market, exploitation films traced classical Hollywood's production formulas. Though Rothman began directing during the height of second wave exploitation, her films truly do not fit into this template; rather, they oscillate between comedies of manners, bedrooms farces, surrealistic explorations of desire, and futuristic dystopian parables.

Rothman's professional space within the industry (rather than her films themselves) engendered the exploitation label. First working under the auspices of second wave exploitation stalwart Roger Corman, the oft-heralded "King of the B's," Rothman's first directorial credit came from the exploitation industry on the film *Blood Bath* (1966). *Blood Bath* was known in the business as an "Iron Curtain salvage job," an Eastern European film that had been purchased cheaply in order to be reworked for the U.S. market. Rothman rewrote the narrative, reassembled the final film from a hodgepodge of footage and supervised the editing process frame by frame.

The result is a film that strains mightily to maintain a sense of logic and continuity, a near impossible feat considering the mélange of material that Rothman had to manage. Due to the composite and collaborative nature of the film, it is difficult to read her authorship in it, but *Blood Bath* does portend one of the themes that would define Rothman's career: constraint.

In the world of second wave exploitation film, the chief concerns of low-budget productions—the consistent dearth of time and money—were as defining of Rothman's career as any aspect of her vision, intent, and artistry. Despite the lack of resources, Rothman films are not overly compromised in terms of form and style. Her camera moves economically, never wasting film on the ancillary, and she has an uncanny ability to establish scenic time, space, and mood within one or two shots. For example, an early shot in *The Student Nurses* of Nurse Priscilla walking to a café uses costuming, non-diegetic music, and a point of view shot that links her desire to a strange man and his motorcycle to succinctly establish Priscilla as an open-minded woman invested in the free love counterculture and the social rebellions it encouraged, traits that will significantly inform her story and decisions for the reminder of the film. Rothman often shot outside, using contemporary Los Angeles as vibrant backdrop, lending credence to an understanding of her films as tailored chronicles of a time of tremendous social change and friction. Her cited influences (Bergman, Kurosawa, and Cocteau, among others) are on display in her most artistically daring film, *The Velvet Vampire* (1971). A surrealist mediation on desire, love, and death, the film is a thematic and stylistic outlier, in the best way possible, to her overall body of work.

However, the film's precise use of lap dissolves, day for night shooting, and tight control of bleached-out desert sunlight are endemic of Rothman's refusal to allow her films to be hampered by their economic pedigree.

Constraint would not only inform Rothman's filmmaking proper but her career trajectory as well. As one of the only female directors working at the time, Rothman consistently found avenues leading to mainstream film, and even television production, closed to her; female directors were rarely considered employable. This gender bias was compounded by the label of "exploitation" attached to her films. Major studios gave little, if any, attention to the exploitation industry, and certainly did not believe that the professionals working in them held much promise.[1] Because Rothman's films were shown, like most exploitation products, in drive-ins and urban grindhouses, they likewise never had exposure to a range of audiences, audiences who could have looked past the exploitation misnomer. As Terry Curtis Fox notes,

> Stephanie Rothman might as well not exist. Because Rothman has done all her work in what remains of poverty row [...] making horror-sexploiters which never reach beyond the drive-ins and grinds—Stephanie Rothman is invisible. Everywhere but on the screen.[2]

In a cruel twist, the industry partially preventing her career growth was also the only industry that would employ her.

Thankfully, Rothman's talents would not go unnoticed or underutilized, nor would she remain a patchwork director. As a graduate of the University of Southern California's film school and the first woman to win the Director's Guild of America's Student Film Award, Rothman followed *Blood Bath* with *It's a Bikini World* (1967), the first feature to showcase her commitment to foregrounding messages of social consciousness and gender equality. A film in the "beach party" cycle that was popular in the late 1960s, *It's a Bikini World* integrates the standard beach party elements—sun, sand, surfing, rock and roll, pretty teenagers in bathing suits—with a nontraditional battles of the sexes plot. In the film Delilah is determined to beat roguish womanizer Mike at a series of athletic contests. In a more standard film, this determination would stem from the desire to seduce Mike by proving herself "worthy" of him. In a Rothman film, however, Delilah's resolve emanates from her belief that Mike is not intrinsically superior to her simply because he is a man and she is a woman.

Of course, it is still a beach party film and as such the two ultimately end up together, but in a relationship that strongly hints at mutual respect and equality.

Delilah is the first in a series of Rothman heroines whose feminism is positioned as entirely natural. Hers is not a stereotype of the bra-burning feminist killjoy but rather a feminism of the everyday. In this way, Rothman's feminism is revolutionary. When Chris, the ostensible center of *Group Marriage* (1973) decides that her current boyfriend is not satisfying her sexually, she recruits another man to be part of their relationship. For Chris, her new partner is a sensible solution to a realistic problem, rather than an opportunity for sexual exploitation. Rothman's feminism exists in the mode of the practical. In another exploitation film Chris would likely have been portrayed as a vamp, incapable of sexual satisfaction, and constantly on the prowl. This type of fetishistic spectacularization of female desire would speak to how feminism was understood, or misunderstood, by an industry populated overwhelmingly by men. But in *Group Marriage* Chris is simply a woman who understands, and takes control of, her own desire. Rothman does not frame feminism as a radical notion or as a countercultural ideal associated with fringe groups; it is simply the way women live their lives.

In line with the idea that feminism exists as a natural component of everyday women's lives, one that takes on revolutionary form in its normalness, is the idea that this feminism extends to *all* women. Rothman's heroines exist on a spectrum of class, employment, and race. Her characters are variously employed, underemployed, and unemployed.[3] More critically, and in direct opposition to a majority of the films of the 1960s, 1970s, and unfortunately still today, Rothman's women are not by default white. Chris is Asian-American; Lynn in *The Student Nurses* (1970) is Mexican-American; Carmen, of *Terminal Island* (1973) is African-American. These women of color all play main roles in Rothman films. In this way, Rothman prefigures later debates about the exclusion of women of color from the second wave feminist movement. Again, this commitment to inclusion speaks to Rothman's investment in a naturalized feminism—if feminism as a mode of living is to be one understood as the practical outgrowth of living as women, it must be a feminism that is accessible and usable for all women as opposed to the province of the privileged few. As Dannis Peary, one of the few scholars who wrote on Rothman during her contemporaneous moment, notes:

> Stephanie Rothman is important because she is that rare commercial filmmaker who has consistently shown a concern for

women in her work, who clearly *likes* women. It is not an accident that Rothman's heroines are not violated, that all rapes fail, all lovemaking is tender, even when the male involved is a scoundrel; that the only woman hit by her lover—Jill in *The Working Girls*—walks out on him *after* hitting him back.[4]

What is so striking, and significant, about Rothman is her ability to infuse her films with these characteristics that are simultaneously radical and fundamental, and do so within the second wave exploitation industry, a genre whose products so often highlighted the exact opposite.

Concerned with equality not just in gender relations but across the social spectrum, Rothman's films also hold the promise of positive social change, a focus that is often realized through a cinematic reorganization of society. In *Group Marriage*, three men and three women enter into a single relationship with one another with the goal of creating new ways to experience love and togetherness. Under one roof, they struggle to create new forms of interpersonal communication, reorganize divisions of labor, and partake in community decision making, all in an effort to create a micro-utopia as a panacea to the perceived macro-dystopia of the outside world.

Similarly, in *Terminal Island*, where convicted murderers are sent to live out their last days on a maximum-security open air island prison in the Pacific Ocean, themes of utopia/dystopia and social reorganization loom large. Oppressed and abused by a sadistic killer and his henchman, a group of convicts break away from the main camp and attempt to overthrow the barbarous regime. In the process, the rebel group creates a utopic society where men and women live, love, and labor equally, away from the divisions and resentments of mainland life. *Terminal Island* is one of Rothman's most violent films, a violence that marks it as distinct from her earlier work.

Rothman's relationship to violence, sex, and nudity in her films is complicated and fraught. Indeed, as long as she included the requisite amount of the three in her films—hallmarks of second wave exploitation—she was free to create the films as she saw fit. Under these conditions, Rothman often couched her sex and violence in dramatic role reversals and comedy, and developed a set of ideological guidelines through which she incorporated these more normatively exploitative elements into her work.[5] *The Student Nurses* opens with the attempted rape of Nurse Sharon by a patient in the hospital, but instead of her body and victimization being put on display, she fights off her attacker and calls on two orderlies to subdue him with a tranquilizer shot in his bare buttocks. Paradoxically, then, the first scenes of violence and nudity in the film are organized around a male body, and a de-centering of heteronormative pleasure in spectacle. Through this reversal, Rothman discharges the performance of sex and violence expected by second wave exploitation audiences. This dismissal strikes a bargain with the audience: "[…] you came for sex and violence, here's sex and violence, now we'll go on to things which are more interesting (including political violence and nonexploitative sex)."[6] Like her portrayal of feminism, sex and nudity are refreshingly practical and normalized. Moments of nudity, both male and female, are contained within everyday situations: showering, changing clothes, etc. Sex is treated similarly naturally; it is variously erotic, uncomfortable, pleasurable and boring. It is, like the majority of spectacle in Rothman's films, normalized as a strategy of subversion.

Perhaps the most essential fact about Stephanie Rothman and her films is that both she and they have been virtually wiped out of memory and history. In a time when low-budget independent films labeled as "exploitation" are valued by fans and scholars alike as cult fetish objects rather than as embodiments of the collective social experience, perhaps this loss of remembrance is not entirely surprising. But, indeed, it is a disservice, especially considering the unique and pioneering place that Rothman and her films of fierce social consciousness hold in cinema history. Given the critical reluctance to give serious consideration to work saddled with the exploitation label, it is clear that the label that held back Rothman's career also crippled her legacy. Terry Curtis Fox, one of Rothman's earliest champions, perhaps articulated it best when he noted that

> The most bitter irony of Stephanie Rothman's career is that the one woman filmmaker of the Seventies with a consistent and solid body of work—a body of work that expresses the possibilities of American society—seems to have a better future as a cause then as a director.[7]

Biography

Stephanie Rothman was born in 1936 in Paterson, New Jersey, and has resided in California since the age of eight. An accomplished dancer at a young age, Rothman grew up in a household that valued art, music, and literature. After graduating high school at the age of sixteen, she earned a degree in sociology from the University of California Berkeley. In 1962 she entered USC film school, where she became the first woman to win the Directors Guild of America student award. At USC she met her husband and long-time collaborator/producer, Charles S. Swartz. Producer and director Roger Corman hired Rothman as his assistant in 1964. Under Corman, Rothman began her first professional directorial efforts, receiving her first director's credit in 1966. In 1970, Rothman and Swartz joined Corman in his new production/distribution company, New World Pictures. In 1972 Rothman, Swartz, and New World colleague Lawrence Woolner formed the production/distribution company Dimension Pictures, where Rothman served as the Vice President in charge of creative development. At the time, she was one of the only female production executives in the system. Rothman and Swartz left Dimension in 1974, and she attempted to move into mainstream filmmaking, but found all doors closed to female directors. After nine years of trying to break the gender barrier for directors, Rothman retired from the film industry.

Notes

1 This stigma would change in the mid to late 1970s when the crop of "New Hollywood" directors such as Francis Ford Coppola and Martin Scorsese emerged from the "training ground" of second wave exploitation filmmaking to transform Hollywood feature films. Unfortunately, Rothman would never be afforded this opportunity, which leads Cook (2005) to question whether or not the much celebrated "training ground" of second wave exploitation operates as successfully for female professionals as it does for male professionals.

2 Fox, T.C. "Fully Female." *Film Comment* 12.6 (1976): 46–50, 50.

3 Some examples of the spectrum of employment in Rothman films are as follows: In *Group Marriage*, Elaine is a lawyer, while Jill in *The Working Girls* (1974) is a law student; the four women of *The Student Nurses* are just that; Denise in *The Working Girls* is sign painter and her friend Honey is unemployed with a degree in math (and at the beginning of the film, homeless); Chris and Jan in *Group Marriage* are a car rental customer agent and a retired flight attendant, respectively.

4 Peary, Dannis. "Stephanie Rothman: R-Rated Feminist," *Women and the Cinema*. Eds. K. Kay and G. Peary. New York: E. P. Dutton, 1977, pp. 179–92, 192.

5 Rothman's self-developed guidelines for integration of necessarily spectacularized sex and violence include but are not limited to: equitable male and female nudity; avoiding filmic rape and when forced to include rape scenes filming them as non-voyeuristic; avoiding nudity as a form of vengeance; forsaking violence whenever possible, and when it

is represented, showing it as harsh, non-eroticized, and with significant consequences; and scripting female characters who make choices irrespective of their relationships with male characters.

6 Fox, p. 47.
7 Ibid., p. 50.

Filmography

Blood Bath (1966) aka *Track of the Vampire*
It's a Bikini World (1967)
The Student Nurses (1970)
The Velvet Vampire (1971)
Group Marriage (1973)
Terminal Island (1973)
The Working Girls (1974)

Further reading

Cook, Pam. "'Exploitation' Films and Feminism." *Screen* 17.2 (1976): 122–27.
Peary, Dannis. "Stephanie Rothman: R-Rated Feminist." *Women and the Cinema*. Eds. K. Kay and G. Peary. New York: E. P. Dutton, 1977. 179–92.

JOHN WATERS

By Dana Heller

For most of his filmmaking career, John Waters worked with a steady cast and crew known as "The Dreamlanders," named after his Baltimore film company, Dreamland Productions. The inner circle, which shifted and expanded over the years, included Divine (Harris Glenn Milstead), George Figgs, David Lochary, Susan Lowe, Edith Massey, Pat Moran (his casting director), Cookie Mueller, Mary Vivian Pearce, Vincent Peranio (his production designer), Van Smith (his costumer and hairdresser), Maelcum Soul, Mink Stole, and Channing Wilroy. With Dreamland, Waters developed an independent, DIY production technique and an underground cinema aesthetic that drew on the experimental energies of the 1960s counter-culture as well as elements of camp sensibility, exploitation cinema, Antonin Artaud's concept of a "Theater of the Absurd," and the transgressive attractions of the carnivalesque. A showman at heart, Waters orchestrated these elements to create a singular body of work represented by "cult" classics such as *Pink Flamingos* (1972) as well as the commercially successful comedy, *Hairspray* (1988). While the latter would make him famous, it was his early films—above all the films that constitute his "Trash Trilogy" – that would cement his reputation as an auteur, a reputation best encapsulated by the writer William Burroughs who dubbed Waters, "the Pope of Trash."

In the 1960s, Waters was influenced by a pioneering group of underground filmmakers, most under thirty years of age, which included Jack Smith, the Kuchar Brothers, Ron Rice, Ken Jacobs, Kenneth Anger, and eventually Andy Warhol, who became the personification of New York City's glamorous underground movement. Waters' *Roman Candles* (1966), a forty-minute tribute to Warhol's *Chelsea Girls*, was a triptych composed of three synchronized movies projected by three adjacent 8-mm projectors. Billed as a "trash epic," the film was never commercially released.

Eat Your Makeup (1968), a short shot on 16-mm film, starred Maelcum Soul as a maniacal governess who kidnaps fashion models and tortures them by forcing them to model before audiences until they drop dead from exhaustion. Not long after the film's opening Soul died of a drug-overdose at the age of twenty-seven, thus opening the way for Waters' childhood friend and future muse, Divine, to take center stage in Dreamland's first feature-length project, *Mondo Trasho*. Featuring a musical soundtrack comprised of unlicensed original tracks, *Mondo Trasho* starred Divine as a trashy blond-bombshell, a gum-chewing Jayne Mansfield look-alike. While filming an outdoor nude scene on location in Baltimore, Waters, along with several of his cast and production crew, were arrested for "indecent exposure" and "conspiracy" to commit indecent exposure. The charges were eventually dropped.

Shot on a budget of $5,000 loaned to him by his father, *Multiple Maniacs* (1970) was the first Waters film to incorporate synchronized dialogue. The title pays tribute to Herschell Gordon Lewis' graphic horror/gore film, *Two Thousand Maniacs* (1964). Lady Divine (Divine) is the operator of a depraved traveling sideshow, the "Cavalcade of Perversion," which features fetishistic performances such as "puke-eating." In a scene that reflects Waters' on-going fascination with the twin themes of Roman Catholicism and sexual perversion, Divine is anally penetrated with a set of rosary beads during an anonymous sexual encounter that takes place in a church with a woman who describes the Stations of the Cross. The film ends on a surreal note, with Divine's rape by a fifteen-foot shellfish named "Lobstora," which sends her on a random killing spree until she is shot by the National Guard to the musical accompaniment of Kate Smith's "God Bless America."

The production of *Multiple Maniacs* coincided with the grisly and sensational 1969 murder of Sharon Tate, the actress and wife of film director, Roman Polanski, by the Charles Manson "family" in Southern California. The Tate-LaBianca murders, which occurred just as production of *Multiple Maniacs* began, and the arrest of the Manson family members, which took place near the completion of the project, obsessed Waters. That obsession has lasted throughout his career, evidenced by the fact that most of his films contain some reference to the Manson crime. A dedicated follower of true crime in general and a noted expert on the Manson case in particular (he is a longtime friend of former Manson follower, Leslie Van Hauten), Waters remains a frequent attendee at celebrity trials wherever and whenever he can gain admittance.

More to the point, one of the central and lasting preoccupations of Waters' work takes on definition at this stage of his career: the glamour of notoriety, or the celebrity status that American culture lavishly confers on the (typically female) taboo-breaker. Nowhere is this theme more extravagantly exploited than in Waters' next film, the first of his Trash Trilogy and his first color feature, *Pink Flamingos* (1972). The plot revolves around two families who become locked in a deadly feud for the title of "The Filthiest People Alive." On one side, there is Divine, her hippie son (Danny Mills), and her deranged 250-pound mother (Edith Massey) who remains through the film in a playpen, eating eggs and wearing nothing but a bra and girdle. On the other side, there are the Marbles (David Lochary and Mink Stole), a couple who make their living by kidnapping runaway girls, inseminating them with sperm, and selling their babies to childless lesbian couples. With its low-budget aesthetic, freakish characters, scatological humor, and scenes of graphic sexual perversion, critics were mostly appalled by *Pink Flamingos'* unprecedented celebration of cinematic bad taste. The film's notoriety resulted in no small part from its final segment – shot in one continuous take, with no editing, special effects, or cut-away – of Divine eating dog feces freshly expelled from a small poodle. The moment occurs quickly, and without great fanfare, yet it remains one of the best-known and most frequently referenced moments from any John Waters movie.

Pink Flamingos transformed Waters from a Baltimore filmmaker to a national filmmaker, famous for having positioned his unglamorous home city as a raw cinematic trope of the American grotesque. In a larger sense, Waters' films served an unapologetic critique of the mainstream Hollywood film industry, its labor economy and consumer ethos. Divine was also transformed from a relatively unknown character actor to an internationally celebrated drag performer whose underground celebrity imitated the fame-starved women she often played in Waters' movies. *Female Trouble* (1974), the second installment of the Trash Trilogy, draws as much from the commercial and material excesses of American celebrity culture as it does from Jean Genet's correlation of violent crime and aesthetic experience. Inspiration for the film came to Waters while he was visiting one of the Manson family convicts, Charles "Tex" Watson at the California Men's Colony in San Luis Obispo. During these visits, Waters became fixated on criminal "celebrities" and their fawning groupies who flitted around the prison visiting room. He decided that the theme of his next film would be outlaw beauty.

Divine plays two roles in *Female Trouble*, one female and the other male (in one scene that was especially difficult to shoot, the male character rapes the female). The starring role is Dawn Davenport, a delinquent, suburban teenager who desperately wants cha-cha heels for Christmas. When she doesn't get them, she throws a violent tantrum on Christmas morning, topples the tree over on her mother, and runs away from home. The plot traces her development from petty thief and unwed mother, to unhappy wife of a philandering hippie beautician, to fashion model and lab rat for the maniacal experiments of beauty salon owners, Donald and Donna Dasher (David Lochary and Mary Vivian Pearce). The couple seduces Dawn with the promise of achieving unparalleled beauty and fame through crime. Brainwashed by the Dashers and grossly disfigured by her vengeful mother-in-law, Dawn's performance at a local nightclub ends in mayhem when, in the name of "art," she goes on a shooting rampage and murders her audience. She dies in the electric chair, deliriously convinced that she has at last reached the pinnacle of stardom, her final words an appeal to her fans: "Please remember, I love every fucking one of you."

The collaboration of Waters and Divine produced a critical deconstruction of the classical Hollywood articulation of the movie star. If stars variously embody contradictions produced by their dichotomous positioning as cultural commodities and private persons, Divine (whose drag name seems to have been derived from Genet's fictional alter-ego in *Our Lady of the Flowers*, although Waters cannot recall its origins) represented the predicament of defective embodiment in an industry that equates gender, sexual, class, and racial deviations with monstrosity and terror. Indeed, the "stars" of Waters' early films exploit all manner of physical deformity and invert all codes of bodily conduct. And yet they always manage to overcome their oppressors, who often appear far more conventional in their middle-class manners and styles of class and gender embodiment.

Notably absent from the cast of *Desperate Living* (1977), the third and final installment of the Trash Trilogy, is Divine, who at the time was touring in the stage production of Tom Eyan's *Women Behind Bars*, and David Lochary, who died from a drug overdose. Produced on a budget of $65,000, Waters recruited the talents of some new cast members, such as Jean Hill. He also initiated the practice of casting real-life celebrities to star in his films. For *Desperate Living*, he enlisted the former Mafia moll, convicted felon, and burlesque performer, Liz Renay, whose memoir, *My Face for the World To See*, impressed Waters so much that he traveled to Boston where Renay was performing in a strip club and invited her to play the role of Muffy St. Jacques, the femme lesbian partner of butch Mole McHenry (Susan Lowe).

By the 1980s, the underground aesthetic of shock and exploitation that had fueled the counter-culture's midnight movie circuit was appropriated by the Hollywood film industry. Waters' approach to filmmaking changed. *Polyester* (1981) and *Hairspray* (1988) were more commercially viable projects than any he had previously undertaken, but they were no less deliberate in their critique of conventional beauty and morality. *Polyester*, which restored Divine to star billing alongside former teen idol, Tab Hunter, is a case in point: the film is an homage to the popular 1950s melodramas of Douglas Sirk, whose influence is evident not only in its lighting techniques and cinematography, but in its conspicuously stylized theatricality, which satirizes gender and sexual norms. As Francine Fishpaw, a middle-aged suburban housewife whose world collapses when she discovers that her husband, Elmer (David Samson) who runs a local porn theater, is having an affair with his secretary, Divine plays a "normal" woman for the first time in any Waters film. Without the monstrous persona, makeup and hairstyle that had come to dominate Divine's screen presence, reviewers could observe for the first time Divine's natural gifts as a comedic film actor and her effective onscreen chemistry with Hunter. By strategically casting Hunter as Francine's lover, an actor whose early screen career was tainted by Hollywood press revelations of his off-screen homosexual relationships, Waters also galvanized his reputation for casting off-beat pop culture icons, a practice he continued in latter films which featured convicted criminals (Patty Hearst), porn stars (Traci Lords), and celebrities (Sonny Bono, Johnny Depp, Melanie Griffiths, Deborah Harry, Lili Taylor, Kathleen Turner, Tracey Ullman).

Polyester was also noteworthy for its introduction of "Odorama," Waters' tribute to William Castle's theatrical film gimmicks of the 1950s and especially to Mike Todd, Jr., who in 1960 introduced the short-lived gimmick, "Smell-O-Vision" with the release of the film *Scent of Mystery* (1960). For *Polyester*, audiences were provided with numbered scratch-n-sniff cards that were to be used with corresponding numbers on the screen to enliven the olfactory dimensions of the narrative, which include a rose, feet, glue, pizza, and a fart. *Polyester* highlighted Waters' maturing skill as a satirist and critic of American social and political trends, in particular the rise of the conservative right and the feckless hypocrisy, sexism, homophobia, and priggishness of the so-called "moral majority."

With the release of *Hairspray*, all of the elements that had marked Waters' evolution as an anarchic filmmaker and critical observer of American social taboos and cultural mythologies came together in a surprising new configuration: a congenial teenpic about the civil rights movement. When Waters completed the script for *Hairspray* he presented it to New Line Cinema, the independent studio that had overseen most of Dreamland's previous projects. Over the years, a loyal working relationship had evolved between Dreamland and New Line that had proved as beneficial for the latter's reputation as an independent outfit that spotlights non-commercial cult and foreign films as it had for Waters' reputation as a fringe artist. For this reason, studio executives at New Line expressed marketing concerns when they realized that *Hairspray* would garner no more than a PG-rating from the Motion Picture Association of America. When asked if he would throw in some four-letter words to boost the rating to R, Waters refused.

With its mainstream appeal and optimistic message of youth empowerment and racial justice, *Hairspray* did succeed in alienating a significant portion of Waters' hardcore underground fan base. However, and despite its squeaky-clean veneer, Waters considers *Hairspray* to be the most subversive film he has made to date. Indeed, *Hairspray* marks a point of peculiar aesthetic convergence in popular American cinema, a convergence perhaps best underscored by David Edelstein's description of the film as "a family movie both the Bradys and the Mansons could adore." With low-budget horror franchises and *Porky's* style sex comedies driving the box office, Waters did the thing that seemed most radical: he made a family-friendly film that champions social non-conformity, civil disobedience, interracial romance, and a fat female heroine whose parents are both men.

Hairspray is based on Waters' memories of growing up in Baltimore during the turbulence of the Civil Rights era and the dawn of the 1960s youth counter-culture. Consistent with Waters' long-established reliance on original music to drive filmic narrative, *Hairspray* nostalgically recreates the popular R&B music, dance steps, and fashions of the period. Above all, the film centers on Waters' teenage obsession with *The Buddy Dean Show* (1957–64), a televised dance party that was Baltimore's racially segregated version of Dick Clark's nationally syndicated, *American Bandstand*. Like *Pink Flamingos*, *Hairspray* stages a feud between two families – the working class Turnblads (Divine and Jerry Stiller) and the bourgeois Von Tussels (Debbie Harry and Sonny Bono). Their daughters, Tracey (Ricki Lake) and Amber (Colleen Fitzpatrick), compete for the affections of Link Larkin (Michael St. Gerard), the title of Miss Auto Show 1963, and the coveted position of most popular girl on *The Corny Collins Show*.

Tracey's audition scene highlights the film's equation of gender and racial prejudice, when a member of the Corny Collins council distastefully asks Tracy if she would ever "swim in an integrated swimming pool." "I certainly would," Tracy replies. "I'm a modern kind of gal. I'm all for integration." Visibly disgusted by this response, Amber shifts the focus of conversation away from the polluting morphology of blackness to the filth of female corpulence, pointedly declaring, "This girl's a trash can!" Here we are again reminded that trash, while appearing on the surface a source of cheap amusement, has remained throughout John Waters' career a potent aesthetic and cultural metaphor, a challenge to oppressive power relations of privilege and taste, and a fierce expression of the wish to rewrite the laws of proper social embodiment from the outlaw margins of society.

From *Mondo Trasho* to his most recent film, *A Dirty Shame* (2004), the allure of filth, deviancy, abjection, and all manner of irreverent sexuality and violence has coexisted alongside the work-a-day banality of ordinary middle-class religious, familial, and romantic values. Attending to almost every aspect of writing, directing, editing, financing, producing, and marketing, John Waters created an independent cinema aesthetic that correlates with its mode of production and a deliriously campy vision of American life.

Biography

John Samuel Waters, Jr. was born on April 22, 1946 and raised in suburban Lutherville, MD, in an upper-middle-class Roman Catholic home. He began making movies with an 8-mm Brownie movie camera that his grandmother gave him for his seventeenth birthday. He attended the University of Baltimore for one year, and then moved to New York City where he briefly studied filmmaking at NYU before being expelled. Waters went on to form Dreamland Productions with the group of friends that would constitute, for most of his filmmaking career, his cast and crew. A writer, visual artist, stand-up comedian, and art collector, Waters resides to this day primarily in his home city of Baltimore.

Filmography

Hag in a Black Leather Jacket (1964)
Roman Candles (1966)
Eat Your Makeup (1968)
Mondo Trasho (1969)
The Diane Linkletter Story (1970)
Multiple Maniacs (1970)
Pink Flamingos (1972)
Female Trouble (1974)
Desperate Living (1977)
Polyester (1981)
Hairspray (1988)
Cry Baby (1990)
Serial Mom (1994)
Pecker (1998)
Cecil B. Demented (2000)
A Dirty Shame (2004)
This Filthy World (2006)

Further reading

Egan, James. *John Waters: Interviews (Conversations with Filmmakers)*. Jackson: University of Mississippi Press, 2011.

Heller, Dana. *Hairspray*. Malden, MA & Oxford, UK: Wiley-Blackwell, 2011.

Ives, John G. *John Waters (American Originals)*. New York: Thunder's Mouth Press, 1992.

Pela, Robrt L. *Filthy: The Weird World of John Waters*. Los Angeles: Alyson Publications, 2002.

Waters, John and Simon Doonan. *Shock Value: A Tasteful Book About Bad Taste*. New York: Thunder's Mouth Press, 1981, 1995, 2005.

Waters, John. *Crackpot: The Obsessions of John Waters*. New York: Scribner, 1983.

—. *Role Models*. New York: Farrar, Straus, and Giroux, 2011.

INDEX